Toward a Critical Political Economics

A CRITIQUE OF LIBERAL AND RADICAL ECONOMIC THOUGHT

Dwayne Ward

Goodyear Publishing Company, Inc.
Santa Monica, California

Library of Congress Cataloging in Publication Data

Ward, Dwayne.
  Toward a critical political economics.

  Bibliography: p. 309
  1. Economics—History—United States.   2. Social
sciences—History—United States.   I. Title.
HB119.A2W26   330'.0973   76-29795
ISBN 0-87620-905-3

Y-9053-3

Current printing (last digit):
10 9 8 7 6 5 4 3 2 1

Printed in the United States of America

Cover and interior design by Kathleen Trainor

For Barry

The nation's hoop is broken and scattered.
There is no center any longer
and the sacred tree is dead.

Black Elk

follow leading
          ideas
not leaders

          James O'Connor

CONTENTS

PREFACE

On a winter night in upstate New York I had, once again, been attempting to clearly grasp the economic dynamics described in Baran and Sweezy's *Monopoly Capital*. I was especially confused by and intrigued with their concept of the economic surplus and the process of generation and absorption of surplus. Upon running into someone I knew on the way to the library coffee room, I was asked "How's it going?" My response was "I feel like there is some sort of missing link." He, not surprisingly, returned this comment with a puzzled look which prompted me to go into a bit more detail about my struggle with theory. Later I quit work and went home to get some sleep. However, even asleep, I continued to struggle with this intellectual puzzle. I was trying, unsuccessfully, to juxtapose theory and reality.* During the night, the intellectual quest was eventually

*Which, as developed later in Chapter 1, is an error which confuses a description for what is being described. There was in fact not a missing link at all since the connection I was trying to make was founded on a misunderstanding of what science is. The resolution of my conflict about the concepts in Monopoly Capital is presented in Chapter 4.

abandoned unresolved and a vivid dream appeared in full color in which I was walking through a beautiful wooded mountainous area in the Rockies when a huge boulder crashed down from one of the mountains, bounced into the valley where I was walking and smashed into infinitesimally small particles and disappeared before my amazed, but not aghast, eyes. I was much more impressed by the experience than any intellectual interpretation I might have formulated to explain or understand it.

I kept walking through this wonderland of nature; and after passing through more woods, I came upon a clearing in which Merv Griffin, a television personality who annoys me so much in "real life" that I cannot turn him off quickly enough, was sitting surrounded by children who were poking him playfully and kidding him when he disclosed his despair at going soft in the belly. The children cheered him up substantially and then disappeared into the woods leaving him by himself. As I was strolling by, he said, "Come here. I want to tell you something." I walked over to him and he told me "The world is full of people who are anxious to share *their* impressions on the nature of existence, on the way things work. Watch out for that." He added "Everything is the same but I am experiencing it differently." My perception was that he was telling me that he was becoming more involved in tuning into reality and shedding his preconceptions, while at the same time being more concerned with *practice* and living rather than theory. He was warning me of the danger of listening to others' conceptions of reality and the way this attention to others can get in the way of *experiencing* reality itself.

This is a difficult lesson for an intellectually inclined person to accept. Indeed, to take this lesson absolutely seriously might lead to abandoning a search for social science, *qua* science since it might be an exercise in futility interfering with existence itself. But my fate is to ponder. Therefore, it is still necessary to entertain alternative interpretations of social reality. My need for "social science" still exists. Objective views of the world around us aided by the most sensible conceptual frameworks and open and honest dialogue would be valuable not simply to seek truth but to assist in the quest toward rational living as well as living, period. Objectivity, though elusive as love, is something to seek.

I do not believe that Marxian social science provides all of the answers or poses all questions worth asking. Nor is it totally adept at sorting out science from ideology. But I think that in a world of apparent relativity, it has much to say that conventional social science does not or will not say because of the social classes conventional social science generally represents and the interests it commonly promotes. I think that Marxian social science does provide a powerful intellectual orientation at its best and in its least dogmatic formulations, especially when it does not exclude other ideas in the air for sectarian/ideological reasons.

This book is an attempt to "bridge the gap" between conventional economic and, to some extent, social thought and Marxian social science, to work toward a critical political economics that recognizes theory as theory and reality as reality. Some theories are more plausible than others. They work from more realistic assumptions and raise some of the more crucial issues in a comparatively holistic fashion, seeing personal and social existence as very interdependent. It is in the latter sense that I am much more attracted to Marxian social science than to conventional American economic and social thought. Marxian social science is much more able to transcend ethnocentric bias and the chauvinism of Western economic reality and conceptions. It is able to do so, I suspect, because the drafters of Marxian social thought in this country are mainly outsiders; they are not part of conventional social science and the institutions from which it is practiced because of their social class or national origin. Those social scientists who offer the Marxian interpretation of events are commonly not enthusiastic about the usual American reality. They have not experienced or believed in the "American Dream," and they see our history as one in which there has been a great deal of involvement in the exploitation and subjugation of peoples, particularly nonwhite peoples. The authors of this critical thought are marginal people. I believe it to be an unsurprising irony of history that these outsiders are now moved to interpret events, to further expose the myth of the American Dream, and to point to it as generally dysfunctional in this highly interdependent world. Insiders who are also social scientists mainly think of ways to keep the dream alive while leaving consequent implications for the world system conveniently out of mind. Those who do not seek membership in this exclusive, but questionable, club ask, "What does the dream have to do with everything else? How does material affluence of the U.S. variety relate to the exhaustion of the globe itself?"

It is time that, in the interest of the world majority, a broader view be developed and that the myth be shown to be a myth. I hope that the development of a critical political economics inside the U.S.—an atypical island socioeconomically—will, in the relatively short run, provide a powerful argument in favor of a more rational world economic and social system that will address itself to the needs of the majority of the earth's inhabitants. If this rubs the proponents of the American Dream the wrong way, so be it. I see the world, sadly or not, as the battleground of classes, interests, cultures, and peoples. But change emerges through conflict and new perceptions and even social realities come through the clear articulation of opposing arguments. Social science is unavoidably intertwined with its subject.

This book compares and contrasts a few intellectual positions that exist in contemporary American economic and social thought. They suggest that a critical view of our society is appropriate and persuasive, but such a view lacks the following it deserves. This disinterest is a social phenomenon and can be explained by class hegemony extended to ideas.

This critical view demands that contemporary Marxian and "radical" thought be heard if our goal is to listen to all paradigms which relate to an understanding of what is going on. I believe that an eclectic critical political economics which draws heavily from the best of radical and Marxian thought and selected parts of conventional social science (including, certainly, some of its methodology) can provide the key elements of a powerful paradigm that can go far toward relating to the economic, social, and political realities of the late 20th century. But I also think that the warning to beware of others' descriptions should be heeded since these conceptualizations should never be confused for the often elusive real thing. At most, these descriptions are only close approximations to the way social dynamics are actually occurring. Although I am skeptical of social "laws," I think a general tendency exists as long as the inertia founded on past social creations is not fundamentally altered by new developments (e.g., social revolutions). I confess to being quite impressed by a general continuity in history which is expressed so well by scores of writers. If this continuity provides a glimpse of our plausible future, the vision is not a comfortable one. But if anything can alter our course—which I believe to be open to re-evaluation and dramatic change—it is an *awareness* of where we are and what we are doing, or at least an awareness of the most persuasive *perceptions* of contemporary economic, social, and political reality. I think that critical political economics is useful in the task of assisting society to understand itself.

ACKNOWLEDGMENTS

This is a book in theory, but it is clearly grounded in my life experiences—the social processes I have observed and lived within. As such, it is extremely difficult to acknowledge everyone who contributed to the development of this work, so only those who come immediately to mind are mentioned.

An early spark of critical thought was provided by the state of Montana whose Department of Highways blew away a mountain on my grandparent's ranch in order to build an interstate highway. That mountain was dear to me and provided peace and stability during my childhood. I see that event as symbolic and as a dramatic example of the way in which people's connections with the land have been severed in a short span of time. Other sparks were provided by the corporations I worked for in the mid to late 1960s immediately after graduating from the University of Montana. It became clear to me, from working inside these corporations, that capital is something to which I must object. The educational system, while providing much of the time and some of the money for this book, planted other seeds of contempt for hierarchical institutions and affirmed my view that critical thought is allowed in the United States only at a high personal price emotionally, and then only if one is resigned to being fired at whim. The radical movement of the 1960s provided a very central spark in its partially organized opposition to racism, imperialism, poverty, war, alienation, sexism and other social maladies, as well as its often convoluted presentation of alternatives. The energy from that movement still lives—however pained and tortured—and its opposition to the capitalistic system's attempt to destroy the environment and blow the ground out from under the people for very maldistributed profit, has provided another basis for this book. The literature of that radical movement, and that related to struggles of long ago, is the labor to which my writing is most indebted. What follows in this book is an expression closely tied to what others have written, and to the strange and painful, but also weird and sometimes wonderful seas in which I have swum, from Montana to California, to New York and back again many times since the mid-1960s.

More specifically, directions for this work stem from the San Francisco Bay Area collective and journal *Working Papers on the Kapitalistate*. Seeds of thought planted earlier—especially while I was a graduate student at San Jose State University in 1966 and 1967— were nurtured by that collective's study of James O'Connor's *The Fiscal Crisis of the State* and other classic and contemporary Marxian literature. The result was that tentative directions came together during the summer of 1973 while I conducted an introductory macroeconomics course at the College of San Mateo. The participants in that course—especially Kyle Katherine Roat—and those enrolled in others I offered at State University of New York College at Oswego, Onondaga Community College in Syracuse, New York, Skyline College in San Bruno, California, San Jose State University, Syracuse University, and California State University, Chico deserve thanks for listening to my sometimes half-baked ideas and helping with the cooking.

Those to whom I owe a very special debt include James O'Connor— an unfailing, amazing and more than generous friend and correspondent who provided criticism and comments on the entire manuscript in its various stages of development, and who suggested very central ideas in the first place. His contribution to political economics and critical social science is enormous and is sprinkled throughout this book. While his dedication to his work has not been without a high personal price, the least Jim should expect is the recognition he is due as one of the country's leading social theorists. The greatest tribute to Jim would be in the form of great strides forward in progressive social change for which he has been fighting as long as I've known him, and before.

A. Dale Tussing also critically reviewed the entire manuscript in great detail and provided much of the motivation to get it together. He is entitled special note for arranging the institutional support for my works more than once. I harbor no grudge against him for the frequent very pointed, and to the point, sarcasm he penned in the margins of my first drafts. Those drafts deserved it, and I have nearly recovered. Jesse Burkhead was central in the development of this work while it was in process and also compiled an extremely useful critique that aided me in preparing the manuscript for publication. He proved to be especially patient with my several aborted starts and tolerant of my allergy to the orthodox thought in economics which he has had the task of conveying to scores of students (along with more critical thought). Nikola Uzunov, a visiting professor from Yugoslavia and a colleague while at California State University, Chico in 1975–76, read the entire manuscript and caught some weak analysis, especially in politics, and eliminated some loose talk. Thanks go to Gunter Remmling for informing me of the sociology of knowledge, reading the manuscript, and providing encouragement when it seemed in short supply. Stephen Ward, my brother, receives my appreciation for reading and commenting on parts of the early drafts. Thanks go to Oliver Clubb for looking over the manuscript.

Many former colleagues at the Educational Policy Research Center at Syracuse are due warm thanks for contributing in ways I expect they, and more certainly I, were not very conscious of at the time. Some of these are Jane Ackley, Susan Baillie, Fred Baldwin, Ross Burke, Carol Burmingham, Louis Clark, Miriam Clasby, Thomas Corcoran, Laurence DeWitt, Paul Hartley, Emily Haynes, Sheila Huff, Nancy Jones, Bernard Kaplan, Kerry Klockner, Wendy Kohli, Kathy McCarthy, David Mathieson, Mary-Beth O'Neill, Steven Porter, Nancy Ryan, A. Dale Tussing, Gordon VanDeWater, Maureen Websters, Naomi and Peter White, Warren Ziegler, as well as others in and around the EPRC. The environment at the EPRC was especially fertile with ideas and was a key base while the manuscript was drafted, and the ongoing dialogue there helped me sort things out.

Courses I conducted at California State University, Chico, helped me reconsider the manuscript for this book. In particular, a workshop consisting of more than 30 bright and inquisitive people examined the structure of industry as well as the relationships between industry, the financial nexus and the state (especially the antitrust and regulatory arms of the state). The findings of this group reinforced earlier conclusions reached and provided the basis for some revisions. There were several helpful and supportive critics of the political economy and society at Chico during the year, but a few must be mentioned by name: Richard Bryant, Neta Gladney, Rich McKinley, Pamela Swift,

Candy and Norm Wasson, Jim Williford, and, especially, Michael Wilson. The visits of James Ridgeway and Paul Sweezy to the campus provided additional reinforcement for the ideas in this book, and the hope that critical thought cannot be easily starved. Though they are themselves comparatively untainted by a formalized deep steeping in, or concern for, the social sciences, I must gratefully thank Lawrence Mackles, Diane Dayton MacLeod, Michael McCloskey, and Fredda Orol for being my close friends and confidants. For frequent shelter from the storm and very patient tolerance during the difficult formative stages of this work, I am indebted to Judy and Martin Reiner as well as to Diane and Jim Mahshie, Bob and Marilin DeMore, and Carl and Sheri Bailey. Nancy Ryan once rightfully requested my special thanks for enduring with me the period during which the manuscript was drafted; she and I both know how often words are inadequate to express feelings. Thanks are also due to my mother, Margaret Dickgraber, my grandparents, Mary and William Bennett, and the rest of my family for trying to understand what I was doing.

Jane Frost's magical typing fingers put the first drafts of the book together, Paulette Jacques wrote scores of letters to publishers and authors to obtain permissions, and a small and friendly army of people at Goodyear made this book a reality: Editor Steve Lock, production editors Colette Conboy and Derek Gallagher, proof-readers Carolyn Conboy and Georgia Griggs; Pamela Novak, Pamela Tully, Patricia Sweeny and Christopher Wain are also due appreciation and thanks. Kathy Trainor did the interior and cover design.

The greatest debt—my greatest source of inspiration, strength and occasional optimism—is owed my son Barry who has undergone, with tender innocence and enthusiasm, dramatic upheavals in his life as I have necessarily explored ideas and practice in mine. To him, this book is dedicated in struggle, love and hope that all of us can move past the forces of darkness to the life-generating forces of light.

I extend apologies to those many people who contributed to this book whom I have not mentioned by name. No guilt by association is intended for those I have mentioned, for I have found that while friends who think like I do aided in generating insights, the same is true for those who do not.

CREDITS

1

THE EMERGENCE OF A CRITICAL POLITICAL ECONOMICS IN AMERICAN ECONOMIC THOUGHT

The purpose of this book is: (1) to serve as a critique of selected ideas in economic thought; (2) to serve as a critique of aspects of the contemporary U.S. political economy; and (3) to work toward a synthesis which provides a theoretical framework.

Four Paradigms: Keynesian, Galbraithian, Marxian, and Radical Thought

The ideas explored are those of four paradigmatic archetypes, which turn out more nearly to be two on close examination. The first is Keynesian thought, a body of ideas which emerged from the work of a whole generation of economists. This school was the dominant one throughout the 1960s. Although it contains many ideas that are likely to remain, much of the applicability of Keynesianism is awash.

Keynesian economics addresses itself mainly to macroeconomic stability and the regulation of aggregate demand through fiscal and monetary policies. It is concerned with employment, the price level, and economic growth. A second body of inquiry into the U.S. political economy is penned by one man, John Kenneth Galbraith, but is representative of an archetypical stance to which many economists adhere to a greater or lesser extent. This post-Keynesian set of ideas goes beyond the microeconomics taken for granted in Keynesian thought. There is a particular focus on centralized and concentrated capital. The state is advised to consider a variety of policy recommendations or ignore them at its own, and the people's, peril. Knowledge is the basis of power. From the Galbraithian perspective, the best possible society of the future would be a "social democracy." Policy to generate economic stability is seen as possible both within capitalism and the state changed—but moderately—in the direction of Western European varieties of economic systems. Both Keynesian and Galbraithian thought suppose a stabilized capitalism to be possible and desirable.

Marxian economics, the third archetype explored, remains the most important body of ideas, which criticizes the economic system in the U.S. from a highly skeptical perspective. Originating in the 19th century, Marxian thought experienced a rebirth of interest among some economists and other social scientists in the 1960s and is experiencing, seemingly, even more of a resurgence during the 1970s. This neo-Marxism has been deeply influenced by events in the 20th century, has benefited from the work of many scholars over the decades (mostly from abroad), and is a tradition which is linked ideologically to an international socialist movement. But in the United States, Marxian scholars are usually viewed as heretics, and they do, indeed, deviate from the main thrust and expressed values of their culture. Of particular interest to contemporary Marxian writers in political economics are centralized and concentrated capital, the state, and the relationship among these and instability, imperialism, inequality, and choices between laissez faire and planning. The relationships between and among the social classes and the institutions provide central topics of study. Implicit in Marxian thought is an analysis of the "laws of motion" which are thought to result from the relationship between the political economy and society. Social change is founded upon social conflict—capital versus labor, socialism versus capitalism, developed nations versus the Third World. Contradictions in the system breed conflict and social transformation. Capitalism is viewed within the perspective of world history.

The fourth set of ideas is difficult to separate from the third in practice. Radical (or New Left) political economics paralleled the radical action and protest of the 1960s, which stood in opposition to inequality, imperialism, and alienation. It went beyond these to include a rather free-wheeling sociology which provided analyses of racism, sexism, power, alienation, and alternatives to capitalism, to single out but a few areas of study. Its practitioners were those who could not accept the economic orthodoxy or the more classical Marxian stance. Indeed, the general political climate in the U.S. during the 1950s contributed to a general ignorance of the Marxian paradigm, since most Marxian social scientists in the U.S. were denied employment in the educational system. A residual and purely ideological anti-Marxism is commonplace in the country, which probably contributed to the attraction to a more vague radicalism. Still another reason for the creation of a New Left perspective was the often mistaken identification of Marxism with Soviet practice and the somewhat curious sectarian left in the U.S. Leftist university students could not, on the whole, identify with the Communist Party or other leftist organizations that had one specific ideology or another. The university students of the 1960s who were attracted to the political left took on a different sort of radicalism. Cultural heroes were Lenny Bruce, Jack Kerouac, James Dean, Bob Dylan, Joan Baez, and the Beatles rather than Karl Marx. In social science C. Wright Mills was, for example, among the few critical voices in the universities.

With the emergence of a more eclectic Marxism and problems of macroeconomic instability, continuing and chronic inequality, alienation, imperialism, and other problems of capitalism in the 1970s, it is increasingly difficult to tell the difference between radical political economics and Marxian political economics. Perhaps the main reason is that the radical political economists became more educated in the diversity of Marxian thought as it increased in relevance and availability. And many who experimented with countercultural alternatives found that they would fail or be but moderately successful within the superstructure of monopoly state capitalism.

Both Marxian and radical political economists see a stabilized capitalism possible only under unacceptable conditions, if at all, and see the U.S. society as a pernicious order that should be changed in fundamental ways. Thus, although liberals often stand torn between Keynesian/Galbraithian and radical/Marxian perspectives, those who are more unequivocally anticapitalism find the paradigm that relates to their ideology in the latter but must also notice the former if only to be in tune with possible or likely developments. Keynesian and Galbraithian thought prescribe policy to reform capitalism, and sometimes those prescriptions are adopted by the state.

The ideas explored here can be but a rough mirror of social reality; thus, an exploration of economic thought becomes also an exploration of the political economy, the second purpose of this work. The main foci are economic instability, centralized and concentrated capital, and the state. Economic instability is a key problem of capitalism and is one which both the defenders and detractors of the system analyze. Economic instability, therefore, becomes a key part of this exploration of ideas.

Centralized and concentrated capital is also important to this exploration. The presence of the largest corporations cannot be overlooked since everyday life is permeated thoroughly by them. The 500 largest corporations produce—various guesses suggest—more than half of all commodities in the country. The monopoly capital center of the economy may employ as much as one-third of the work force. And it is possible that the state system employs another third. The ideas explore in some depth the structural realities of our times and offer theories about the implications of these realities.

The exploration of the political economy leads to the third purpose. A set of observations emerges. The observations are some selected ideas which are rooted in the varieties of economic thought mentioned. Although limited in scope, this general theoretical stance presents a view of the structure of the U.S. political economy, sketches some of the interrelationships between the key sectors, and offers a view of the economic system's dynamics, its tendencies toward instability, and its impact on broadly defined social classes. As an exploration in theory, all issues are not resolved. But if stability is to obtain while private ownership of the means of production with its implied inequality is retained, it will exist in a state-corporate regime that should be seen as what R.E. Pahl and J.T. Winkler have termed "fascism with a human face," what Bertram Gross refers to as "friendly fascism," and what James O'Connor calls "the social-industrial complex." The alternative to this political-economic state is a fundamental reorganization of American society which would require the socialization of the means of production and a revolution in the social relationships surrounding production. As Leonard Rapping put it (at a teach-in on the economy at Syracuse University in February 1975), the choices ahead, given the enormity of the problems, may be those of a national socialist or democratic socialist variety. The question may not be so much one of planning as one of the *kind* of planning and the social classes benefited and represented.

If the decisions are left to those who are currently politically powerful, a more specifically national socialist future seems likely, although state indecision which prolongs economic stagnation is possible. If, on the other hand, the working people of the country and their allies organize themselves and avail themselves of a program yet to be invented as well as a political vehicle yet to be created, a democratic socialism might be consciously sought. This activism would be a way out of cynicism and despair which are their own punishment.

The following is, in part, a search for grounded theory in political economics using the method of comparative analysis similar to that suggested by Barney G. Glaser and Anselm L. Strauss.[1] With a comparision of theoretical views on instability, centralization and concentration in industry, and the state, some theories emerge as more persuasive than others. A final summary, critique, and beginning toward a synthesis are presented in the last chapter as part of this third purpose.

The remainder of this chapter discusses related issues, which serve as an introduction and provide the context for the more specific inquiry into the different paradigms on economic instability, the centralization and concentration of capital, and the state. A sense of the controversy that surrounds contemporary political economics is constructed, and the difference between critical political economics and orthodox thought is shown. Critical political economics itself will be defined shortly, but it can be said at the outset that its foundation is radical and Marxian thought. The discussion is placed in the context of social science. The social basis of critical political economics and the literature which makes it up are the final areas that must be covered in this introductory chapter. Critical political economics provides rich perspectives which are useful in understanding the contemporary economic system in the United States and alternatives to it. The central thread of thought throughout the following discussion is that Marxian and radical political economics provide especially useful conceptual frameworks. It is time for discussion of Marxian and radical thought to be brought out into the open even more and its status as unwanted stepchild of the social sciences to be ended. It is time that the best of Marxian economics be better used in the development of conceptual and empirical work in the social sciences.

Marxian readers may consider these introductory statements quaint. To them the issue is resolved. The merits of Marxian thought are obvious and only the task of resolving disagreements among themselves remains. They may even contemptuously refer to mainstream social science as bourgeois and see its practitioners as conscious or unconscious ideological opportunists (and the politically naive), who are servants of the state and the ruling class and who are technocrats, not *scientists,* often working under contract oblivious to the end results of their efforts. It also may be argued that the university and higher education in general are simply part of the political economy as a whole, the training ground for an important part of the work force and, to a smaller extent, the emerging ruling class.[2] In this context, it may well be argued, it should come as no surprise that there are very few professors articulating the best and most relevant critical social science. It would be considered quite naive to look for penetrating analysis in the service stations maintained for capital and the state.

Yet, a good deal of good critical thought in political economics, much of it from an academic base, has been written. The Marxian perspective is alive and well and is addressing itself to attempting to understand economic, social, and political problems and prospects. This attempt is positive because there is much that needs to be explained, and conventional economics has not proved itself adequate. An alternative to piecemeal social science, which may be good at analyzing small parts of society, is needed. Marxian thought attempts to be holistic, and there is a need to perceive the big picture. And there is a crisis in conventional economic thought. This is not surprising, as Marcus Raskin has put it, "since there is a crisis in political authority, . . . there is a crisis in what is to be known and understood."[3]

Critical Political Economics in Social Science

The issue of a crisis in thought is discussed in Chapter 2. But part of the discussion, which is far from resolved, should establish the context of the emergence of critical political economics more solidly.

Thomas S. Kuhn[4] is perhaps one of the most cited authors on conflict and change in the general perspectives held in scientific inquiry. He introduced the idea that there is competition among *paradigms,* which, Sweezy once explained, "is very close to . . . a conception of reality (or some aspect of reality)"[5] and that the competitors attempt to establish a grip on the body of inquiry. Kuhn says about times of disarray and dissonance in scientific activity:

> This is the period . . . during which individuals practice science, but in which the results of their enterprise do not add up to science as we know it. And . . . during periods of revolution

when the fundamental tenets of a field are once more at issue, doubts are repeatedly expressed about the very possibility of continued progress if one or another of the opposed paradigms is adopted. Those who rejected Newtonianism proclaimed that its reliance upon innate forces would return science to the Dark Ages. Those who opposed Lavoisier's chemistry held that the rejection of chemical "principles" in favor of laboratory elements was the rejection of achieved chemical explanation by those who would take refuge in a mere name. A similar, though more moderately expressed, feeling seems to underlie the opposition of Einstein, Bohm, and others, to the dominant probabilistic interpretation of quantum mechanics. In short, it is only during periods of normal science that progress seems both obvious and assured. During those periods, however, the scientific community could view the fruits of its work in no other way[6]

Jack D. Douglas makes this comment about Kuhn's general position and its applicability to sociology. His perception would apply equally to economics:

Sociology, like every other science, is in fact a *multiple paradigmatic* discipline. That is, there are many different paradigms which can be legitimately used by any sociologists in various fields. (As in any science, we have our *paradigm-Imperialists:* in *The Structure of Social Action* Talcott Parsons tried to show that there was an implicit paradigm for all social actions in the works of Durkheim, Weber, Marshall, and Pareto; Kingsly Davis and others argue that structural-functionalism *is* sociology—the whole truth and the only truth; Otis Dudley Duncan and others argue that *only* the ecological model will allow us to achieve the true goals of sociology. But, of course, these conflicting imperialistic slogans themselves show us that there are many paradigmatic approaches from which everyone can choose the one he considers most appropriate to his own purposes. Just as in physics the complexity of the physical world and man's knowledge about it have prevented any successful unified field theory, so in sociology the complexity of the social world and our knowledge about it have maintained our freedom of choice between paradigms.)[7]

The general point that Douglas is making in this discussion of the various schools of thought that exist in sociology is that

Kuhn has argued very persuasively that the normal (non-revolutionary) work in science is done within the context—*and* confines—of classical works known to all scientists in that area. These works serve as *paradigms* for this normal work: they provide implicit and explicit assumptions about the "relevant" realm of reality which provide an overall, "adequate" view of that reality; and, very importantly, they *show* the scientist by example just *how to go about doing* his work so that he will get "worthwhile" and "valid" results.[8]

Citing Kuhn and part of the discussion[9] surrounding the application of his perceptions about the nature of science to the social sciences shows that there is no adherence here to a "true believer" stance in science or social science. And it has been argued that the validity of applying Kuhn's ideas to social science is not itself entirely defensible.[10] But this unresolved debate is, perhaps, somewhat unresolvable; and the discussion here is presented within the context of Western thought, leaving deeper questions to professional philosophers who are probably locked in the same dilemma.

The general task here, then, is to alleviate the general "paradigm-imperialism" of conventional economics, knowing full well that many of the pitfalls of knowledge that apply to social science in general also apply to critical political economics. That is the state of the art.

One major working assumption is that much of social science provides useful perspectives in the attempt to assist society in understanding itself even though, as the Gestalt therapist Richard Weaver (of Cold Mountain Institute in British Columbia) once argued, this may well be the age of scientism with its practitioners (especially, an ever increasing number of Ph.D.'s) its high priests. Further, because there is so much material appearing in print, it takes more time to sort the gems from the trivia, and, as David M. Gordon has written, energy is put into "plunging down blind alleys, reading volumes of material which ultimately" obfuscate the issues more than they clarify them.[11]

The development of a solid critical political economics can help clear the obfuscation and assist in seeing society as it is, relatively free of unconscious ideologies. This requires being clear on the implicit working assumptions and theories particularly, as well as possessing the knowledge that to have described a social phenomenon is not the same as to have explained it. The former is the task of empirical observation, of which a massive amount is done in this society, whereas the latter requires theoretical and conceptual frameworks.

The contemporary Marxian paradigm, in particular, and critical political economics, in general, should be considered in this task because although Marxian political economics is not ideology-free, it tends, as do Marx's writings, to be aware of its stance of advocacy. At its best, it is successful in sorting out its analysis of what is from its argument of what is likely to develop in the future and, most certainly, what would be nice to create. Joan Robinson points out that conventional economic thought does not share this awareness:

The orthodox economists, on the whole, identified themselves with the system and assumed the role of its apologists, while Marx set himself to understand the working of capitalism in order to hasten its overthrow. Marx was conscious of his purpose. The economists were in general unconscious. They wrote as they did because it seemed to them the only possible way to write, and they believed themselves to be endowed with scientific impartiality. Their preconceptions emerge rather in the problems which they chose to study and the assumptions on which they worked than in overt political doctrine.[12]

Actually, there is really no absolutely satisfactory term to capsulize the variety of social inquiry that comprises this book. Critical political economics is a rough label. The term *radical* is usually used to talk about what is termed critical here. There are problems with this use because it is not particularly radical to see things as they are, even if seeing means noticing that society is not harmonious and that there are serious generic economy-wide problems which make capitalism as we know it unviable in the long run.

Critical political economics is, in essence, a synthesis of much of the existing theory explored in this work. The cornerstone of critical political economics is a radical/Marxian meld. The remainder of critical political economics is an eclectic mix. Of particular importance is the eclectic work of economic dualism theorists. Critical political economics has been influenced by Keynesian thought. Empirical studies on the structure and performance of the political economy and society are also part of critical political economics. The most precise statement about such economics is not altogether satisfactory, but it can be said that critical political economics is radical political economics that makes no pretense about radical action. It is an analysis of the political economy, not a call to arms. It is an intellectual framework, not a strategy for action. Action may logically emerge from critical political economics, but it would be an error to see writers of critical political economics as revolutionaries in fact as long as there is no political strata to which critical political economists can relate. One might turn radical, but that is another story. As long as the writers of critical political economics remain only analysts of the system, they should not be presumptuous enough to think of themselves as radical political economists. In sum, then, *a working definition of critical political economics includes what is usually called radical political economics, Marxian political economics, and selected eclectic work.*

Norman Birnbaum used the term *critical* in about the same fashion in a discussion of critical sociology (at the American Sociological

Association annual meeting in Montreal, August 1974). There is a basis for the use of the adjective *critical* in the works of the authors of the Frankfurt School and the Institute of Social Research, particularly those of Theodor Adorno, Max Horkheimer, and Herbert Marcuse,[13] as well as in other European thought.[14]

The basis for this critical political economics must be seen as the seminal work of Karl Marx (1818-1883). The rediscovery of Marx's contribution by yet another generation is most likely due to the faltering domestic economy as well as to general skepticism about the accompanying society and knowledge about economic trauma in the history of capitalism. Still another factor is the tragic war against the people of Vietnam and others in the Third World, which led to a broader critique of the U.S. economy and society and its general tendencies in the 1960s and 1970s. The emergence of critical political economics is founded in an awareness of a harsh social reality. And this reality is, by and large, something to which conventional thought has consistently and persistently failed to address itself adequately.

In conventional economics, this inadequacy has usually emerged in the form of underlying assumptions in the models offered. For example, neoclassical thought is based largely on individual behavior and the construct of the competitive firm. Although *some* competitive firms may exist in the contemporary economy, this, as we will argue in some detail in Chapters 4 and 5, is not a reality that represents the *primary* structural arrangement of the economy. This sector is but one within a broader social structure. And critical political economics focuses on the interdependence of people and their institutions.

Conventional economics is inadequate in still another way. Typically, all of the relevant variables are not included in the analysis. The economy is abstracted out of its social and political setting (which, too, are abstractions from everything that is happening in "reality"). Thus, for example, to be devoid of a realistic theory of the state is to deal unsatisfactorily with a large and important part of the determinants of economic stability (a topic covered extensively in Chapter 5).

In addition, the international dimensions affecting the domestic economy must be included if a theoretical stance is to be holistic. For example, the economies of France, England, Italy, Japan, and Canada have much to do with what is happening in the United States and vice versa; these countries appear to be experiencing many of the same difficulties as the U.S. Structural similarities, therefore, must exist just as fundamental dissimilarities exist between these countries and, for example, the Scandinavian countries since measured economic outcomes are shown empirically to be quite different in these two broad groupings. Still different and dramatic structural differences exist between these two groups and the socialist countries, such as Cuba, China, and others. A discussion of these broad economic types in this cursory way demonstrates a host of assumptions, theories, and measured "realities" which are the stuff of which political economics is made.

Critical political economics forms a general paradigm which is based on assumptions that are more realistic, which includes more variables coupled with empirical observation, and which arrives at a relatively holistic view. In so doing, it must be defensible in some of the usual ways to merit a place in social science. It cannot be mere dogma, propaganda, or journalism.

Robert M. Solow, in a spirited exchange with John G. Gurley over the exclusion of developments in radical political economics from a collection assessing the state of economics, responded in particular to this point in his general opposition to radical political economics. He said:

> I don't think it's wrong for a survey of economics to talk mostly about technique and the availability of data. There is a difference between a survey of medicine and a survey of health, or between a survey of meteorology and a survey of the weather. So why not between a survey of economics and a survey of economic life? I presume that knowledge of technique and acquaintance with certain bodies of data . . . distinguish the radical economist from the radical journalist, or the radical sociologist, or the radical clarinetist . . .[15]

It is interesting to note that Solow was talking about the radical political economics of the 1960s which he charged was "more a matter of posture and rhetoric than of [any] scientific framework at all." But he says in a parenthetical note, which now merits discarding the parentheses:

> Classical Marxian economics is a different matter, of course, though there is a problem about its relation to the classical paradigm. Anyhow that is another story. "It is no accident," as they say, that modern radicals are not much interested in the old man who wrote *Capital*. They are much more interested in the Hegelian Marx and the author of the Paris Manuscripts of 1844.[16]

Solow, of course, was responding to his sense of where he took radical political economics to be in 1970—at the time being associated with the Union for Radical Political Economics—and was ignoring the work of the more specifically Marxian political economists in his critique. At best, Solow was partly right. There was in some of early radical political economics a substantial amount of "loose thinking."

This was partially a reaction to the usual curriculum offered by departments of economics at the time and a relative ignorance about the best of Marxian thought. There were even jokes (made by conventional economists) about how economics was not really about people. And those who wanted to ponder questions about how the economic system was related to the broader society and to politics and government were not able to pursue those questions in even the "best" and "most prestigious" university economics departments in this country.

The boundaries of economic thought have broadened somewhat since the more rigid definitions that permeated the graduate curricula in the 1960s, and political economics has become more legitimate in faculty rhetoric if not in actual courses offered and critical political economists hired. This broadening is probably a function of the standard paradigms in economics not relating all that well to a *comprehensive* view of the workings of the economy, particularly the role of government (a key focus in Chapter 5). Many of the working assumptions of standard economics are under question and are even ridiculed on many fronts. In addition, the radical criticism has made a subtle, but real, impact on the variety of ideas being entertained. Some students have expressed an interest in more challenging thought; and established members of the economics profession, Gurley, for example, have gone through meaningful changes in their intellectual orientation which has helped to legitimize the stances of like-minded younger colleagues.

It is useful to offer Gurley's definition of political economics and radical political economics to put the discussion of this work as a whole in context:

> Political economics, as distinguished from . . . conventional economics, studies economic problems by systematically taking into account, in a historical context, the pervasiveness of ruler-subject relations in society. "The realm of the political," as political scientist Robert Tucker has written, "is the realm of power and authority relations among people . . ."
>
> I will add that it is these pervasive relations of domination and servitude, these relations of power and authority that lead to conflict, disharmony, and disruptive change. A political economist sees these power structures and puts them at the forefront of his analysis; a conventional economist—who sees society as free, self-interested economic men interacting as equals in the marketplace—does not.
>
> To extend the discussion of these differences, the conventional economist, because he sees harmonies of interest almost everywhere, can visualize himself as a neutral technician, applying his techniques as objectively as possible. If class or group conflicts

do not exist, one can, of course, work for the "general interest." The political economist turned radical, on the other hand, not only studies economic problems within the historical context of ruler-subject relations, but he actively takes the side of the poor and the powerless, and he generally sees the system of capitalism as their oppressor. He believes, therefore, that the conventional economist not only fails to take account of relations of power and authority, and so fails to grasp the most socially relevant aspects of the problem, but, by being so blind to class interests and so caught up in his data and his techniques, he in effect supports a system that maltreats large numbers of people.[17]

This definition is not totally persuasive in that economists can be political, and usually are, without knowing it. In conventional economics, politics and power come up mainly in the form of exclusion. For example, the Keynesian may assume it is possible to implement his or her fiscal policy recommendations to stabilize the system (the worth of which is, itself, a political judgement). The position taken here is that all economics is inherently political and ideological, and, therefore, the terms *economics* and *political economics* can be used almost interchangeably. Critical political economics is generally conscious of its politics, and it is possible to sort out its analysis (using the scientific method) from its political hopes and positions of advocacy. It should be added that critical political economics need be cautious about its use of language and the ideologies that emerge linguistically. Gurley, for example, uses the masculine pronoun above, rather than those for both sexes.

Charges that one paradigm or another is unscientific are not particularly valid or useful. The scientific method is a *limited device* to structure the argument, but it cannot ask the questions. The questions which occur to political economists—social scientists who study the economy would be a better term—are broader in scope and are, therefore, less subject to rigorous *quantitative* treatment than the topics of regular economics. But that reason hardly suggests that the questions should not be raised, that attempts to explain phenomena in the political economy cannot be a "scientific" activity, or that only quantitative expositions constitute the stuff of which scientific activity is made.

Perhaps Elliot Liebow put it as simply as possible when he recalled the favorite expression he gleaned from his discussions with Hylan Lewis in their work which resulted in Liebow's well-known study of black streetcorner men: "The scientific method is doing one's darndest with his [or her] brains, no holds barred."[18]

It may be easier to suggest what social science does not have to pretend to be in order to construct a sense of the extent to which critical political economics is defensible as part of it. It need not be assumed or expected that science has as its function the reproduction or "reality" since this would be an error which

> . . . rests on a confusion between a description and what is described. Albert Einstein once remarked, it is not the function of science "to give the taste of the soup." To be a description of the taste of soup is clearly not to be the taste of soup. On reflection there is surely no reason whatever for anyone to suppose that a description of some characteristic of soup should, itself, taste like soup. Yet a muddle just as egregious is involved in disparaging science's alleged failures in this respect. Of course, if we are intelligent and lucky, and employ sensibly the information conveyed by the statements of science, we may be able to put ourselves into the position of tasting soup. But this is, of course, quite different from expecting that the statements of science (the ones *about* the taste of soup) are defective, or somehow fail, because *they* don't taste like soup.[19]

A Definition of Social Science

Let me briefly summarize what I take social science to be. It is the use of theory—which can be seen as easily as hypotheses, notions, conceptualizations, and even guesses or hunches—and empirical observation augmented by the most penetrating and illuminating questions to discern as nearly as possible what is occurring in social reality. This can be undertaken in any number of ways with the employment of any number of methods. But sophistication in method should never be confused for a necessary or sufficient condition for the task at hand to be considered social science. In short, social science is a general approach to discern what is going on.[20]

The term *social science* is used here as a convenience in the usual sense. But Mills put it well when he said:

> I feel the need to say that I much prefer the phrase, "the social studies" to "the social sciences"—not because I do not like physical scientists (on the contrary, I do, very much), but because the word "science" has acquired great prestige and rather imprecise meaning. I do not feel any need to kidnap the prestige or to make the meaning even less precise by using it as a philosophical metaphor. Yet I suspect that if I wrote about "the social studies," readers would think only of high school civics, which of all fields of human learning is the one with which I most wish to avoid association. "The Behavioral Sciences" is simply impossible; it was thought up, I suppose, as a propaganda device to get money for social research from Foundations and Congressmen who confuse "social science" with "socialism." The best term would include history (and psychology, so far as it is concerned

with human beings), and should be as noncontroversial as possible, for we should argue *with* terms, not fight *over* them . . . With the hope of not being too widely misunderstood, I bow to convention and use the more standard "social sciences."[21]

That work in the social science which is the most clearly and simply stated seems the most useful. Social science should not represent an elitist cult whose members speak only to each other, but rather social science should assist in the task of helping society understand itself. This is not to say that there is no place for the more abstract, formalized, and mathematized presentations. But neither should the latter be confused as the *only* valid social science.

Further, social thought has much to do with, and is founded in, the social existence of its authors. In this sense, economics is quite sociologically based. That is, the kinds of questions economists ask depend, to no small extent, on where they are in the social order. This connection is often quite subtle and elusive but exists nonetheless.[22] As is argued later, the social existence of the 1960s and 1970s was particularly instrumental in the emergence of developments in critical political economics.

A New Eclecticism in Economic Inquiry

The main focus that follows is on selected parts of what John Kenneth Galbraith has called "the lower economics."

> He pictured the prestige structure of economics as a hollow pyramid or cone. At the base the sides are transparent and have many openings to the outside. As one approaches the apex, the sides become increasingly opaque and impermeable. Economists dealing with practical matters dwell at the base, and they have easy communication with the outside world. Their economics is adulterated by foreign admixtures of politics, moral judgements and sociology. The practitoner at this level merits little esteem. In contrast, economists dealing with pure theory can be found near the top of the pyramid. They are protected from outside influence. Their work is formal and mathematical. It has little or nothing to do with reality, and is highly regarded by the profession.[23]

It is possibly in the lower economics that the most controversy is presently occurring. Some have gone so far as to argue that a *revolution* truly exists in economic thought.[24] Others perceive the situation as a *crisis* in economic thought.[25] My view is that the conventional wisdom is under considerable fire but has retained its somewhat shaken hegemony insofar as the formulation of public policy is concerned. This hegemony is largely unjustified, but it is not surprising. It is simply a reflection of the hierarchical stratification which exists in our society. That is, those ideas which gain access to the centers of power, particularly the executive branch of the federal government, must be supportive of the general social and economic status quo. Ideas which threaten the status quo and the hierarchical nature of society are an anathema, by definition, to the arena of decision making. Thus, although a critical political economics is developing in part of economics, there is still a strong basis for the persistence of conventional economic thought in most of economics. It is too simple to suggest that a revolution in thought is taking place because the implementation of Marxian notions into intellectual and popular consideration has been a rather slow process with surges and setbacks over the last one hundred years. If there is a revolution, it is also being accompanied by a formidable counterrevolution. A discussion of the context and content of critical political economics requires developing in much more detail the new eclecticism in economic thought which is a part of the questioned hegemony of the conventional wisdom, particularly Keynesian thought. Chapter 2 will give particular attention to the development of a Marxian critique of central Keynesian notions (see also Chapter 3) as well as discuss the idea that a crisis exists in the legitimacy of Keynesianism. Chapter 4 makes the Marxian critique more specific by focusing in on Baran and Sweezy's contemporary classic, *Monopoly Capital*, and comparing it with Galbraith's *The New Industrial State*, a more widely known, accepted, and, as we will argue, quite deficient view of the place of capital in the society as a whole. This is an important and timely contrast because it is not impossible that Galbraith's work could take on the following significance to which one could be very much opposed:

> Today the cry is heard: "Where is the New Keynes?" The majority of economists, the monetary-fiscalists, are in disarray; they know how to handle inflation and recession separately but not simultaneously. If they intend to wait for a new Keynes who will think up a clever device to alleviate stagflation while leaving all social, political, and economic relations intact, they are likely to have an extremely long wait. That leaves the monetarists, who would cure inflation with a resounding recession; and the planners, headed by Galbraith, whose program and strategy are set out in all necessary detail in the last third of *Economics and the Public Purpose*. Considering the prospects of the first two groups, both free market loyalists to the end, it is just possible that the day will arrive in the not too distant future when the President will say: "We are all Galbraithians now." [26]

The discussion of the Marxian paradigm raises further questions on theories relating to the dual economy, the state, and the problem of economic instability within the context of the general social and economic structure. To answer them, Chapter 5 draws heavily on James O'Connor's *The Fiscal Crisis of the State,* a work written in the Marxian tradition, which provides the elements of one of the most profound theories of general macroeconomics, the nature and role of the political state, and to new economic, social, and political directions. O'Connor's argument is contrasted with Galbraith's *Economics and the Public Purpose,* which is an ideological defense of state capitalism. Thus, the development of a critical political economics seems far reaching in its possibilities for a thoroughgoing analysis of the conventional wisdom and its Galbraithian "alternative." The final chapter, Chapter 6, draws the discussion together as a whole and argues that Myron Sharpe's critique of the main schools of economic thought is something with which one can agree but that his zeal for a Galbraithian future is something about which severe skepticism is in order. However, Sharpe did not consider the critical political economics alternative. The work of James O'Connor, in particular, provides the theoretical basis for further studies that help in understanding the general macroeconomics of our time and for anticipating the sociopolitical directions that may emerge in response to contemporary economic realities. It is no exaggeration to suggest that a critical political economics in a more developed form could offer a powerful analysis of the current era which deserves a full hearing as a key part of the lower economics. Chapter 6 presents a final critique and a synthesis of theories of economic instability, centralization and concentration in industry, and the state. In this way an attempt is made to construct a "grounded" view of some aspects of the U.S. political economy from the perspective of critical political economics.

Again, the main thesis explored here is that Marxian and radical political economics provide rich perspectives for understanding contemporary capitalism in the U.S. and for the development of critical political economics. This argument exists in the setting of American economic thought where Keynesian, neoclassical, and Institutional economics (where Galbraith is placed by some) comprise the main schools.

Articulate statements of all of these views are widely available.[27] The basis of the laissez faire stance[28] characteristic of neoclassical thought may be found in Adam Smith's classic *An Inquiry Into the Nature and Causes of the Wealth of Nations,* which first appeared in 1776. This view has been formalized, revised, and restated often in this century (as in, for example, Milton Friedman's *Capitalism and Freedom*, published in 1962) and contains the notion that the "invisible hand" of the market[29] effectively deals with the question: what is to be produced, how will it be created, and who will get it? Government, in this view, is best when it is nonexistent or nearly so. Neoclassical thought differs from Smith's position primarily in the methodological formalization of the argument and in the abandonment of the labor theory of value when Marx brought Ricardo's discussion to threatening conclusions.

Marxian political economics is in direct contradistinction to neoclassical thought. Its basis is Karl Marx's three volumes of *Capital*, the first of which appeared in German in 1867 and in English 20 years later. In this view government is part of the state which is, more or less, the executive committee for the owners of the means of production.[30] Capitalism produces and reproduces social classes who engage in struggle over the what, how, and for whom questions posed above. Theories of macroeconomic instability, which should be seen as standing apart from his ideas about where this would lead sociopolitically, appeared in Marx's seminal works which provide fundamental theories, categories, and ways of thinking for the basis of modern discussions of the phenomenon of instability in capitalist societies.[31] To this day, as this work as a whole documents and as contemporary events underline, Marx's rejoinder to the laissez faire position provides a challenging argument. As G.A.D. Soares put it in 1968, "Eighty years have elapsed since Marx's death, and Marxism undoubtedly still is the main ideological issue nowadays."[32] This is because the decades since Marx's passing have "witnessed the transformation of Marxism from a sociological and economic theory into the official ideology in several countries and into the prevalent socioeconomic doctrine in certain academic subcultures in Western countries as well."[33]

Sweezy distinguishes Marxian thought from that of conventional economics articulately:

> Orthodox economics takes the existing social system for granted, much as though it were part of the natural order of things. Within this framework it searches for harmonies of interest among individuals, groups, classes, and nations; it investigates tendencies toward equilibrium; and it assumes that change is gradual and nondisruptive. I don't think I need to illustrate or support these propositions beyond reminding you that the foundation of all orthodox economics is general and/or partial equilibrium (the two, far from being incompatible, really imply each other). And as for the point about gradualism, I need only recall that printed on the title page of Alfred Marshall's *magnum opus*, the *Princi-*

ples of Economics, is the motto natura non facit saltum—nature makes no leaps.

It might perhaps be plausibly argued that equilibrium provided a workable axiomatic base for a real social science at a certain time and place—the time being roughly the half century before the First World War, and the place Britain and a few other countries of advanced capitalism. For my part, I do not believe this was true even then. I think economics by the time of what may be called the "marginalist revolution" of the 1870s had already practically ceased to be a science and had become mainly an apologetic ideology. Putting harmony, equilibrium, and gradualism at the center of the stage was dictated not by the scientific requirement of fidelity to reality, but by the bourgeois need to prettify and justify a system which was anything but harmonious, equilibrated, and gradualistic.

It was almost at the same time as the marginalist revolution, when economics (as distinct from classical political economy) was being born as an apologetic ideology, that Karl Marx put forward a radically different and opposed mode of analyzing the dominant economic systems. In place of harmony he put conflict. In place of forces tending toward equilibrium he stressed forces tending to disrupt and transform the status quo. In place of gradualism he found qualitative discontinuity . . .[34]

But this was not simply carping, negativism, or fatalism. Although it was profoundly argued that capitalism was a system that generated antagonistic social classes and interests and produced anything but social harmony, progress, equilibrium, and stable growth, the possibility of conflict existed at the emergence of a more rational and humane system—socialism. Marx pointed to tendencies that he perceived to be generic and system-wide; he drew on the works of the Classical School—those of Smith, Say, Malthus, Ricardo, James, and John Stuart Mill, to mention but a few of the most prominant—to bring discussion of capitalism to quite different conclusions than those of the laissez faire advocates.[35]

Out of this deadlock between paradigms sprang neoclassical and—when capitalism entered a highly problematic period in the 1920s and 1930s—Keynesian economics. At the same time work in Marxian political economics proceeded and, as Soares pointed out, some of the ideas about socialism were actually attempted in various parts of the world in the present century.

Yet these experiments in the creation of a new basis for society—with the possible exceptions of Cuba, China, and, perhaps, Yugoslavia—did not, on the whole, provide inspiration for even socialist-inclined critics of capitalism in the United States. Therefore, the more vulgarized Marxism became quite unattractive and often irrelevant to the radical political economists of the 1960s. This economics was perhaps founded more in a critical sociology and was often characterized by a theoretical vacuum in which there was more an opposition to the orthodox theory than the presentation of a rigorous alternative paradigm. After a few years of a preoccupation with practice and a relative lack of respect for theory, it came to be shown that the former was not enough. When a search for theory that related to real events was once more undertaken, there was nowhere else to turn except to classical and contemporary Marxian thought and its analysis of capitalism.

Critical Political Economics and the Movement

At its core American critical political economics[36] embodies the spirit of the Movement—"that novel and loose Left amalgam born in the 1960s of the civil rights, antiwar, campus, feminist, and other struggles"[37]—in its search for peculiarly American answers to the dilemmas of our times. Critical political economics and the Movement, of course, should be seen as intellectual and political responses to the concrete realities generated by the economic system of capitalism. A critical depiction of social reality has resulted in calling the system as a whole into question. Therefore, this critical political economics is not unrelated to practice. The discovery of social meaning has been synonymous with the discovery of social problems and the general economic environment. The topics of study undertaken by practitioners of critical political economics reveal staggering inadequacies and social facts which disclose serious instability and inequity. In this view society as we know it is quite likely to be passing folly. Its hierarchical structure stands as ultimately vulnerable, but there is also an awareness that the problems of capitalist society can provoke and have provoked in many historical instances rather hysterical and violent responses. Germany's tragic experiment with fascism in the 1930s and 1940s following the Great Depression is one such example. In this critical political economics, the meaning of the material world is clarified. Obvious discrepancies in the struggle over material objects emerge. The existence of a stratified society becomes obvious. It becomes apparent that there exist two main classes—owners and workers.

It is also probable that contradictions and conflicts are based on the class nature of society. In critical political economics, capitalists are seen as a parasitic class. Social reorganization would end the division between those who work and those who appropriate the value of the labor of workers. Although socialism has demonstrated major difficulties, it remains the only option that seems at all sensible in the medium-to-long run. A revised capitalism working hand-in-hand with the state may prolong the existence of private ownership of the means of production, but the legitimacy of this arrangement seems ultimately vulnerable. Privately owned empires are conspicuously apparent, and it seems very possible that such massive concentration would make the task of acquiring or seizing control all the easier, particularly if it came to be widely believed that these corporate empires are instrumental in the creation of a troubled economic, social, and political environment. And if it came to be widely thought that centralized and concentrated capital is the basis of a distributional problem that threatens the viability of an unplanned capitalism.

For example, huge profits for the owners of the oil reserves must be rechanneled into investment outlets of some type, saved, or consumed. In any of the three cases, an initial redistribution is followed by a problem of intensified concentration of wealth that results in a shifting balance of power. In a sense, multinational corporations in this industry (and others) form a huge company store in which the delineation between owners and workers becomes much more pronounced and in which a hierarchy of ownership has emerged in a more distinct and visible fashion. As this single example suggests, the phenomenon of the private ownership of the means of production has taken on a new meaning in this century. The general orientation of critical political economics can assist in clarifying the meaning of this phenomenon. That is the task of all of the following chapters.

To establish a plausible argument that the analysis contained in critical political economics is close to those who struggle for a new society requires delving into our recent past.[38] The anguish of this struggle is all too familiar to those who experienced the antiwar movement of the 1960s, which was preceded in spirit by the civil rights movement in the earlier part of the decade. Both of these movements form the basis of the American New Left. This New Left must be distinguished from the "new liberalism," which the 1960s spawned as well. However, the New Left and the new liberalism have some interests in common. Both, for example, opposed the war in Vietnam and blanket anticommunism, and both were sensitive to moral issues. The new liberalism identified with Freedom Now, with community action programs in preference to the welfare bureaucracy, and with a genuine concern with the quality of life rather than with the worn rhetoric of the Democratic Party. Both the old left and the old liberalism were common thorns in the sides of the New Left and the new liberalism.[39]

It can be argued that a key difference is: "the new liberalism, like the old, remains firmly fixed within the ideological and political framework of corporate rule."[40] The new liberals seek compromise and reform. For example, what is needed, in this view, is a reallocation of resources away from the military to the cities to deal with their problems. The fundamental nature of the social structure is not questioned; basic change is thought to be unrealistic, although responses to surface manifestations of deeper problems in the social structure are cause of a great deal of anguish and discussion.

The New Left, in contrast, went far beyond the position of the new liberalism. This is not to say that some folk heroes and past battles were not held in common. It is to say that the New Left sought change which was perceived to be much more fundamental. A key difference is that the new liberalism did not have a sound critique of the system of capitalism, whereas this system was usually rejected nearly in its entirety by the New Left.

Evidence to support this view is, at best, scattered. But personal recollections of the 1968 Democratic convention in Chicago suggest that there were two distinct responses to the realization that then-President Lyndon B. Johnson was nowhere near the image of the "peace candidate" he promoted in his 1964 campaign. The new liberals supported the candidacy of Eugene McCarthy; the New Left primarily advocated street politics and symbolically supported Eldridge Cleaver, the Black Panther who was the Peace and Freedom Party candidate for President in a few states. The new liberals appeared to feel that McCarthy had a real chance to receive the nomination and were aghast when Hubert Humphrey, who was strongly identified with Johnson, was nominated. One McCarthy supporter, who had gotten "clean for Gene," was, in fact, crying on Michigan Avenue after McCarthy's defeat, proclaiming, "It's all over." The New Left, on the other hand, never entered the Hilton Hotel or McCarthy's suite there but were across the street in Grant Park often engaged in direct confrontation with the Chicago police and the National Guard. Perhaps the charge of naivety is too harsh for the many McCarthy supporters who had gotten involved in politics for the first time. But the debacle of the convention, broadcast for all to see and accompanied by CBS's vetern newsman Walter Cronkite losing his composure, suggests that the new liberals were, indeed, naive. It can hardly be argued that the 1972 election and its accompanying Watergate scandal, which deposed Nixon and left us with Ford and Rockefeller, gave a breath of fresh air and new confidence to the new liberals. And even with the Democrats in power the critique of society offered by those in the Movement remains instrumental, and the deeper conflicts of our times—including capitalism vs. socialism—are far from being resolved.

The New Left of the 1960s is generally perceived as having been radical and revolutionary, maintaining a style which was often bizarre and without purpose and functioning with no clear ideology except for opposition to the American Dream. Herbert Marcuse called this stance "The Great Refusal."[41] The refusal, one can speculate, appeared in two main forms—socialistic and anarchistic.[42] The former sought some sort of political solidarity and collective action. Yet, a specific socialist party that could attract those who were involved in this strain of the New Left did not emerge.

The anarchist strain, on the other hand, turned more to "doing their own thing" and often attempted to behave as if the revolution had been won and the task of creating a self-actualizing life style were on the immediate agenda. This behavior was expressed most profoundly by those who sought out and created the commune movement of the 1960s, which remains in various and amorphous forms. Some belonged to both strains simultaneously and at different times during this volatile period. It is quite safe to say that this distinction still seems valid; both strains still exist. If a political vehicle came to exist, it is likely that both strains would be part of a revolutionary strata. And if a revolution were successful, it is entirely possible that a postrevolutionary struggle between the two would be next on the agenda.

It is possible to put these two strains in more traditional terms as well since enough time has not yet passed to see the situation clearly and objectively. Among the ranks of the New Left are those who see Proudhon's pronouncement that "property is theft" as essentially correct. Others see classical and contemporary Marxian analyses as not only viable, but completely necessary, if the understanding that is needed to act as a foundation for meaningful change is to be developed. Still others gain their intellectual heritage from the style of the Wobblies and the Luddites. Others are identified with the counterculture without any intellectual heritage, seeking personal liberation and avoiding theorizing. Most are probably a combination of all these—consciously or unconsciously. There are academics, revolutionaries, and those who "revolutionize themselves" by changing their life styles and attempting to weed out the contradictions between their values and their activities. The majority are probably marginal to both the new world and the old. Alienation is without a doubt a driving force and an afflicting ailment. And many former members of the New Left have probably given up the struggle and exist, however uncomfortably or comfortably, once more in the mainstream. But the mainstream itself is not secure.

It should now be clear that the New Left is not an easily understood phenomenon, but its existence cannot be denied nor can it be shown to be irrelevant to the 1970s. Evidence on the latter is difficult to produce; it will only be demonstrated when historical perspective exists. A remark made by Theodore Roszak should be offered to those who do not share this perception.

> I have colleagues in the academy who have come within an ace of convincing me that no such things as "The Romantic Movement" or "The Renaissance" ever existed—not if one gets down to scrutinizing the [microscopic phenomena] of history. At that level, one tends only to see many different people doing many different things and thinking many different thoughts. . . . It would surely be convenient if these perversely ectoplasmic *Zeitgeists* were cardcarrying movements, with a headquarters, an executive board, and a file of official manifestoes. But of course they aren't.[43]

The Movement is still around, but it is very scattered and without focus, and many of its former adherents burned themselves out on radical politics. But perhaps a remark made by Jacobs and Landau still holds, "Those in the Movement now restlessly seek to find a new politics and a new ideology that will permit them to link existential humanism with morally acceptable modes of achieving radical social change."[44]

The Radical Movement in the Post–World War II Period

The origins of the Movement, which as a social development parallels contemporary critical political economics, are elusive. They have many strands which will be pointed out only fleetingly since this is not the place to lay down the detailed historical accounts that others have written.[45] In these works, there is general agreement on some main issues.

The New Left probably has its beginnings in the mid-1950s during which a few intellectuals sought to come to grips with the brutality of the Stalinist Soviet Union and Western imperialism. In Jacobs' and Landau's view, significant beginnings for the Movement occurred in England where the publication of two new journals, *The New Reasoner* and *Universities and Left Review*, began in 1957. In 1959 these two joined to form the *New Left Review*. The intellectual underpinnings of the New Left Review included those who saw the failure of Marxism resulting from its vulgar application rather than from its theoretical foundations. In these journals the humanism of socialism was rediscovered along with the plight of the common person. Alienation and humanism could not be comfortably discussed within the confines of the old left because of its general alliance with the Soviet Union, one of the few socialist experiments. Therefore, a new forum needed to be invented. The events following this modest intellectual rebirth seem remarkable in retrospect. However, cold realities, not theories, made a new intellectual and ethical commitment necessary.[46]

The beginnings in the United States are a bit later than those in Europe and for good reason. The American Dream was at least breathing steadily, if not based on a healthy foundation, and Senator Joseph R. McCarthy had rekindled substantial interest in a traditional American scapegoat, the political left. Radicalism was discredited in many circles, and its adherents put on the defensive by this classic political demagoguery.

It was not until the late 1950s that a small group of intellectuals began to form around the universities of Wisconsin, California at Berkeley, and Chicago. At Wisconsin, historian William Appleman Williams thought Marxism was useful to understand the history of America. A Wisconsin group began *Studies on the Left*, "a journal of research, social theory, and review." The publication of *New University Thought* began in Chicago. In 1960 a meeting was held in Madison to consider combining the two journals. The debate centered around the use of the word "left." The Chicago group, whose members had some experience in communist youth groups, thought the use of words, such as *left* and *socialism*, were so discredited as to be useless. The Madison people, who also had communist youth group experience, argued "that since they were socialists and Marxists, they should say so."[47]

Jacobs and Landau see the American New Left originating at least in part from these beginnings. The editors of these journals were committed to both socialism and critical thought and came to view themselves as seeking to be "a new breed of university professor." The issues went beyond politics and socialism and included human freedoms in general.[48] It seems very reasonable to suggest that in these journals the New Left had clearly spotted the issues. The push was for a democratic, decentralized socialism which would place people and their lives over the primacy of property. A dichotomy was posed. Capitalism and bourgeois democracy allowed the owners of the means of production freedom to pursue their interests but in the process, and under the protection of the Fourteenth Amendment to the U.S. Constitution, trampled over the human rights of most people in the society; a socialism compatible both with security and the absence of exploitation could be invented that would allow everyone to participate in decision making within the general framework of collective but decentralized ownership of the means of production. The New Left argued that the alleged freedoms under democracy along with capitalism were largely illusory; and socialism was not, as myth also held, necessarily accompanied by totalitarian, centralized, and bureaucratic domination. These remain as the central issues surrounding the debate between capitalism and socialism and within socialism itself.

A change came to the emerging Movement in the early 1960s, with the arrival of another generation, which was more concerned with activism than with intellectual activity. The university came to be regarded as a part of the enemy, the Establishment. The new members of the Movement knew little, and cared less, of the debates of the 1930s. Stalinism, Trotskyism, and social democracy were, for them, academic constructs and quaint anachronisms rather than relevant existential realities or contemporary issues. The new genera-tion saw its enemies as "American society and its Establishment,"[49] the forms of domination and control which existed but had been mystified by popular ideology,[50] the gap between what the nation claimed to represent and what it actually represented both at home and abroad, and the one dimensional mentality[51] and aspirations that were expected of young adults raised in relative affluence.

Intellectuals, such as Marcuse, provided discussions of issues that one could read, but the more direct and feeling forms of expression were offered by the disenfranchised generation itself in its outpour-ing of music. The deep alienation was better expressed, for example, by Simon and Garfunkel in their many albums than by sociologists. In his song "It's Alright, Ma (I'm Only Bleeding)," Bob Dylan brought home to us the insight that even our president must sometimes stand naked, and other incredibly concise one liners.[52] The Moody Blues and Beatles were hardly one dimensional.

One of the first new political heroes was Fidel Castro, a man of action apparently without an ideology, whose concern was being instrumental in forming the political foundations for a better life for people. Such a life could not be anticipated under the bankrupt Batista regime, which was closely tied to American capitalist inter-ests.[53] "Fair play" was demanded for the Cuban revolution. In May 1960 the House Un-American Activities Committee (HUAC)[54] provided the emerging movement with a chance for action of its own, and demonstrations against the Committee's San Francisco hearings

took place. HUAC charged that the demonstrators, like the participants in many demonstrations that followed, were communist inspired. The demonstrators knew that they were not and that this issue
was fundamentally irrelevant subterfuge.[55]

Freedom Rides in the South in 1960 and 1961 followed. Caryl
Chessman was executed. Students and Bohemians came together and
formed "the loose and overlapping segments of what was to become
known as The Movement.[56]

The sentiments expressed by the Movement were that

> American society supported facism, oppressive institutions,
> capital punishment, and wars against popular movements in
> underdeveloped countries. "Alienation" was used to describe the
> society's effects on its citizens, and American society was seen as
> the source of injustice and suffering everywhere. While opposed
> to injustice and suppression of liberty in general, the activists did
> not feel the same outrage against Castro or Mao or Khrushchev
> that they could against their own rulers. It was "our" fault.
> Brought up and nurtured on the United Nations and liberal
> political values, hearing them articulated so well by President
> Kennedy and Adlai Stevenson, they demanded purity at home
> first, and when it was not forthcoming, quickly became con-
> vinced that it was impossible, there was something rotten at the
> core of American society.[57]

So a revulsion against the liberal rhetoric and end-of-ideology
platitudes developed. The new members turned to "talking from the
gut" in the style of Bob Dylan and other folk singers. There was an
increasing commitment to action. The Student Nonviolent Coordinating Committee (SNCC), which was, at first, relatively free of an
ideological stance, and the Students for a Democratic Society (SDS),
which emerged from a gathering in Port Huron, Michigan in 1960,
came to provide two specific forums from which to direct this
commitment.[58]

Jacobs and Landau summarize their interpretation in this way:

> What began perhaps as a rebellion against affluence and
> liberal hypocrisy grew in a few years into a radical activism that
> protested injustice at the very core of the society. But when even
> this was tolerated by the structures under attack, some of the
> young radicals began to think about something beyond rebellion
> or radical protest. The Movement now is struggling to develop an
> ideology that will guide them toward building an organization
> that can compete for political power.[59]

Critical political economics can be viewed as a part of the task
Jacobs and Landau perceive if ideology is taken to mean the manner
of thinking characteristic of a class or social grouping. The political

mechanism, on the other hand, still does not exist and only history will reveal if Jacobs and Landau are correct that organization will follow the clarification of ideas. *Indeed, the fragile U.S. left could be obliterated if fascism became dominant.*

The Movement Today At best, the Movement as a whole remains fragmented, and the current period is probably one in which the various people who compose the Movement or who might come to compose it are struggling with their own identities and have, at least temporarily, dropped out of the overtly political activity and organization building. Also, in a depressed economy (the widely ignored reality of the 1970s) personal survival is a problem which seems to generate individualism and more intense competition as people attempt to maintain their socioeconomic status.[60] However, in recent times there have been continual guerrilla underground strikes against the system, but it can only be concluded that these have so far failed to rally *mass* political action.[61]

Blacks and women have been most effective in recent years in creating solidarity among themselves to deal with common issues. Given the socioeconomic situation of these two parts of the population, it is no wonder that there is a substantial amount of fervor. For white males, however, the situation has been different, and more vague—even for those who experienced participation in the more active years of the New Left.

Karl Marx, in earlier times, might be considered as a model to emulate for those white males who feel superfluous today. For Marx, the son of a white lawyer, the process of forming an identity as a revolutionary who provided conceptual directions for understanding the workings of society was more psychological, philosophical, and intellectual. He chose the scientific method. To him, and many of those who empathize with his general intellectual stance, the approach was necessarily one of reason and the development of an awareness of society and history. Such an approach makes clear what specific action is likely to occur and where it makes sense to become politically involved personally. Marx's writings turned out to be his most significant political contribution for the development of an alternative to capitalism.

One can only speculate about the basis for a revulsion toward a mindless pursuit of the refinement of trivial parts of the conventional wisdom among those psychologically similar to Marx. It is not an easily explained anathema. Theory is absent, but limited observation serves as well. Perhaps identification with the Movement is partly a function of social class, at least for many. In any case, there is a continuing development of a revolutionary strata containing different peoples and a parallel and corresponding emergence of a critical political economics. It continues to this day, however subterranean it has been driven and however difficult it is for this critical political economics to emerge in the face of job discrimination against adherents to the paradigm.[62]

One plausible explanation for the continued interest and adherence to critical studies might be related to the continued fact of a crisis in the economy and society and a crisis, therefore, in the basis for human existence. The crisis includes most of the population which must sell its labor to live,[63] and from this stratum have emerged intellectual workers as well.

The General Orientation of Critical Political Economics

Theories of the basis of the Movement itself are highly speculative. It is easier and more conclusive to point out some of the literature which can be seen as the documents of the part of the Movement, critical political economics, in this work. Part of this literature has been noted in the preceding pages, but there are other works that must be mentioned at least in passing before turning to the more narrow focus of economic instability, the centralization and concentration of capital, and the state. [64]

A main journal is the *Review of Radical Political Economics* *(RRPE)* published by The Union for Radical Political Economics (URPE). Founded in 1968, this organization has provided a forum for a variety of dissidents who are involved in work in political economics.[65] The published works appearing in the *RRPE* come from a variety of left perspectives, reflecting the diversity that exists in the Movement.

Among the conference papers which URPE released in 1968, for example, there were conventional Marxian thought and New Left articles which negated the conventional neoclassical paradigm. Still others were written in an empirical and descriptive vein drawing on a combination of educated common sense and sociology.[66] In the organization itself it is no secret that political differences and divisions exist and that parts are thought by other parts to be "elitist." Women members have made charges of sexism against some men who are URPE members. In fact, sexism is a matter of continuing dialogue in URPE as in other parts of the Movement. Still, the organization is the major alternative and supplement to the American Economic Association, and it has maintained a membership and activities in which people can participate. Rather than being a group that simply reacts to conventional wisdom, it conducts its own sessions at gatherings of professional economists; and it has generated a difficult-to-measure but substantial interest and following.

For critical responses to URPE, one need only peruse the organization's newsletter. People who are deeply involved in the more activist dimensions of the Movement sometimes criticize URPE members as being armchair radicals. Certainly part of the membership fits this description. What is more, in some ways URPE is little different than the American Economic Association with many URPE members holding dual membership. But URPE seems no more or less vulnerable to ongoing criticism than other Movement groups. In fact, criticism is a large part of the stuff of which URPE is made. As in other parts of the Movement, critiques of itself are nearly as common as analyses of the broader society of which it is a part.

The Review of Radical Political Economics has had much more staying power and is better known than some other quite good Movement publications.[67] There is substantially less underground press in the 1970s than there was in the 1960s. At least one very good explicitly socialist journal, *Socialist Revolution*,[68] lacks the following that the *RRPE* has generated. The reason is probably that *RRPE* is coupled with an *organization* and is responsible for generating activities both of its own and at gatherings of the economics profession as a whole. The development of critical political economics owes much to The Union for Radical Political Economics. In particular, URPE provides those who are working in the vein of critical political economics with a forum—a medium, an organization URPE represents a symptom of a broader sentiment. The existence of critical thought in economics is undoubtedly much more widespread than that which is displayed by the presence of this one organization.[69]

Radical political economics, of course, has also captured the attention of the Establishment journals,[70] and mention of the radical critique and Marxian economics, often distorted and superficial, appears in most contemporary introductory textbooks in economics.[71]

One of the best and most comprehensive guides to this literature is provided by the Union for Radical Political Economics. In 1970 URPE put out a two-volume set entitled *Reading Lists in Radical Political Economics*. In 1974 URPE offered another two-volume set entitled *Resource Materials in Radical Political Economics*. The list of topics covered by the literature included is long: methodology, general political economy, thought, poverty and inequality, social change and social movements, minorities, alienation, Marxism, production of the working class, women, cities and the urban environment, the military-industrial complex, ideology in social science, contradictions of capitalism, economic history, economic development, imperialism, national liberation, socialism, comparative economic systems, and so on. There are volumes on socialist alternatives for America in both the 1971 and 1974 editions of the URPE guides to the literature. Much of the guides is presented in the form of reading lists for courses and therefore suggests an order in which the uninitiated might pursue some of critical political economics. It is no exaggeration to state that these reading lists are a rich contribution, a real directory of critical economic, social, and political thought. Pursuing the literature presented would be to undertake a curriculum lasting for some time. But it would be well worth the effort.

In addition to the directory of literature provided by URPE, a number of collections of readings in critical political economics exists which might provide the dabbler with a more manageable introduction.[72] These collections help fill what was previously an intellectual void. In many instances, they are part of the work done by those who developed a critical awareness of society especially during the 1960s.

The topics mentioned previously in connection with URPE are also the general topics covered in these introductory volumes. The main focus is on the structure of the economy and the way in which capitalism generates instability, insecurity, inequality, alienation, racism, sexism, irrationality, imperialism, and war. The authors present the view that some sort of socialism is the way out of the dilemmas of capitalism, and many discuss the varieties of socialism that exist in practice and in theory. David Gordon's *Problems in Political Economy* stands apart from the rest in that its focus is spatial, i.e., it talks about urban problems within the context of capitalism.[73]

Two journals deserve special recognition as part of critical political economics. They have provided a critique of capitalism for many years. These are *Sciences and Society* and *Monthly Review*. *Monthly Review* has existed for more than 25 years, and Paul Sweezy—who is undoubtedly the most recognized American Marxist economist—is one of its editors. It has probably made the greatest contribution to the development of Marxian economic thought in the United States.[74]

In addition, a new journal—*Working Papers on the Kapitalistate*—has emerged, which has as its focus, as the name of the journal emphasizes, the capitalist state.[75] There is available at least one introductory textbook, now in its second edition, which offers the radical critique in contrast to conventional economics to beginning students of political economics and the general reader.[76]

To cover all of the issues pointed to fleetingly and to document the argument that critical political economics offers an interpretation of the social world worth considering is, of course, too huge a task. Thus, the following has the more narrow focus of economic instability, centralization and concentration of capital, and the state. Through comparative analysis, it will be argued that the development of a critical political economics, which draws heavily on radical, Marxian, and the more eclectic political economics and social science, offers an interpretation that is useful in understanding the workings of contemporary U.S. capitalism. The general mood in which this is done was stated well by the late C. Wright Mills: "I have tried to be objective. I do not claim to be detached."

NOTES

1 Barney G. Glaser and Anselm L. Strauss, The Discovery of Grounded Theory: Strategies for Qualitative Research (Chicago: Aldine Publishing Co., 1967).

2 See, for example, James O'Connor, "The University and the Political Economy," Leviathan, vol. 1, no. 1 (March 1969), pp. 14–15. This article also appears in the Maxwell Review, vol. VI, no. 1 (Winter 1970), pp. 49–54.

3 Foreword to Judith Carnoy and Marc Weiss, eds. A House Divided: Radical Perspectives on Social Problems (Boston: Little, Brown, 1973), p. vii.

4 Thomas S. Kuhn, The Structure of Scientific Revolution (Chicago: The University of Chicago Press, 1970), p. 163. Copyright © 1970 by the University of Chicago Press.

5 Paul Sweezy, "Towards a Critique of Economics," Monthly Review, vol. XXI, no. 8 (January 1970), p. 3 and The Review of Radical Political Economics, vol. 2, no. 1 (Spring 1970).

6 Kuhn, The Structure of Scientific Revolution, p. 163. In connection with this, stands, as a parallel in economics, the hegemony of Keynesian thought. When it was not under question, especially in the early to middle 1960s, great progress appeared to be underway in economics as a science. Contemporary events suggest that this was an illusion held by a part of the economics community. Further discussion of this example appears in the next chapter.

7 Jack D. Douglas, "The Rhetoric of Science and the Origins of Statistical Thought: the Case of Durkheim's Suicide," in Edward A. Tiryakian, ed., The Phenomenon of Sociology: a Reader in the Sociology of Sociology (New York: Appleton-Century-Crofts, 1971), pp. 45–46.

8 Ibid., p. 45.

9 See also Sweezy, "Towards a Critique of Economics," pp. 2–3; David M.

Gordon, Theories of Poverty and Underemployment: Orthodox, Radical, and Dual Labor Market Perspectives *(Lexington, Mass.: D.C. Heath, 1972), Chapter 2; and Hyman R.* Cohen, "Dialectics and Scientific Revolutions," Science and Society, *vol. XXXVII, no. 3 (Fall 1973), to mention but three.*

10 *By, for example, Robert Wolfson of the Department of Economics at Syracuse University.*

11 *David M.* Gordon, Theories of Poverty and Underemployment, *p. ix. Gordon's book is a good introduction to critical political economics in general; it also provides a contrast of perspectives, including that of critical political economics, on poverty and underemployment.*

12 Joan Robinson, An Essay on Marxian Economics *(London: Macmillan Press, Ltd., 1966), p. 1.*

13 *See, particularly, Martin Jay,* The Dialectical Imagination *(Boston: Little, Brown, 1973); Max Horkheimer,* Critical Theory *(New York: Herder and Herder, 1972); and Albrecht Wellmer,* Critical Theory of Society *(New York: Herder and Herder, 1971).*

14 *E.g., Robin Blackburn, ed.,* Ideology in Social Science: Readings in Critical Social Thought *(New York: Random House, 1973). Blackburn has been associated with the British* New Left Review. *The American sociologist who perhaps most fits the spirit in which we use the term critical is the late C. Wright Mills, particularly in his fine little book* The Sociological Imagination *(New York: Oxford University Press, 1959).*

15 *Robert M. Solow's discussion of John G. Gurley, "The State of Political Economics,"* The American Economic Review, *vol. LXI, no. 2 (May 1971), Papers and Proceedings of the 83rd Annual Meeting of the American Economics Association, p. 65.*

16 *Ibid., p. 64*

17 *Gurley, "The State of Political Economics," pp. 54–55.*

18 *Elliot Liebow,* Tally's Corner *(Boston: Little, Brown, 1967), p. 235.*

19 *Richard S. Rudner,* Philosophy of Social Science *(Englewood Cliffs, N.J.: Prentice-Hall, 1966), p. 69.*

20 *A complex issue in social science is that of prediction, which many social scientists see as something social science is obliged to undertake. Personally, I am inclined to make predictions only if I preface them with a lot of caveats employing the rhetoric of centeris paribus which can often prove to be a kind of sorcery or a fancy dance which is pseudoscientific, at best. Yet in practice it could be argued that to pretend to be aware of "what is going on" is to have implicitly become wrapped up in a prediction or hypothesis verification. Forecasts should be seen as a closely related but separate matter. Forecasts occur with respect to the future, and in the social sciences, as a matter of fact, they are sometimes even made with the idea that they can be altered if an undesirable scenario emerges on paper. These issues suggest that the application of the method of the physical sciences does not totally apply to the social sciences. More accurately, it should be used with caution, which orthodox economists—often lacking a sociological frame of mind—frequently fail to do.*

21 C. Wright Mills, The Sociological Imagination, p. 18, footnote.

22 See, for example, Gunter W. Remmling, ed., Towards the Sociology of Knowledge: Origin and Development of a Sociological Thought Style (New York: Humanities Press, 1973); Gunter W. Remmling, Road to Suspicion: a Study of Modern Mentality and the Sociology of Knowledge (New York: Appleton-Century-Crofts, 1967); and Werner Stark, The Sociology of Knowledge (London: Routledge & Kegan Paul, 1958). I applied the perspective of the sociology of knowledge to economic thought in "An Inquiry into the Roots and Content of the World View of Paul Baran," unpublished, 1970, and "An Exploration in Social Theory and Social Structure: a Critical Appraisal of the Classical School of Economics," unpublished, 1970. Also see Peter Berger and Thomas Luckmann, The Social Construction of Reality (Garden City, N.Y.: Doubleday, 1966).

23 Myron E. Sharpe, John Kenneth Galbraith and the Lower Economics, 2nd ed. (White Plains, N.Y.: International Arts and Sciences Press, 1974), p. 1.

24 Ibid., Chapter 1 and Benjamin Ward, What's Wrong With Economics? (New York: Basic Books, 1972) provide some guidance on this question.

25 See, for example, Rendigs Fels, ed., The Second Crisis of Economic Theory (Morristown, N.J.: General Learning Press, 1972). This is a collection of papers from the American Economic Association meeting, December 27–29, 1971. The title of the work is taken from the title of a paper given by Joan Robinson. Also see Robert Lekachman, Economists at Bay: Why the Experts Will Never Solve Your Problems (New York: McGraw-Hill, 1976). Lekachman argues that economics has become little more than a branch of applied mathematics and has lost touch with the great tradition of political economy. Yet, he seems to hold the view that contemporary problems can be attributed, at least in part, to blunders by those economists who have been listened to by political leaders, especially presidents. Radicals who think in terms of social class would be highly skeptical of this interpretation.

26 Sharpe, John Kenneth Galbraith and the Lower Economics, p. x.

27 A popular and well-known introduction to economic thought in general is Robert L Heilbroner's The Worldly Philosophers (New York: Simon & Schuster, first published in 1953). Also see Eric Roll's A History of Economic Thought (Englewood Cliffs, N.J. : Prentice-Hall, in its various editions since 1953); Joseph A. Schumpeter, History of Economic Analysis (New York: Oxford University Press, 1954); John E. Elliott and John Cownie, eds., Competing Philosophies in American Political Economics (Pacific Palisades, Calif.: Goodyear Publishing Co., 1975); E.K. Hunt, Property and Prophets: the Evolution of Economic Institutions and Ideologies (New York: Harper & Row, 1975); Jacob Oser and William C. Blanchfield, The Evolution of Economic Thought, 3rd ed. (New York: Harcourt Brace Jovanovich, 1975); and Everett J. Burtt, Jr., Social Perspectives in the History of Economic Theory (New York: St. Martin's Press, 1972).

28 One of my favorite interpretations of the consequences of laissez-faire is Karl Polanyi, The Great Transformation (Boston: Beacon Press, 1957). Here it is shown that the laissez-faire stance is much more than academic. Polanyi persuasively argues that it was the basis for world conflict in the 19th and 20th centuries, including wars.

29 *Douglas F. Dowd, in* The Twisted Dream: Capitalist Development in the United States Since 1776 *(Cambridge, Mass.: Winthrop Publishers, 1974) provides a clever updated term for this general notion: "the invisible fist." This is also another good introductory work on economic thought as well as a good interpretation of our times.*

30 *The state system includes, in Douglas Dowd's words, "government; administration and bureaucracy; military, paramilitary, and security forces; the judiciary; lesser (local and state) governments; legislative assemblies (federal and other)." Ibid., p. 249. This is not a complete definition; more will be said later in Chapter 5. An attempt to avoid the usual confusion about this term is made here.*

The classic statement by Marx and Engels in The Communist Manifesto *(New York: International Publishers, 1848) is: "The executive of the modern state is but a committee for managing the common affairs of the whole bourgeoisie." (p. 11)*

31 *E.g., among others, James O'Connor,* The Fiscal Crisis of the State *(New York: St. Martin's Press, 1973); Joan Robinson,* An Essay on Marxian Economics; *Michio Morishima,* Marx's Economics: a Dual Theory of Value and Growth *(New York: Cambridge University Press, 1973); Paul Mattick,* Marx and Keynes: the Limits of the Mixed Economy *(Boston: Porter Sargent Publisher, 1969); Victor Perlo,* The Unstable Economy: Booms and Recessions in the U.S. Since 1945 *(New York: International Publishers, 1973) and, of course, Paul Baran and Paul Sweezy,* Monopoly Capital: an Essay on the American Social and Economic Order *(New York: Monthly Review Press, 1966), as well as other writings by Sweezy. Especially see his* The Theory of Capitalist Development: Principles of Marxian Political Economy *(New York: Monthly Review Press, 1968);* Modern Capitalism and Other Essays *(New York: Monthly Review Press, 1972); and Paul M. Sweezy and Harry Magdoff,* The Dynamics of U.S. Capitalism *(New York: Monthly Review Press, 1972). Extremely important in this vein is Ernest Mandel,* Marxist Economic Theory, *2 vols. (New York: Monthly Review Press, 1970); An* Introduction to Marxist Economic Theory *(New York: Pathfinder Press, 1970); as well as other works by Mandel noted in the bibliography. A focus on labor and its relationship to capital is contained in Harry Braverman,* Labor and Monopoly Capital: The Degradation of Work in the Twentieth Century *(New York: Monthly Review Press, 1974). An important Marxian work that analyzes the role of education is Samuel Bowles and Herbert Gintis,* Schooling in Capitalist America: Educational Reform and the Contradictions of Economic Life *(New York: Basic Books, 1976).*

32 *A.D. Soares, "Marxism as a General Sociological Orientation,"* British Journal of Sociology, *vol. 19 (1968), p. 365.*

33 *Ibid.*

34 *Paul Sweezy, "Towards a Critique of Economics," pp. 1–2. An earlier version of this paper was presented at, what those who attended will remember to be, an enlightening and lively session of an early meeting of The Union for Radical Political Economics, at MIT, November 1–2, 1969. Sweezy must be seen as a key contributor to the development of a critical political economics in the U.S.*

35 *For an excellent discussion of the relationship between classical political*

economy and the conclusions to which it was taken by Marx see Ernest Mandel, The Formation of the Economic Thought of Karl Marx (New York: Monthly Review Press, 1971). A good work on Marx's life and thought is Werner Blumenberg, Portrait of Marx (New York: Herder and Herder, 1972).

36 No pretense of laying down a critique of the massive literature in European critical political economics is made here. But a couple of works that provide an introduction to European thought in addition to that of the Belgian Ernest Mandel who has already been mentioned, and the British Joan Robinson should be noted. There is the New Left Review, in London, a particularly lively Marxian journal which is useful to keep up on developments in European Marxian thought. Also see Dick Howard and Karl E. Klare, eds., The Unknown Dimension: European Marxism Since Lenin (New York: Basic Books, 1972).

37 George Fischer, ed., The Revival of American Socialism (New York: Oxford University Press, 1971), p. v.

38 It is important to note that the Movement is not a new entity in American society, nor is the radical political economics of the 1960s without historical parallels. Jack London, in particular, articulated the sentiment of some people early in the 20th century in his many stories, books, and polemics. His War of the Classes, published by Macmillan in 1905 falls into the polemical category. Joan London (Jack London's daughter), in Jack London and His Times (Seattle: University of Washington Press, 1939), sketches the milieu in which her father existed. He was the son of an astrologer who left Jack's mother before he was born, and the San Francisco of the late 19th century was a haven for those with interests similar to some contemporary countercultural types there.

39 Robert Wolfe, "Editorial Statement: Beyond Protest," Studies on the Left, vol. 7, no. 1 (January–February 1967), p. 3.

40 Ibid.

41 See, among other works, Herbert Marcuse, An Essay on Liberation (Boston: Beacon Press, 1969).

42 One could also see Gil Green, The New Radicalism: Anarchist or Marxist (New York: International Publisher, 1971).

43 Theodore Roszak, The Making of a Counter Culture: Reflections on the Technocratic Society and Its Youthful Opposition (Garden City, N.Y.: Doubleday, 1969), p. xi.

44 Paul Jacobs and Saul Landau, The New Radicals (New York: Vintage Books, 1966), p. 7. Copyright © 1966 by Random House, Inc.

45 One history of the New Left is James O'Brien, "A History of the New Left, 1960-1968," originally in three installments in the May–June, September–October, and November–December, 1968 issues of Radical America. This history was reprinted by the New England Free Press. Another is Christopher Lasch, The Agony of the American Left (New York: Random House, 1968), especially from Chapter 5 on. Also see George Fischer, ed., The Revival of American Socialism (New York: Oxford University Press, 1971); Peter Clecak, Radical Paradoxes: Dilemmas of the American Left: 1945-1970 (New York: Harper & Row, 1973); and Priscilla Long, ed., The New Left: a Collection of Essays (Boston: Porter Sargent Publishers 1969).

46 Jacobs and Landau, The New Radicals, p. 9.

47 Ibid., p. 10.

48 Ibid., p. 11.

49 Ibid., p. 12.

50 Many good ideas on this from a theoretical perspective are contained in Ralf Dahrendorf, Class and Class Conflict in Industrial Society (Stanford: Stanford University Press, 1959).

51 The modern classic here is Herbert Marcuse, One-Dimensional Man (Boston: Beacon Press, 1964).

52 On his fifth album, "Bringing It All Back Home," which appeared in 1965. Dylan did a national tour in 1974 and sang the song "It's Alright, Ma (I'm Only Bleeding)" which contains this line and was received with standing ovations. Dylan must be seen as a central Movement philosopher, poet, and song writer.

53 Jacobs and Landau, The New Radicals, p. 12. See also James O'Connor, The Origins of Socialism in Cuba (Ithaca, N.Y.: Cornell University Press, 1970).

54 Which finally was abolished in January 1975. For an account of its activities, see Walter Goodman, "A Farewell to HUAC, Whose Glory Was Behind It," The New York Times, The Week in Review section, (January 19, 1975), p. 20.

55 Jacobs and Landau, The New Radicals, p. 12-13

56 Ibid., p. 13.

57 Ibid., p. 14.

58 Ibid.

59 Ibid.

60 For example, the School of Management at Syracuse University sponsored seminars in early 1975 to teach people how to be more impressive at a job interview. The flyer announcing the seminars began with "Can't get a job" and went on to suggest that it might be attributed to not being suave enough. Obviously, people would see through this if they all took lessons in how to do an interview and remained unemployed. But in the earlier stages of an economic contraction many might believe that their employment difficulties could be overcome by competing more vigorously.

61 An interesting document which is the political statement of the Weather Underground is Prairie Fire: The Politics of Revolutionary Anti-Imperialism (San Francisco: Communications Co., 1974), in which the Weather Underground lists bombings and other acts of armed struggle it has carried out.

62 This point is touched on again, later. Other examples are reported in the Union for Radical Political Economics Newsletter, (December, 1974). Three adherents to the general stance of critical economics were dismissed from San Jose State University at the end of the 1973-74 academic year and were reported to have been replaced with four conservative economists. In addition a Marxist political economist was fired from Lehman College (CUNY) in New York City. These firings sparked the formation of an informational picket line in San Francisco at the Allied Social Science

Associations convention in December 1974 at the inaugural address of the new President of the American Economic Association. URPE views political firings of critical political economists as a systematic phenomenon. I agree on the basis of personal knowledge and experience. An excellent account of job discrimination in universities against radicals in Lawrence F. Lifschultz, "Could Karl Marx Teach Economics in America?" Ramparts, vol. 12, no. 9 (April 1974).

   Job discrimination against radicals is, of course, nothing new in the U.S. One case is that of Scott Nearing who was fired from the University of Pennsylvania in 1915 and the University of Toledo in 1917 in the midst of war fever. Dr. Nearing's account in The Making of a Radical: A Political Autobiography (New York: Harper & Row, 1972) presents the view that progressive ideas were not conducive to surviving within universities essentially dominated by business interests whose representatives sat on boards of trustees. Thorstein Veblen underscores all of this in his The Higher Learning in America: A Memorandum on the Conduct of Universities by Business Men (New York: Sagamore Press, 1957), first published in 1918.

63 See Andrew Levison, The Working Class Majority (New York: Coward, McCann and Geoghegan, 1974) for documentation of the obvious point that the U.S. is a society where the majority are members of the working class "no matter what the color of their collars" as Paul Sweezy is fond of saying.

64 The main focus throughout this work is political economics because a focus is needed and because critical political economics is more a part of my experience than other thought founded in the Movement. Parallel thought exists elsewhere. For example, in sociology there is The Insurgent Sociologist and The Berkeley Journal of Sociology. Similar endeavors exist in psychology and even in the natural sciences (e.g., the journal Science for the People).

65 An early attempt, partially successful, to explain URPE was James H. Weaver, "The Union for Radical Political Economics," Maxwell Review, vol. vi, no. 2 (Spring 1970), pp. 41–49. One could also see Tom Riddell, "A Note on Radical Economics and the New Economists," Review of Radical Political Economics, vol. 5, no. 3 (Fall 1973), pp. 67–72. The latter is an outline of the role of the "new economists" as "hand-maidens" of the Establishment and what the role of radical economists should be (about which Riddell doesn't come to firm conclusions). He suggests the obvious—practice—which is difficult to implement in the absence of a more coherent and broad based Movement.

   The best way to get a sense of URPE is to read its Newsletter and The Review of Radical Political Economics. There were, as of December 1974, around 1,300 individual subscribers to the RRPE and the review is sent to around 2,200 people and institutions. There also have been recent increases in membership reported by the national office as well as the addition of a few new chapters (which are largely made up of faculty and graduate students on university campuses) as part of the organizational structure. In contrast, the American Economic Association, the major professional organization for economists in the U.S., which was founded in 1885, sends its American Economic Review and Journal of Economic Literature to 17,966 individuals; and when institutions, mainly libraries, are added, circulation is about 25,000 (as of December 1974). The URPE publication, then, has an individual circulation that is a bit over 8 percent of the AEA's circulation of the AER and the JEL.

66 URPE, Conference Papers of the Union for Radical Economics (Ann Arbor, Mich., 1968).

67 For example, Leviathan, which appeared in 1969 and disappeared after a few issues in 1971, was a high quality Movement journal.

68 This journal was founded in 1970 in San Francisco. Its founders included some former editors of Studies on the Left, which ceased publication in 1969.

69 One example is The Union of Marxist Social Scientists, originating in 1974.

70 See, for example, the previously mentioned article by John G. Gurley, "The State of Political Economics," The American Economic Review, vol. LXI, no. 2 (May 1971), pp. 53–68; Martin Brofenbrenner, "Radical Economics in America: a 1970 Survey," The Journal of Economic Literature, vol. viii, no. 3 (September 1970), pp. 747–766, as well as "What the Radical Economists Are Saying," Harvard Business Review, vol. 51, no. 3 (Sept.–Oct. 1973), "A Skeptical View of Radical Economics," The American Economist, vol. XVII no. 2 (Fall 1973), and "Samuelson, Marx, and Their Latest Critics," Journal of Economic Literature, vol. XI, no. 1 (March, 1973), all by Brofenbrenner. Also see S. T. Worland, "Radical Political Economy as a 'Scientific Revolution'," Southern Economic Journal, vol. 39, no. 2; October, 1972).

71 One of the least superficial discussions is in Paul Samuelson's Economics, which is the archetypical expression of Establishment economics. Also see, for example, Edwin Mansfield, Principles of Macroeconomics (New York: Norton, 1974) for an incredibly naive and superficial look at Marxian economics. Or look in the index under Marx in almost any textbook on economics published in this country and be prepared for an absolute vulgarization and misrepresentation of Marx's ideas.

Still another work that should be noted is Assar Lindbeck, The Political Economy of the New Left: an Outsider's View (New York: Harper & Row, 1971). Samuelson provided a foreword to this. Lindbeck, a Swede, wrote the book "to facilitate a dialogue between the New Left and academic economists" in the background of a speaking tour at various U.S. campuses during 1968–1969. Although this is not a comprehensive little book, it is provocative and touches on many of the main issues, but it is ultimately inconclusive.

72 Four examples are Edwards, Reich, and Weisskopf, eds., The Capitalist System: a Radical Analysis of American Society (Englewood Cliffs, N.J.: Prentice-Hall, 1972); David M. Gordon, ed., Problems in Political Economy: an Urban Perspective (Lexington, Mass.: D.C. Heath, 1971); David Mermelstein, ed., Economics: Mainstream Readings and Radical Critiques, 2nd ed. (New York: Random House, 1973); and Maurice Zeitlin, ed., American Society Inc.: Studies of the Social Structure and Political Economy of the United States (Chicago: Markham Publishing Co., 1970).

Still another work which is a contribution to the literature in this vein and which is a good introduction is Howard Sherman, Radical Political Economy: Capitalism and Socialism from a Marxist-Humanist Perspective (New York: Basic Books, 1972).

73 See also, in this regard, Daniel R. Fusfeld, The Basic Economics of the Urban Racial Crisis (New York: Holt, Rinehart and Winston, 1973) and his shorter, and in some ways more lucid, work "The Basic Economics of the Urban and Racial Crisis," Conference Papers of the Union for Radical Political Economics, (Ann Arbor, Mich.: 1968), pp. 55–84.

74 See Lifschultz, "Could Karl Marx Teach Economics in America?," for more on this. There is also Monthly Review Press which is a key resource for publications in critical political economics. A review of the bibliography of this work indicates many of these. An overview of Monthly Review from the perspective of its editors is "Twenty-Five Eventful Years," Monthly Review, vol. 25, no. 13 (June 1974), pp. 1–13.

75 Working Papers on the Kapitalistate was created by James O'Connor and others and looks at the state in several capitalist societies, particularly the U.S., Japan, Italy, and Germany, with members of "the redaction" from all of those countries.

76 E.K. Hunt and Howard J. Sherman, Economics: an Introduction to Traditional and Radical Views, 2nd ed. (New York: Harper & Row, 1975). If a textbook has to be used to teach introductory economics, I prefer this one. It begins by putting the contemporary economic system in historical perspective and then moves on to contrast conflicting views on microeconomics and macroeconomics. It offers a thorough and realistic treatment of government in relation to the economy and provides a great deal of empirical data. The book ends with a thin but interesting discussion of comparative economic systems and the problems and prospects under socialism. Importantly, Hunt and Sherman are generally careful in their documentation. Many orthodox texts, on the contrary, substitute the authority of the authors for the careful presentation of ideas.

2

THE QUESTIONED HEGEMONY OF KEYNESIAN THOUGHT

Chapter 1 showed that a critical political economics based on a Marxian and radical theoretical foundation is needed to fill a vacuum which many think exists in contemporary economics. For this view to be plausible, it is necessary to discuss the alternative to critical political economics. It is also necessary to elaborate on the theme that a theoretical vacuum does exist because the most prominent paradigm in contemporary macroeconomic thought—the Keynesian paradigm—does not relate to reality as well as alternative perspectives on the political economy and society. Thus, this chapter develops the idea that the hegemony of Keynesian thought is in question on a variety of grounds and that alternative analyses of the political economy should be considered. The view developed here is that Keynesian policies both ameliorate and exacerbate economic instability. Michal Kalecki has argued that Keynesian policies as applied in the United States (and elsewhere) actually serve to change the structural foundations of the economy and reinforce centralization and concentration in both capital and labor.[1]

The discussion will first establish the relationship between the thought of John Maynard Keynes and modern economics. In this chapter and in this work, Keynesianism is taken to be an archetype in economic thought as well as a popular ideology. Keynesianism extends beyond the theoretical work of John Maynard Keynes to form a school of thought which promotes a paradigm containing "scientific" and ideological aspects.

A second task is to look at the foundations of Keynesianism, that is, Keynes' general theory. The theory will be put in an economic, social, and political context. This chapter will discuss Keynes' theoretical reaction to the Great Depression of the 1930s as well as the relationship of his ideas to macroeconomic instability and problems of income distribution in more recent times.

A third task is to develop in more detail the first introductory undertaking on the relationship between Keynes' general theory and Keynesianism. But an added dimension is the connection between Keynesian thought and the modern lower economics. Much of contemporary lower economics is quite Keynesian, but there are also other strands of thought in this literature. A look at some of it suggests that many tenets of Keynesianism are under question and that the hegemony of Keynesian thought as a popular economic doctrine is in serious doubt. The closely related ad hoc policy suggestions which have been added to a Keynesian foundation also should be considered suspect from the perspective of critical political economics.

The Keynesian Paradigm: Archetype and Ideology

Keynesian thought means here those ideas put forth first by John Maynard Keynes in The General Theory of Employment, Interest and Money published in 1936 and developed and embraced by a whole generation of economists and policy makers. The essence of Keynesian thought is that capitalism by itself does not necessarily generate a full employment level of production, and a capitalist economy could, therefore, languish indefinitely with people unemployed and production facilities underused unless government action to stimulate aggregate demand is consciously and adequately undertaken. Later Keynesians, once the Great Depression was past and the price level (inflation) became a matter of concern, adopted the ideas developed by Keynes to this latter phenomenon as well. Keynesianism, then, means those ideas on aggregative economics held by Keynes and his followers that came to dominate the lower economics as well as the more formalized theory which reached its apex in the early and middle 1960s. These ideas dominated college and university curricula then; many undergraduates learned about the Keynesian doctrine. This learning was often helped by Paul Samuelson's *Economics,* an introductory textbook epitomizing post-World War II economic thought in the U. S. Samuelson's textbook was presented in ten editions between 1948 and 1976, and Keynesian economics in its modern introductory form remains the macroeconomics Samuelson's book propounds. Thus, even though many advocates of Keynesianism no longer feel much of the optimism and zeal, that paradigm remains the most prominent and commonplace in the conventional thought. The Keynesian paradigm is one of the most important archetypes in 20th century economic thought as well as one of the more important political economic ideologies in the society at large.

However, the general Keynesian stance came under fire in the late 1960s for a variety of reasons, and the criticism has continued into the 1970s. Many have grave reservations about the promise of the so-called Keynesian revolution. Marxian thought has reasserted its challenge in the face of fiscal and monetary policies (key tools of Keynesian medicine to regulate the level of aggregate demand, output, and employment) failing to be embraced in central government in a fashion that generates relatively full employment, stable prices, and a reasonable rate of economic growth. The view that only more direct forms of state intervention, such as conscious national planning, will stabilize the economy seems to be gaining prominence among those who were formerly optimistic adherents to the more indirect Keynesian policies. Discussion of national planning was underway among many prominent liberal economists by early 1975 as unemployment and inflation continued at rates generally considered unacceptable.[2] Dialogue and controversy surrounding comprehensive planning, public employment, and wage price controls is in its infancy.

The first half of the 1970s was a time when Keynesian suggestions for increased government expenditures during times of unemployment and decreased government expenditures during times of inflation could not be applied so simply for political reasons or for assured success for deep structural reasons. The economy and society face a seemingly continuing state of disarray as well as disillusionment about the promise of the Keynesian paradigm. Although, it is too early to proclaim the end of the Keynesian revolution since no clear consensus exists to push for alternative policies and theories, the

Keynesian era will probably end by the latter part of the 1970s or early 1980s.

Others—particularly radical and Marxian economists and socialists—have always been skeptical of the ability of Keynesian policies to stabilize the economy. More accurately, the kind of "stability" these policies would deliver, if they could deliver it at all, would be a hierarchical solidification. The view in these circles is that any policies embraced by the state in capitalist society would be policies which would benefit the upper socioeconomic strata disproportionately. The Nixon administration, lasting from 1968 to 1974, for example, is known to have formulated wage-price controls of a variety which were specifically designed to "zap" labor.

Michael Harrington coined the term "Adam Smith's John Maynard Keynes" in a polemical discussion to dramatize that Keynesian notions did not deviate from thought which serves as an ideology supportive of capitalism. Although this may have been a controversy only among liberals and conservatives, Harrington argued that New Deal economics had become a conservative force in American life and that even a comparatively stabilized capitalism characterized by the dominance of corporate interests was more than suspect. His argument was that the corporate interest and the "common good" do not coincide, a large underclass remained, and, besides, it was not Keynesianism as applied economic science that removed the nation from the Great Depression of the 1930s. Rather the main boost to the economy was the entry of the United States into World War II.[3] In practice, apparently *military* Keynesianism was the most likely form to emerge.

The latter view is, of course, controversial and has generated arguments to the contrary—that military expenditures have, over time, drained the economic vitality of the United States and have been undertaken with a corresponding decline in more essential investment in plant and equipment, the results of which are problems of productivity vis-à-vis the rest of the capitalist world. Seymour Melman, for example, has presented this view. Wasteful military expenditures *may* have been instrumental in moving the nation out of the Great Depression, but a continued expansion of the military part of federal spending, the argument goes, has been dysfunctional in the postwar period.[4] It seems reasonable to believe that military expenditures have done both; thus, it may not be surprising to note that the opposing theses of the Harrington and Melman varieties have played a part in moving others towards still another view which states that there have been *conflicting* functions existing in the U.S. military expenditures. Keynesianism as applied can thus be seen as generating as well as abating the contradictions of capitalism. Clarence Y. H. Lo, drawing on the theoretical work of James O'Connor and Claus Offe, puts it this way:

> The existing Marxist literature has been correct in pointing out that the military budget (1) deters the U.S.S.R., China, and the left (armed confrontation), (2) affects international trade and capital flows, (3) supports the overall level of aggregate demand and sometimes regulates demand (military Keynesianism), and (4) provides profitable investment opportunities for military contractors as well as for the civilian economy (subsidized investment). But the military budget cannot successfully perform *all* of these functions simultaneously. Policies that resolve one set of problems create new difficulties. Often, military spending upsets these four necessary functions, rather than satisfying them. Thus, the existing Marxist literature does not develop the notion that military spending is only a partial, temporary, and self-contradictory resolution of capitalist economic problems. By the single minded concentration [of how military spending is functional for the economy], Marxists have left themselves wide open for criticism by writers such as S. Melman and R. Barnet, who have been quick to attack the Marxist position by pointing out the obvious ways in which military spending is detrimental to the economy.[5]

Lo, who uses and is involved in developing the framework of the contemporary Marxian theory of the state (discussed in Chapter 5), points to the contradictions existing between these different functions. This theory of the state shows why macroeconomic stability does not emerge even when there is government intervention on a large scale, the *purposes* to which the expenditures are directed aside. His emphasis on contradictions, characteristic of Marxian thinking, seems very useful, and this theme will appear again.

Contradictions in the way in which expenditures are undertaken by government lead to the argument that it is not surprising that simplistic Keynesian ideas are under considerable fire. In response, alternative paradigms are being constructed, with some founded on both orthodox and more eclectic Marxian notions.

It is not enough to suggest that government should "push or pull," as Stanford Professor of Economics Lorie Tarshis once put it when summing up the wisdom that Keynesian macroeconomics had to offer. Those Keynesians who insist that the problem is how the ideas have been misapplied by ignorant and short-sighted legislative and executive branches of the federal government are left to prove why the outcome should be different. Political economics must have a realistic theory of the state which goes beyond orthodoxy if it is to be fact rather than an academic game. Political economics must explain what is happening in reality if its ideas are to be taken seriously and considered useful even if such economics leads to suggestions for far-reaching structural changes and exposure of deeply rooted conflicts and contradictions in capitalism.

Here are some reasons why contemporary economics is in a state of disarray and why there is heated debate. Stability, the main promise of Keynesian economics, has not been attained. With the increasing concern about the environment, economic growth, which is part of the modern macroeconomic program based on a Keynesian foundation, is not as surely defensible as previously thought.[6] More accurately, economic growth is not a sensible policy to promote over the long run. This topic will be discussed later, but an irony of the American society is that it may become necessary to produce *less* using the labor of more people.

Even mainstream economists who are not deeply troubled by continuing economic and social inequality but who are bothered by a persistent price level and employment instability which knows some, but few, class barriers have rethought their intellectual positions. The relevance of the dominant paradigm in contemporary economic thought has been questioned particularly in the face of unemployment and underemployment as well as falling GNP during most of 1974 and 1975, both of which were accompanied by inflation. Even a new term, stagflation, has been invented to label the phenomenon.

Joan Robinson saw what she called "the second crisis of economic theory" by late 1971 and pointed out that "there are now many more economists to suffer from the second crisis than there were to be discredited in the first."[7] The crisis deepened and changed to contain aspects of the first crisis—problems in the level of employnent—in the years following her observation. Some of the dimensions of what Joan Robinson sees as the first and second crises of economic theory, which mirror crises in reality, must be spelled out in some detail.

The Crises of Capitalism and Keynes' General Theory

Perhaps Adolf Hitler demonstrated to the world in the most dramatic fashion that there are distinct ways in which a nation's government can intervene in an economy to redress accumulated economic instability and accompanied social and political turmoil both at the microeconomic (e.g., using enforced slave labor to maximize industrial output in firms in some specific industries as well as undertaking government enterprises) and at the macroeconomic (e.g., massive central organization and stimulation of production by infusions of central government spending) levels. From 1933 to 1945, Germany engaged heavily in conscious fiscal and monetary and many other state interventionist policies and brought product markets and resource markets together in a way not previously thought of by economists working in the framework of the "neoclassical synthesis" without abolishing capitalism.

Keynes (1883–1946), who was very much a contemporary of Hitler (1889–1945), also took it as his task to deal with the limitations of laissez faire and came to promote government policies to generate employment since he felt that if government did not intervene, a depressed capitalism would languish indeterminantly. The key difference between the two, a central and important difference, was the *tasks* that government *should* undertake. Keynes was not stamped from a militaristic or fascistic mold, and he thought his proposals should be used for peaceful purposes. He sought no political office personally but approached the powerful as an adviser. Military Keynesianism was not really what Keynes himself had in mind, and as the Yugoslavian economist Nikola Uzunov has pointed out (in conversation with this author), fascism, or national socialism, is the result of a political system coming to dominate an economic and social system. Nationalism, in fascist Germany and Italy, for example, led the middle class to turn against the lower class, using the financial backing of the upper class. Eventually the political system came to dominate even the upper class. Thus, the correlation of fascism with military Keynesianism is at best controversial since fascism is a political form that can (and has) grow(n) out of economic policy designed to deal with extreme social agony.

Joan Robinson sees the crisis in economics and the economy as a continuation of problems of capitalism that were so visible in the 1930s. That is, the problems of laissez faire have not been laid to rest by Keynesian-type intervention into the economy. One comment sums up an important point:

> The second crisis of theory is already far advanced. I do not regard the Keynesian revolution as a great intellectual triumph. On the contrary, it was a tragedy because it came so late. Hitler had already found how to cure unemployment before Keynes had finished explaining why it occurred. This time also the real situation is crowding upon us before we have begun to discuss our problems.[8]

Robinson's general argument is that although the second crisis is part of the first, there are also some ways in which it is different. The issues involved here are some to which critical political economics addresses itself.

Robinson notes that Lionel Robbins' well-known essay, published in 1932, described economics "as the subject that deals with the allocation of scarce means between alternative uses." She adds, "It was just a coincidence that the book appeared when means for any end at all had rarely been less scarce." In Great Britain there were three million unemployed workers, and in the United States the gross national product was around half of its pre-Depression level.[9]

Orthodox thought at the time argued that part of the problem was that wages were too high because trade unions kept wage rates from falling. Another part of the problem, it was thought, was that the central bank was inconsistent in its monetary policy and was behind widely fluctuating money supplies, which probably affected price-wage structures. Still other parts of the problem were thought to be barriers to international trade, national budgets, and other infringements on the free play of the market which, it was thought, left to its own mechanisms would tend toward a full employment equilibrium. But, the collapse of the system in the 1930s was too much of a test for these ideas. They are now in the dust bin of history. "Out of this crisis emerged what has become known as the Keynesian revolution."[10] It seems unlikely that, given the structural basis of contemporary state capitalism, there can ever be a return to a laissez-faire economy.

The Keynesian "revolution" can be viewed in many ways. There are many different aspects of theory in the writings of John Maynard Keynes and of those who drew from, refined, and expanded upon his theoretical perspective. Still another dimension includes the varieties that the application of the thought of Keynes and his followers actually took in *practice* in an effort to influence the functioning of the economy as a whole. There is voluminous literature; there are scores of economists who subscribe to this school of thought, and the federal government of the United States uses policy suggestions which could be considered very Keynesian, however erratically applied. Further, there are many who would argue that all of the dimensions of Keynesian policy suggestions have never been given a fair chance because of the politics of the nation. Others argue that Keynesian economics does not really address itself to the key issues which must be considered if a stable and humane society is to be constructed. Utopianism reigns in both pro- and anti-Keynesian camps.

It is now nearly a statement of the obvious to point out that Keynes' *The General Theory of Employment, Interest and Money* was conceived as an act of relevance, as a response to a worldwide depression which required new perspectives on massive unemployment and underuse of productive resources and the associated human suffering and developing social turmoil. [11] A theory was necessary which would address itself to the realities of the times and which would also be acceptable to those in power, those who would actually decide what would be done.

Keynesian economics can be thought to be a remarkable shift away from the laissez-faire ideals of the classical economists and their neo-Classical followers who developed more refined models. It can also be seen as simply a mechanism by which to prop up a pernicious order which benefits the few and oppresses the many. However one judges it, it is necessary to understand the fundamentals of Keynesian economics since it is a part of national policy and is the basis of theoretical discussions and policy recommendations that are regularly seen in the scholarly literature and news media. Indeed, even Nixon proclaimed himself a Keynesian in 1970. Contemporary macroeconomics is mostly Keynesian thought refined (and often vulgarized), and the bare bones of the Keynesian paradigm can be picked out of virtually any college-level introductory economics textbook available in the United States.

Further, in introducing his budget in early 1975, President Ford spoke on the one hand, of tax cuts and a budget deficit of around $52 billion and, on the other hand, hoped for a balanced budget by fiscal year 1976-77. [12] Ford's budgetary address in January 1976 included an estimated deficit of $43 billion for fiscal year 1976-77 and data revealing an estimated $76 billion deficit for fiscal year 1975-76. He expressed the hope that a balanced budget would be attained in three years. [13] In view of the fact that deficits have been the rule in the postwar period, Ford's statement must be regarded as more political in nature than his sense (and his advisers') of what will actually happen. More will be said about the latter, but here the issue is left with a newspaper headline: "Count Ford Among the Keynesians." [14] This is a profound statement on the impact of the ideas of John Maynard Keynes or any writer.

Keynes' General Theory[15]

What Keynes recognized, of course, is that the economies of capitalist nations would not automatically provide the full employment of the work force, growing production, or stable prices. Massive unemployment and idle resources could not help but be noticed. Solid evidence opposing the notions of laissez-faire economists could not help but press for new theoretical formulations which would become the basis for practice. Keynes' focus on aggregate demand as determined by the level of income was a step in a much different theoretical direction than that previously existing in economic thought which had gathered a following. Perhaps Keynes was pointing to the obvious which had been obscured by the former economic ideology masquerading as science.

Keynes was amazingly succinct in his statement of his general theory. *All* of his first chapter, "The General Theory," reads like the following:

> I have called this book the *General Theory of Employment, Interest and Money,* placing the emphasis on the prefix general. The object of such a title is to contrast the character of my arguments and conclusions with those of the classical theory of the subject, upon which I was brought up and which dominates the economic thought, both practical and theoretical, of the governing and academic classes of this generation as it has for a hundred years past. I shall argue that the postulates of the classical theory are applicable to a special case only and not to the general case, the situation which it assumes being a limiting point of the possible positions of equilibrium. Moreover, the characteristics of the special case assumed by the classical theory happen not to be those of the economic society in which we actually live, with the result that its teaching is misleading and disastrous if we attempt to apply it to the facts of experience.[16]

The last line in this first chapter also applies to Keynes himself when his theory of the 1930s was carried beyond the point in history when it made sense. But other comments must be made about this packed paragraph of ideas.

Interestingly, Keynes uses the term "classical economics"—a term invented by Marx—to include Ricardo and James Mill as well as their predecessors, the most notable, or at least noted, of whom was Adam Smith. Keynes at the same time goes beyond Marx's definition to also include the followers of Ricardo who worked in the same paradigm seeking to perfect it. Some he mentions are John Stuart Mill, Alfred Marshall, F. Y. Edgeworth, and A. C. Pigou.[17]

Here it is important to point out an apparent dissonance in economic thought. Keynes, who was schooled in, but moved beyond, the classical school included those whom others have termed neo-Classicists (such as Marshall, Edgeworth, and Pigou) in addition to Ricardo, who produced conflicting strains of thought, as classicists. Those who seized upon Ricardo's theory of value comprised the radical wing, the most important of whom were the Marxists, who were hardly of the same mind as the neoClassicists. Ricardo himself, in fact, had some proletarian disciples and one, Thomas Hodgskin,

> . . . was a name to frighten children in the days following the repeal of the Combination Laws in 1824. It was probably inevitable, therefore, that many of the more conservative economists should come to regard Ricardo's theory of value not only as logically incorrect but also as socially dangerous.[18]

Economic thought, as evidenced here, is hardly a neutral art. It is the battleground of communists and capitalists, of labor and capital.

To realize the extent to which Keynes was steeped in Classical economics, one only need read Harrod's biography of him. This account, which is as droll as the cultural milieu in which it is set, offers a great deal of insight into the intellectual development of Keynes, the son of John Neville Keynes. The latter was a Cambridge don, lecturer in logic and political economy and, later, administrator. This one quote from Harrod sets the tone of the younger Keynes' heritage: "Here was a happy, late-Victorian family, living in moderate circumstances but solid comfort, the house well staffed with domestic servants, the passing days full of activity and the future secure."[19]

On reflection the first chapter of Keynes' *magnum opus* is quite vague and does not reveal what the general theory is—the view of the way Keynes thought the economy actually worked in contradistinction to the classical "special case." The latter which, as Keynes so revealingly put, "dominated the economic thought" of the governing and academic classes of [his] generation as it [had] for a hundred years past."[20]

The focus in this classic work is on the basic circularity of the whole economy. Products and resources—human and other—come together with money as the "fuel and tractor that do the actual pulling of the plow."[21] That is, Keynes attempts to show how capitalist society works where labor and other commodities alike are bought and sold in the market with money—all of this a fact of everyday life.

This idea of a circular flow was a very useful one, and it was not surprisingly picked up when it was reinvented and legitimized by Keynes: the aggregate demand for commodities, in turn, provided income for industry, which in turn caused them to both need workers and to compensate them. In other words, supply does not create demand. Income creates the wherewithal for demand which generates supply, profits, and the purpose for labor to be employed.

But before developing these ideas in considerable detail, Keynes offers a critique of classical economic thought. He pointed out that the Classical theory of employment was founded on two postulates:

(1) "The wage is equal to the marginal product of labour"; and (2) "The utility of the wage when a given volume of labour is employed is equal to the marginal disutility of that amount of employment." Then he says that

> . . . the volume of employed resources is duly determined, according to the classical theory, by the two postulates. The first gives us the demand schedule for employment, the second gives us the supply schedule; and the amount of employment is fixed at the point where the utility of the marginal product balances the disutility of the marginal employment. [22]

Keynes adds that if the above is true then there are four ways in which employment might be increased: (1) an improvement in

> organization or in foresight which diminishes "frictional" unemployment . . . (2) a decrease in the marginal disutility of labour, as expressed by the real wage for which additional labour is available, so as to diminish "voluntary" unemployment . . . (3) an increase in the marginal physical productivity of labour in the wage-goods industries (to use Professor Pigou's convenient term for goods upon the price of which the utility of the money-wage depends) . . . (4) an increase in the price of nonwage-goods compared with the price of wage-goods, associated with a shift in the expenditure of nonwage-earners from wage-goods to non-wage-goods. [23]

It would take some doing to make this sound much less like mumbo jumbo, but perhaps license can be taken to make a few leaps and go directly to what Keynes concluded in his critique of the classical theory of employment since the intervening steps can be studied in the original, and the argument is very technical and dry. He concluded that the classical theory depends on these assumptions:

> (1) that the real wage is equal to the marginal disutility of the existing employment;
> (2) that there is no such thing as involuntary unemployment in the strict sense;
> (3) that supply creates its own demand in the sense that the aggregate demand price is equal to the aggregate supply price for all levels of output and employment.
>
> These three assumptions, however, all amount to the same thing in the sense that they all stand and fall together, any one of them logically involving the other two. [24]

These assumptions, of course, did not square with observed social reality and there was the need for a theoretical breakthrough. Keynes changed the focus to "the principle of effective demand" (the title of the third chapter) and away from wage rates and spoke of "the propensity to consume" (the subject of Book III) and "the inducement to invest" (the topic of Book IV) as the key determinants behind what level of employment would actually obtain. Further, Keynes gave credit to these ideas where it was due:

> The great puzzle of Effective Demand with which Malthus has wrestled vanished from economic literature. You will not find it mentioned even once in the whole works of Marshall, Edgeworth and Professor Pigou, from whose hands the classical theory has received its most mature embodiment. It could only live on furtively, below the surface, in the underworlds of Karl Marx, Silvio Gesell or Major Douglas. [25]

Keynes says that he thought that this was "something of a curiosity and a mystery" but that "It must have been due to a complex of suitabilities in the doctrine to the environment into which it was projected." He explains this position clearly:

> That it reached conclusions quite different from what the ordinary uninstructed person would expect, added, I suppose, to its intellectual prestige. That its teaching, translated into practice, was austere and often unpalatable, lent it virtue. That it was adapted to carry a vast and consistent logical superstructure, gave it beauty. That it could explain much social injustice and apparent cruelty as an inevitable incident in the scheme of progress, and attempt to change such things as likely on the whole to do more harm than good, commended it to authority. *That it afforded a measure of justification to the free activities of the individual capitalist, attracted to it the support of the dominant social force behind authority.* [italics added][26]

Keynes adds "It may well be that the classical theory represents the way in which we should like our Economy to behave. But to assume that it actually does so is to assume our difficulties away."[27]

On reflection it is apparent that a lot of politics (and, perhaps, even mysticism) were wrapped up in a scientific suit of clothing which was useful and functional to "the dominant social force behind authority." Here the "radical" Keynes emerges with a sociology of knowledge, seeing the owners of the means of production behind the structure of power. This may be reading too much into Keynes here, but it probably is not. If Keynes' sociology of knowledge is correct for the paradigm preceding him, what of his since it became the dominant paradigm? It is possible that Keynes had more than one general theory. He existed in a place in society where he would know what ideas were likely to be propagated and which were not.

Keynesian economics focuses on the economic system as a whole, and the level of aggregate demand that must be generated to produce relatively full employment. Keynes did not, however, totally abandon thought on the way in which this might affect the whole of society, particularly in the closing chapter of *The General Theory* entitled "Concluding Notes on the Social Philosophy Towards Which the General Theory Might Lead." To put Keynes' social philosophy in perspective Keynes is best quoted where he says this at the outset:

> The outstanding faults of the economic society in which we live are its failure to provide for full employment and its arbitrary and inequitable distribution of wealth and incomes. The bearing of the foregoing theory on the first of these is obvious. But there are also two important respects in which it is relevant to the second. [28]

Keynes points out the way in which *The General Theory* relates to the question of the distribution of wealth and income in this fashion:

> Our argument leads towards the conclusion that in contemporary conditions the growth of wealth, so far from being dependent on the abstinence of the rich, as is commonly supposed, is more likely to be impeded by it. One of the chief social justifications of great inequality of wealth is, therefore, removed. I am not saying that there are no other reasons, unaffected by our theory, capable of justifying some measure of inequality in some circumstances. But it does dispose of the most important of the reasons why hitherto we have thought it prudent to move carefully. [29]

To elaborate a bit, then, Keynes is simply saying that inequality cannot be justified on the grounds that the rich provide the basis, through their saving, for the expansion of capital, and therefore the growth of economic output, because if broad based consumption is not large enough capital is not going to be formed. Notice, however, that Keynes did not say that all inequality should necessarily be abolished.

But all of this adds up to rather vague speculation or at least it does not move views on the distribution of income into the realm of purely scientific discussion. One could easily and simply agree with Joan Robinson's assessment of the contribution of Keynesian thought on this point: "In short, we have not got a theory of distribution." [30]

Keynes' second point with respect to extreme inequality being unjustified centers around his theory of the rate of interest. Previously, it had been argued that a high rate of interest was needed to induce saving, and this also served to fatten the bank accounts of the wealthy rentiers. Keynes argued that a low rate of interest served to induce investment (i.e., expenditures by enterprises for the expansion of plant and equipment as well as the buildup of business inventories). Thus, he moved to the conclusion that a kind of socialization of investment through the manipulation of the interest rate would probably be necessary for the maintenance of full employment and this manipulation could go against the interests of the monied, nonentrepreneurial rich and thus lessen inequality.

In short, Keynes was arguing that the economic machinery might function better if the economic interests of some members of the society were undermined, specifically the very rich. But he seems nowhere near arguing for the abolition of the private ownership of the means of production, even in highly concentrated sectors. The reason is that he seems to have thought that the composition of production was essentially socially acceptable. In his own words:

> I see no reason to suppose that the existing system seriously misemploys the factors of production which are in use. There are, of course, errors of foresight; but these would not be avoided by centralising decisions . . . It is in determining the volume, not the direction, of actual employment that the existing system has broken down.[31]

This view—a central, most important observation—is expressed early on in the book as well:

> . . . the analysis of the Propensity to Consume, the definition of the Marginal Efficiency of Capital and the theory of the Rate of Interest are the three main gaps in our existing knowledge which it will be necessary to fill. When this has been accomplished, we shall find that the Theory of Prices falls into its proper place as a matter which is subsidiary to our general theory.[32]

Keynes, then, seems not so far afield from the classical economists as he is sometimes thought. About this he is quite specific:

> Our criticism of the accepted classical theory of economics has consisted not so much in finding logical flaws in its analysis as in pointing out that its tacit assumptions are seldom or never satisfied, with the result that it cannot solve the economic problems of the actual world. But if our central controls succeed in establishing an aggregate volume of output corresponding to full employment as nearly as is practicable, the classical theory comes into its own again from this point onwards. If we suppose the volume of output to be given, i.e., to be determined by forces outside the classical scheme of thought, then there is no objection to be raised against the classical analysis of the manner in which private self-interest will determine what in particular is produced, in what proportions the factors of production will be combined to produce it, and how the value of the final product will be distributed between them . . . Thus, apart from the necessity of central controls to bring about an adjustment between the propensity to consume and the inducement to invest, there is no more reason to socialize economic life than there was before.[33]

Keynes was "simply" seeking to establish a broad structural framework of stabilization within which the capitalist system could function without the problems of disequilibrium which manifested themselves in the Great Depression.

Keynes undoubtedly had reasons for this position. He appears to have felt that a stabilized market system under private ownership would fulfill the economic criteria of efficiency within a framework of decentralization of decision making and the play of self-interest. But even more importantly, Keynes argued that under this system "individualism" could be maintained, if it could be purged of its abuses, such as that evidenced by the drive toward monopoly control. Inaccurately, Keynes had apparently identified socialism with totalitarianism, which the Soviet experience of his time tended to substantiate.

Keynes, in this last chapter of *The General Theory*, seems to believe that a stabilized capitalism would be more favorable to peace as well since it would help to eliminate some of the economic causes of war, "namely, the pressure of population and the competitive struggle for markets."[34]

He argues that the system of laissez-faire capitalism left itself open for problems. He writes:

> Under the system of domestic laissez faire and an international gold standard such as was orthodox in the latter half of the nineteenth century, there was no means open to a government whereby to mitigate economic distress at home except through the competitive struggle for markets. For all measures helpful to a state of chronic or intermittent underemployment were ruled out, except measures to improve the balance of trade on income account.[35]

At a time when the world of private enterprise was in a state of collapse, Keynes remained an optimist about the possibilities for the future and the role that professional economists could make in a contribution to public policy. The last paragraph of this monumental book is prophetic, perhaps even in a macabre fashion given contemporary fear about the power of huge institutions:

> I am sure that the power of vested interests is vastly exaggerated compared with the gradual encroachment of ideas. Not, indeed, immediately, but after a certain interval . . . But, soon or late, it is ideas, not vested interests, which are dangerous for good or evil.[36]

It is understandable that Keynes would be more interested in short run changes in the political economy than anything else given the dismal times much of the world was experiencing. It was important to come up with quick measures which would serve to put people back to work to deal with massive human suffering. He was justifiably impatient with those who argued that things would get better over the longer haul through the usual means available to an economic system in which laissez faire was the guiding principle. He is famous for his wry observation that "In the long run we are all dead."

From Keynes to Keynesianism

Unfortunately, aspects of Keynes' short run suggestions became part of the long run that was not his focus and not without problems. As Joan Robinson puts it, "So-called Keynesian policy has been a series of expedients to deal with recessions when they occurred."[37]

> The very essence of his problem was uncertainty. He started from a Marshallian short period. Here we are today with whatever stock of capital equipment, training of labor, and business organization that the past has produced; decisions are being taken today on the basis of expectations about the future . . .[38]

It is not surprising, then, that others had reservations about the *longer run* implications of Keynesian policy suggestions. For example, Michal Kalecki thought that with a low-unemployment situation, there would be a corresponding decline in "discipline" in the factories with resulting price increases.

> In this situation a powerful block is likely to be formed between big business and the rentier interests, and they would probably find more than one economist to declare that the situation was manifestly unsound. The pressure of all these forces, and in particular big business, would most probably induce the government to return to the orthodox policy of cutting down the budget deficit. A slump would follow.[39]

Robinson draws this analysis out further and paints a quite plausible description of the roots of secular inflation which adds up to a useful short-run policy turning into a longer run crisis. Her general argument is that

> The advocates of "Keynesian" policies accepted only half of Keynes' diagnosis of the instability of capitalism. He described how the level of output is determined (in given technical conditions) by investment and consumption. He described how the level of prices is determined by the level of money-wage rates. It was sufficiently obvious that if continuous near-full employment was maintained without any change in traditional institutions

and attitudes in industrial relations, there would be an irresistible pressure to inflation. I think that in the United States this element in Keynes was somehow swept under the carpet. . .[40]

Robinson argues that the second half of Keynes' theory was accepted later, under the Nixon administration, when a decision was made "to alter the rules of the game in industrial relations by decree"[41] (i.e., the imposition of wage-price controls).

It is in this sense that the "second crisis" of which Robinson speaks is related to, but is, at the same time different, from the first: "The first crisis arose from the breakdown of a theory which could not account for the *level* of unemployment. The second crisis arises from a theory that cannot account for the *content* of employment."[42] That is, Keynesian doctrine provided a set of policy suggestions to stimulate aggregate demand but minimized analysis of the power of centralized and concentrated capital and labor. Robinson sees the power of capital as part of the first crisis which was never resolved and, in fact, became more extreme. Attempts to resolve the first crisis eventually ushered in accompanying secular inflation and the reinforcement of the centralized and concentrated structure of industry which determined the characteristics of the work force. The problem of unemployment was not alleviated; it was changed. Robinson is not totally clear on the way in which the content of employment is not explained as a key part of the second crisis of economic theory, but the answer can be found. A. Dale Tussing, for example, sees the contemporary labor market as one including a large but unknown number of teenagers, women, nonwhites, and older workers whose status in the work force is in flux, which is in contrast to the more stable labor market for white prime-age males. Those who are not white prime-age men hold jobs for a shorter duration at lower wages and in and out of the labor force.[43] The usual term for this force is the secondary labor force, and there is little reason to believe that typical Keynesian policies will go far to alleviate the plight of those who are part of this disadvantaged group.

Actually, it would be accurate to say that the capitalism in the U.S. in the middle 1970s suffers from both the first and second crises that Joan Robinson describes with some new difficulties thrown in as well.[44] There is (at this writing) unemployment and underemployment, declining GNP and real wages, continuing inflation, unabated inequality as measured by the distribution of income, and more. It may be accurate to suggest that the U. S. has moved beyond the first and second crises, to use Joan Robinson's terms, and into a third and still different crisis which has thus far resisted any absolutely satisfactory interpretation.

But the Joan Robinson and Michal Kalecki observations point to a fundamental flaw that emerges when Keynesian macroeconomic policy is applied to capitalist society over time. Although it does serve to abate massive underuse of resources, it seems not to alleviate the struggle over relative income shares between and within capital and labor. Thus, the process of growth in capitalist society remains one of disruption with some people climbing the socioeconomic ladder and many people getting wiped out.[45] The growth path is not one of social harmony or of tendencies toward the equalization of income among the population, and at this writing, there is not even growth in the U.S., the knowledge of Keynesianism not withstanding.

Keynesian "solutions" (and here I am thinking more of the popular ideology that emerged as much as the thought of Keynes himself) to problems involving the level of employment cannot be looked at in static terms and cannot be used for long-term application without difficulties. Part of this may be an increasing distributional problem in the face of policies which

> . . . persuaded successive presidents that there is no harm in a budget deficit and left the military-industrial complex to take advantage of it. So it has come about that Keynes' pleasant daydream was turned into a nightmare of terror.[46]

This distributional problem is that increasing wealth, which accompanied military Keynesianism, was not spread around so that the bottom of the socioeconomic strata would feel the impact of growth. Robinson is not speaking in relative terms but in absolute terms.

> Growth requires technical progress, and technical progress alters the composition of the labor force, making more places for educated workers and fewer for uneducated, but opportunities to acquire qualifications are kept (with a few exceptions for exceptional talents) for those families who have them already. As growth goes on at the top, more and more families are thrown out at the bottom. Absolute misery grows while wealth increases. The old slogan, "poverty in the midst of plenty," takes on a new meaning.[47]

Yet this is not to suggest that Keynes was totally oblivious to the shallowness of capitalist values and the longer term transformation of capitalism or that he should be held reponsible for the application of some of his ideas. In fact, when thinking about the longer run he definitely was more visionary. In an essay entitled "Economic Possibilities for Our Grandchildren" he said this:

> . . . when the accumulation of wealth is no longer of high social importance, there will be great changes in the code of morals. We shall be able to rid ourselves of many of the pseudo-moral

principles which have hag-ridden us for two hundred years, by which we have exalted some of the most distasteful of human qualities into the position of highest values. We shall be able to afford to dare to assess the money-motive at its true value . . . All kinds of social customs and economic practices affecting the distribution of wealth and its reward and penalties which we now maintain at all costs, however distasteful and unjust they may be in themselves . . . we shall then be free, at last, to discard.[48]

It need hardly be mentioned that the generation of the grand-children of Keynes has come and then some, and the money-motive he mentions remains a central one.

It can be argued, in sum, that Keynes sought to suggest ways to make capitalism work and hoped for a longer run evolution of the system to something more humane, which would provide more security and certainty as a framework for people to live out their lives without being denied basic human freedoms.

With this perspective about the longer run the question "Was Keynes attracted to Marxian ideas?" seems to logically follow. If Harrod's account is accurate, the answer to this is an unambiguous, if highly curious, no. This account of Keynes' life indexes references to Marx only twice. One story is in the mid-1920s where Harrod and Keynes are in dialogue over the proper works to assign their students. The works of Marshall, Pigou, and Keynes himself are thought by Harrod appropriate to assign at Oxford. Keynes, Harrod says, gave "defence of the Oxford method" though the former was at the rival Cambridge. This method was the reading of Plato and Aristotle.

> This was the right way to introduce the young to knowledge. Let them study texts of which one knew that, whether they were true or false, they were the product of master minds. In econom-ics the next best thing was to read Adam Smith and Ricardo. (Marx might certainly be discarded.) A hint could be dropped, of course, that to fill in gaps they should take a quick look at Alfred Marshall.[49]

The second account of Keynes' response to Marx comes directly from a letter written by Keynes to George Bernard Shaw in 1935 which is well worth quoting at length.

> Thank you for your letter. I will try to take your words to heart. There must be *something* in what you say, because there gener-ally is. But I've made another shot at old K. M. last week, reading the Marx-Engels correspondence just published, without making much progress. I prefer Engels of the two. I can see that they invented a certain method of carrying on and a vile manner of writing, both of which their successors have maintained with

fidelity. But if you tell me that they have discovered a clue to the economic riddle, still I am beaten—I can discover nothing but out-of-date controversialising.

To understand *my* state of mind, however, you have to know that I believe myself to be writing a book on economic theory which will largely revolutionise—not, I suppose, at once but in the course of the next ten years—the way the world thinks about economic problems. When my new theory has been duly assimilated and mixed with politics and feelings and passions, I can't predict what the final upshot will be in its effect on action and affairs. But there will be a great change, and, in particular, the Ricardian foundations of Marxism will be knocked away.

I can't expect you, or anyone else, to believe this at the present stage. But for myself I don't merely hope what I say,—in my own mind I'm quite sure.[50]

Of course, Keynes was correct in his prediction of his own impact but, perhaps, not in the way he had quite intended. It might not be outrageous to suggest that if he were around to say so, he might in fact deny being a "Keynesian," and he might be bothered by the way in which his ideas were vulgarized, used loosely to formulate longer run policy, and even applied as a doctrine to allow presidents who really had no political choice to label his policy Keynesian while, as Joan Robinson said it so well, sweeping a part of the program under the rug. In short, although price theory[51] may be a matter subsidiary to the general theory, it has now become a central issue. It may be right here that some of the elements necessary to understand and explain the contemporary crisis of capitalism exist. It seems that Robinson and Kalecki astutely put their fingers on one of the major places where Keynesianism as applied economic medicine went wrong.

To summarize, Keynes provided a persuasive critique of the economic orthodoxy which preceded him as a part of *The General Theory.* But he provided an analysis of the macroeconomic issues with only the short run in mind. There were structural implications as time passed. However, Keynes persuasively argued that general equilibrium might exist in the economy at a point where much of the work force and plant and equipment were idle as easily as not. Under the laissez faire doctrine, he found economic instability and even a prolonged depression an unsurprising outcome and provided a theoretical argument for state intervention. This argument had previously been widely regarded as anathema among those in power, most economists, and perhaps the general population. Government fiscal policy, through tax and expenditure powers, was seen by Keynes as particularly effective in providing income which would increase consumer demand and business investment and thereby create jobs. When people had jobs, they had income which allowed consumption which required production, business investment, and employment. Applied Keynesianism, then, was a periodic "pump-priming" operation that was seen as leaving the ownership of the means of production intact, though it might contain some theoretical arguments which would run counter to the interests of an idle class of rentiers. But problems were also created by Keynesianism. In fact, one might say that Keynesianism as an applied doctrine has ended up as much a part of the problem as a part of the solution for contemporary society.

Although wars, war related expenditures, and preparation for future wars were not consciously invented simply to use a military Keynesianism to enhance profits and create jobs, the resulting prosperity, once underway, provided fewer reasons—from a narrow self-interested and short-term point of view—for people to question the system's ability to deliver the goods. It is possible that the post-World War II period in the U. S. has had a military Keynesianism as its economic engine. There has also been a transformation in the structure of capitalism. The changing industrial mix and the centralization and concentration in industry at the same time have profoundly affected the population as a whole and those who are work-force participants. The system has, as its cornerstone, corporations which are, as David Gordon has put it, "profit junkies on prosperity highs." The driving mechanism behind the functioning of the system is not the wish to create employment, output, or human activity. These are all derived in the process of capitalist profit seeking.[52]

Continued contradictions are a part of contemporary capitalism. The issues which must be examined in an analysis of the system are those of a macroeconomic nature spotted by Keynes, but attention to the structure of industry, the distribution of income, and the impact of the financial nexus are also important. The view here is that one must go beyond Keynesianism to construct a persuasive analysis of the political economy which untangles even the macroeconomic phenomena of the level and composition of output and employment and the genesis of inflation. Although a more comprehensive sketch of the way in which the political economy is structured and performs must wait until the final chapter, a plausible first view is that the interrelated and combined problems of inflation, unemployment, declining real wages among parts of the work force, and wavering industrial production are rooted primarily in the corporate structure and its sphere of influence. Simple Keynesian thought hardly relates adequately to the extent of the crisis in the 1970s. This crisis probably centers in and around corporate and upper socioeconomic strata economic and political hegemony, which is maintained in a contradictory fashion by the state. Although this can only be an assertion here, the extent of the underconsumption, overproduction, and distributional set of problems is likely to usher in a new era in the American political economy with proposals for planning emerging out of necessity. But other paradigms must be explained before this can be seen as a totally plausible view.

The next task in this chapter is to discuss the modern lower economics a bit more and establish the link between this literature and the thought of Keynes and the Keynesians. In this way some of the prevailing economic doctrines will be sketched and an elaboration on the place of the Keynesian paradigm in present times will be discussed. It will become apparent that those who seek a stabilized capitalism have added ad hoc measures to fundamental Keynesian thought in recent times. The conventional economics of the present is moving toward an eclecticism with a Keynesian base. But even with changes and additions, economics which is supportive of capitalism has yet to demonstrate its scientific validity. If its hegemony is intact, it is an ideological hegemony.

From Keynes to Contradictions in the Modern Lower Economics

Keynes' theoretical contribution is important because it formed the foundations of a world view, a paradigm about the economy, which was accepted—at times reluctantly, at times embraced—by the state. The Employment Act of 1946 is probably the most striking commentary. A government which promises to do what it can to maintain relatively full employment and to stabilize production and prices while not changing the economic system of capitalism in other significant ways appears to be one which has accepted Keynesian ideas.

Further, as touched on earlier, the Keynesian paradigm is one which is unquestionably the most frequently presented in macroeconomics textbooks which appear in print in the United States. Even the most "radical" introductory textbook takes the position that "we are all Keynesians now."[53] Paul Samuelson, of course, is probably the single most significant economist to pass this paradigm on to scores of undergraduates in institutions of higher education in the many editions of his well-known introductory textbook. Even recently published principles of macroeconomics works take the revised and developed Keynesian paradigm to be "the modern theory."[54] The notion that government can stabilize the economy by engaging in deficit spending during times of unemployment has possibly become "common sense," thanks to the many popularizations of what Keynes had to say on that subject.

A well-known example which reached a large audience in the 1960s and converted at least one balanced budget fanatic into a Keynesian was Robert L. Heilbroner and Peter L. Bernstein's *A Primer on Government Spending*. The first edition of this book was published in 1963 and a second edition in 1972 in which it was noted that one reason for the appearance of the book was specifically to influence President Kennedy. It was thought, correctly, that he would be sympathetic to the Keynesian perspective. The book is now out of print which may be a commentary on the simplistic "push or pull" ideas which it promotes and which have little or nothing to say about unemployment and inflation existing simultaneously.

Nonetheless, this book is a very clear and easy to read introduction to popularized Keynesianism, and it covers key concepts in a limited space. Personal experience shows that economics students, who do not know where to begin when attempting to understand a series of vaguely related textbook chapters, get the point which this little book conveys. That is, the presence of a nation's wealth—the stuff for human use—is not a sufficient condition to assure that it will be cranked out or that everyone will be involved in the process or will receive a share of it. Central government is in the unique position of being able to use its tax and revenue powers to intervene in the economy when necessary to stimulate or retard production and associated activity on the part of labor. That same government can, in any particular time period, create debt because, in its nonfinite life, it can deal with this debt later by repaying or refunding; the government also has the power to tax, to legislate, and to create money and, therefore, is quite different from individuals and businesses.

But there is a key point that the book fails to mention. It is probably one key issue of our times: Although government debt is owned publicly and is "a debt that members of a community owe to one another,"[55] some have more of a claim on future revenue and others foot the bill. Fiscal and monetary policy have everything to do with the class composition of society. The future generations that pay off the debt or who pay interest on it are those who are taxed; however, the tax system favors the upper socioeconomic strata, a small percentage of whom also own the corporations that stabilization policy attempts to keep intact.[56]

In short, even if it worked, the popularized version of Keynesian thought has avoided some very important issues and has especially danced around the phenomenon of income distribution and what it has to do with the economy as a whole and specific parts of the population. Indeed, as Paul Baran put it, "in our time . . . faith in the manipulative omnipotence of the State has all but displaced analysis of its social structure and understanding of its political and economic functions."[57]

Robert Lekachman in presenting a collection of essays assessing the impact of Keynes made this statement:

> . . . everybody is a Keynesian now: eminent conservative economists admit as much. But what is badly needed is a theory to arm the vision of the second, more radical Keynes. For neither Keynes nor anyone else has told us how to socialize investment, invent wholesome "compromises by which public authority will cooperate with private initiative," content all the social classes, and preserve at the same time the freedom and variety of which capitalism at its best was capable. Until a powerful theory does emerge—here is the task ,for the new Keynes—economists will continue to advocate with decreasing relevance the policies of the conservative Keynes. How Keynes might have laughed to see the sight. How cheerfully he would have set to work to amend or discard his own theories in favor of better substitutes.[58]

Although one might not agree with all of the statement above (freedom, in particular, has been distributed, obviously, in a highly unequal way), with much, or with any of it, it is still another piece of evidence that Keynes, indeed, did make an impressive impact on ideas.

The work of Keynes seems to be the most influential (in industrialized economies characterized by the private ownership of the means of production) of any economist that has emerged in the 20th century. Joan Robinson would probably encounter virtually no disagreement in her opinion that the economic crisis of the 1930s which confronted the capitalist world led to "what has become known as the Keynesian revolution."[59] Indeed, one doctoral candidate was moved to entitle his dissertation *The Keynesian Revolution* as early as 1944,[60] only a few years after the publication of Keynes' masterpiece.

Lawrence R. Klein is probably right on target when he says that "it was undoubtedly the simplicity of the final construct that led to such wide acceptance of the theory at an early stage."[61] Klein is also reasonable in his judgment that "the Keynesian system as a mathematical model would have come into being without Keynes, as a natural outgrowth of the economic discussions of the 1930's."[62]

But we are no longer living in the decade of the 1930s, and the economic difficulties facing the capitalist world suggest that Keynesianism is hardly enough, not that it ever was in terms of broad criteria which could be used to evaluate the success or failure of the political economy of a nation. Paul Sweezy has even gone so far as to say that the imposition of the Keynesian paradigm in actual economic policy making is a debacle.[63] The discussion is far from over, but there is reason to suspect that Keynesian policies are likely to be of short-run worth at best. And even then sensible programs to cope with serious inflation *and* subemployment have not been constructed.

It is very possible that the optimism of the 1960s, a period which may have been the "golden age" of Keynesian influence on society (but also the age of U. S. military aggression in Indochina), is a stance which is very out of touch with the realities of the 1970s. The "new economics" founded on Keynesian thought and extolled by Walter W. Heller, Chairman of the Council of Economic Advisers under Presidents Kennedy and Johnson, in his book *New Dimensions of Political Economy,* seems antiquated today. In the preface to the book, Heller poses some important questions which he says put "the 'new economics' . . . to a series of stern tests." He asks, "Could economic policy hold inflation in check without direct controls? Could economic policy be nimble and selective enough to keep total demand moving up while restoring balance to the economy?" He asks, when mulling over the economic impact of the end of the war in Vietnam (a very premature question when the 1967 edition of the book was published): "Would the 'new economics' succeed in minimizing the problems and maximizing the opportunities?" He answers in this way:

> Grounds for optimism in answering these questions will be found in this book, especially in its development of the theme that modern economic intelligence and advice have been woven into the everyday fabric of White House decision-making for good.
> One's optimism is strengthened by the flexible and responsive adaptation of policy to economic change in the months since this book was written.[64]

In fairness to Heller, it should be added that he ends the preface by admitting that "Modern economic policy, both here and abroad, has yet to demonstrate that it can deliver full employment and vigorous growth and at the same time maintain, in a free economy, reasonable price stability and balance-of-payments equilibrium."[65] Developments since the book was written strongly suggest that what "modern economic policy . . . has yet to demonstrate" has not been demonstrated and that his optimism was at best premature and at worst blind. Further, the assumption that "vigorous growth" is something public policy *should* seek is being questioned by people in various socioeconomic strata and by those in academe. It is not at all obvious that "more" is consistent with the longer run survival.

The discussion of this matter has only recently begun and is associated with the formative work coming out of the Club of Rome world model which was constructed by internationally prominent people who have been meeting since 1968 to discuss selected problems of today's world. The focus of the Club of Rome has been the whole earth and currently existing trends in population, pollution, the depletion of natural resources, and world food supplies, as well as industrialization. In putting together a systematic analysis of all of these trends, Jay W. Forrester of MIT was commissioned to do a quantitative model of the world system.[66]

Forrester's work has been criticized in various ways and is said to be highly simplified, as one would expect it would have to be, and highly aggregated. Yet it should be viewed as a pioneering effort on which others can build. Some issues have been clarified, and whether one disagrees or agrees one thing is clear, or nearly so. It is not *obvious* that economic growth is in fact desirable over the longer run for a particular nation or for the world, that is growth of the Western industrial variety. Perhaps a more crucial issue is one of distribution since part of the world's population is starving while a minority has enormous surplus. And perhaps the *composition* (e.g., automobiles compared to tractors which are instrumental for food production) of a nation's and the world's output is the key issue.

> Separating hysteria from truth is a difficult task, but the questions raised by the Club of Rome report deserve recognition and some serious thought. What is the optimal rate of economic growth? What definition of growth is to be attacked? Should actions be taken to curb growth here and now? If so, what are the proper actions? How do we deal with the more specific problems posed within the growth-no-growth framework? Can technological progress provide for the future? Is there an optimal population size? How would a no-growth policy affect the incomes of disadvantaged groups? Will the available energy supply limit growth? What are the growth problems of other nations? How would individuals adjust to a no-growth policy?[67]

In short, the issues are these even if there are no conclusive answers.

1. Is continued growth possible?

2. Is continued growth necessary?

3. Is continued growth desirable, that is, is it needed to make people "happy"?[68]

There seems to be wide agreement on the first of these three issues.

There do seem to be limits to growth. The main disagreement is on how soon these limits will be reached. The Club of Rome model suggests that they will be approached in 70 years. To others the issue is mainly up in the air, and it is not known if "the growth horizon [will] be approached slowly and asymptotically or at an accelerated rate followed by a violent collapse, as predicted by the Club of Rome study groups."[69]

Alan Watts (1915–1974), the late philosopher and interpreter of Zen to a large and eager American audience, touched on the latter two issues in his autobiography when discussing the impact he hoped to have on "very rich and powerful people" by showing them "how to use their imaginations and enjoy themselves through being disabused of the notion that money and prestige have, in themselves, material reality. Love of money and imagination in spending it seem to be mutually exclusive." He said,

> People do not generally realize that those who govern states and great corporations are not really in control of these monstrous organizations of human action. They are like the drivers of runaway trucks which will disintegrate if brought to a sudden stop, yet cannot be slowed because they are carrying emergency supplies to a scene of disaster. But it is not happiness to cultivate ulcers and heart disease while amassing millions of paper dollars and covering the world with smog and greasy grime.[70]

In connection with this latter point are a few thoughts on a book written by a noted economist who has offered fundamentalist Keynesianism to scores of the uninitiated both in the previously mentioned *Primer on Government Spending* as well as in his introductory textbook *The Economic Problem*. Robert Heilbroner is perhaps different and more diversified than many economists. He has written on economic thought and economic history and has been concerned with the lesser developed nations as well as the domestic situation in the United States and the economic systems of capitalism and socialism.[71] He writes for the popular audience as much or more than for his academic colleagues.

Heilbroner's *An Inquiry Into the Human Prospect*, published in 1974, is important because it is seen by many as a kind of Malthusian doomsday book which suggests the need for more centralized authoritarianism or a revolutionary plan of social reorganization if the earth is to survive for very long. Heilbroner gives the reader every reason to believe that he is not optimistic.

> The outlook for man, I believe, is painful, difficult, perhaps desperate, and the hope that can be held out for his future prospect seems to be very slim indeed. Thus, to anticipate the

conclusions of our inquiry, the answer to whether we can conceive of the future other than as a continuation of the darkness, cruelty, and disorder of the past seems to me to be no; and to the question of whether worse impends, yes.[72]

Heilbroner admits that "much in [his] estimate of the human prospect must rest on generalizations for which there exist no objective data at all."[73]

But he presents some data in developing his argument, which can be seen as a less doomsday perspective than is often thought. He points out that the problems the world faces are formidable, if not ultimately fatal, and they surround the pressure of population against other resources over time with industrial production and associated growth in productivity adding up to a short-term necessity, as perceived by the rulers of various nations, but a longer run calamity if current trends continue.

His view has much in common with that held by the Club of Rome, which he cites, and one comes away from the book with the sense that the hegemony of Keynesianism should be questioned even if it worked since it would be very much a large part of, if not the basis of, the problem in the longer run. These ideas are from one of the foremost popularizers of Keynesian thought!

The Human Prospect is a book about the consequences of an unplanned world society, both in its population and in its use of other resources. The dilemma is that although planning is desirable for the survival of the species, it is not at all certain that it will be undertaken in the parts of the earth that it most certainly should be, e.g., the United States where huge per capita consumption requires large quantities of natural resources, and India and much of the Third World, with the exception of China, where the population is increasing at frightening rates. But one really disturbing aspect of Heilbroner's vision is the possibility of even more nations producing nuclear weapons to use as instruments of political blackmail. Wars of redistribution may be the only choice which some very poor nations can follow. Then, even if the consumption of unrenewable resources is abated, population growth is checked, and random nuclear wars are prevented, the threat of heat emission—thermal pollution—from industrial production appears to be growing exponentially. One estimate Heilbroner cites suggests that the earth's temperature could increase by about 50 degrees centigrade in 250 years which would make the planet uninhabitable. [74]

This problem suggests that it is necessary for the economic system of capitalism to be dramatically turned around, to engage in production for use paying special attention to ecological matters and avoiding waste wherever possible. But Heilbroner does not really explore the possibility that change could emerge from a severe breakdown of the U. S. economic system. Heilbroner's focus is on the longer run which has probably colored his vision somewhat; his implicit assumption that "business as usual" is possible in the United States seems somewhat dubious.

The less pessimistic aspects of Heilbroner's position are that this should not necessarily be seen as a particularly devastating situation for world society as a whole over time. It means, rather, that new directions probably must be sought as a matter of practical necessity. The price being paid by many people (especially those of lower socioeconomic status) in the meantime is, of course, a high one.

Heilbroner updated his scenario in an article written a year following *The Human Prospect* in which he had, however, become even more certain of his assumptions, and was aware of even more problems such as world hunger and economic struggles such as that involving petroleum. In this article he sees the late 20th century as "a period of historic inflection from one dominant civilisational form to another." Heilbroner noted that of existing societies only China contains the array of features necessary for survival with the most freedom that might be expected under the circumstances. These features are "a careful control over industrialisation, an economic policy calculated to restrain rather than to whet individual consumptive appetites, and above all, an organising religiosity expressed through the credos and observances of a socialist 'church'."[75]

There is no doubt that there are limits to growth, according to Heilbroner. Others do not share that perception and see the more alarmist discussions as bordering on the lunatic fringe.[76] If those who see no limits, or few limits, to growth are correct, then the hope of Keynesian policies, for those of that persuasion, might not be under fire so much as containing but part of a program to stabilize capitalism. If those who hold Heilbroner's view are correct, the Keynesian archetype will be of very limited relevance in the future.

Thus, it may not be unreasonable to assess Keynesianism in the following way: to the extent that it works, it reinforces an economic and social order that is both dangerous and on the side of a hierarchical stability. Admittedly this view is presented here in the form of a yet-to-be-verified hypothesis. But many are arguing on the side of this assessment.

Still another observation that can be made about the Keynesian perspective is the class nature of different policies. It can be argued that in the short run, Keynesian policies affect different parts of the population in different ways with the trade-off between unemployment and inflation being class programs. Policies designed to assure that there are jobs for everyone, for example, are in the interest of the lower socioeconomic strata and particular parts of it. The upper socioeconomic strata and those who have stable and assured employment would care most about inflation and would not care if policies to abate it required some unemployment, as long as they themselves were not unemployed. For example, it is reported that as many as 41 percent of black teenagers were jobless in early 1975 when the general unemployment rate was 8.2 percent.[77] Although a continuing problem of inflation is of concern to this particular part of the population, having little or no income that can be legally obtained makes the problem of inflation secondary or nearly irrelevant. Granted, this case is an extreme one, but it is also one that should not be minimized, glossed over, or thought not to be a symptom of a broader problem. Further, it is an issue which policy makers know exists but have not dealt with it decisively. Piecemeal and reformist techniques have been discussed and sometimes introduced, but because of politics, little has been actually done, except in a partial and symbolic fashion, that approaches the magnitude of the situation of the lowest socioeconomic strata of U. S. society. It would seem that the explanation for this absence of intervention is that action from the federal government would threaten the class interests that those policy makers, both congressional and executive branch, represent. And the federal level of government is the only place in which any redistribution policy at all is discussed that relates to the problems of the lower socioeconomic strata. Perhaps "crime" against property is the policy that part of the lowest socioeconomic strata has been forced to produce.[78]

By 1972 Daniel R. Fusfeld was not alone in his perception that the promise of Keynesianism as an economic doctrine was shattered. The meld of Marshallian microeconomics and Keynes' macroeconomics did not add up to a harmonious whole. Fusfeld points to several distinct problems that brought the neo-Classical synthesis into severe question even before the level of unemployment was again a serious issue (as it was by 1974). Inflation, the troubled international monetary system, continued militarism, inequality, and alienation were apparent and seemingly worsening.[79] Perhaps Fusfeld goes too far when all of these problems are pointed to as evidence of contemporary Keynesianism being "the shattered synthesis." It could as easily be said that Keynesianism should be faulted for failing to cure cancer or predict the weather. But, on the other hand, Fusfeld's reaction to the contemporary economic orthodoxy in the face of deepening problems may be one that is somewhat justified on the grounds that the orthodox economists promised so much so confidently for so long and were actively promoting their paradigm in the public domain. Reality did not agree much at all with the textbook accounts of the way a Keynesian capitalism is supposed to work, nor did it appear likely that it ever would.

By the fall of 1974, Nixon had been pushed out of office because of his involvement in the well-known Watergate scandal. Gerald Ford, the replacement for the deposed Spiro Agnew, who had left the Vice Presidency because of a different scandal of his own, invited many well-known economists to Washington shortly after his rapid ascent to the Presidency for "summit meetings" which were ultimately inconclusive. But it is remarkable to note that the reported consensus among the economists was that "rapidly rising wages formed the major inflationary threat." [80] This consensus was reached at a time when real wages had been declining and many corporations were revealing record profits! The major issue that was reported to have been addressed was inflation and the second big issue was "to build broad support for policies to which the Ford Administration [was] already committed, such as reductions in government expenditures."[81] By May of 1975 the unemployment rate was 8.9 percent, the highest it had been in three decades. Industrial production dropped 3.6 percent during the month of January 1975, which was the largest monthly decline since December 1937, and the decline between September 1974 and February 1975 was 9.5 percent. Indeed, gross national product *fell* 1.8 percent in 1974 and 2 percent in 1975.[82] But many corporate earnings reports showed a different picture:

> Lykes, Youngstown, quarterly earnings $1.96 a share vs. 56¢ in the year-earlier quarter . . . Gruman, $2.12 vs. $1.12 . . . General Telephone, 86¢ vs. 83¢ . . . International Paper, $1.49 vs. $1.06 . . . Goodyear, 52¢ vs. 50¢ . . . R. J. Reynolds, $1.52 vs. $1.49 . . . Columbia Broadcasting, $1.14 vs. 85¢ . . . Colgate -Palmolive, 61¢ vs. 36¢ . . . [83]

It cannot be said that the economists sought only the ear of the President. A long list can be made of economists who met with Speaker of the House Carl Albert and other members of the Democratic Steering Committee as early as June 27, 1974 to attempt to formulate a program for the Democrats' consideration. This list included Otto Eckstein, Walter W. Heller, Leon Keyserling, Arthur M. Okun, Paul S. Samuelson, Charles L. Schultze and James Tobin presenting one set of proposals and John Kenneth Galbraith and Robert Lekachman presenting a dissenting view.[84] Months later the adoption of any program by the Democrats was not apparent if it existed at all. Further, the situation had to be watched on a day-to-day basis with practicalities sometimes taking precedence over politics inasmuch as both the Republicans and the Democrats wanted to keep the system as a whole functioning. Therefore, the compromise that seemed to be emerging was one of a debate over *how large* a tax cut was needed and what income groups should be the primary beneficiaries. [85]

Although the Republicans were philosophically opposed to massive intervention in the economy, they were involved in the debate about how much to intervene; the Democrats had found advocates of two somewhat different positions.

The first view of what should be done can be summarized easily because there was a certain expectable coherency to it. The group pointed out that the problem was the worst since World War II and was different in that unemployment was high, growth of the economy had been low and even negative, the "peacetime" inflation was the largest in U. S. history, interest rates were higher than at any previous time, real wages had fallen, and profits were "inflating in a nonsustainable way." [86]

Their collective response is that no *dramatic* action should be taken because there was no quick solution. Rather cautious fiscal and monetary policy was advised "that [would] carefully simmer down the boiling inflation"; tax reform was suggested to get real wages in shape and to correct the maldistribution of income. [87]

Since policies to deal with inflation are contradictory to those that are needed to deal with unemployment the group advocated a "greatly expanded program of public service employment" to maintain incomes and work habits. It was also suggested that federal priorities be re-evaluated and social programs be given preference over the military portion of the budget. The group also recommended a monetary policy that would bring interest rates down and not be so harsh on the housing construction. [88]

This is not all of the group's program, but it is most of it. Lekachman and Galbraith offered a critique and an alternative program:

> With regret, for we respect the careful efforts of those participating, we are refraining from signing the Report on Inflation for the Democratic Steering and Policy Committee. The United States is suffering from the worst inflation since World War I. We are asked for remedies. The report (for good reason) does not recommend a tighter monetary policy than at the present. It proposes a highly justifiable redistribution of tax burdens but no additional tax restraint. It expresses oblique concern about military spending but makes no firm recommendation for a reduction. It is feeble on the subject of wage and price policy—a

dialogue but not controls. If the government cannot use fiscal policy, cannot use monetary policy, cannot use controls, the reader will ask, what is left? The answer, alas, is nothing. Or, at most, there are prayer and hopeful prediction, both of which the administration has already exploited to the full.[89]

Lekachman and Galbraith argued that there should be a "stiff surtax on upper income—say, above $15,000 or $20,000." In addition, "Given the present level of profits, equity also requires a solid increase in the corporate income tax." Further there should be an excise tax on large automobiles and "other heavy users of energy or scarce materials for luxury purposes." They also suggested that there be a reduction of military spending and a ban on tax cuts as well as monetary restraint that would be eased when possible to expand housing.

There should . . . be vigorous government-sponsored action to expand food, fertilizer, and fuel supplies and, where appropriate, to conserve use. [What is more], in the modern, highly organized economy there must be firm, fair, and strongly administered wage and price controls. . . . Against the very real chance of increasing unemployment as inflation is brought to an end, there must, as the report recommends, be an adequate fund for direct employment in useful civic tasks for those who cannot find jobs. Such directly financed employment is in place of general macroeconomic action to stimulate the economy with its consequent and unacceptable inflationary effect.[90]

The major thrust was against inflation in this part of the report, but Galbraith and Lekachman conclude on this note:

A recession may come; we now know that economic prediction, our own included, is not sufficiently valid to serve as a basis for action. We must be willing promptly to change course as necessary but we must act on the basis of the present reality. The present reality, one that is deeply distressing to millions of people, is inflation.[91]

What emerges from the commentary above, the sketch of ideas being offered by economists who believe themselves to be addressing the crisis of capitalism and who perceive themselves influential enough to be heard in circles of power, is a sense of considerable confusion and contradiction, a continuing and deepening problem, substantial disagreement on fundamental issues and suggestion of contradictory policies. If there is little concensus among economists one can expect less zeal for their programs in the Congress and the executive branch of the federal government.

The Keynesian paradigm does not adequately relate to the current situation. What was being suggested by the economists mentioned above was partially a Keynesian program, partially a system of controls (from the Galbraith-Lekachman school of thought), a bit of redistribution of income, and perhaps some public employment. The hegemony of Keynesian thought seems at an end with the emergence of a mixed bag of eclectic political economics which displays the absence of a solid grasp of the state system to which it is being addressed. Economics that appeals to the powerful appears to be in a very makeshift, patchwork state. Does it really merit a vote of confidence? More accurately, should it be seen as little more than an upper socioeconomic strata ideology?

Indeed, as much is acknowledged by a good many "well-known" economists themselves with respect to the legitimacy of economic policy suggested by them and their colleagues.

> A bevy of economists and social thinkers got together here yesterday at a conference on full employment, and one of the few things that emerged was that there is no more agreement in academe on what ought to be done than there is in government.
>
> "I don't know why anybody listens to economists anymore," Prof. Robert Lekachman, an economist at Lehman College, cautioned his audience at the outset. That may have been the only thing that anyone was convinced of during the day-long affair.[92]

It might be added that this questioned legitimacy is hardly based on new developments. There is evidence that economists have been less adept at dealing with understanding the economic environment than is thought as a matter of course.

> A modest survey of economists' predictions has shown why their reputation has suffered along with the economy. Among other shortcomings, the accuracy of their predictions of the path prices will take in a given year is what one would expect to get by tossing a coin.
>
> The evidence on his brethren's performance was compiled by Geoffrey H. Moore of the National Bureau of Economic Research and published recently in the newsletter of the Morgan Guaranty Trust Company. Mr. Moore studied the predictions of both government and private economists over a 13-year period for the rate of inflation and the gross national product. Generally, private and official forecasts agreed and both groups erred together. Here is what Mr. Moore reports.
>
> -On G.N.P., 10 times out of 13 the forecasts of the change in growth rate were in the right direction.
>
> -On prices, the forecasts of whether they would rise or fall were correct in four years, wrong in four and ambiguous in five, because either the forecast rate or actual rate remained constant.
>
> -Both official forecasts and private ones tend to err on the optimistic side.[93]

Perhaps the central issue of this chapter, in view of the preceding discussion, should be the questioned hegemony of economists as well as of Keynesian thought. Perhaps the structural arrangements on which our lives are founded are too important to allow an elitist group of paradigm-imperialists to formulate be they radical, liberal, conservative, eclectic or whatever. Perhaps the *role* of the economist needs to be taken much less seriously in an effort to end divisions between people. Perhaps then a wide spread and broadly based discussion of the *issues* might be generated, which are much more important than the *labels* we have given phenomena and the legitimacy that has been awarded persons who get paid to think and offer policy which ultimately affects the lives of everyone. Economists could draw on their knowledge to act as facilitators, to be sure, but there seems little reason for them to be set apart as *experts* or neutral *scientists.*

With these criticisms of simple-minded Keynesianism, the eclecticized recent thought, and even economists, it need be asked: Why is it that academic economics has any legitimacy at all? Gerald Peabody offers some ideas that point to the answer to this question:

> No paradigm is declared invalid unless a replacement is at hand. A decision to replace the old with a new paradigm involves comparisons of both with nature and of each with the other. A proposal for a new paradigm is often accompanied by strong resistance since a change requires that previous standards of beliefs and procedures must be discarded. A paradigm change involves a reconstruction of the field from new fundamentals. The profession must make a complete transition: it must change its view of its field, its methods, and its goals and learn to see nature in a new way.[94]

These problems need not lead to absolute despair and pessimism, though it is not difficult to understand why much of both exists. Rather, the opportunity may be upon us for social reconstruction. It is unlikely that change ever occurs unless from necessity, and it is in the self-interest of the mass of people to support it. Naturally, there is reason to worry about the specific kind of change that is likely to take place since a look at history does not provide much solace. But neither does the evidence show a need for fear. Indeed, perhaps some inspiration can be gleaned from the struggle for self-determination by the people of Indochina.

At this point it is useful to step back to gain perspective. A lesser sense of hysteria can be found in the Marxian literature because from this point of view the current crisis has been going on for some time in spite of the chauvinistic paradigm presented and conducted by an academic and governmental power elite. For example, if the flip side of U.S. affluence were a huge military budget, a military Keynesianism that generated contradictions and crisis, it would seem that systemic readjustment would be absolutely desirable even though it would create many changes. Perhaps the emerging death of, or at least severe conflicts in and challenges to, military Keynesianism can also be seen as the *birth* of the search for new answers and as being unable to sustain a system that is ambivalent in its values and contradictory in the ideology it professes and the activities it permits and undertakes. The decline of feudalism was also the rise of a new kind of social order. The possible decline of the U.S. economy—and capitalism everywhere—could be the beginning of the creation of a new way to arrange our economic, social, and political affairs. It is not clearly a disappointment or a problem when Establishment economists of the various types do not have the answers. Their power is probably overestimated to begin with and what actual events occur will probably be forecast when they are already powerfully in motion.

Although the current crisis is not new, it is certainly affecting different parts of the population in new ways. For example, people attempting to enter the work force for the first time or after an extended absence are encountering difficulties not encountered by others in the past. Individuals with college degrees, for example, are not necessarily going to find the place they thought they would "with all the rights and privileges pertaining thereto." More and more people are finding out that they really are part of the working class and must sell their labor to live regardless of what their values are. These people often happen to be more visible and more vocal than others who encounter hardship in U. S. society. It *appears* that there is more of a problem when a college educated person from, for example, an affluent suburban family reared in comfort cannot pursue the intended career as a high school teacher, child development specialist, or other professional pursuit. For many parts of the work force and for the hard-core "surplus population" there has been a serious problem for some time. John Lee Hooker's song "I'll Never Get Out of These Blues Alive" sums up the feeling for many people. The situation *seems* to be worsening when it begins affecting those who *publicize* ideas (or know publicizers). Thus, the current crisis may really be the *continuing* crisis, which has many dimensions that are broadening and deepening. More people may come to struggle to create meaningful change of a variety that potentially goes far beyond the thought of Eckstein, Heller, Keyserling, Okun, Samuelson, Schultze, Tobin, Galbraith, Lekachman, and others—the elite who appeal to government policy makers to implement their policies to save capitalism again. The ability of the media to make public and legitimate the ideas of a mere handful of idea makers and policy formulators, whose thoughts have captured the minds of the people, may be near the end. Perhaps we are on our own and need to think for ourselves. Perhaps what is being witnessed is the questioned hegemony of authority supportive of the old order.

These conclusions are not surprising in view of the general historical and political climate of the United States. The quest for a stabilized corporate monolith or an expansive multinational capitalism complete with imperialism, obviously, could not offer much appeal for a portion of the population. But then neither does unemployment when it implies personal disaster. So two main factors may put Keynesian economics to the final test. First, the economic orthodoxy is under challenge and others are attempting to construct scientific and ideological opposition. Second, everyday reality in the 1970s seems surrounded by a mild hysteria, chaos, and apparent *general* insecurity. In this environment, Keynesian policies may look like empty rhetoric that has had its day. A new reality that is perceivable and includes the increasing centralization of industry and the state along with the expansion of the market and the proletarianization of the *world* population has led to ideas which challenge theory which well may be hopelessly bankrupt.

The remainder of this work then, seeks to present two competing views—those of Galbraith and those of critical political economics, especially Marxian economics—comparing one against the other and ending up, in the final chapter, with a final critique and synthesis of Keynesian, Galbraithian, Marxian, and radical thought in political economics. The next chapter continues this discussion of the crises of capitalism and criticizes Keynesian thought from a Marxian perspective while at the same time looking critically at Marxian thought. This necessitates, in Chapter 4, taking a deeper look at the structural foundations of U. S. industry from both a Marxian and Galbraithian point of view and then, in Chapter 5, looking more closely at the state in capitalist society from these same two points of view as well as expanding the discussion of theories about the structure of the economy as a whole. This leads, in Chapter 6, to final observations on thought in political economics and on the structure and performance of the U. S. political economy.

NOTES

1 See Michal Kalecki, "Political Aspects of Full Employment," Political Quarterly, vol. 14 (October–December 1943). This article is included in Selected Essays on the Dynamics of the Capitalist Economy, 1933–1970 (Cambridge: Cambridge University Press, 1971).

2 See, for example, The Initiative Committee for National Economic Planning, "For a National Economic Planning System," Challenge, vol. 18, no. 1 (March–April 1975), pp. 51–53.

3 Michael Harrington, Toward a Democratic Left (New York: Macmillan, 1968), Chapter 2.

4 Seymour Melman, American Capitalism in Decline: The Cost of a Permanent War Economy (New York: Simon & Schuster, 1974). Also see Pentagon Capitalism: The Political Economy of War (New York: McGraw-Hill, 1970), by the same author.

5 Clarence Y. H. Lo, "The Conflicting Functions of U. S. Military Spending After World War II," Working Papers on the Kapitalistate, no. 3 (1975), p. 26.

6 See, for example, E. G. Schumacher, Small is Beautiful: Economics as if People Mattered (New York: Harper and Row, 1974). Especially see Barry Commoner, The Closing Circle: Nature, Man and Technology (New York: Alfred A. Knopf, 1971).

7 Joan Robinson, "The Second Crisis of Economic Theory," in Rendigs Fels, ed., The Second Crisis of Economic Theory (Morristown, N. J.: General Learning Press, 1972), p. 1. A collection of papers from The American Economic Association Meeting, December 27–29, 1971.

8 Ibid., p. 8.

9 Ibid., p. 1.

10 Ibid., pp. 1–3.

11 A history too vast to even begin to list exists on the depression of the 1930s. But a very fine collection in which real people tell their own stories about life during this time is Studs Terkel, Hard Times: An Oral History of the Great Depression (New York: Avon Books, 1970).

12 John Herbers, "Count Ford Among the Keynesians," The New York Times, The Week in Review section (January 19, 1975), p. 4.

13 Office of Management and Budget, The United States Budget in Brief: Fiscal Year 1977 (Washington, D.C.: U. S. Government Printing Office, 1976), pp. 7 and 56.

14 Herbers, "Count Ford Among the Keynesians." It must be noted that this is a highly confused Keynesianism in light of the fact that Ford's key economic adviser and head of the Council of Economic Advisers, Alan Greenspan, was sworn into office with Ayn Rand at his side. Greenspan and his mentor, Ayn Rand, basically do not like government, are adherents to the laissez-faire position, and would like "to try to undo what the Federal government has been doing since the days of Franklin Roosevelt's New Deal," according to Newsweek (February 24, 1975), p. 61.

15 See Appendix A for a highly abridged discussion of Keynesian economics including the graphic depiction of the Keynesian cross.

16 John Maynard Keynes, The General Theory of Employment, Interest and Money (London: Macmillan, 1936), p. 3. Reprinted by permission of Macmillan London and Basingstoke. A well-known interpretation of this work is Alvin H. Hansen, A Guide to Keynes (New York: McGraw-Hill, 1953).

17 Ibid., footnote.

18 Ernest Mandel, The Formation of the Economic Thought of Karl Marx (New York: Monthly Review Press, 1971), p. 45, drawing on the work of Ronald L. Meek.

19 R. F. Harrod, The Life of John Maynard Keynes. Copyright, 1951, by R. F. Harrod. Reprinted by permission of Harcourt Brace Jovanovich, Inc.

20 Keynes, The General Theory, p. 3.

21 To borrow a phrase I like from Michael Meeropol in "A Radical Teaching a Straight Principles of Economics Course," The Review of Radical Political Economics, vol. 6, no. 4 (Winter, 1975), p. 3.

22 Keynes, The General Theory, pp. 5–6.

23 Ibid., p. 7.

24 Ibid., pp. 21–22.

25 Ibid., p. 32.

26 Ibid., pp. 32–33.

27 Ibid., p. 34.

28 Ibid., p. 372.

29 Ibid., p. 373.

30 Robinson, "The Second Crisis of Economic Theory," p. 9.

31 Keynes, The General Theory, p. 379.

32 Ibid., pp. 31–32.

33 Ibid., pp. 378–379.

34 Ibid., p. 381.

35 Ibid., p. 382.

36 Ibid., p. 384.

37 Robinson, "The Second Crisis of Economic Theory," p. 5.

38 Ibid., p. 4.

39 Kalecki, "Political Aspects of Full Employment," p. 330.

40 Robinson, "The Second Crisis of Economic Theory," p. 4.

41 Ibid., p. 6.

42 Ibid.

43 A. Dale Tussing, "Emergence of the New Unemployment," Intellect, vol. 103, no. 2363 (February 1975), p. 305.

44 A good analysis is David M. Gordon's "Recession Is Capitalism as Usual," The New York Times Magazine (April 27, 1975). Arguing that the system functions with profit for capitalists as the driving force, Gordon finds it unsurprising that periodic slumps are tolerated since they serve the function of disciplining labor and restoring profits.

45 Michael Meeropol, "A Radical Teaching a Straight Principles of Economics Course," makes this point similarly.

46 Robinson, "The Second Crisis of Economic Theory," p. 7.

47 Ibid. Keynes of course saw this quite differently: "This analysis supplies us with an explanation of the paradox of poverty in the midst of plenty. For the mere existence of an insufficiency of effective demand may, and often will, bring the increase of employment to a standstill before a level of full employment has been reached." Keynes, The General Theory, pp. 30–31.

48 John Maynard Keynes, "Economic Possibilities for Our Grandchildren," Essays in Persuasion (New York: Harcourt, Brace and Co., 1932).

49 Harrod, The Life of John Maynard Keynes, pp. 382–383.

50 Ibid., pp. 532–533.

51 Price theory is used as a term in the traditional sense in economic thought. One focus is on the varieties of industrial structure (including competitive, oligopolistic, monopolistic) and the relationship between structure, conduct, and performance. Thus prices are part of the analysis but so are wages and the relationship between capital and labor. This, of course, is hardly a comprehensive description of price theory.

52 David Gordon, "Recession Is Capitalism as Usual."

53 Instructor's Manual to accompany E. K. Hunt and Howard J. Sherman, Economics: An Introduction to Traditional and Radical Views (New York: Harper & Row, 1972), p. 84 of the manual.

54 For example, Edwin Mansfield, Principles of Macroeconomics (New York: Norton, 1974).

55 Robert L. Heilbroner and Peter L. Bernstein, A Primer on Government Spending, 2nd ed. (New York: Vintage Books, 1972), p. 57.

56 This complex set of issues has obviously been treated a bit thinly. More will be said on it throughout this whole work. Also see, in this regard, John Gurley, "Federal Tax Policy (A Review Article)," National Tax Journal, vol. xx, no. 3 (September 1967).

The U. S. Treasury Department reported that 402 individuals with incomes of more than $100,000 paid no federal income tax in 1972 for a variety of perfectly legal reasons. Some were large deductions for interest paid on money borrowed for business ventures, the oil depletion allowance, fast depreciation writeoffs for real estate, large capital gains. A dramatic example was President Nixon who paid $792.81 in 1970 and $873.03 in 1971— less than three-tenths of one percent of his $260,000 a year annual income. And this was after a "minimum tax" law was enacted in 1969 to require that wealthy people pay at least some tax! By contrast, someone making $10,000 and having a spouse and two children would have paid about $905. The 402 untaxed individuals were reported in Eileen Shanahan, "No-tax List Rose for Rich in 1972," The New York Times, (March 3, 1974), p. 27. Senator Mondale expressed the view that nonpayment of federal taxes by people with high incomes merely represented the "tip of the iceberg." Nixon may not be the best example here because of his visibility and subsequent problems with the Internal Revenue Service.

57 Paul A. Baran, The Longer View: Essays Toward a Critique of Political Economy (New York: Monthly Review Press, 1969), p. 262. This originally appeared in "On the Political Economy of Backwardness," Manchester School of Economic and Social Studies (January, 1952). The Longer View is a posthumous collection of Baran's essays.

58 Robert Lekachman, ed., Keynes General Theory: Reports of Three Decades (New York; St. Martin's Press, 1964).

59 John Robinson, "The Second Crisis of Economic Theory," p. 3.

60 Lawrence R. Klein, The Keynesian Revolution, 2nd ed. (New York: Macmillan 1966), p. vii.

61 Ibid., p. 213.

62 Ibid., p. 224.

63 Paul Sweezy, in a public lecture at the State University College at Cortland, New York, March 12, 1974.

64 Walter W. Heller, New Dimensions of Political Economy (New York: Norton, 1967), preface to the paperbound edition.

65 Ibid.

66 W. E. Schiesser, "The Club of Rome Model," in Andrew Weintraub, Eli Schwartz, and J. Richard Aronson, eds., The Economic Growth Controversy (White Plains, N.Y.: International Arts and Sciences Press, 1973), p. 220. It is interesting to note that the idea for the symposium that produced the papers compiled in this volume was attributed, in the preface, to the president of the Pennsylvania Power and Light Company who was concerned about the energy crisis as "a symptom of the broader problems surrounding the economic growth controversy," (p. v).

One basic presentation of the general argument is in Donella Meadows, Dennis Meadows, Jorgen Randers, and William Behrens III, The Limits to Growth: a Report for the Club of Rome's Project on the Predicament of Mankind (New York: Signet, 1972). The ideas contained in this book are crucial and merit detailed study and discussion. Here the props are knocked out from under current policy founded on Keynesian thought, and planning becomes the central issue. The debate becomes one of the sort of planning that is likely to occur and is possible. Here enters the struggle between Marxian and Galbraithian thought with the latter providing the model for national socialism and the former the model for democratic socialism, to put it in highly simplistic terms. Of course there are varieties of Marxism. For democratic socialism to exist, the Marxist stage of development must be that in which decentralization is prevalent: a huge bureaucratized state has either been avoided or it has withered away.

67 From the Introduction, Weintraub, Schwartz, and Aronson, eds., The Economic Growth Controversy, p. xiii.

68 Ibid., p. xiv.

69 Ibid.

70 Alan Watts, In My Own Way: An Autobiography, 1915–1965 (New York: Random House, 1972), p. 87.

71 In the order of topics mentioned see Robert Heilbroner's The Worldly Philosophers (New York: Simon & Schuster, 1967); The Making of Economic Society (Englewood Cliffs, N. J.: Prentice-Hall, 1962); The Future as History, (New York: Harper & Row, 1959); The Great Ascent (New York: Harper & Row, 1963); The Limits of American Capitalism (New York: Harper & Row, 1966); and Between Capitalism and Socialism (New York: Random House, 1970).

72 Robert Heilbroner, An Inquiry Into the Human Prospect (New York: W. W. Norton, 1974), p. 22.

73 Ibid., pp. 23–24.

74 Ibid., pp. 60–61. This is of course highly controversial. My colleague Joe Elliott, a botanist with the Northern Powder River Coal Basin Environmental Impact Study Group in Montana, offered the opinion that thermal pollution would be catastrophic long before it reached the extent Heilbroner discusses.

75 Robert Heilbroner, "Second Thoughts on the Human Prospect," Futures, vol. 7, no. 1 (February 1975), pp. 36–37.

76 Geoffrey Barraclough, "The Great World Crisis I," The New York Review of Books, vol. 21, nos. 21 and 22 (January 23, 1975), pp. 20–28.

77 An editorial account of this may be found in James Reston, "41% of Black Teen-agers Jobless!" The New York Times, Week in Review section (February 23, 1975), p. 3.

78 To deal with this idea is, of course, a whole other work. But it would seem that an analysis of crime is possible using some composite measure of economic activity as the independent variable and crimes of various types as the dependent variables. For example, one inmate awaiting arraignment in the Public Safety Building in Syracuse, New York (in November of 1974) said he preferred "boosting" (shop lifting) to welfare because he was able to maintain a sense of self more distinctly and was actively involved in society, autonomous and not dependent on others. My account is a paraphrase of this person's interpretation which was put in much more direct/earthy terms but I think it accurate.

79 Daniel R. Fusfeld, "Post-Post-Keynes: the Shattered Synthesis," in Annual Readings in Economics '73/'74 (Guilford, Ct.: Dushkin Publishing Group, 1973), pp. 12–14.

80 Edwin L. Dale, Jr., "President Told Nation Does Not Now Face Big Depression," The New York Times (September 6, 1974), p. 16.

81 Eileen Shanahan, "Economists Open Inflation Talks in Capital Today," The New York Times (September 5, 1974), p. 1.

82 "A Frightening Momentum," The New York Times, Week in Review Section (February 9, 1975), p. 1. U. S. Department of Commerce data for all of 1974 and 1975.

83 "Highlights of the Week," Business and Finance Section, The New York Times (February 16, 1975), p. 14.

84 "Toward a Democratic Economic Policy," Challenge, vol. 17, no. 4 (September–October 1974), p. 58.

85 Philip Shabecoff, "Ford is Reported Ready to Accept House Tax Plan," The New York Times (February 23, 1975), pp. 1 and 36.

86 Toward a Democratic Economic Policy."

87 Ibid.

88 Ibid., p. 59.

89 Ibid., p. 60.

90 Ibid.

91 Ibid.

92 Lee Dembart, "The Economists are Confused, Too," The New York Times (February 16, 1975), p. 51.

93 "Economic Forecasting: A Toss-Up," The New York Times, Business and Finance Section (February 16, 1975), p. 1. Copyright © 1975 by The New York Times Company. Reprinted by permission.

94 Gerald E. Peabody, "Scientific Paradigms and Economics: an Introduction," The Review of Radical Political Economics, vol. 3, no. 2 (July, 1971), p. 3. This entire issue of RRPE is a comparatively early attempt to construct a reorientation in economic thought. It should be seen as a contribution to critical political economics. Personally, I would discard the word "nature" and put "social reality" in its place.

3

SOME MARXIAN IDEAS ON THE CRISES OF CAPITALISM: CONTRAST WITH ORTHODOXY

The hegemony of Keynesian economics and the modern orthodoxy in general is in question on a number of grounds. Chapter 3 develops this theme more fully by introducing some ideas on the way in which Marxian political economics is useful in analyzing the economic system in the United States and in providing an alternative to the Keynesian perspective. At the same time in moving from classical to modern Marxian analyses, one can believe that aspects of Keynesian thought are useful to supplement Marxian thought and that modern Marxian thought is to no small extent quite eclectic and somewhat ad hoc itself. Thus, the tasks here are to, *first*, continue the critique of Keynesian thought and the conventional wisdom in general; *second*, present some Marxian analyses of capitalism; *third*, point to some problems of Marxian thought; and *fourth*, introduce some admittedly sketchy and highly impressionistic data about the condition of the

U.S. political economy in the first half of the 1970s in comparison to the post-World War II period in general. What emerges is a sense that Marxian interpretations and criticisms of the political economy and of the economic orthodoxy are useful if underdeveloped. But it is also revealed that a sketch of some of the surface manifestations of the economic system requires a deeper look into the *structure* of centralized and concentrated capital, the financial nexus (which is but touched on superficially in this work), competitive capital, and the state.

As this is written, the U.S. political economy is in the midst of economic difficulties which are generally acknowledged to be the most serious since the Great Depression of the 1930s. It is not known if the trough of the contraction in employment and output has been reached yet or not, and there is a danger of presenting a view which is unduly influenced by this perhaps transitory situation. Thus, parts of this chapter—which provides an admittedly thin depiction of aspects of the political economy of the first half of the 1970s—touch on matters which will only be understood when additional historical perspective exists. On the other hand, the recent recessionary situations exist at least to some extent as a matter of conscious federal policy to counteract double digit inflation. It is clear that fiscal policy will be undertaken to counteract the recession even before inflationary pressures have been fully abated though the rate has decreased in 1975 and 1976 as unemployment has soared. One policy was that of tax rebates of $100 to $200 per return for 1974 and a decreased withholding of federal taxes. But while federal injections into income flows are occurring, state and local governments—which are obliged under law to avoid budgetary deficits—are cutting back in expenditures and public employment in response to fiscal difficulties. It is not known if the economic contraction will be abated or if it will worsen. Yet it can be said that to some extent the 1970s to date has been a period of crisis for at least a part of the population which has been reflected in but goes beyond the usual statistical measures. There has always been a lower class in the United States. But a new unemployment and underemployment has emerged in labor markets where the people in question are skillful. This has particularly been noticed by recent graduates of higher education and others attempting to get established in careers. Indeed, even some holders of Ph.D.s are underemployed, and forecasts of the future paint a bleak picture.[1] Perhaps everyone knows a college graduate working as a security guard or taxi driver. The so-called educationally disadvantaged who work in the secondary labor market, who are unemployed, or who simply drop out of the work force (and become "discouraged workers") have been discussed for years by policy researchers and federal and state policy makers (while collecting handsome salaries) who have not reached any conclusive answers or firmly admitted (as many suspect) that there are no answers within the structure of capitalism. The recession spoken of here is not a new crisis at all but is more part of a deepening and continuing one. This crisis in its more apparent stage is important, however, in that it could be the prelude to general economic collapse, continued unresolved problems of substantial official rates of unemployment and inflation, and/or new forms of state intervention as well as (in any of these cases) resulting sociopolitical developments.

Although the nature of the economic crisis of the 1970s is not well understood at this writing, it is useful to draw on Marxian writings about it to give a flavor of Marxian interpretations. A deeper critique and comparison of contemporary Marxian thought in contrast to the archetype represented by John Kenneth Galbraith's work in the following chapters focuses on the structure of the political economy more than on the surface manifestations. Both levels of discussion suggest that, as a tentative view, the crises of the system could usher in new forms of state intervention in a dramatic and greatly accelerated fashion. This direction is precisely the one for which Galbraith and others are arguing and what Marxists and radicals see as a dangerous possibility insofar as "stability" would occur within the general structure of the private ownership of the means of production with "public" control implying the solidification of existing social stratification. The emergence of a streamlined monopoly state technocracy would imply a society similar to that depicted by George Orwell's 1984, if planning is instituted without changing ownership and control. It would be the corporatist era of "fascism with a human face" described by R. E. Pahl and J. T. Winkler. Those who favor workers' power, ownership and control, as most Marxists and radicals do, would be in opposition to this corporatism—not simply philosophically but in practice. And the struggle between labor, capital, and the state would enter a new stage as state intervention would be accelerated along with the reinforcement of centralized and concentrated capital. The dialogue among the various decipherers of the political economy is spirited; many are attempting to make sense of the labyrinth of institutional and human behavior in these complex times. The view here is that economic and social conditions, which have been unfolding in the 1970s and which previously pointed to an emerging state corporate superstructure, might well be accelerated in response to serious economic contraction affecting more of the population. Thus the choice has been made to speak of some things in part of the following where a more cautious approach would be to wait for the unfolding of events.

First, some central aspects of Marxian critique of capitalism will be sketched. *Second,* this critique is contrasted with the Keynesian perspective. The latter can be seen as a useful complement to the Marxian perspective, to understand that the state intervention advocated by the Keynesians can serve to remove capitalism from chronic depressions and prolong its life as well as alleviate pressures of opposition to it. Keynesianism can be seen as the link from laissez faire capitalism to state capitalism. What is more, the move toward a more formalized state capitalism (and Keynesian policies, it should be remembered, have been in existence in the U.S. for but four decades at most) seems accelerated as (1) deficits in the federal budget are accepted and are enlarged; (2) the financial structure is reinforced and bank failures are prohibited; and (3) the failure of major corporations is not allowed. Thus a *third* feature to be explored in the following is the thesis that the state and especially the central government is the willing partner of centralized and concentrated capital. This relationship seems to be in a new stage of development in the 1970s. The state monopoly capitalist nexus seems to be of an unprecedented magnitude. At the same time, serious difficulties remain. The most noticed of these are unemployment and inflation. A tentative view is that higher rates of unemployment are consistent with higher rates of inflation in the 1970s as compared with the rest of the post-World War II period to date, aside from the serious contraction of employment and output beginning in 1974. All of this leads to the rationale for a deeper look at the structure of industry in the U.S. and the state in capitalist society in Chapters 4 and 5 on the way to a final critique and theoretical synthesis based on the comparative analysis in this work as a whole in Chapter 6.

Marx and Keynes: Complementary Dissonance

Economics: An Awkward Corner, By Joan Robinson, is a good summary statement of the current situation in economic thought, especially since it comes from a member of "that brilliant Cambridge group which surrounded John Maynard Keynes during the years when he was constructing first the *Treatise . . .* and next that epochal volume *The General Theory of Employment, Interest and Money.*"[2] By 1966 Robinson had come to this conclusion about the British economy and society and the world situation.

It seems to me that the people of this country are not in the mood for radical change. They prefer a loose-jointed, ramshackle economic system to one streamlined for efficiency and speed. They are willing to accept much that is irrational and unjust for the sake of preserving the continuity of our political institutions and the glorious flummery of Church and State.

But, at least the rising generation resents privilege and snobbishness and demands genuine equality of opportunity for everyone to use what talents he [or she] may have. They are perfectly ready to shed the last rags of empire and settle down to being a small country devoted to neutrality and peace.[3] . . .

Two menaces hang over the world today—the rise of population ahead of economic development which is spreading desperate misery in the southern continents, and the American crusade against communism, which threatens worse horrors than it is already perpetrating and meanwhile prevents each economic system from settling into peaceful co-existence with the other and using its resources to meet its urgent needs.[4]

Joan Robinson herself has defied being easily classified, though Lekachman refers to her as a radical Keynesian. James O'Connor has labeled her a "Cambridge Marxist" in that her underlying value theory is Ricardian, not Marxist. That is, she does not agonize over the labor theory of value, which troubles some Marxists. Here the level of the discussion is most often on *circulation*, and the labor theory of value is taken to be an obvious underpinning of what is said on a different plane of abstraction (i.e., human beings and their work activity are at the root of material creation but the story, especially of economic instability and the centralization and concentration of capital, does not begin and end here). But perhaps this disagreement among Marxian writers and others is just as well since it really does not matter what one labels a social scientist because this is but a convenience for those who need things in their (often arbitrary) place. One can see Ms. Robinson as "Marxist" as most academic Marxist economists in that she is a scholar of Marx even if she does not engage in Marxist *praxis*. Most western Marxists do not, even though they call themselves Marxists. In fact, in the U.S. or Britain (as well as elsewhere) it seems a contradiction for a person to work in a hierarchical university, engage in unilateral decisions, exercise power over those who are in fact "subordinates" (including "students"), and see oneself as a *Marxist*. This behavior is not Marxist; but those who do not behave in a Marxist way can know a great deal about Marx. Joan Robinson is, perhaps, such a person. She has provided useful and clear interpretations of Marxian economics, and she has some insightful things to say.[5]

Perhaps the secret to Joan Robinson's work toward a Keynesian/ Marxian synthesis is to be found in this passage:

> Keynes' system of thought operates within a restricted field. He does not touch at all upon the major questions with which Marx was concerned, and he has undermined the orthodox theory of long-period equilibrium without putting anything very definite in its place. Thus Marx's theory, or at any rate some theory on the questions which Marx discussed, is as much required to supplement Keynes as Keynes' theory is to supplement Marx.[6]

Before she reached this conclusion, Robinson made her case well. She suggested that there are reasons that Marx should be recognized by economists and also reasons for that recognition being mixed.

> Academic theory. . .has. . .arrived at a position which bears considerable resemblance to Marx's system. In both, unemployment plays an essential part. In both, capitalism is seen as carrying within itself the seeds of its own decay. On the negative side, as opposed to the orthodox equilibrium theory, the systems of Keynes and Marx stand together, and there is now, for the first time, enough common ground between Marxist and academic economists to make discussion possible. In spite of this there has still been very little serious study of Marx by English academic economists.
>
> Apart from political prejudice, the neglect of Marx is largely due to the extreme obscurity of his method of exposition. There are two serious defects in the Marxian apparatus, which are quite superficial in themselves, and can easily be remedied, but which have led to endless misunderstandings.[7]

Robinson offers a succinct explanation of these defects. First,

> In Marx's terminology C, constant capital, represents productive equipment (factories, machinery, etc.), and raw materials and power; V, variable capital, represents the wages bill; and S, surplus, rent interest, and profits. Now if we write (as Marx habitually does) $C + V + S$ to represent the flow of production, say per year, then C is not the stock of capital invested, but the annual wear-and-tear and amortization of capital [and ingredients used up].
>
> $$\frac{S}{C + V}$$
>
> is the share of profits in turnover, and not the rate of profit on capital invested. The rate of profit which (for Marx as in orthodox systems) tends to equality in different lines of produc-

tion, and the rate of profit which tends to fall as capital accumulates is not

$$\frac{S}{C + V}$$

but the rate of profit on capital invested.[8]

Ms. Robinson says that Marx was aware of this point but his use of the expression above

> . . . for the rate of profit on capital is excessively confusing. Moreover, lumping raw material and power along with equipment in the single concept of constant capital makes it impossible to distinguish between prime and overhead costs, since prime costs consist of V and part of C (raw materials and power), while another part of C is overhead. Thus Marx's apparatus is useless for many of the problems in which academic economists have interested themselves, especially in connection with short-period supply price and the influence of monopoly on the share of wages in output.[9]

With regard to the second problem in Marx's *Capital* Robinson says the following:

> The second main difficulty arises from Marx's method of reckoning in terms of value or labour time. With technical progress and capital accumulation, output per man-hour tends to rise, so that the *value* of commodities is constantly falling. Academic economists are much concerned with output, and with concepts such as the "real national income," the "level of real wages," and so forth. To measure these in terms of *value* is to measure with a piece of elastic. Thus academic economists, if they get as far as considering Marx at all, are apt to form the impression that his methods of thought are quite useless, and to dismiss the whole of his analysis as an inextricable mass of confusion, which it is not worth the trouble of understanding.[10]

Importantly, Robinson notes still another part of Marx's analysis.

> This impatience has been further encouraged by the perennial controversy over the labour theory of value. In my opinion, this has been much ado about nothing, and the pother that there has been over it has disguised both from the academics and from the Marxists and the real nature of the question at issue. To the academic economist, the "theory of value" means the theory of *relative* prices—the prices of commodities in terms of each other. Now Marx's theory of relative prices, as set out in Volume III of *Capital,* is quite simple. The rate of profit on capital tends to equality in all lines of production. Wages of labour also tend to

equality in all occupations (allowing for differences in skill). The amount of capital per unit of labour employed is governed by the state of technical development. The normal price (apart from errors and perturbations of the market) for, say, a year's output of any commodity, is equal to the wages of the labour employed in producing it *plus* profit, at the ruling rate, upon the capital invested. Prices would be proportional to *values* if capital per unit of labour (the organic composition of capital) were the same everywhere, but, in fact, for technical reasons, proportionately more capital is employed in some industries than in others, and since the rate of profit on capital invested tends to equality, profits, relatively to wages, tend to be high where the ratio of capital to labour is high. Thus normal prices are equal to long-run costs of production, and the ruling average rate of profit on capital is the supply price of capital to any particular line of production. Conditions of demand determine the amount of each commodity produced.[11]

Though not simple, careful reading and reflection help to clarify Marx's theory of value[12] and lead Robinson to conclude that the gap between this theory and orthodox theory is not as wide as it may appear at first glance. It is simply the "first starting point for any theory of relative prices." She adds

The academic economist may consider it too simple and primitive . . . but he has no reason to regard it as fundamentally erroneous. Equally, the Marxist has no reason to regard the labour theory of value, *as a theory of relative prices,* either as particularly important or as fundamentally opposed to orthodoxy.
What divides Marx's theory from others is not at all the question of relative prices of commodities but the question of the *total* supply of capital and the rate of profit on capital *as a whole.* On this question there is a sharp difference between Marx and the pre-Keynesian academics.[13]

Another quote is useful to get to the root of the matter:

The real differences between Marx and the orthodox schools concern the question of what governs the accumulation of capital and the distribution of the total product of industry between workers and capitalists. Compared to these problems, the determination of relative prices of commodities appears as a secondary question which has been too much flattered by all the attention that has been paid to it. It is precisely upon these large questions that the old orthodox system has been profoundly shaken. Thus, as between Marxists and Keynesians, the labour theory of value is a totally irrelevant issue. [Italics added.][14]

Robinson, then, sees Marx as a great economist in much "the same sense as Ricardo, Marshall, and Keynes were great economists, and

. . . his merits simply as a theorist have been concealed by the prophetic robes in which he has been dressed up."[15]

The central issues surround theories of crises. Although Volume II of *Capital* contains similarities to Keynes' analysis, it is obscure and was not fully completed by Marx at the time of his death in 1883.[16] And although while there are similarities, there are also differences. In Marx's system the amount of surplus which capitalists have succeeded in extracting influences the amount of investment.[17] For Keynes investment is determined by the likelihood of future profit which explains the onset of a slump following a period of intensive investment and the emergence of unemployment along side expanding wealth and increased productive capacity. But for Marx this problem of inadequate effective demand, in this instance, is not the issue and the notion that separate decisions to save and invest is not entertained "which, in Keynes' system, appears as the root cause of crisis and unemployment." Marx's reasoning on this score is not in tune with his main thrust.[18] Marx does not question the existence of investment opportunities. He has agreement on this in much of modern investment theory which is closer to Marx than Keynes.[19]

For Marx, of course, unemployment does exist as a central problem endemic to capitalism with his focus on "the reserve army of labour," the size of which depends on the amount of capital which exists. Unemployment emerges when there is not enough capital (which is a flow not a stock) to employ those who are available. In turn, new technology increases productivity when a short-term relative shortage of labor exists, and the reserve army is once more created in the next time period. This is quite different from unemployment that is the result of insufficient demand.[20]

> It seems, then, that Marx and Keynes are discussing two different problems, and that each theory is required to supplement the other. Marx, however, regarded his system as all-inclusive, and he purported to derive from it an explanation of the crises which develop in advanced capitalist economies. It is here that, in the light of Keynes' argument, Marx's analysis appears inadequate and unconvincing.[21]

There are still two more important issues that need to be pointed to, if but fleetingly. First, according to Ms. Robinson, Marx argued in the first Volume of *Capital* that

> Real wages (broadly speaking, with exceptions and reservations) tend to remain constant at subsistence level (though the subsistence level contains a "moral and historical element" due to the customary standard of life). As productivity increases with capital accumulation and technical progress, the rate of exploita-

tion (the ratio of profits to wages) therefore tends to rise. Capital at the same time tends to be concentrated in ever fewer hands as large units prevail in the competitive struggle over smaller units. Thus there is an ever-growing difference between the wealth of the few and the poverty of the many which in the end will lead to an explosion—the overthrow of capitalism and the "expropriation of the expropriators."[22]

The increased impoverishment thesis is one of the more controversial areas raised by various interpretations of Marx. Others claim that Marx did not make this argument at all but it was, rather, imputed by anti-Marxians who were anxious to show Marx's theory inadequate on the grounds that it did not meet the criterion of prediction that many social scientists hold must obtain if a theory is to be thought valid. In other words, if Marx did not adhere to the argument that increasing absolute exploitation would exist under capitalism, the event of increasing real wages in 20th century capitalist society does not prove him to have had a false sense of the dynamics of the system.[23] The issue is left unresolved here in that *Capital* is exceedingly difficult to decipher on this score. It seems more important to note that Marx was aware of the essential conflict and struggle between labor and capital. Thus it is difficult to disagree or agree with Ms. Robinson's claim that "Marx did not foresee to what an extent capitalism would be able to buy off the workers with refrigerators and Ford cars."[24] It seems more accurate to suggest that Marx could not conceive of the emerging state as a driving force and willing servant of capital, though scholars of Marx's work could point to some passages in his assorted writings (other than *Capital*) that indicate the contrary. The general contention here is that Marx did not generate a theory of the state that goes beyond that expressed in *The Communist Manifesto,* and it is not worthwhile to agonize over the point. Rather, Marxist theory of the state should be *primarily* attributed to more recent Marxian writers.

Much of the modern Marxian literature, further, gives the sense that an explanation for the absence of increased *general* impoverishment under capitalism is due. But perhaps this is a retort to the anti-Marxians. In this literature one argument is that workers in developed nations have experienced increasing real wages partly because of the relationship of their countries to those in the Third World. In short, imperialism may have served to export the crises.[25] But the staying power of capitalism thus far has been formidable and cannot be shrugged off, and those such as Robinson seem persistent in claiming that Marx's analysis is deficient on that score. If it is, Joan Robinson offers this explanation:

Thus it appears that Marx's prediction of "increasing misery" of the workers has failed to be fulfilled. At this point Keynes once more supplements Marx, for he shows how increasing wealth brings its nemesis in a different way. Growing susceptibility to unemployment appears instead of growing poverty of the masses as the weakness at the heart of developing capitalism.[26]

How long this will be so remains to be seen, and it should be pointed out that capitalism may, indeed, contain the seeds of its own destruction but in a way Marx did not consider. Here one must consider the "limits of growth" controversy, and Robert Heilbroner's discussion in *The Human Prospect*, which point alarmingly to the system's ecological worldwide impact. But, of course, an industrialized socialism contains many of the same dangers.

The second point is

> There is a . . . strand of thought in *Capital* which is quite different from the first, and which, indeed, is hard to reconcile with it. This is the Law of Falling Rate of Profit, elaborated in the third volume. In this argument (once more with exceptions and qualifications) it is the rate of exploitation, not the rate of real wages, which tends to remain constant. If the rate of exploitation is constant, real wages rise with productivity, the workers receiving a constant share in a growing total of real output. Now, according to Marx, there is a broad tendency for the organic composition of capital to rise as time goes by; that is to say, capital-using inventions are the predominant form of technical progress, so that capital per unit of labour employed is continuously rising. If capital per unit of labour is rising, but profit per unit of labour is constant (or rises more slowly) then the rate of profit on capital is falling. Thus capitalists undermine the basis of their own prosperity by their rage for accumulation. The connection between this theory and the theory of crises is made in the most tangled and confusing passages of Volume III, and has been the subject of many conflicting interpretations. Instead of plunging into that jungle, it is better to concentrate upon the first stage of the argument—the rising organic composition of capital.[27]

When this is done problems arise since it is conceivable that the organic composition of capital need not necessarily rise since "Marx (or rather Engels for him) clearly admits that it is not the case that all technical progress increases capital per unit of labour." In addition, improved transportation and time saving inventions such as electronic communications may "save capital."[28]

> Certainly many great capital-saving inventions (such as wireless in place of cables) have been made in recent times. . . . A world in which organic composition is constant (or, for that matter, falling) is perfectly conceivable. To such a world, Marx's analysis would have no application, and the whole of that part of

his theory of crises which depends upon the declining tendency
of profits would fall to the ground. His case for a tendency to
ever-deepening crises as a necessary and inevitable feature of
capitalism thereby cannot be sustained. If there is a fundamental
defect in capitalism it must have deeper roots than in a mere
accident of technique.[29]

Keynes, on the other hand, does not rely on tendencies in organic
composition of capital, but when a capital-saving invention occurs,
there is a likelihood that a lessened outlet for investment would also
"tend to make a smaller contribution to maintaining effective demand."[30]

> Thus it appears that whichever branch of Marx's theory of
> crises we follow, it is necessary to call in Keynes' analysis to
> complete it, and neither part of Marx's argument can stand up by
> itself.[31]

At the same time, Keynes' system—as has already been argued at
length—is limited in a number of ways, especially in that it does not
deal with the structural implications of the longer run application of
the suggestions for economic engineering. It would seem, then, that
many important parts of Marx's thought are useful in the construction of a holistic view; and many who agree with this stance have,
over the generations, done precisely that. Often these social scientists
have been called "revisionists" by those who were attracted to a more
orthodox Marxism. But to such charges it might be said, so what if the
thought of Marx is used as a general intellectual tradition and as but a
loose and general starting point for economic and social inquiry so
long as that inquiry is insightful?[32] Indeed, those who are skeptical of
the viability of capitalism cannot advise those whom they seek to
convince that the answers are obvious or clear in classical Marxism.
It would seem that the point is to explain particular dynamics and
phenomena rather than to remain true to ideas that are fuzzy, even if
one must, at the same time, admire the seminal attempts of those
ideas. A sensible stance seems to be this: Marxian thought seems
useful to develop a science of society; but some parts are more useful
than others, and whatever supplements and replacements make sense
should be undertaken.

One perception that does clearly emerge from Frederick Engels'
short synopsis of *Capital* is the notion that the transformation of
labor power into capital and the growing proletarianization of the
population are intertwined events. While much of the accumulation
of surplus value is plowed back into increasing the stock of capital,
the productive capability of the society increases over time. Thus,
although the proletarianized population is at the mercy of capitalists
(and the state in modern times) for the provision of the wherewithal

to live (especially as rural to urban population shifts occur and a move toward nonagricultural life styles are pushed into existence), the means of production are more vulnerable to appropriation and control by the workers. In this way the labor theory of value makes sense, and Marxism as a revolutionary doctrine appears, rates of profit and the more esoteric debates aside. But a problem exists in that Engels seems (at least in this instance) not to acknowledge the absence of homogeneity in the work force. That is, while many exist as the industrial reserve army and while impoverishment is the lot of a part of the population, other workers have secure and well-paid employment. Rather than a "mass of oppressed workers," some are and some are not. This probably explains why, in the U.S. at least, there seems to be no unified "social class which is more and more compelled to claim the utilization of . . . wealth and . . . productive forces for the whole of society—instead of as today for a monopolist class."[33] This is also why it seems extremely important to entertain modern Marxian and other work which sees capital and labor as more complex than depicted in the view that Engels offers.

Perhaps one of Marx's main contributions was one of a general method and an incredible ability to integrate and synthesize huge amounts of theory and data toward a holistic and, at the same time, an interdisciplinary view of economy and society. If some specific analyses offered by Marx do not apply or are not clear, this hardly proves his work useless. Indeed, to look at the development of his thought from early writings to *Capital* and his move from philosophy to the science of society is an inspiration, albeit one that is somewhat intimidating to others who would hope to write penetrating studies drawing from whatever resources seem useful. Marx dared to be experimental and struck out without the support of society's institutions. But he did have the support of his family and friends, a dedication to the workers of the world, and a belief in himself.

Thus *a summary* (and superficial) *view* is that both Keynes and Marx focused on flows of income among the population, though, of course, Marx's *central focus* was always on *social relationships surrounding production*. Keynes, on the other hand, did not explicitly touch on matters of social class based on one's relationship to the means of production much at all. Each recognized the existence of unemployment and crisis as features that one could expect to emerge and not of themselves disappear under capitalism. Marx is generally thought to have held the view that the dynamics of capitalism would result in the emergence of a crisis from which it would be difficult to recover without the workers capturing the productive facilities and reorganizing them. Keynes, on the other hand, in introducing the notions of aggregate demand, the propensity to consume, and the like, opened the door to reasoning which suggested that the highest civil authority, the state, could transcend both labor and capital and through its fiscal and monetary policies recreate the circumstances through which the periodic crises of capitalism could be alleviated. Marx's theory of distribution appears to have been one where capital was favored and therefore the productive possibilities of the system would fail to be realized as workers did not have the wherewithal to purchase their own product. Keynes essentially did not have a theory of distribution or saw problems of distribution being circumvented through state intervention. Clearly these issues are not yet totally resolved. The state has become the body through which both labor and capital (and those who are part of neither) struggle.

Joan Robinson's interpretation points to elements in Marx's *Capital* that were rediscovered by Keynes and shows how the latter failed to be as holistic as Marx and indeed did not see that as his purpose. It can be said that Marx and Keynes, to some extent, had different time horizons as have their followers. The main issues *include,* nonetheless, the distribution of income between property and labor as well as theories of the bases of economic crises.[34] Others agree on the origins of these issues and the controversy continues.

Hunt and Sherman put it well in their introductory textbook. Here, as in most contemporary accounts of the functioning of the economy, the link between capital and labor is spoken of in terms of the basic circularity of the economy. Money is the intermediary between capital and labor, between the product markets and the resource markets. They point out that

> Many economists have labored to map this circulation of money and goods in the nation—just as biologists map the circulation of blood through the body. The two most famous economists who have labored at this task are Marx and Keynes.[35]

More accurately, it should be added that Marx derived the idea of circulation from the French Physiocrat (a body of economic theory in the eighteenth century) F. Quesnay's "Tableau oeconomique" (first printed in 1758) and perhaps through others since the idea was picked up by many economists. In Keynes' work the idea is implicit and was drawn out by later economists working in the same vein. In particular, many introductory textbooks introduce a circular flow chart and then go on to discuss Keynesian economics.

Hunt and Sherman make the now nearly apparent observation: Marx had provided the essential focus long before Keynes but this analysis was ignored by the mainstream probably because Marx had gone one step beyond Keynes in that he analyzed "not total flows but flows by class—thus, not just total income but workers' income and capitalists' income."[36]

Marx more or less excluded the "public" sector in his analysis seeing it mainly as a mystified, and small, part of the capitalist class. Keynes, on the other hand, can be seen as having provided some of the ideological and scientific weapons to help revitalize capitalism through the use of the state. In fact, it seems to be no exaggeration to claim that his thought was primarily a bridge to state capitalism thinking of little more than the comparatively short run. This in turn provided a highly useful set of rationalizations for a whole generation of economists and policy makers to suggest that the state could provide longer term stability. These programs were acceptable, importantly, to those who had the immediate power to act and did not create massive opposition among the population at large. The view here is that Keynesian doctrine was used as a rationalization because the most immediate action by capitalist governments was that of worldwide violence with deficits in the federal budget emerging as a matter of course which—thanks to Keynes—had scholarly legitimacy. As Lekachman put it:

> We cannot be really sure that as a nation we possess the will to create full employment except to the accompaniment of considerable quantities of military spending.
> The economic history of the last four decades is not terribly reassuring on this score. The Second World War, not the New Deal, ended the Great Depression. It is still disconcerting to recall that American unemployment as late as 1940 was nearly six million men and women, or 14.6 percent of the labor force—after two terms of Franklin Roosevelt. [37]

Joan Robinson and Michal Kalecki[38] contributed the implications of the *longer run* application of Keynesian stabilization policy. Marxian thought of this variety is useful, and one finds a substantial Marxian critique of Keynesian ideas with but a bit of looking. Marx had himself focused on problems of circulation as a malady that faced capitalism. An elaboration on this is needed.

Joan Robinson's position is persuasive when she argues that

> Keynes' theory gives strong support to Marx's contention that "the real barrier of capitalist production is capital itself." . . .

> Marxist economists have on the whole tended to gloss over the underconsumption element in Marx's theory, and Rosa Luxemburg, who developed it most clearly, is generally regarded as heretical. Underconsumption theories have been associated with an appeal for reform rather than revolution—with the view that capitalism *might* be made to work satisfactorily—and for this reason they are uncongenial to the Marxist creed.
> The association of underconsumption theory with a desire to preserve freedom of enterprise and a distaste for revolution is once more exemplified in Mr. Keynes, who regards his own

theory as "moderately conservative in its implications," and finds the philosophy of Gesell more sympathetic than the philosophy of Marx. But this association is superficial, for the maldistribution of income is quite as deeply imbedded in the capitalist system as Marx believed the tendency to falling profits to be, and cannot be eliminated without drastic changes in the system. The case for revolution, as opposed to reform, might have been argued just as well on the basis of the analysis in Volume II of *Capital* as on the basis of Volume III.[39]

There is agreement here with Robinson's stance which was touched on earlier. On reflection, it is difficult to see how capitalism could be a system which engages in a great deal of income redistribution and remain *capitalism*. And if reform worked to "stabilize" a system characterized by substantial inequality, a normative position could easily be that one could not be zealous about stability since it would be a hierarchical stability. But, of course, it must also be admitted that a Pandora's box has been opened. It cannot really be *known* if capitalism is likely to collapse soon or late or even at all, though economists can be found who believe collapse to be possible. In fact, as is suggested later, and drawn out in Chapter 5, the growth of a social-industrial complex is the more likely direction that might be undertaken by capital and the state which could contain crises for a time.

The social-industrial complex is similar to capital's relationship with the state under the military-industrial complex. However, rather than arms, the state engages in "peacetime" activities such as the launching of telecommunications satellites or promoting an expanded educational system. Although this is not a full definition, the social-industrial complex can be seen as the state nexus existing in an expanded fashion relating to the lives of people in their everyday activities while maintaining capital and the private accumulation with which it is associated. The idea of the social-industrial complex is attributed, by James O'Connor, to IBM board member Lyle Spencer who, in 1966, looked forward to its emergence.[40] The social-industrial complex can be seen as a formalized state capitalism, or a capitalism characterized by private ownership and state "control" and funding. In essence, the social-industrial complex is somewhat similar to social democracy attributed to Britain's Labour Party and the planned capitalism prescribed by John Kenneth Galbraith's *Economics and the Public Purpose* as well as that proposed by The Initiative Committee for National Economic Planning.

Opposition to the social-industrial complex and the state in general would not be on the grounds that absolute economic and social disarray made that opposition necessary. Rather, opposition would emerge from a more ideological basis where if given the choice between the sort of national socialism (the integration of capital and the state at the comparative expense of workers) that a social-industrial complex would imply and democratic socialism, many people might not only favor the latter but would do everything possible to help build it. This issue is one on which there can only be speculation, but it can be argued that a social-industrial complex does not coincide with working class (broadly defined) interests. If the social-industrial complex were to exist more certainly, it is likely that academic economics (to the extent *economics* were to remain the handmaiden of capital and the state) would take on even more engineering/technocratic directions; and it would be about as fascinating as accounting. Then it would be more fruitful for critical social scientists to undertake sociological investigations of the impact this sort of society has on its people and to wonder if the seeds of revolution, as some argue, are planted more during "stable" but more subtly or overtly oppressive times than during an economic slump.[41] There would probably be opposition to a bureaucratic, authoritarian, and hierarchical state capitalism. The New Left and the Counterculture represented (and to some extent still represent) a turning away from monopoly state capital forms which would be even more pronounced under a social-industrial complex. During the 1960s many who were attracted to the Movement could have behaved more conservatively and retained a teaching, corporate, or other job; but an emphasis on personal freedom and growth as well as the quest for identity and some good times seemed much more important, much less one-dimensional, and extremely less alienating. It is unlikely that the authoritarianism and bureaucracy of a stabilized state monopoly capitalism would exist for long without producing responses to these alienating forms.

Keynesianism as the Link to State Capitalism: Paul Mattick on Keynes and Marx

Ideas related to much of what has been said on Marx and Keynes can be found in a very good and, curiously, not-so-well-known book written "during a time hailed by the President of the United States as 'the greatest upsurge of economic well-being in history'."[42] In his contrast of Marxian and Keynesian thought, Paul Mattick, in an objective fashion, pointed to many of the key issues and implications surrounding a prolonged Keynesian application and reached this position while a boom economy still existed:

> It is my contention that the Keynesian solution to the economic problems that beset the capitalist world can be of only temporary avail, and that the conditions under which it can be effective are in the process of dissolution. For this reason the Marxian critique of political economy, far from having lost its pertinency, gains new relevance through its ability to comprehend and transcend both the "old" and the "new" economics.[43]

Mattick, however, felt that there were areas in Marx's theory of change with which he could not agree even if he states the view that change of a socialist variety would have to emerge with the push for it coming from the working class including the industrial proletariat. Further, he indicates that he sees the choices ahead as being either socialism or barbarism.[44] By socialism Mattick means this:

> . . . a socialist revolution must mean precisely the creation of a social structure in which the producers *themselves* control their product and its distribution. It is conceivable only as one made by the working-class which ends social class relations. What Marx—and before him, in 1843, Flora Tristan—formulated in one single proposition, namely, that "the emancipation of the working class must be conquered by the working class itself," remains the implicit postulate of all genuine socialist thought.[45]

The point of disagreement with Marx emerges in this fashion:

> Marx did not envision an intermediary stage between private-enterprise capitalism and socialism. His rather clean-cut differentiation between feudalism, capitalism, and socialism made for a certain "orderliness" and "simplicity" in his revolutionary expectations. He recognized, however, that his history of the rise of capitalism pertained solely to Western Europe, and he opposed any attempt to turn it into "a general historical-philosophical theory of development valid for all nations, no matter what their historical conditions might be." Marx, as well as Engels, allowed for courses of development different from those in Western Europe, and for a shortening of the road to socialism for precapitalist nations, in the wake of successful proletarian revolutions in the West. They recognized the state-capitalist tendencies in developed capitalist nations as indications of the coming socialist revolution without foreseeing their role in transforming precapitalist into state-capitalist systems of production.[46]

Mattick clearly points to the distinction between state capitalist systems and socialism. Many, such as John Kenneth Galbraith in *Economics and the Public Purpose,* persistently confuse one for the other. But if one agrees with Mattick's interpretation, the emergence of state capitalism could hardly be thought to usher in the end of antagonistic relationships in society. Rather the conflict between labor and capital would be different.

We know now that social revolutions in capitalistically-under-developed countries do not, and cannot, repeat the pattern of development of Western capitalism, but tend to introduce state-capitalist structures. They are not socialist revolutions in the Marxian sense even if they do avail themselves of Marxian ideology. The idea that state-capitalist revolution means the victory of socialism even in industrially-advanced nations gains some credibility because such revolutions appear to bring to its logical conclusion the increasing government-determination of production and of social life in general, and because they follow the pattern set by the established state-capitalist systems, which are quite generally perceived as socialist. In these systems, however, the institution of state-capitalism had the function not of abolishing the proletarian class but of aiding in its quick formation and thereby in the formation of capital. In indus-trially-advanced countries, state capitalism would be as irra-tional a system as that which preceded it, for the difficulties of capital production can here be resolved not through an increase of exploitation but only through its abolition.[47]

Although Mattick is abstract enough that it cannot be known for certain what countries he specifically has in mind, it seems reason-able to suggest that he would also include, for example, the Soviet Union in his category of state capitalism. This would trouble many people, but others would tend to agree. A more accurate view, it would seem, is that countries such as the U.S.S.R. are a state socialism where a centralized state shows few tendencies of "withering away" so that a combination of social ownership and participating work relationships can be attained.

Mattick argues that the sort of revolution and resultant society that Marx had in mind has never occurred. Such a society would have involved "the contradiction between the growing social forces of production and the narrow capitalist relations of production . . . being overcome through a revolution which, by ending the class structure of society—its basic antagonism—would open the way towards a socialist world."[48]

But this does not smash the relevance of Marxian thought since

Keynesianism merely reflects the transition of capitalism from its free-market to a state-aided phase and provides an ideology for those who momentarily profit by this transition. It does not touch upon the problems Marx was concerned with. As long as the capitalist mode of production prevails, Marxism will retain its relevance, since it concerns itself neither with one or another technique of capital production, nor with social changes within the frame of capital production, but only with its final abolition.[49]

Mattick hits upon perhaps the most important observation about the place of Keynesian thought in the transformation of capitalism when he points out that this body of knowledge is quite useful for the state-aided phase of capitalism. Further, this state-aided phase can and does take many directions including the use of fiscal and monetary policy as well as controls, direct intervention in labor markets in the form of limited public employment to alleviate part of the inability of the private sector to use everyone who wants to work, and even discussion—though limited action or consensus in the U.S.— of comprehensive economic planning[50] in the style of that underway in other capitalist countries. The problems of instability in modern capitalist countries seem to be such that there are pressures to move beyond Keynesian policies toward more direct forms of state intervention. As movement occurs, it is useful to draw on modern Marxian interpretations of events in that critical and skeptical views of state intervention are held in contrast to orthodox economics which often seeks through its work to assist in the transition to a more specific state capitalism. What is more, classical Marxian thought proves to be inadequate as an intellectual resource to help understand the contemporary situation since it was developed when the state was not large in comparison to the political economy as a whole. It is plausible that it was in "the ruling classes' best interests . . . to be served by a poor rather than a rich State"[51] in the last century when Marx was developing his seminal work, and he, therefore, essentially omitted a "public" sector from his analysis. It was not really until the 20th century in the U.S. and elsewhere that a large central government existed so it is not hard to understand why this theoretical vacuum is present in earlier Marxian thought and was left for later Marxian scholars to remove.

Eclectic Neo-Marxian Thought and the Financial Nexus, Fiscal Policy, and Economic Crisis in the Post–World War II Period

Much of the preceding discussion indicates that there have been significant problems and unresolved issues during the state-aided phase of capitalism. To get a clearer picture of these phenomena, it is useful to point to some additional analysis that exists.

Paul Sweezy and Harry Magdoff, two American Marxian writers and the editors of the *Monthly Review* (M.R.) are of the belief that

> The monopoly capitalist economy is always in danger of sinking into a state of deep stagnation. The basic reason is that

capitalists seek to keep the wages and hence the purchasing power of workers at a minimum, while expanding their capital as rapidly as possible.[52]

They find an explanation in the following written by Marx.

> To the extent that the productive power develops, it finds itself at variance with the narrow basis on which the condition of consumption rests. On this self-contradictory basis it is no contradiction at all that there should be an excess of capital simultaneously with an excess of population. For while a combination of these two would increase the mass of the produced surplus value, it would at the same time intensify the contradiction between the conditions under which this surplus value is produced and those under which it is realized.[53]

Sweezy and Magdoff note that this source of stagnation—"excess of capital" along with "excess of population" equalling unused plants and people out of work—is a problem of capitalism in all of its stages of development but that this difficulty is exacerbated when the system is in a stage of monopoly capitalism

> . . . because of the enormous power of giant corporations to control prices and wages in their own favor. Furthermore, in the monopoly stage consumers are regularly fleeced (for the second time in the case of workers) in the sphere of circulation by monopolistic middlemen, retailers, usurers, racketeers, etc. The result is further to reduce social consuming power and to concentrate additional income in the hands of those whose modes of expenditure are luxury consumption goods and increased capital investment. The whole system is rigged in favor of the haves and against the have-nots. The only trouble is that the more it works that way, the worse it works.[54]

It has already been pointed out that Keynesian policies were devised to counteract tendencies toward stagnation. Sweezy and Magdoff say

> . . . otherwise the whole system would have gone down the drain long ago. On the one hand there must be massive injections of purchasing power to supplement the restricted consumption generated by the normal workings of the system; and on the other hand there must be continuously maintained incentives, chiefly in the form of a steadily rising price level, for the rich minority to invest their lavish incomes. Like a leaking tire, the economy must be unflaggingly pumped up if it is not to go flat and come to a full stop.[55]

This leaking tire metaphor is simple and useful but

> . . . fails in one respect. As long as the economy is pumped up enough to keep going, all the monopolistic forces within it work

overtime to increase their share of the take. This means higher prices, higher rates, higher fees, higher costs all along the line. And this perpetual scramble for more on the part of the powerful and the privileged exacerbates the underlying disproportions which are at the root of the system's malfunctioning. To complete our analogy we would have to say that both the tire and the leak grow with the passage of time, thus requiring a continuously larger and more active pump.[56]

Here we have the elements of a plausible "theory of inflation under conditions of monopoly capitalism."[57] Since Sweezy has been a long-time analyst of monopoly capitalism, there is much behind this view which must be left for a more intensive critique in the next chapter. The focus offered in this article is not on monopoly capital but rather on the "pump," or fiscal and monetary policy undertaken at the federal level of government and the credit system.

This focus is an important one, and the gross aggregate data indicate that many important changes have been underway in recent decades in these three main pumping mechanisms, which seem, thus far, to be very much at the root of keeping the "tire" from going flat but have, plausibly, generated new problems at the same time. A line of reasoning is suggested by a look at government finances, the activities of the central bank (the Federal Reserve System), and the credit/debt system in the U.S.

Deficit Spending by the Federal Government and the "Leaking Tire"

The central ideological accomplishment of Keynesian economics, as has already been discussed in some detail, is probably that it gathered ruling class and mass support (or at least squashed effective opposition) for the government policy of laying out more in expenditures than it receives in revenues, borrowing the difference from selected parts of the population and its institutions, and repaying or refinancing this debt later. This process provides an additional injection into the economy as a whole which offsets leakages that would otherwise result in deficient aggregate demand. All workers who wanted employment could not find it if demand were not adequate, and this would cause excess productive capacity, that is, idle plants and equipment. The sociopolitical implications of a prolonged economic crisis are not certain, but there are far ranging sociopolitical implications.

As profits are maintained by injections into the economy from government and the banking system, "business as usual" becomes possible along with the maintenance of class relations which provides continuity in society over time. Those at the apex of the socioeconomic pyramid seem to have devised a way to avoid changing the nature of the economic system, if but for a while. Federal government finances have played an especially important part in this.

> It is of course commonplace that deficits are the rule rather than the exception nowadays; it remains only to give the notion a bit more quantitative definiteness. One way is to divide the post-Second World War period into four periods and observe the changing ratio of deficit to surplus years. In the decade 1945–1954 there were five deficit years and five of surplus (including one year of a balanced budget). In the next decade, 1955–1964, there were seven deficit years and three surplus. And in nine years, 1965–1973, there were eight deficits and one surplus. But even more striking is the way the size of the deficits has been growing.[58]

What is more, "the cumulative deficit of the first four years of the 1970s was more than 80 percent greater than the cumulative deficit of the last four years of the 1960s.[59] Admittedly, the difference this makes is not obvious, thus the implications of an expanding deficit are left to emerge.

A similar statement can be made about the expansion of the money supply by the Federal Reserve System. From 1966 through 1969 the cumulative expansion of currency in circulation plus demand and time deposits in addition to deposits at nonbank thrift institutions was about 26 percent. In comparison, for the four years 1970 through 1973 the cumulative growth was 43 percent.[60]

Even with a very expansionary fiscal and monetary policy in the early 1970s in comparison with the latter part of the 1960s one "might . . . expect that this most recent period would have been one of relatively full utilization of labor and manufacturing capacity."[61] But a look at Table 1 indicates that this has not been the case. Here it can be pointed out that the lowest "official" unemployment rate for the 1970s is higher than the highest unemployment rate between 1965 up to and including 1969. Conversely, the highest percent of manufacturing capacity used in the early 1970s was less than the lowest percent for the years 1965 through 1969. With the percent change in consumer prices (inflation), the pattern is not so neat as with the other two measures; but the rate for 1973, 8.8 percent, was unusual in the U.S. and food prices in that year increased a startling 20.1 percent. The following year, 1974, general price inflation was substantially worse. Further, for all items the average change in prices for the 1961–1965 period was 1.3 percent, for 1966–1970 it was 4.5 percent, and for 1971–

1973 it was 5.2 percent.[62] One might therefore have little difficulty in agreeing with the *Monthly Review* editors when they said that there was "apparent establishment of new norms in the 1970s as compared to the second half of the 1960s." Further, "except in the area of prices, the responsiveness of the system to more and more vigorous pumping systems seems to be on the decline.[63]

TABLE 1   INFLATION, UNEMPLOYMENT, AND MANUFACTURING CAPACITY USE

Year	Percent Change in Consumer Prices	Unemployment as a Percent of Civilian Labor Force	Percent of Manufacturing Capacity Used
1965	1.9	4.5	89.0
1966	3.4	3.8	91.9
1967	3.0	3.8	87.9
1968	4.7	3.6	87.7
1969	6.1	3.5	86.5
1970	5.5	4.9	78.3
1971	3.4	5.9	75.0
1972	3.4	5.6	78.6
1973	8.8	4.9	83.0
1974	12.2	5.6	78.9
1975	7.0	8.5	68.7

Source: U.S. Bureau of the Census, *Statistical Abstract of the United States: 1974* (95th edition). Washington, D.C.: U.S. Government Printing Office, 1974; Joint Economic Committee of the Council of Economic Advisers. *Economic Indicators.* Washington, D.C.: U.S. Government Printing Office, February 1976; Board of Governors, Federal Reserve System, *Federal Reserve Bulletin*, vol. 62, no. 3 (1976).

The Credit/Debt System and Aspects of the Financial Nexus

The *Monthly Review* editors present data on commercial bank loans, consumer installment credit, and mortgage debt and observe that the average annual increase in commercial bank loans during the years 1965–1969 (which they remind us were the Vietnam War boom years) was 9 percent. In contrast the annual rate of increase for 1971, 1972, and 1973 was 15.2 percent, or 70 percent higher than the Vietnam War boom years.[64]

In consumer installment credit there was a remarkable increase in 1972 and 1973 with additions being about double (in constant dollars) the rate of that in other years back to 1965. It is argued that "this was doubtless an important factor in maintaining the demand for consumer durables (especially automobiles) during the latest cyclical upswing." It is also argued that the need for especially heavy repayments during the next couple of years will exercise a depressing effect on consumer demand, quite apart from other factors such as increased unemployment and the energy-crisis-related decline in the demand for automobiles. . . .

Finally, mortgage debt, which in the aggregate is much larger than all other types of consumer credit put together. It used to be that most mortgage debt was incurred in order to build new housing, but in recent years more and more people have been mortgaging or remortgaging their homes to acquire money for other purposes. . . . From our present point of view the most important thing about this . . . is the sensational jump in the rate of increase in mortgage debt formation since the relatively depressed year 1970 (the additional debt formed in the first half of 1973 was running at an annual rate nearly double that of 1970). No doubt whatever that this part of the credit system was pumping at or near full capacity. The [data] also show clearly the trend to greater non-housing uses of mortgage debt. It is interesting that this item now runs consistently ahead of the increase in installment credit. . . . In other words, quite apart from new housing, borrowing on real estate has become the largest source of consumer debt financing. It seems that as old mortgages are paid off and real estate values rise, people find it necessary or cannot resist the temptation (and/or the blandishments of banks eager for additional business) to step up their "buy now, pay later" way of life.[65]

It is useful, at this point, to supplement the *Monthly Review* observations on the credit system with some of Michael Tanzer's work to get a picture of debt by class in an attempt to depict the vulnerability of contemporary capitalism and its population to crises.

The basic danger to the U.S. economy is one that is always present in a capitalist economy—the possibility that monetary conditions will get out of line with physical production and consumption needs. In my view, a crucial source of potential imbalance results from the tremendous post-World War II growth of credit that has helped fuel the real economic growth in production and consumption.

In a sense, the last twenty-five years have witnessed a new development of capitalism, what one might call "credit capitalism." Earlier, the most important developments in capitalism were in the area of production (assembly lines and mass manufacturing), and somewhat more recently in the area of marketing (advertising, mass distribution, etc.). Today the emphasis in the business world is increasingly on the selling of credit. While sales on credit are not new, what is new is both the scale and the fact that, as Hillel Black notes: "Credit has become an end in itself. In many instances more profit is derived from credit than from the goods and services being sold."

"Credit capitalism" is really the highest and purest form of capitalism. For one thing, nothing tangible is produced, so that there are few labor problems; computerized records are substituted instead. Second, credit capitalism has the potential of being automatically self-perpetuating, in that interest on the debt continually adds to the amount of debt outstanding. The ultimate success lies in getting a person so addicted to credit that he borrows more money simply to pay back his old debt.[66]

Tanzer argues that the growth of "credit capitalism" results in an increasingly "illiquid" economy and an increasing vulnerability of a downturn in the economy snowballing into a major crisis which would be difficult for the federal government to contain.[67]

By "illiquid" Tanzer means that the ratio of money to debt and the ratio of money to liquid assets have declined. Further

. . . liquidity may be defined as the extent to which relatively simultaneous attempts by large numbers of individuals or businesses to turn the particular asset into money could be effectively realized. This in turn partly hinges on the extent to which a mass attempt to exchange a particular asset for cash could be facilitated by the government without serious negative consequences for the economy.

. . . a real danger point is reached when the ratio of debt to money is so high that debtors, seeking to obtain new loans to make interest payments or to refinance their old debt, help drive interest rates to very high levels. "Tight money" and high interest rates tend to slow real economic activity by curtailing home construction, business investment, and state and local governmental borrowing and spending capability. Concurrently they also tend to cause a slide in the stock market, partly as a result of investors selling stocks in order to buy high-yielding bonds. This in turn may put further downward pressure on real economic activity because serious declines in the stock market can trigger a shriveling of business and consumer confidence that leads to reduced production and spending plans. This in turn, leads to greater unemployment, further lowering of income and purchases, even greater unemployment, and so on.[68]

The question becomes: How possible or likely is a "monetary crackup"? To answer this question, one must look, Tanzer argues, at liquidity by income class and sectors rather than at the gross changes in liquidity for the economy as a whole when looking at the entire postwar period. For example:

Following the Penn Central Railroad bankruptcy, the squeeze on corporate treasuries has been widely discussed. (Corporate holdings of cash and government securities as a proportion of their current liabilities had dropped from 73 percent in 1946 to 19 percent in 1969.) Less publicized is the drop in household liquidity. Thus, the net worth of individuals has increased fourfold since 1945, but in that year 14 percent of all household financial assets were in currency and demand deposits, and another 19 percent were in U.S. government securities; in other words, one-third of individual assets were highly liquid. By 1968 the proportion had declined to only 11 percent. On the other hand, back in 1945 corporate stock accounted for only 30 percent of all household assets. By 1968, corporate stock made up 47 percent of household assets.[69]

Like the editors of the *Monthly Review,* Tanzer points out that the huge increase in individual borrowing probably has much to do with the postwar growth of the economy. But importantly, it is noted that the largest increase in individual debt is that owned by the lower and middle classes while the largest increase in individual assets, the holding of corporate stock, "which have risen from $110 billion in 1945 to $870 billion in 1968 . . . are owned overwhelmingly by the top 1 percent income class." What exists then is a debt-asset split which requires a closer look at both the debtors and the stock owners.[70]

> The most striking aspect of the debt picture is that consumer installment credit is already a major burden on the poor and the working class. More than 10 percent of the families who earn under $7,500 per year (45 percent of the entire population) have to devote more than 20 percent of their income to debt repayment; only about 5 percent of middle-income families ($7,500 to $15,000 income) have a similar debt burden, and only 2 percent of the upper-income group (over $15,000) must worry about debt repayment. Even worse, among the most debt-ridden families—those who use more than 40 percent of their income for debt repayment—the majority have incomes under $3,000 per year.[71]

Further, the installment debt burden of blacks, the gross statistics indicate, is significantly greater in relative terms than that for whites as is the case for younger families as compared with older ones. In contrast, home mortgage debt—not surprisingly—is more a phenomenon of the middle class. Families with under $7,500 in income accounted for about 20 percent of total mortgage debt while those with $7,500 to $15,000 accounted for 60 percent.[72]

In Tanzer's view, then, the debt-asset situation existing in 1968 was one in which the greatest debt burden was a problem of lower socioeconomic people who probably would also be first-hit in the event of an economic downturn. The second hardest hit would be middle class mortgage holders. "The upper-income group's vast holdings of corporate stock would be of little support to the debt structure in recession, because the upper-income group has relatively little debt."[73]

Many implications follow from the structure of debt which has emerged since World War II and the above points to but a few salient features. It is certain, though, that this period of expansion is different from those previously and that the problems that are likely to continue require period-unique analysis.

But before returning to the other "pumps" that have kept the "tire" from going flat, it is necessary to comment on other aspects of the credit/debt system.

Tanzer alleges the following with respect to American banking:

> Perhaps most dangerous of all, the commercial banks, the backbone of the monetary system, . . . threw caution to the wind in their activities. For one thing, these banks are trustees for vast pools of capital, and in an attempt to stem the outflow of these funds to the then highly successful "go-go" mutual funds, they sought to improve their own investment performance by increasing speculation in the stock market. At the same time, with the enormous demand for loans, business and personal, the banks reduced their own liquidity to levels that would never have been tolerated in a more rational period. More conservative banks frequently were dragged into the performance race, since failure to take the risks that all other banks were taking would make the conservative bank less profitable, at least in the short run. And, it is this short run that is characteristically of the greatest concern in a speculative period. After all, whether it be investment in chain letters or Dutch tulips at $10,000 each, who worries about the underlying reality when there is always a sucker to whom you can sell them at a higher price? Only when growing numbers of people begin to see that the emperor may in fact be naked do reality considerations, followed by panic, begin to intrude.[74]

Although the issues raised here are many and it would require a major study to cover them adequately, comments on the banking system and credit and debt will be left with a few more observations gleaned from other secondary sources:

> The specter haunting today's capitalist world is the possible collapse of its financial institutions and an associated world economic crisis. The miasma of fear is hardly surprising in the light of the coincidence in many capitalist countries of seemingly uncontrollable inflation, declining production, and instability in financial markets. The banking and credit community is showing increasing signs of weakness.[75]

Certainly this interpretation is controversial, but at the same time, it gives reason to pause and ponder. Indeed, fears are expressed by "the more responsible financial leaders of the capitalist class. . . ." As Robert V. Roosa put it:

> There has been a loss of confidence in the financial machinery most of us took for granted. There is a fear, a kind of foreboding.

[It is] not too much to say that these concerns are similar to the kind that prevailed in the 1930s.[76]

The editors of *Monthly Review* argue that

the important changes, showing increasing sources of instability, are not new, but . . . have been developing since the early 1960s and accelerating since the mid-1960s. . . .
The answers to these questions are not to be found in ignorance, absence of wisdom, or lack of will power. What has to be understood is that the ruling class and government officials could hardly have prevented the present situation from developing no matter how much they may have wanted to. The overextension of debt and the overreach of the banks was exactly what was needed to protect the capitalist system and its profits; to overcome, at least temporarily, its contradictions; and to support the imperialist expansion and wars of the United States. Those who now complain and tremble over excesses are the very same people who helped bring them about, or at the least did nothing to forestall them, for fear of bringing down the whole financial network.[77]

In short, the thesis presented by these Marxian writers is that financial institutions have been instrumental in the protection of profits of U.S. corporations, which corresponded to the self-interest of both. This protection, in turn, has served to drive the system into an inflationary spiral resulting in corresponding pressure for a resounding recession. A recession weeds out financially unsound business enterprises, restores discipline in the labor force as workers' demands become the desire for a job rather than a larger piece of the action or a voice in decision making, and in the process, profit margins are restored for the dominant corporations and the financial superstructure. The general argument, which is surely controversial, is that, as Marx would have put it, the post-World War II period has been one of "driving capitalist production beyond its own limits."[78]

The editors of the *Monthly Review* make the observation that the overall liquidity of both banks and corporations has changed over the postwar period. The period between 1960 and 1974 was especially active, with corporations becoming more reliant on bank loans, bonds, and mortgages. It is pointed out that this is not a problem so long as profits are adequate to meet interest payments. But it is posited that at least a part of inflation in recent times can be explained by an examination of corporate debt.

As interest burdens increase—the result of larger debt as well as higher interest rates stimulated by the huge demand for money capital—capitalists raise prices to meet these obligations. And as price hikes spread throughout the economy, the need for even

> more borrowing follows. Thus, debt obligations, interest charges, and prices chase each other in the upward spiral of inflation.[79]

What is more, the relationship between the corporations and the banks, in the Sweezy and Magdoff view, has implications for bank liquidity:

> . . . we are beginning to see obstacles emerging in the ability of the banks to keep on supplying credit at the accelerated rate of the past. It is true that the banks, in pursuit of ever more profits for themselves, have tried to keep up with the demand for loans. But in doing so they have stretched themselves so thin that their liquidity is in question, and legitimate fears have been raised about the possible collapse of the financial system.[80]

Admittedly, this at first glance appears to be a rash statement. Their reasoning is based on a comparison of very recent times with the rest of the postwar period and the general argument is that the boom associated with the Vietnam War years kindled the

> flames of inflation [and] induced an expansion of the bank-lending activity beyond any traditional understanding of the so-called fiduciary responsibility of the banks, a process that endangers the safety of the money left for safekeeping and begins to bump against the ultimate ceiling of how much money banks can lend.[81]

Loans as a percent of deposits were 36 percent in 1950 among all banks with deposits of $100 million or more. In 1955 the percentage was 46 percent; by 1960 it was 56.3 percent; by 1965 it was 66.2 percent; by 1970 it was 70.8 percent; by 1974 it was 82 percent.[82] The pattern was similar for the large New York City banks while the percentage was somewhat higher for each year noted.

> While there is no trustworthy guide to the "proper" ratio of loans to deposits, the persistent rise in the ratio, especially since 1970, reveals that even apart from their responsibility as safe-keepers of other people's money, the banks are fast approaching the absolute limit (100 percent) of the deposits that could be loaned out.[83]

Such a high percentage (as 82 percent) is unprecedented between 1900 and 1970. A figure of 79 percent was reached in only one year, 1921, while in the year of the most famous crash of the stock market, 1929, the ratio was 73.1 percent.[84]

Other changes occurred as well, such as in the composition of deposits. For example, "No less than 40 percent of the deposits of the large New York City banks consists of large certificates of deposit, money borrowed to facilitate the rapid growth of loans beyond otherwise practical limits . . ." and so on.[85] But the pressures of profit seeking in a competitive environment of sorts, it is argued by the *Monthly Review* editors, "lead to a larger and larger share of relatively unsafe loans in the banks' portfolios.[86]

Thus a two-pronged situation which is suggestive emerges. On the one hand, as corporations have turned to maintaining a lower ratio of liquid reserves compared to debt,[87]

> the harder it becomes for the corporations to repay their bank loans (because of declining liquidity), the more the banks are obliged to grant further loans to prevent borrowers from going bust and thus defaulting on the backlog of loans. As willing or unwilling collaborators in the process by which the large corporations operate closer and closer to the edge of the precipice, the banks are themselves drawn nearer to the same edge, for they can manage to lend at such a furious rate only by impairing their own liquidity.[88]

It should be apparent that an increasing ratio of loans to deposits implies at the same time decreasing bank liquidity. On this score the editors present data from the Federal Reserve System which shows a secular decline in liquidity if one takes liquidity of large commercial banks (those with deposits of $100 million or more on December 31, 1965) to be cash plus all U.S. Treasury bonds and short-term notes. Cash plus all treasuries as a percent of total deposits fell from 54 percent in 1950 to 42.7 percent in 1955 to 34.7 percent in 1960 to 22.3 percent in 1965 to 18.3 percent in 1970 to 13.6 percent in 1974.[89]

> Yet even this meager liquidity ratio exaggerates the reserve position of the large commercial banks. First, in order for a bank to qualify as a depository for U.S. Treasury funds, it must keep a specified reserve of U.S. treasuries to back up the government's deposits. Hence, not all of the treasuries included in this liquidity ratio would be available to meet sudden large drains on deposits. Second, the data shown on liquidity represent what the banks originally paid for the bonds. (This is standard accounting practice for bank assets.) The market prices of bonds, however, go up and down: as interest rates rise the prices of bonds go down and vice versa. For example, if a bank wanted to sell a 20-year, 3 percent Treasury bond which had been bought for $1,000 (and so recorded on the bank's books), all that could be realized on that bond in the market at the end of 1974 would have been about $550. Furthermore, if several big banks began to unload their bond holdings quickly, the market price would drop even further.[90]

Thus, a more conservative estimate of liquidity would be cash plus short-term U.S. Treasury notes.

> And here we see the same pattern: a persistent decline in
> liquidity, dropping by almost half from 17.5 percent in 1960 to 9.6
> percent in 1974. . . . [But] Liquidity ratios are not the only way of
> looking at the safety problem. Traditional theory of good banking
> practice points out that while loans are a source of risk, banks
> protect themselves by maintaining special reserves in reasonable
> anticipation of a certain percentage of defaults, and in the final
> analysis rely on the bank's equity capital (bank stockholders'
> original investment plus accumulated profits) to make good on
> unexpected loan losses (thus preventing loss of deposits). But
> here too the ratio of equity capital to outstanding loans has been
> steadily dropping, most noticeably since 1960. . . .[91]

This factor was noted by Arthur Burns, chairman of the Federal
Reserve Board, in an address to the American Bankers Association at
their convention on October 21, 1974:

> At the end of 1960, equity capital plus loan and valuation
> reserves amounted to almost 9 percent of total bank assets. By the
> end of 1973, this equity capital ratio had fallen to about 6½
> percent. Furthermore, the equity capital banks had been lever-
> aged in some cases at the holding company level, as parent
> holding companies have increased their equity investments in
> subsidiary banks by using funds raised in the debt markets. Thus,
> the capital cushion that plays a large role in maintaining con-
> fidence in banks has become thinner, particularly in some of our
> largest banking organizations.[92]

Other important features must be pointed to in order to grasp the
situation more clearly:

> We should know something about bank holding companies. A
> "loophole" in the amendments to the 1956 Bank Holding Com-
> pany Act has been used by most of the big banks to expand their
> activities into a diverse range of nontraditional financial opera-
> tions. What happens is that a holding company is set up which
> owns a bank and at the same time may own, for example,
> mortgage, finance, and factoring businesses. A number of these
> bank holding companies have gone to the money market to
> borrow funds in order to carry on this variety of operations, and
> in the process have used some of the borrowed money to increase
> their equity investment in their own banks. This is what Burns is
> referring to: even that small ratio of equity capital to assets is
> overstated, since some of the equity is really only debt owed by
> the parent company.[93]

The question then emerges: how were banks able to keep increasing loans as a percentage of deposits to reach the unusual level,
among large banks, of 82 percent in 1974? This situation is not fully
the result of "increasing their capital, attracting additional deposits,

or selling off investments in bonds." Rather, "banks themselves have become major borrowers in order to . . . indulge in their furious rush to lend." And in the process a complicated network of lending and borrowing emerged which "further stimulated the inflationary process, but also resulted in a kind of delicately balanced debt structure that is constantly in danger of breaking down."[94]

This allegation is not a loose one, bur rather emerges from still more data which merits review by the interested reader in this analysis of the banks by the editors of the *Monthly Review*. What is revealed is a large increase in short-term borrowing as a percent of total loans outstanding. (For the large commercial banks this went from 2.2 percent in 1950 to 4.5 percent in 1960 to 20.8 percent in 1965 to 28.7 percent in 1970 to 48.5 percent in 1974.) Among this source of funds are those from the Federal Reserve Bank, large negotiable certificates of deposit, and Eurodollars (which "in effect means the borrowing by U.S. banks from their branches abroad, and is based on the dollar deposits in these foreign branches").[95]

The implications, according to the *Monthly Review,* are that the bank's enormous debt expansion as both borrowers and lenders is of a speculative nature.

> On the one hand, the banks are gambling that businesses will be able to repay their loans despite (a) declining corporate liquidity, and (b) the fact that many firms are borrowing to pay for investment in plant and equipment that will take longer to produce the income needed than is required by the loan repayment schedules. On the other hand, the banks are speculating on being able to support this large and growing lending by having recourse to the mercurial money markets.[96]

This blunt conclusion is reached: "In short, the commercial banking structure, and the entire business world that relies on this structure, is skating on thin ice that is getting progressively thinner."[97]

To this conclusion many would ask: but aren't there safeguards such as the Federal Deposit Insurance Corporation (FDIC) and others that would make sure the whole banking system does not come tumbling down like a house of cards? The answer is that the FDIC is probably more effective in providing an illusion of safety for depositors rather than providing safety itself. Although the FDIC is really an insurance company and supposedly can rescue depositors "only to the extent that it has enough assets to cover bank losses,"[98] in practice it serves the function of maintaining the public confidence that would make its extensive use unnecessary. It is here that the view presented in this chapter differs from that of Sweezy and Magdoff. It probably matters but little that, as they point out, the deposits covered by FDIC insurance amounted to $465.6 billion at the end of 1973. Against this the FDIC had $8.6 billion: $5.6 billion of assets, plus the right to borrow, according to existing law, $3 billion from the U.S. Treasury.[99]

It is not being claimed that corporate and bank liquidity is not as Sweezy and Magdoff describe it, but rather the important relationship is that between the financial and corporate nexus and the state which, as is argued in Chapter 5, serves the dual and contradictory functions of accumulation and legitimization. Thus far the state has been generally successful in maintaining both of these functions with respect to the credit/debt system and the financial nexus as a whole. Although a careful reading of the *Monthly Review* analysis and the work of others[100] cannot help but plant a seed of doubt in one's mind about the ability of these functions to be maintained infinitely, it can be posited that the position of these seemingly vulnerable institutions is more likely to usher in a more pronounced and obvious state capitalism than to bring about a collapse of the corporate and financial structures and a corresponding accelerated and abrupt downward spiral. Elsewhere Sweezy and Magdoff discuss the attitude of the First National City Bank of New York (appearing in their *Monthly Economic Letter*) where it is argued that there is little cause for panic about the possibility of bank failures because central banking would not act passively as it did in the 1930-33 period and that the FDIC has virtually underwritten deposits of up to $40,000 per account as a federal obligation. As Sweezy and Magdoff put it, "What New York's largest bank is saying here is that the Federal Reserve will take care of the big boys and the FDIC of the little fellows."[101] Although it remains to be seen if this is really true since it would signal in a new era in U.S. capitalism, it seems plausible that the First National City Bank is accurate in its assessment of the relationship between the people, the financial nexus, and the state. And, indeed, some economists would argue that it is not the private sector that needs to be closely scrutinized so much as the public sector. This is especially the case, some point out, as fiscal crisis is experienced in New York City and other large cities to the point that the vast City University of New York had to be closed before the scheduled end of the academic year in 1976 because it was broke. This was also the case with Chicago elementary schools. Public finance economist Jesse Burkhead expresses the view that the plausible scenario is for more cities to experience similar difficulties.

Thus while the liquidity picture has changed in recent times among both corporations and financial institutions, so have attitudes in the business world and perhaps the population. Everything possible is done to avoid the bankruptcy of major corporations. The financial institutions to which they are in debt seem, in turn, to be functioning in a new environment.[102] And even in times of isolated bank failures or sinking confidence, "runs" are infrequent. Further, when banks do fail, comebacks are experienced. For example, a European group of investors gained control of the Franklin National after it failed. A major American airlines was acquired by an oil-rich Middle Eastern country in 1975 when it faced bankruptcy. And Lockheed was bailed out by the federal government itself. In short, it seems to be no exaggeration to say that capitalism relates to the *world* of capitalists and is underwritten by the state. Its power should not be underestimated. It is a clever (cunning may be a more apt description) system however much one may dislike it because of its obvious inequities.

At the same time, it must be pointed out that the Marxian literature is not the only place where warnings about the debt structure of the U.S. are to be found. For example, a supplement to the droll and staid *Business Week*—a magazine addressed mainly to business executives—entitled "The Debt Economy" appeared in its October 12, 1974 issue with the following description.

> The U.S. economy stands atop a mountain of debt $2.5-trillion high—a mountain built of all the cars and houses, all the factories and machines that have made this the biggest, richest economy in the history of the world. . . .The U.S. is the Debt Economy without peer. It has the biggest lenders, the biggest borrowers, the most sophisticated financial system. The numbers are so vast that they simply numb the mind: $1-trillion in corporate debt, $600-billion in mortgage debt, $500-billion in U.S. government debt, $200-billion in state and local government debt, $200-billion in consumer debt. To fuel nearly three decades of postwar economic boom at home and export it abroad, this nation has borrowed an average of $200-million a day, each and every day, since the close of World War II. . . .
> And there are signs of tension everywhere: corporate debt-equity ratios are way out of line, consumer installment-debt repayment taking a record share of disposable income, the huge real-estate market in desperate trouble despite all the federal government has done to save it. Never has the Debt Economy seemed more vulnerable, with a distressing number of borrowers and lenders in precarious shape.[103]

It may well be, then, that the editors of the *Monthly Review* are accurate when they see the expansion of the U.S. economy in the period since World War II as one which was related to the unusual liquidity in the finances of people and business. This liquidity was generated during World War II as the economy was going full tilt with accompanying rationing, price controls, shortages that were endured in the name of patriotism, and the nature of government finances used during that period. People had therefore been able to both liquidate their debt and accumulate savings while businesses were in a favorable liquidity position as well. In the case of nonfinancial corporations with more than $100 million in assets the "average liquidity ratio (cash and government securities divided by short-term debts) was well over 100 percent. . . ."[104]

Other factors in the postwar period which led to unprecedented economic expansion in the U.S. were probably "automobilization," including building cars and roads and the whole interstate highway network. Suburbanization, the extension of cities, urban sprawl and intercity decay were experienced as part of this expansion. Accompanying industries emerged in a multitude of varieties as well. The assistance of the U.S. in the reconstruction of Europe and accompanied exports, the engagement in military intervention in Korea and Vietnam, and the military buildup as part of the "Cold War" and its aftermath were still other events that spurred the economy. In other words, the decades after World War II

> inaugurated a new period which (for the United States) lasted an extraordinarily long time by previous capitalist standards—a period of some 30 years of expansion, interrupted only by more or less regularly recurring mild recessions. The driving forces this time were world war, preparation for new wars and waging of large-scale regional wars (Korea and Vietnam), and the second great wave of automobilization.[105]

Rather than a typical period, the post-World War II period may well have been quite unusual. It is the view of the *Monthly Review* editors that "the *normal* state of the system in its monopoly stage is one of cyclical ups and downs in a context of continuing stagnation."[106] A look at the evidence seems to powerfully substantiate their case.

But the ability to attain what many would see as a "stability" of employment and prices seems possible in the short run so long as state responsibility for the economy is maintained and expanded. And it seems reasonable to predict that state intervention in the economy and society will increase, must increase, if profound difficulties are to be averted. In the process, new problems will emerge, but they, too, are likely to be approached in an incremental fashion.

To allow a deep depression to emerge in an effort to deflate the economy and the price structure and then begin anew with some of the most vexing distortions weeded out of the economy is not a course that is appealing to many. People whose political futures as well as those whose wealth and power would sink with the economy and the working class as a whole are united in opposition to a depression.

> Thus since the Second World War every time a recession looked as though it might get worse and turn into an old-fashioned depression, the reaction of the governing circles was to turn on the deficit spending and money-and-credit spigots. It was conceded that this would involve a certain amount of inflation— maybe two or three percent a year—but that has always been considered better for capitalism than price stability, not to speak of price deflation. For a long time all seemed to be for the best in the best of all possible worlds.
>
> What was ignored—and still seems to be recognized only by Marxists on the Left and financial conservatives on the Right—is that this strategy necessarily involves a secular increase in society's debt structure, with a parallel decline in corporate and individual liquidity. Thus the economy became more and more vulnerable to the kind of shocks which in the old days used to touch off panics; and in order to guard against this recurring threat, the need for still more inflation becomes increasingly acute. Thus the near panic triggered by the Penn Central bank-ruptcy in 1970 was countered by a massive injection of Federal Reserve credit. Price increases, a bloated credit structure, fever-ish speculation all had to be tolerated and actually spurred on in order to stave off the dreaded deflation which in times gone by was capitalism's "natural" cure for such ills. [107]

Capitalism: Sinking or in Transition?

The state answer to inflationary pressures does seem, however, to remain recessions in current times followed by action to prevent the economic contraction from becoming too pronounced. As the reces-sion beginning in 1974 deepened in 1975 and as both the Executive and Congressional branches of the federal government acted slowly to attempt to abate it, discussion of national planning surfaced with a focus not so much on the recession itself as on the longer run course ahead. Perhaps this is because, as David M. Gordon has put it, "recession is capitalism as usual." [108] One plan was constructed where planning would be undertaken at the highest level of government by a small group, which would have the obligation to analyze the alterna-tive courses the government might take on economic issues. When Herbert Stein made a similar proposal in December of 1973 when he was chairman of Nixon's Council of Economic Advisers, there was little support for such a plan. If the health of the economy becomes worse, as fiscal crises at all levels of government deepen, and as awareness deepens that a host of problems can stand in the way of obtaining the petroleum on which the nation runs, it seems that there might be more support for a national planning group. There is opposition, to be sure, but it can be posited that powerful support or resistance to the idea will be directly related to the rates of corporate profits, inflation, and unemployment. At the same time a great deal of business opinion might echo that of John D. Harper, chairman of Alcoa and head of the Business Roundtable, a group of 150 leading businessmen, when he said about national planning: "I'm very strongly against it. I've seen too many countries where it simply does not work. When corporations do their own planning, it works because the markets control it. But governments are too remote from control and the responsibility for the decisions made."[109]

Nonetheless, if the state is not successful in its application of policies—and it does not seem at all obvious that success is assured—then it can be posited that capitalism is not likely to yet sink so much as enter a new phase where state capitalism of a more direct and visible form will emerge. The financial situation as depicted in this chapter is but a reflection and a part of the country's economic activity, but it appears that difficulties existing in the financial circles could be part of the many realities which could accelerate and exacerbate the emergence of a more formalized state capitalism. Associated with pressures which could result in conscious planning is the growing insecurity of the "new economics." As the vacuum in "acceptable" economic theory continues to exist it seems likely that a national planning policy controversy is the course that discussion among social scientists, policy makers, and government officials will take.[110] This view is based on a sense of both the surface manifestations which display economic disarray emerging from this chapter and Chapter 2; the perception that the economic orthodoxy is in a state of transition as the hegemony of the economics founded on the thought of Keynes comes to be seen as less and less relevant to the actual economic problems of the nation; and, most importantly, the sketch of the *structure* of the political economy that emerges from the following two chapters. Though this is at best an impressionistic and tentative view, the economic problems of the 1970s seem to be founded upon a structure which is full of contradictions. This reality will necessitate the state plunging down new avenues of policy as a matter of practical necessity. These policies may continue to be piecemeal at first but they are likely to become the doctrine embraced by the state, like Keynesianism, over time. Critical social scientists and many people including socialists will have new analyses to make and battles to fight if this view is accurate.

At the same time it is no rash observation to suggest that U.S. capitalism is in a lot of trouble and that the course ahead is one which cannot be easily forecast, if at all. There is no general agreement among those economists and policy makers who seek to maintain capitalism. Orthodox economics seems highly suspect in its ability to provide longer run policy suggestions for the maintenance of the system to deliver relatively full employment, price stability, consistent growth, and an equitable (whatever that might mean coming from the orthodox framework) distribution of income. It is even more suspect as a social science qua science. The irrelevance of orthodox theory in turn necessitates entertaining alternative paradigms and undertaking additional theoretical and empirical work to explain the situation. A persuasive view is that economic crises in the latter part of the 20th century are generic to the economic system of capitalism. This is a view which is expanded in the following chapters along with a look at the structure of the system—particularly industry and the state.

The possibilities for the not-too-distant future include economic collapse, more vigorous state policies that are somewhat effective for the short run, or moves toward workers' reorganization of various types. What seems most likely to occur is that the state will be moved as a matter of practical necessity to intervene into the economy and society even more dramatically and that state capitalism will become even more "advanced" in the United States as the decade of the 1970s unfolds.

There appears to be emerging agreement among Marxian and radical economists (and, undoubtedly, others) in the view here that a more definite state capitalism is likely.[111] At the same time a difficult dilemma will be faced by state formulators of policy if this system develops. The structure of centralized and concentrated capital will be reinforced by an intolerance of recessions, and it is likely that renewed pressures of inflation will be part of a program of economic recovery. This changing structure in turn, to the extent that future recessions are considered intolerable, will require more state intervention in the form, most likely, of wage-price controls which imply a lessened reliance on the marketplace for the determination of economic events. A deeper look into the structure and functioning of the U.S. political economy is necessary to understand the basis for the emerging debate not about whether there should be state intervention so much as over the form and extent of state intervention. The next chapter, then, looks specifically at the centralization and concentration of capital and draws out contemporary Marxian interpretations of the meaning of this concept as well as the view of John Kenneth Galbraith (whose archetype may be the Keynesianism of the near future). It is plausible that some of the seeds of contemporary instability and inequality emanate from this structure.

NOTES

1 This is touched on in Dwayne Ward, "Labor Market Adjustments in Elementary and Secondary Teaching: the Reaction to the 'Teacher Surplus'," Teachers College Record, vol. 77, no. 2 (December 1975), pp. 189–218. Also see Laurence B. DeWitt and A. Dale Tussing, The Supply and Demand for Graduates of Higher Education: 1970–1980 (Syracuse, N.Y.: Educational Policy Research Center, 1971).

2 Robert Lekachman's introduction to Joan Robinson, Economics: An Awkward Corner (New York: Random House, 1967), p. v. Copyright © 1967 by Pantheon Books, a division of Random House, Inc.

3 Joan Robinson, Economics: An Awkward Corner, p. 63, 64.

4 For more on this see Frank Roosevelt, "Cambridge Economics as Commodity Fetishism," The Review of Radical Political Economics, vol. 7, no. 4 (Winter 1975).

5 Some Marxists would urge not using Robinson's interpretation of Marx, but rather going to Marx himself or perhaps Paul M. Sweezy's The Theory of Capitalist Development (New York: Monthly Review Press, 1968). For myself, Robinson's interpretation provides a good first look for a nonscholar in classical Marxism (which can be a quagmire in thought). Additional works by Robinson that are worth checking out are her An Essay on Marxian Economics (London: Macmillan, 1966); On Re-reading Marx (Cambridge: Students' Bookshops, 1953); and, among others, Marx, Marshall and Keynes (Delhi, India: The Delhi School of Economics, University of Delhi, 1955).

6 Joan Robinson, "Marx and Keynes," in David Horowitz, ed., Marx and Modern Economics (New York: Monthly Review Press, 1968), p. 115. Much of this article first appeared in 1948. Reprinted by permission of Monthly Review Press.

7 Ibid., p. 107.

8 Ibid., pp. 107–108.

9 Ibid., p. 108. James O'Connor points out that a key reason orthodox economists do not find Marx's categories useful is not technical at all. Orthodox economists want to find ways to make capitalism work while Marxists want to tear it down and replace it with socialism.

10 Ibid., pp. 108–109.

11 Ibid., p. 109.

12 For another very good account of Marx's theory of value also see James O'Connor, The Corporations and the State (New York: Harper & Row, 1974), Chapter 2, "The Theory of Surplus Value." Also see the late Stephen Hymer's "Robinson Crusoe and the Secret of Primitive Accumulation," Monthly Review, vol. 23, no. 4 (September 1971), pp. 11–36.

13 Robinson, "Marx and Keynes," p. 109.

14 Ibid., p. 110.

15 Ibid.

16 For the view that there are affinities between Marx and Keynes, see Robinson, An Essay on Marxian Economics, chapter 6.

17 As A. Dale Tussing put it (in personal communication), "The capitalist's consumption comes from surplus, so the reinvestment of surplus is not formally determined in Marx's system. You have to add something like a propensity to consume."

18 Robinson, "Marx and Keynes," pp. 110–111.

19 As A. Dale Tussing points out.

20 Robinson, "Marx and Keynes," pp. 111–112.

21 Ibid., p. 112.

22 Ibid.

23 A. Dale Tussing, for example, disagrees with Joan Robinson's interpretation and thinks mention of "subsistence" is not to be found in Capital and the claim that "real wages tend to remain constant" at the subsistence level is not accurate. James O'Connor's view (in a critique of an earlier version of this chapter) is that the absolute impoverishment thesis is to be found in Marx's writings but refers to the proletarianization process of the pre-capitalist producing class.

24 Robinson, "Marx and Keynes," p. 112.

25 See, for example, Harry Magdoff, The Age of Imperialism (New York: Monthly Review Press, 1969), and Paul Baran and Paul Sweezy, Monopoly Capital (New York: Monthly Review Press, 1966), as well as Paul Baran, The Political Economy of Growth (New York: Monthly Review Press, 1957).

26 Joan Robinson, "Marx and Keynes," p. 113.

27 Ibid., pp. 113–114.

28 Ibid., p. 114.

29 Ibid., pp. 114–115.

30 Ibid., p. 115.

31 Ibid.

32 The question of "revisionism" seems to be mainly the concern of those involved in the sectarian left who seem to fight among themselves as much as against those who support the system of capitalism. It is my view that those Marxists who disagree with other modifications of Marxist theory tend to see it as revisionism; when the anti-"revisionists" modify Marxist theory it is seen as "development" or "advancement" of Marxist inquiry.

33 Frederick Engels, On Capital (New York: International Publishers, 1937), pp. 13–20. This work apeared in the Leipzig Demokratisches Wochenblatt, nos. 12 and 13, March 21 and 28, 1868 and is reprinted by International Publishers.

34 Joan Robinson, An Essay on Marxian Economics.

35 E. K. Hunt and Howard J. Sherman, Economics: an Introduction to Traditional and Radical Views, 2nd ed. (New York: Harper & Row, 1975), p. 367.

36 Ibid., p. 368.

37 Lekachman's introduction to Robinson, Economics: An Awkward Corner, p. xii.

38 In addition to the already cited work—M. Kalecki, "Political Aspects of Full Employment," Political Quarterly, vol. 14 (October– December 1943), see Kalecki's last published work, "Theories of Growth in Different Social Systems," Monthly Review, vol. 23, no. 5 (October 1971), pp. 72-79.

39 Joan Robinson, An Essay on Marxian Economics, p. 72.

40 James O'Connor, The Fiscal Crisis of the State (New York: St. Martin's Press, 1973), p. 61, footnote 41, and pp. 51-58.

41 One who classifies his perspective as Marxist/Leninist—Victor Perlo, in The Unstable Economy: Booms and Recessions in the U.S. Since 1945 (New York: International Publishers, 1973), p. 208—says this, for example: "There is a widespread belief that revolutions occur only in times of economic crisis; in fact, not a single one of the fourteen successful socialist revolutions took place during a crisis of overproduction."

42 Paul Mattick, Marx and Keynes: The Limits of the Mixed Economy (Boston: Porter Sargent Publisher, 1969), p. vii.

43 Ibid., p. viii.

44 Ibid., the entire Epilogue, pp. 332-341.

45 Ibid., p. 333.

46 Ibid., p. 332.

47 Ibid., pp. 332-333.

48 Ibid., p. 333.

49 Ibid., pp. 333-334.

50 Chapter 5 looks at this in more detail. According to Thomas E. Mullaney in "A Look at Economic Planning," The New York Times, Business and Finance section (March 9, 1975), p. 14, "The subject of Government planning may become a live issue on a broad scale. . . . It is expected that enabling legislation to create [a planning] agency will be introduced in Congress, and then debate will burst into the open." Earlier on in the article Mullaney points to the reasons: "While the public and the political world are worriedly scanning the periodic economic reports these days, economists and businessmen are beginning to look beyond the current recession to the climate that will prevail in the United States and the world for the rest of this decade." Some people who are pushing for national planning are former Assistant Secretary of the Treasury (now a partner in a Wall Street investment firm) Robert V. Roosa; Wassily Leontief, a Harvard professor and Nobel Prize-winning economist; Leonard Woodcock, president of the United Auto Workers; Harvard economics Professor John Kenneth Galbraith and others mentioned later. Developments in this area, it should be obvious, must be watched carefully and perhaps social scientists have a

responsibility to the people to provide analyses of the perhaps frightening implications of a more refined state-capitalism. James O'Connor's The Fiscal Crisis of the State is very important in this regard.

51 Rudolf Goldscheid, "A Sociological Approach to Problems of Public Finance," ed. Richard A. Musgrave and Alan T. Peacock, Classics in the Theory of Public Finance (New York: St. Martin's Press, 1967), p. 204.

52 "Keynesian Chickens Come Home to Roost," Monthly Review vol. 25, no. 11 (April 1974), p. 1. This is basically the substance of a lecture given by Paul Sweezy at the State University College at Cortland, New York, March 12, 1974. It is apparent that capital is being discussed in classical Marxian flow terms here. Reprinted by permission of Monthly Review Press.

53 Ibid.

54 Ibid., pp. 1–2.

55 Ibid., p. 2.

56 Ibid.

57 Ibid.

58 Ibid., p. 7. The deficit is taken to be the difference between all federal government receipts and outlays.

59 Ibid.

60 Ibid., p. 8.

61 Ibid.

62 U.S. Bureau of the Census, Statistical Abstract of the United States: 1974, (Washington, D.C.: U.S. Government Printing Office, 1974), p. 405.

63 "Keynesian Chickens Come Home to Roost," p. 8.

64 Ibid., p. 4.

65 Ibid., pp. 4–5, 5–6.

66 Michael Tanzer, "Depression Ahead," ed. David Mermelstein, Economics: Mainstream Readings and Radical Critiques, 2nd ed. (New York: Random House, 1973), p. 167.

67 Ibid., p. 168.

68 Ibid.

69 Ibid., p. 169.

70 Ibid. Hunt and Sherman, in the second edition of Economics, (New York: Harper & Row, 1975), put it this way: "it was shown that in 1956 the wealthiest 1.6 percent of the population owned at least 80 percent of all corporate stock and virtually all of the state and local government bonds." (p. 400). The authority they cite is Robert J. Lampman, The Share of Top Wealth-holders in National Wealth, 1922–1956 (Princeton, N.J.: Princeton University Press, 1962).

71 Tanzer, "Depression Ahead," p. 168.

72 Ibid., p. 170.

73 Ibid.

74 *Ibid., p. 173.*

75 *"Banks: Skating on Thin Ice,"* Monthly Review, *vol. 26, no. 9 (February 1975), p. 1. This paragraph continues in a fashion that some might see as a leap. "Thus in the span of one year the United States witnessed the two largest bank failures in its history (U.S. National Bank in San Diego and Franklin National Bank in New York). In addition, according to a report in the* Wall Street Journal *of December 18, 1974, more than a dozen European banks reported big losses or failed in 1974." Reprinted by permission of* Monthly Review Press.

76 *Ibid., p. 2.* (Reported by the Boston Globe [August 5, 1974].) *Of course, the view of those involved in keeping the banking system going cannot express skepticism publicly without actually causing a panic in confidence which would underly a collapse of the financial system. James E. Smith, Comptroller of the Currency in the U.S. Department of the Treasury admitted to serious difficulties but presented an optimistic forecast for 1975 arguing that the two dramatic bank failures mentioned previously were the result of poor management and that the banking system is essentially sound and safe. He said that there was a "need to play catch-up ball with the larger banks" and 1974 had been "a year of substantial loan losses" but that a million dollar study had been recently completed by a large accounting firm which suggested the need for a computerized information system which would relay the foreign currency situation to the central authorities more quickly. Mr. Smith presented these views on Louis Rukeyser's program, "Wall Street Week," on the Public Broadcasting System, March 14, 1975.*

77 *"Banks: Skating on Thin Ice," pp. 3, 4.*

78 *Ibid., p. 5.*

79 *Ibid., p. 7.*

80 *Ibid., p. 8.*

81 *Ibid., p. 9.*

82 *Ibid., p. 11.*

83 *Ibid., p. 9.*

84 *Calculated by the editors of the* Monthly Review, *and presented in the above on pages 9 and 10, from U.S. Bureau of the Census,* Historical Statistics of the United States, Colonial Times to 1957, *(Washington, D.C.: U.S. Government Printing Office, 1960).*

85 *"Banks: Skating on Thin Ice," p. 10.*

86 *Ibid., p. 12.*

87 *"The Long-run Decline in Corporate Liquidity,"* Monthly Review, *vol. 22, no. 4 (September 1970).*

88 *"Banks Skating on Thin Ice," p. 12.*

89 *Ibid.*

90 *Ibid., p. 13.*

91 *Ibid., p. 14.*

92 *Arthur Burns, cited by the editors of* Monthly Review, *ibid., pp. 14–15.*

93 "Banks: Skating on Thin Ice," p. 15.

94 Ibid.

95 Ibid., pp. 16–18.

96 Ibid., p. 18.

97 Ibid., p. 19.

98 Ibid., p. 14, footnote.

99 Ibid.

100 Another example which is more journalistic in style than the Monthly Review analysis is Martin Mayer, The Bankers (New York: Weybright and Talley, 1975). This is reviewed by Nicholas von Hoffman, under the caption "Money on the Brink," The New York Review of Books (March 6, 1975), pp. 6 and 8.

101 "The Economic Crisis in Historical Perspective," Monthly Review, vol. 26, no. 10 (March 1975), p. 7. Reprinted by permission of Monthly Review Press.

102 An important structural question is the extent to which the financial nexus has control over the corporations. This is touched on in the next chapter. It is important to note that the extent of this control is controversial not only in social science as a whole but among Marxian writers. For alternative Marxian views see Paul M. Sweezy, "The Resurgence of Financial Control: Fact or Fancy?" Monthly Review, vol. 23, no. 6 (November 1971), pp. 1–33. This is a good rejoinder to Robert Fitch and Mary Oppenheimer's "Who Rules the Corporations?" Socialist Revolution, vol. 1, no. 4 (July-August, September–October, vol. 1, no. 6. November–December 1970). The latter seek to demonstrate that financial institutions control corporations while Sweezy argues that corporations are fairly autonomous which was also argued in Monopoly Capital. James O'Connor discusses the Fitch and Oppenheimer view in "Fitch and Oppenheimer's Theory of Finance Capital," which first appeared in Socialist Revolution, vol. 2, no. 1 (January-February 1971) and is included as chapter four in O'Connor's The Corporations and the State (New York: Harper & Row, 1974). O'Connor's view is that the Fitch-Oppenheimer discussion is useful in that a lot of Congressional committee materials are used to develop their argument and they seek to unravel the relationship between banks and corporations. But he concludes that bank wheeling and dealing has not captured the corporations. The most plausible view, it is thought here as a result of conducting a university research workshop involving more than 30 people, is that the banks and the corporations are quite interrelated both financially and in terms of interlocking boards of directors, many of whom emanate from the upper income population which can be seen as the ruling class standing behind and benefitting from the activities organized by the banks and corporations. There is agreement here with Michel De Vroey that "reality will probably be closer to a mixture of the two hypotheses than to a black or white situation" ("The Separation of Ownership and Control in Large Corporations," The Review of Radical Political Economics, vol. 7, no. 2 (Summer 1975), p. 9).

103 This Business Week article was cited in "The Economic Crisis in Historical Perspective," Monthly Review, pp. 6–7.

104 Ibid., p. 5.

105 Ibid., p. 4.

106 Ibid., p. 2.

107 "Keynesian Chickens Come Home to Roost," *pp. 10–11.*

108 David M. Gordon, "Recession Is Capitalism as Usual," The New York Times Magazine (April 27, 1975), pp. 18 and 49–63.

109 Thomas E. Mullaney, "A Look at Economic Planning."

110 In fact, a bill sponsoring national planning was introduced into the Senate by Senators Hubert Humphrey and Jacob Javits in May of 1975, according to "Highlights of the Week," The New York Times, Business and Finance Section (May 18, 1975), p. 14. In addition to the resources already cited see Jack Friedman, "A Planned Economy in the U.S.?" The New York Times, Business and Finance Section (May 18, 1975), pp. 1 and 11.

111 See in this regard, David M. Gordon, "Recession Is Capitalism as Usual," and the article, "The Economic Crisis in Historical Perspective—Part II," Monthly Review, vol. 26, no. 11 (April 1975), pp. 1–13.

4

THE CENTRALIZATION AND CONCENTRATION OF CAPITAL: MARXIAN AND GALBRAITHIAN VIEWS

This chapter discusses the tendency toward centralization and concentration in capitalist economies, particularly as they are dealt with
in Marxian and Galbraithian analysis. In order to do this the
necessary elements of capitalism itself must be discussed to put
centralization and concentration in context. Marxian thought is
instrumental in understanding the dynamics of the economic system
in the United States, especially centralization and concentration of
capital. *Centralization* is, in Marx's words, "expropriation of many
capitalists by few."[1] Centralization involves the comparative increase of wealth and power by a part of capital which transcends
industrial sectors of the political economy. *Concentration* occurs
when a particular market in a particular industry comes more under
the control of a corporation or a group of corporations. When it is
observed that U.S. capital is more centralized and concentrated it is

to point out that relatively fewer units of capital (typically corporations and financial institutions) are in charge of all production as compared to the past, and specific industries are dominated by fewer corporations than previously. The contemporary tendency is for the emergence of conglomerate multinational corporations that are vertically and horizontally integrated and are often closely tied to finance capital and the super rich. A corollary is that more of the population is proletarianized than in the past. That is, more and more people have only their labor power to sell. This especially includes descendents of those who worked the land (and produced for use as well as for exchange) and smaller capitalists.

It is, of course, a vast oversimplification to suggest that only contemporary radical and Marxian thought have emerged along side that of John Kenneth Galbraith to fill the vacuum in economic theory sketched in the preceding chapters. There are some problems with Marxian thought. It possesses many of the same antecedents as the conventional wisdom. Marxian thought is, in part, founded upon the economics of David Ricardo of the Classical School. Yet Marxian thought in its modern version has moved far beyond that and the impact of Keynes, Michal Kalecki, Lenin, and a host of neo-Marxian and other writers have supplemented Marx's seminal contribution to a holistic conception of the political economy and society. Although there is little in *Capital* which sheds light on the state, the modern Marxian writings have made major contributions in this area. What is more, the strand in Marx emphasizing the tendencies toward concentration in industry have been drawn out in detail by modern Marxists. This emphasis will be documented more fully here before moving on, in the next chapter, to look at a key Marxian view of the state—an institution which has become more and more important in society as a main actor in concocting various measures, both lethal and benign—to keep the system as a whole functioning. To no small measure it is likely that the growth of the relative size of business enterprise has necessitated the growth of the state if anything resembling stability in employment, relative prices, and output is to obtain (which is a dubious proposition, nonetheless).

For a deeper analysis of the view that corporations and the realities of ownership and control have much to do with the need for the intensified intervention of the state it is necessary to explore the wealth of published information about the structure of industry in the United States, the nature of ownership and control and concentration of influence in the political economy. Since this topic is a huge one, it will be necessary to be impressionistic at times. In addition, there are gaps in the available data; therefore, the theories and hunches of others will be necessary if sometimes imprecise resources.

Baran's and Sweezy's *Monopoly Capital,* and especially their notion of the generation and absorption of surplus, provides tentative focus. But this work is not enough for a plausible picture of the place of large corporations in American society. A number of Marxian and critical studies along with a variety of data will be used to construct a sense of the place of big business in the United States. This sense is an important part of the "grounded" set of ideas about the nature of capitalist society in late 20th century America.

The thought of John Kenneth Galbraith, while influential, should hardly be seen in the same light as Marxian thought—in fact, it is often specifically anti-Marxian—even though Galbraith has pointed to many of the same issues in a seductive fashion which may seem to take the steam out of the Marxian position. Galbraith, for example, provides an analysis of the large corporation and its relationship to society and suggests that patchwork reforms without fundamentally changing the forces and relations of production could result in significant change in the direction of social democracy. He sees a social stratum, the "educational and scientific estate," already existing as the stratum for change. He can be seen as an unwitting (or, perhaps, conscious) ally of the social-industrial complex and the solidification of a dangerously bureaucratized, hierarchical, and streamlined state, capitalist technocracy. It is important to understand Galbraith's position in anticipation of entirely possible responses to the crises of capitalism by the ruling elite. Galbraith's writings in the lower economics can be seen as an important *archetype.* What he is saying for a popular audience is also being developed elsewhere in the more obscure and prestigious economics such as that associated with Wassily Leontief who is an advocate of national planning.

At first glance the Galbraith/Leontief variety of policy suggestions may seem innocuous at worst or as the elements of a really sensible program at best. But as James O'Connor and other radical economists have pointed out, ominous implications exist in the Galbraith/Leontief technocratic suggestions for the reorganization of society. More specifically, Leontief's economics looks at the relationship between industries through input/output models—a useful analytic device, but also one with sociopolitical implications. In a society where the means of production are privately owned and where a corresponding elite hold a highly disproportionate share of wealth and power, the application of planning removes production via the market and places it into the hands of those who would direct it from the top of the socioeconomic hierarchy. Production would be dovetailed industry-by-industry in collaboration with the state, which probably sidesteps the possibility for workers to organize effectively since it would become more and more vague whom and what they were organizing against. O'Connor has called this potentially emerging situation the Big Matrix and notes that the Leontiefian ideas are even more dangerous than those of Galbraith. The application of the Leontief framework quite plausibly provides a serious challenge to the already deficiently exercised power of workers. It is a nonsocialist variety of economic planning that would possibly ameliorate, for a time, the current crisis of capitalism but could conceivably create a social disease as disastrous as economic instability if human freedom and broad-based participation in decision making are worth anything at all. One Marxian position in contradistinction to that of Galbraith and Leontief would be that planning is an essential part of the creation of a more sensible society. However the slogan "Redistribute the Productive Forces on the Basis of Need Not Profit While Revolutionizing the Production Relations on the Basis of Self-Organization and the End of Authoritarianism (including, especially, the end of capital)" could provide the elements of an alternative guide to planning rather than what Galbraith, Leontief and others have in mind.[2] Nikola Uzunov observes that input/output analysis is not theoretical but constitutes a method which can be used under socialism or capitalism. The position taken here is that input/output analysis without socialism and used for a planned capitalism strengthens the power of those on top of the socioeconomic pyramid and is therefore something for which many or most socialists in the U.S. could muster little enthusiasm. The use of this methodology under socialism would be quite a different matter.

Thus, Galbraithian ideas seem to be to the contemporary situation what Keynesian ideas were to the 1930s. Galbraith has a naive view of social class even though he notices and describes in detail a major structural phenomenon of our time; Galbraith sees large corporations as the center of *The New Industrial State*. Baran and Sweezy refer to this phenomenon as *Monopoly Capital*.

In a very important way Galbraith is different from Keynes in that a significant part of the former's analysis deals with a revised theory of the firm. Keynes, it should be recalled, was an adherent to Marshallian microeconomics and even the labor theory of value.[3] Galbraith is a critic of the neo-Classical stance and has attempted to invent a new "institutional" school of thought in microeconomics as well as, in his more recent writings, advocacy with respect to what the macroeconomic setting of the competitive and concentrated (oligopolistic and/or monopolistic) firms and industries should be.

The similarity between Galbraith and Keynes is mainly that they both put forth a program to revitalize capitalism without *fundamentally* changing it—especially the ownership of the means of production and the social relations surrounding production.

This chapter first sketches the necessary elements of capitalism as an economic system through the use of a simple allegorical tale. This provides a plausible view of capitalism as a pernicious social order—one which is founded on conquest and exploitation. This view depicts capitalism as a system which contains inequality as a necessary status for its people and an elaborate socialization process for human beings to accept their lot. A picture of simple capitalism will help to demystify the much more complex variety which currently exists. A *second* important task is to offer some ideas on the tendency for the emergence of concentration in the ownership of the means of production and a corresponding reinforcement of a hierarchical social order. A note on the alternative definitions of concentration is required here. An important part of this discussion includes the empirical dimensions of concentration with a focus on industries and on corporations in the economy as a whole. Salient data from the more traditional industrial organization literature and that generated by the U.S. Bureau of the Census are used. *Third,* an elaboration on centralization and concentration in the context of the economy as a whole will be undertaken. Here is where data are not comprehensive, so that it will be necessary to rely somewhat on impressionistic literature. It is in this area of inquiry that the alternative interpretations of Baran and Sweezy and other Marxists in comparison with Galbraith are pronounced. This contrast provides a somewhat holistic view of the place of the modern corporation in contemporary society.

The Allegory of Robinson Crusoe

One of the most succinct and powerful accounts of many of the tendencies that seem to exist in capitalism—and the psyche of capitalists—is to be found in the late Stephen Hymer's "Robinson Crusoe and the Secret of Primitive Accumulation."[4] Hymer takes the famous allegorical tale about Robinson Crusoe, a mythical 17th-century Englishman (an important factor to notice in view of the historical development of capitalism) who is a long-loved favorite among economists (often, as a starting point for a discussion of international trade).[5] Crusoe provides an archetype for capitalist behavior.

Crusoe's life is put in the context of Marx's analysis of primitive accumulation.[6] Primitive accumulation is meant to be "original" accumulation or the early capitalists' transformation of their social and natural environment into something which they have organized to produce a pecuniary profit for themselves. It is thus the exchange value of objects which matters to the capitalist more than an object's use value. It is the drive to make profit which provides the capitalists' motivation; this profit, in turn, adds to society's output which is disproportionately appropriated. In the thought of Adam Smith and other of the Classical economists this results in a harmonious state of affairs, and Robinson Crusoe is the archetype of the economic man. "He is pictured [by Daniel Defoe] as a rugged individual—diligent, intelligent, and above all frugal—who masters nature through reason."[7]

Hymer turns the latter view around totally and persuasively. He points out that Crusoe is involved in force, slavery, murder, robbery, and conquest. Crusoe of course has qualms at times about his activities, but he is always able to rationalize them. He is not only able to survive, but eventually and with many ups and downs, is successful at turning an initial meager investment of 40 pounds worth of "toys and trifles" into an empire. He becomes the patriarch of an entire isolated society, an island economy, and holds wealth elsewhere. Crusoe, of course, suffers hardship—perhaps the worst of which is many years of isolation—after a shipwreck casts him alone on the island. During his prolonged period of isolation, Crusoe is terrified and anxious much of the time. And though he was an experienced profit seeker before the shipwreck he relates to his environment only on the basis of its use value since there was no one with whom to exchange things and there existed the labor of no one else, at the outset and for a time, to organize for his own benefit. To compile a huge surplus beyond his foreseeable needs made no sense. He was on his own and could not behave as a capitalist. His greed vanished and he functioned, after time, within a wider scheme of values.

It was when a group of Caribbeans came ashore holding a prisoner, after many years have passed, that Crusoe reverted to prior tendencies learned in England. He helped this prisoner—whom he named Friday forever to remind the latter of the day and his debt—"escape." Then the story really begins to move. Crusoe's period of being alone and lonely is gone in addition to much of his fear. He is able to use objects foreign to Friday, such as firearms, to mystify and conquer him—albeit subtly. It is with the arrival of Friday that the origins of Crusoe's empire begin to emerge. But emergence happens only when more people enter the picture and there is, in turn, more labor power to master and coordinate. As Hymer puts it, with the appearance of Friday, "Robinson has his servant. An economy is born."[8]

As time passes, "Friday becomes labor and [Crusoe] becomes capital—innovating, organizing, and building an empire."[9] But this relationship between Crusoe and Friday involves a very intriguing program of resocialization. Indeed, many a contemporary industrial psychologist or behavior modification advocate would learn much from this precursor of Frederick W. Taylor, the father of "scientific management."[10] Eventually, Crusoe's efforts pay off and Friday fits his master's purposes. But in this case

> Robinson cannot depend on the law to guard his property. Instead he uses religion. Europeans do not require so elaborate a socialization procedure as Friday because they have come by education, tradition, and habit to look upon private property as a self-evident law of nature.[11]

Hymer points out that Robinson Crusoe accumulates capital in two different ways throughout his life. In the days before the shipwreck and then again as he regains contact with the outside world, Crusoe was involved in the form that can be expressed in this shorthand way—M-C-M'. First, beginning with some money (M), trading that for commodities (C), and ending up with more money (M'). On the island a second form of accumulation occurs which can be expressed as C-L-C. Beginning with some commodities (C) which are used as bait to gain dominance over the labor (L) of another, Crusoe attracts labor power, which in turn is used to produce more commodities (C). This formula is the secret behind Crusoe's becoming the kingpin of a small empire. Without the labor of others, he is a lonely and frightened figure "content" with only so many commodities as fill his perceived needs. But with both the control over labor and the eventual return to his network of commerce, there is no stopping Crusoe.[12]

The story of Robinson Crusoe makes apparent that capitalism requires more than one person if it is to exist at all. The arrival of just one more person into Crusoe's life was also the beginning of an economic system founded on Friday's labor. Superordination and subordination begin immediately and require an elaborate socialization process. At first force or threats of force are used but later becomes less and less necessary as the rules of the game are established. The organizer, Crusoe, is seen as the brighter of the two—especially by Crusoe—and, because of his entrepreneurial ability, also proves himself able to continue in the role of "wheeler-dealer." Because he is the organizer, it seems fair that he also get a disproportionate share of the product (even housing in the earlier stage of

Crusoe's and Friday's relationship as Friday had to sleep outside the master's more developed facilities). So once the system is in motion, Crusoe has the ability to continue to do more of the same and becomes richer in the process. When the control over labor power and the money economy coexist, accumulation becomes even more possible. Money, then, can be seen as the other form in which commodities can be expressed. With money and control over labor, Crusoe, indeed, is even able to spread his sphere of involvement beyond the island. What is more, he can get the assistance he needs from others who identify with his quest to accumulate and dominate.

> The international economy of Robinson's time, like that of today, is not composed of equal partners but is ordered along class lines. Robinson occupies one of the upper-middle levels of the pyramid. (The highest levels are in the capitals of Europe.) Captains, merchants, and planters are his peer group. With them he exchanges on the basis of fraternal collaboration. (Arab captains excepted.) They teach him, rescue him, do business for him, and keep him from falling beneath his class. He in turn generally regards them as honest and plain-dealing men, sides with them against their rebellious subordinates, and is easy with them in his bargaining. Towards whites of lower rank he is more demanding. If they disobey, he is severe; but if they are loyal, he is willing to share some booty and delegate some authority. Africans and Caribbeans are sold, killed, trained, or used as wives by his men, as the case may be . . . .
>
> The contradictions between Robinson and other members of the hierarchy give the story its dynamics. He is forever wrestling with the problem of subordinating lower levels and trying to rise above his own. The fact that he does not see it this way but prefers to make up stories about himself makes no difference. He denies the conflict between himself and Friday by accepting Friday's mask of willing obedience. And he conceives of his greed as a crime against God instead of against man. But his daily life shows that his social relations are antagonistic and he knows it.[13]

Hymer points out that a close look at *Friday's* grandchildren would also be necessary to see how the repressed antagonistic relationship embodied in the island economy worked out.[14] When this is done the story of incredible concentration as well as conflict and struggle emerges. In but a short span in history a wholly new (sometimes multinational) form of organization—the corporation—has emerged, grown, and expanded, working in full collaboration with the nation-state. But parallel developments are large portions of the world moving in another direction, attempting to abandon capitalism. Antagonism typified by that on the island is expressed on a world scale. Friday's people could as easily be those now in Indochina or any number of places.

With capitalism then it became possible for privately owned organizations to pull together a great deal of labor power over an extended period of time for profit that is accumulated privately. Let us look at some ideas about the tendency toward centralization and concentration and then at concentration itself.

Centralization and Concentration in Industry: Tendencies and Actualities

Centralization is the replacement of many capitalists by a few. Concentration is the control of more of the market in a particular industry by a corporation or a group of corporations. At the same time, centralization and concentration are closely related and often simultaneous; in practice it seems difficult to separate centralization from concentration.

Related to centralization and concentration of capital is the conglomerate corporation, which contains under its aegis units engaged in the production of different kinds of commodities. For example, International Telephone and Telegraph (ITT) diversified through mergers in the 1960s. Previously, since its founding in 1920, ITT had been mainly a telecommunications equipment manufacturer and an operator of telephone companies. Between 1961 and 1968 ITT acquired 55 foreign and 52 domestic corporations. In 1969 alone, the ITT board of directors approved 11 foreign and 22 domestic acquisitions. ITT is involved in many different industries, including chemical cellulose, bakery goods, car rental, hotels and motels, construction, vending machines, fire insurance, finance, as well as its previous activities.[15] There are many corporations that, like ITT, have amassed a network of economic activity in diverse markets. The absolute bigness of ITT in comparison to smaller corporations is an issue in itself even beyond the share of each market ITT possesses. A focus similar to that above is what Baran and Sweezy take in *Monopoly Capital* and what Galbraith takes in *The New Industrial State*. This will be the main level, then, on which the issue of centralization and concentration is addressed here as well.

The editors of *Monthly Review*, Paul M. Sweezy and Harry Magdoff, and most other Marxists believe that there are "laws of motion" which exist in the social relations that make up the capitalist mode of production. They summarize these "laws of motion" in this way:

> (1) Competition of capital generates concentration and centralization, hence the inevitable replacement of competitive by monopoly capitalism.

(2) The accumulation process is inherently unstable and never tends to take the form of a moving equilibrium (a fantasy of bourgeois economics textbooks). Two forms of motion, attributable to related but distinguishable structural features of the system, characterize the accumulation process: (a) the more or less regular ups and downs of the business cycle (in recent times the length of the cycle, from peak to peak or trough to trough, has tended to be around four years); and (b) a long-range and persistent tendency to stagnation manifested in high rates of unemployment and much idle productive capacity.

(3) The process of monopolization has relatively little effect on the business cycle, but it exacerbates the tendency to stagnation.[16]

This view seems plausible if one looks at the history of capitalism. What is more, their contemporary Marxian view is all the more powerful in that it arises out of thought originating more than 100 years ago in the mind of Karl Marx before the great waves of concentration in industry—in the 1890s, in the 1920s and again in the 1960s—actually occurred in the United States. If the test of a theory is its predictive power, it is likely that the detractors of Marxian thought have yet to be proved right and his ideas on concentration, however crude, are attractive.

Yet a bit of reflection on the complex set of issues raised by Sweezy and Magdoff suggests that a deep look into U.S. economic history would be necessary to provide the evidence on which the accuracy of their view would be evaluated. To undertake this here would be to plunge down a tangent from which it would be difficult to emerge and retain a focus on the present. The detailed historical analyses are left to others,[17] and the tendencies toward concentration will be discussed on a theoretical level—highly abridged. Then some data about concentration in industries is presented as a background setting to the contrasting views—Marxian and that of Galbraith—on what difference it makes. Both views, to no small extent, are theoretical and interpretive studies about the observed phenomenon of the huge corporation. At the same time it becomes necessary to be historical in a loose way to establish points of reference.

The claim made earlier that Marx had developed some important ideas about the tendency toward concentration under capitalism is substantiated in a leading industrial organization textbook:

> A century ago, manufacturing was still predominantly the province of the relatively small firm serving local markets, and manufacturing industry was much less concentrated in the aggregate than it is today. (Transportation, on the other hand, already showed signs of growing dominance by large corpora-

tions.) At the time, Karl Marx stood alone among well-known economists in predicting that big business would come to dominate the industrial scene. This development Marx attributed to the corporate form of organization, then acquiring its modern trappings, and to the interaction of scale economies and bitter competition. "One capitalist always kills many," said Marx, leading to a "constantly diminishing number of the magnates of capital, who usurp and monopolise all advantages of this process of transformation."[18]

"[D]uring the next 60 years, the industrialized economies of the world evidently moved a considerable distance toward fulfilling Marx's prediction."[19] What has happened in more recent times—say in the post-World War II period—is less clear though not entirely mysterious. What may be an impressive fact is that the largest 200 or so corporations have not *totally* engulfed the economy and society. In the pathbreaking study by Adolf Berle and Gardiner Means published in 1932 it was

> . . . discovered that the assets of the 200 largest nonfinancial corporations were growing considerably more rapidly on the average between 1909 and 1929 than the assets of all corporations taken together. Without committing themselves to a prediction of what would in fact occur, they noted that *if* the observed disparity in growth rates continued, the 200 largest nonfinancial corporations would account for 70 percent of all industrial activity by 1950 and for practically all industrial corporation assets by 1972.[20]

While the extrapolation did not prove an accurate quantitative guide to events, Berle and Means had obviously looked at an economic phenomenon that merited more study. Indeed, this was a big enough concern that the AFL-CIO Executive Council called on the Congressional branch of the federal government to undertake an in-depth investigation of the structure of the U.S. economy in March 1975. It was the view of the AFL-CIO that U.S. conglomerate corporations were continuing to centralize the ownership and control in economic activity while at the same time spreading its tentacles across other lands as well. The AFL-CIO was dissatisfied with the available information on, especially, the ownership, structure, management, operations, and policies of giant industry in the U.S. and the interlocking relationships with banks but went on to present this data (without indicating the source of their information):

> The 500 biggest U.S. corporations now hold more than two-thirds of all business income. The top 111 manufacturing corporations hold more than half of all assets and get more than half of

all profits in manufacturing. The 50 biggest banks control more than half of all bank assets and hold leverage control stock in more than 5,200 companies.[21]

Douglas Dowd saved others some time and effort by compiling an impressive array of data about concentration in the economy using the measures of organizational control over employment, profits, sales, assets, and the like. In his words,

the 500 largest industrial (manufacturing and mining) corporations in 1972 controlled 65 percent of the *sales* of all industrial companies, 75 percent of their total *profits,* and 75 percent of total industrial *employment.*[22]

In comparison the next largest 500 corporations seem small. The largest 1,000 taken together accounted for 72 percent of all industrial sales (compared with 65 percent for the top 500 corporations); around 80 percent of industrial profits (75 percent for the top 500); around 84 percent of industrial employment (compared with 75 percent for the top 500). Put another way, the second largest 500 corporations account for 6.5 percent of sales, 6 percent of industrial profits and around 9 percent of industrial employment. The contrast shows how dominant the largest 500 corporations are. They are not even approached in sales, profits, and employment by the next largest 500.[23]

What is more, there was an apparent increase of the share of net income among the largest 100 industrial corporations between 1970 and 1973 in comparison to the largest 500. In 1970 the largest 100 got about 68 percent of the net income received by the largest 500, and by 1973 the percentage had increased to roughly 72 percent. Assets of the top 100 increased from about 64.5 percent in 1970 to around 66 percent in 1973, and employment by the largest 100 as a percentage of those employed by the largest 500 remained nearly unchanged. Thus, the net income share of the largest 100 industrial corporations increased somewhat compared to the top 500 between 1970 and 1973 with the proportion of those employed by the top 100 remaining the same.[24] Perhaps this is an index of the power of the largest 100 in comparison to the largest 500, though much more information over a longer period of time would be needed to be conclusive.

The range in concentration among the largest 500 corporations was from the largest in terms of assets—Exxon (formerly Standard Oil of New Jersey)—with $21.5 billion in 1972 to the smallest—Varian Associates—with $188 million. Varian's sales were $203 million while Exxon's were $20 billion.[25]

Altogether the largest 500 industrial companies sold $558 billion worth of commodities in 1972. GNP, in comparison was $1,152 billion.[26] Although a comparison of the sales of the largest 500 corporations with GNP is only a way to show the relative size of economic activity (which should not be confused with the value added to GNP by the largest 500), it is interesting to note that the sales of the largest corporations were 48.5 percent of GNP in 1972. An important measure of centralization and concentration over time would be the percent of *value added* to the entire economy by different groupings of corporations (for example; the largest 50, 100, 150, 200, and so on). Unfortunately, this has not been compiled for corporations in all industries.

But the largest ten corporations (GM, Exxon, Ford, GE, IBM, Mobil Oil, Chrysler, Texaco, ITT, and Western Electric) had *sales* of $133 billion in 1971 (about 10 percent the size of GNP, 24 percent of the top 500, and double that of the second 500). The profits of this same group were $10.3 billion after taxes in 1971 in comparison with total corporate profits of a bit under $50 billion after taxes, or about 20 percent of total corporate profits.[27]

It must be pointed out that there are a good many corporations in the U.S. In 1971 there were 1,733,000.[28] For 500 to emerge so visibly in the midst of so many is remarkable, but is consistent with Marxian thought.

Although the preceding discussion gives a rough sense of the magnitude of the corporate giants, it is also useful to look at concentration by industrial sector. To view the largest corporations in the context of all corporations is perhaps as much a commentary on power in society as economic performance. Table 2 presents some salient data. Here we see that the largest number of corporations were in wholesale and retail trade but they were surpassed in sector share of GNP by manufacturing which was much more concentrated. Three hundred ninety-three manufacturing corporations had more than $100 million in assets and accounted for 61.3 percent of that sector's assets in comparison with 61 corporations in wholesale and retail trade accounting for 18.8 percent of sector assets.

A review of the data in the table shows that 739 corporations held 50.6 percent of all nonfinancial corporation assets in 1964; 325 held 42.1 percent of all nonfinancial corporation assets. The most concentrated sectors (in terms of percentage share of assets held by corporations with $100 million in assets or more) were transportation, communications, electric and gas; manufacturing; and mining. Banking, finance, and insurance were also concentrated with 1,019 corporations holding 65.9 percent of the sector assets. The least concentrated sectors were agriculture, forestry, and fisheries; real estate; services; construction; and wholesale and retail trade.

TABLE 2 THE PERCENTAGE OF ALL CORPORATE ASSETS ACCOUNTED FOR IN 1964 BY CORPORATIONS WITH ASSETS OF $100 MILLION OR MORE

		Corporations With:				
		$100 Million + Assets			$250 Million + Assets	
Sector	Number of Corporations	1965 Sector Share of GNP	Number	Share of All Sector Assets	Number	Share of All Sector Assets
All nonfinancial corporations	1,249,446		739	50.6%	325	42.1%
Agriculture, forestry, and fisheries	25,933	3.7%	2	6.9	1	4.6
Mining	14,487	2.1	30	45.0	10	26.0
Construction	104,134	4.5	5	4.4	1	1.1
Manufacturing	184,961	28.9	393	61.3	171	51.0
Transportation, communications, electric and gas	56,338	8.8	214	84.6	118	75.5
Wholesale and retail trade	421,553	16.4	61	18.8	21	13.4
Services	176,902	10.4	17	10.1	3	2.8
Real estate	259,656	10.5	17	3.8	0	0
Banking, finance, and insurance	124,071	3.1	1,019	65.9	407	54.6

Source: U.S. Treasury Department, Internal Revenue Service, *Statistics of Income: 1964*, Corporate Income Tax Returns, with Accounting Periods ended July 1964–June 1965 (Washington, D.C.: U.S. Government Printing Office, 1969), Table 6, in Frederic M. Scherer, *Industrial Market Structure and Economic Performance*, (Chicago: Rand McNally, 1970). p. 40.

Manufacturing is perhaps the most analyzed industrial sector. Historical data, rough as it is, suggests a long-term trend toward more and more concentration, accompanied by some periods where the extent of concentration is not well known. It appears that about 36 percent of total manufacturing corporation assets were held by the largest 100 firms in 1924. By 1933 the figure reached 44 percent. The period between 1933 and 1947 is a puzzle, but the trend in concentration just after World War II and the late 1960s seems ever upward with about half of total manufacturing corporation assets being held by but 100 firms in 1967.[29] Further, there was an unmistakable upward trend in the 100 largest share of value added in manufacturing—going from 23 percent in 1947 to 30 percent for both 1954 and 1958 and then to 33 percent in 1963 and 1966.[30] The 200 largest manufacturing corporations held 56.7 percent of all manufacturing assets in 1965 while their share of value added was 42 percent in 1966. The gross data indicate that by 1972, 60 percent of total manufacturing assets were held by the 200 largest manufacturing corporations and in 1970, 43 percent of the value added in manufacturing was by 200 corporations (25 percent by the largest 50; 33 percent by the largest 100; and 38 percent by the largest 150). To make a complex story as short as possible, the 200 largest manufacturing companies increased their "contribution" to value added in the post-World War II period (from 30 percent in 1947 to 43 percent in 1970) as well as their share of assets (from 48.2 percent to 60.0 percent). And the largest 100 corporations account for nearly three-fourths of both the value added and the assets of the 200 largest manufacturing corporations.[31]

Part of the apparent increase in concentration among the largest manufacturing corporations in the period since World War II is a result of mergers and acquisition. The period between 1965 and 1969, for example, was one of a great deal of merger and acquisition activity in manufacturing and mining. The 8,213 mergers and acquisitions was nearly double that of 1960–1964 (4,366), and the 1960s as a whole experienced around 12,500 mergers and acquisitions in comparison with about 4,800 during the 1950s. There were about 6,800 mergers and acquisitions in the 1920s, in comparison, which is a period when concentration in manufacturing was increasing substantially.[32]

What has been presented, then, is scattered data on the extent of concentration in industry in the U.S. which should be taken as suggestive but not conclusive. It appears that the comprehensive work in industrial organization is yet to be written and indeed would be a huge research project. It would have to measure, using some composite index, the impact of the largest corporations on the U.S.

economy and society. The important dimensions would be value added to GNP, assets, sales, profits, investment, employment, wages and salaries paid, and so on, and their intertwining ties with the economy as a whole. A key question would be what relationships do corporations have with other key institutions such as banks, government, other countries, and other corporations. There is a large literature on corporations, but everything is not known that it would be useful to know.[33] At the same time, there is not full agreement here with Frederic Scherer when he says "It is futile to attempt a quantitative summary of how much structural monopoly power exists in the whole of the American economy."[34] The issue seems more that the research has not yet been done, and there are few institutions from which to obtain the resources to conduct such research. Admittedly, the ruling class has been effective in covering its tracks when it comes to specifics on ownership and control. But given the right political climate, a great deal could be found out from Internal Revenue Service and other government data. At this stage, and with the resources available for this study, it is necessary to be more impressionistic than is ideal. But an attempt to grasp the whole seems important. Thus, knowing full well that no concise and comprehensive measure of the total impact of large corporations on the U.S. economy and society has been constructed, the next task is to sketch alternative interpretations of this relationship introducing more data from time to time in an effort to untangle the plausible general place of the large corporations in the U.S. political economy.

The preceding does give credence to both the Marxian observation and the position of Galbraith that large corporations play a central role in the economy of the nation and the world. Both see this as an important reality, but perhaps only neo-Classical economists caught up in microeconomic theory would find this startling. The corporations are a power in society that shape and mold social institutions and establish an important part of the framework under which the people live out their lives.

Marxian Views on Centralization and Concentration: Corporations as Monopoly Capital

V. I. Lenin popularized the notion of monopoly capitalism in his famous work *Imperialism: The Highest Stage of Capitalism.* Some decades later, in 1962, another Soviet writer was to look at this phenomenon first hand in the United States after a study of available works on the ownership and structure of the U.S. political economy.

Early in his resulting work, S. Menshikov offers an introductory Marxist/Leninist discussion on the theory of capitalist development in which he appears to be in basic agreement with Lenin's position on finance capitalism drawn from the work of R. Hilferding but modified. But then, in a quasi-empirical discussion, Menshikov wavers substantially and really does not make a convincing distinction between finance capitalism and corporate capitalism or prove that top corporate executives are not drawn from the same circles as the super-rich families which make up finance capitalism. In short, it is not demonstrated that corporate executives are but hired hands of a financial oligarchy, although it is asserted that there are finance capitalists who stand apart from production and, in turn, create a bureaucratic top group of managers with both acting in collaboration with the state to form a state monopoly capitalist superstructure over all of capitalist society. In turn, the view is that the centralized and concentrated structure necessitates and permits a very large number of "competitive" enterprises which are in the oligarchy's interests to maintain. The depiction is one of a neat hierarchy which runs from finance capital to monopoly capital to competitive capital reinforced on all fronts by the state machinery. There is a stratification among capitalists in terms of wealth and power on the basis of their position in this hierarchy with the finance capitalists in the top most stratum.[35]

It is not argued that the financial oligarchy is an idle rentier class. Rather, Menshikov sees this stratum as the one which heads up industrial-banking complexes. But the link between finance capital and corporate operations is not made at all clear, which does not totally resolve a controversial area in Marxian studies.

Ferdinand Lundberg, in his study of the very rich in the U.S., goes so far as to conclude that there is a very real ruling class which relies upon "low-grade stooges" to maintain its power.[36] Many of the key links between the different economic institutions are depicted, and a great deal of information about the upper income stratum's holdings is presented. This huge and polemical best seller is also an informative part of the literature.

Still more promising directions for information about the owners of the means of production are to be found in a case study by James C. Knowles on the Rockefeller nexus, made up of the descendants and their associates of but two brothers—John D. Rockefeller (1839–1937) and William Rockefeller (1841–1922).

What emerges from the Knowles study is a sense that finance capital is probably influential with respect to the operations of at least many large corporations, and it most clearly appears that this part of the super-rich are involved in many spheres including high finance, corporations, and the state. Knowles introduces the idea that there is a core of financial institutions consisting of four huge banks (Chase Manhattan, First National City, and Chemical, all in New York, and First National Bank of Chicago, which were second, third, sixth, and tenth nationally in assets in 1969) and three large mutual life insurance companies (Metropolitan, Equitable, and New York Life which were, in 1969, the second, third and fourth in terms of assets nationally). To make a detailed story as succinct as possible, the relationship between these core institutions is characterized by a multitude of interlocking directorates from members of the Rockefeller group and an alliance with other wealthy families. Although it would take a team of dedicated social scientists to unravel the ties over the generations between these families (including marriages serving to unite them), Knowles has written a great quantity of information on this labyrinth which ties scores of powerful people to the Rockefeller group. It must be studied carefully to be even remotely understood. But no firm conclusions are reached about actual ownership of the core financial institutions' stock since this is a tightly guarded secret. What emerges, then, is a somewhat clouded view of the center of the group's financial empire where an account of a maze of interrelated activities serves as a proxy for actual ownership.[37]

Though the picture of the financial core of the Rockefeller group is murky (and kept that way by design), Knowles believes it to be the basis of still more entanglements with the economy through a number of large nonfinancial corporations. Actual control of some of them is held, it is argued, and less-firm influence is accomplished in four ways: (1) through family stockholdings and management positions; (2) through stockholdings by trusts and other devices of the financial empire; (3) through near-majority or majority representation on the boards of directors; and (4) through dominance over capital sources.[38]

Thirteen corporations are said to be in "firm control." That is, the family itself owns more than 20 percent of the corporation's outstanding stock and in addition at least one member of the family is in a top corporate position (defined as Chairman of the Board, Vice Chairman of the Board, President, Chairman of the Executive Committee, and Chairman of the Finance Committee). The largest corporation included in this group is DuPont (the fifteenth largest nationally in 1969) and Grace (the fiftieth largest according to 1969 *Fortune* magazine rankings). "Working control" (defined as family ownership of at least 10 percent of the corporate stock or more than 5 percent in addition to the family having two or more members in top management positions) is held over another 23 corporations which include five of the largest 50 corporations among *Fortune*'s ranking, three of the biggest 50 retailing concerns, and one of the largest 50 utilities. Control through stock held by bank trusts and other financial institutions is not well documented, though it is alleged that the financial institutions are "locked in" to some corporations for a time and cannot sell vast holdings of stock even when that is desired since holdings are so substantial that to do so would depress the market. It is also argued that a great deal of power is held over corporations because the group had $34.5 billion in trust department assets in 1967 which represented nearly 14 percent of trust assets nationally. Included in this was $22.5 billion in stocks. Knowles argues that since members of the Rockefeller financial group sit on the boards of directors of these four major banks, the voting rights to a significant chunk of U.S. corporate stock are essentially under their control. He goes so far as to say that a large share of control over the American economy is therefore held by this one group when the voting power of their own stock ownership plus that in trust over which they have control is used along with the power held by those who sit on corporate boards and those who are in charge of lending money. And when all of this is linked with those in government who are connected with the Rockefeller group—such as, to name but three of many, Secretary of State Henry Kissinger, Senator Charles Percy, and Vice-President Nelson Rockefeller in the Ford administration—it is apparent that the Rockefeller group has spread its tentacles far and wide.[39]

This information touches on some of the quite thorough but ultimately impressionistic analysis that Knowles presents, but the point is well made. Finance capital cannot be said to be politically and economically impotent. Nor can it be said that a clean distinction between finance capitalism and corporate capitalism is appropriate in this instance or that the hierarchy of control suggested by Menshikov exists in the U.S. political economy.

The question of who controls the corporations is a controversial issue in Marxian political economics as it is in other literature. Possibly this controversy exists because some have been eager to remain more purely Marxist/Leninist, while others have not cared about control at all but have found much of Marxian thought to offer a powerful theoretical core from which to work. Erroneously, those Marxian scholars who have not been adherents to the thesis that finance capital rules the corporations have been categorized as "Marxist managerialists" and have been thrown in nearly the same bag as Berle and Means and other non-Marxians who have written about the American corporation with an emphasis on the so-called "managerial revolution" where the view is that power has passed to those who manage the corporation and away from the actual owners of the corporations. James O'Connor clearly pointed out the fallacy contained in grouping the Marxists and the managerial revolution theorists together when he said,

> To my knowledge, there are no Marxist economists who seriously believe that managers of industry have wrested control from the large owners and exercise that control (for more than a short time, anyway) in their own special interests. Although Paul Sweezy can defend *Monopoly Capital* far better than I can, I cannot help remarking that I think it is a pity that in their rush to "prove" some new "thesis" Fitch and Oppenheimer have to lump Baran and Sweezy's seminal work with the stupid and apologetic doctrines of the bourgeois managerial revolution theorists. . . . Without going into the pros and cons of Baran and Sweezy's own thesis, I would like to recall that these authors write of "the *combined* power of management and the *very rich:* the *two* are in fact *integrated* into a harmonious *interest group* at the top of the economic pyramid."[40]

What emerges is a glimpse of the ruling class which is not monolithic but must be seen as a powerful force in society. Therefore, it seems highly curious that some believe power to be exercised by lower echelon corporate people. Galbraith thinks that the main force in corporations is what he has termed the "technostructure," which consists of those corporate (it is tempting to say workers) employees who possess technical skills and special knowledge necessary to keep the machinery in motion to crank out whatever commodities the corporation is in business to sell. This seems especially hard to believe.

Even Paul Samuelson thinks that power is exercised at a level no lower than top corporate executives. He said, for example, that

> I'd like to think that our MIT students will inherit the earth . . . but reality keeps breaking in. They, like the large corporation itself, are constitutional monarchs who reign only so long as they don't rule. Just let some computer tell Henry Ford, or for that matter the General Motors Board, that they've got to do something he [the computer] wants but which they [Henry Ford or the GM Board] don't think is in their long-run interest, and see how fast he draws his severance pay.[41]

Those who help manage the corporations are hired and fired by those who have control over the corporation.[42] While the controllers may, at times, be some of the same people as top management, a still important force in American society seems to be a more traditional ruling class whose parents and grandparents built their empires in years past.

The existence of a traditional ruling class does not mean that there are not capitalist upstarts who have constructed corporate labyrinths in more recent times. But Sweezy and Magdoff have gone so far as to dub those such as James Ling "underprivileged multimillionaires" who are not part of the top capitalist inner circle. They conclude that the dramatic wave of mergers (what Marx called centralization and concentration of capital) in the 1960s in the form, to no small extent, of the conglomerate corporation complicated a "confused and uncertain political situation" but that

> the kind of viciously irrational and destructive system we have today was fully shaped as far back as forty years ago. Increasing monopolization since then has doubtless made matters worse, but not essentially different.[43]

A more detailed, if flawed, account of this structure is contained in Paul Baran and Paul Sweezy's *Monopoly Capital: An Essay on the American Economic and Social Order*. There appears to be a great deal of agreement among the few Marxian economists in the U.S. that this is a contemporary classic and one of the most widely read works in recent Marxian political economics. Further, the book develops the now popular idea (among radical economists and social scientists and people involved in the Movement) that "monopoly capital" is a central and important part of the structure of the U.S. economy and is very much a part of the society's troubles.

A statement by Robert Heilbroner, made in 1966, can put the Baran and Sweezy view into perspective:

> Working in an isolation from the academic community which was partly enforced, and partly self-imposed, Baran and Sweezy have produced an appraisal of American society, at once bitter and perhaps embittered, that is totally with odds with the interpretation of American society we find in the books of most professors. This flavor of academic heresy is unusual only in America, however. If I judge correctly, the image of American society that arises from their pages approximates (and gives additional substance to) the way our society is seen and understood, not only in Russian and Chinese intellectual circles, but in many important centers of thought in Europe, Latin America, Africa, and Asia. If for no other reason, this fact should be sufficient to justify a careful study of this book.[44]

While Heilbroner sees the Baran and Sweezy presentation "as a moral indictment, as an economic model, and as a theory of power"[45] and finds the first more persuasive than the others, here we will largely avoid discussion of their moral indictment. It has been pointed out in earlier chapters that we are attempting to view political economics within the context of scientific paradigms.

In a review of *Monopoly Capital*, James O'Connor points out that

Baran and Sweezy have come up with a Marxian view which draws heavily on neo-Classical and Keynesian economic theory since the classical Marxist literature does not relate completely to the contemporary situation. O'Connor notes that "Marxist analytic tools were developed to describe the transition from precapitalist to capitalist economies and to unravel the 'laws of motion' of competitive capitalism."[46]

There are important ways in which Baran and Sweezy diverge from Marx's original work. But there are also significant similarities, particularly the intellectual tradition from which they write and their attempt to capture the "whole," or to focus on the total social order, to explain what the significance of large industry is to both the workings of the economy and to point out what the implications are for the people of the U.S. as well as the relationship between the U.S. and the rest of the world.

Economic product, for example, is divided into "socially necessary costs" and "economic surplus." This idea is central to the book, is an attempt to move beyond and draw from the labor theory of value, and is a notion foreign to other schools of contemporary economic thought.

Some major points that Baran and Sweezy make are these: Monopoly capitalism, or huge firms dominating industry, is mainly in charge of the country's production. These firms are directed by a group of self-perpetuating professional managers, they retain much of their earnings, and are quite financially independent. Maximum profits, Baran and Sweezy argue, are sought and new techniques of management, such as market research, are used in this effort. Corporate size and growth as well as horizontal and vertical integration and diversification are goals of management and are encouraged, or at least not blocked, by capital gains seeking stockholders. The economic surplus tends to rise over time as technology advances and capital is substituted for labor in an effort to cut costs. The benefits accruing from lower costs are appropriated by corporations rather than passed on to consumers.[47]

O'Connor offers a statement which can be used as a jumping off point for a more detailed and critical look at the Baran and Sweezy view:

> Working their way carefully from the concrete to the general, from the actual behavior of the dominant economic units to the general process of economic change, they prove as conclusively as it is possible to do in a work modestly subtitled "An Essay on the American Economic and Social Order" that U.S. capitalism fails to automatically generate sufficient investment outlets for

the rising surplus and as a consequence that the system normally tends towards stagnation.[48]

With this preview, an elaboration is in order. It is noted that the central theme on which their analysis is based is "the generation and absorption of the surplus under conditions of monopoly capitalism."[49] A second issue that arises, then, is: what, more specifically, do they mean by monopoly capitalism? What, more concretely, is meant by the economic surplus? Finally, why do they think that stagnation of the economic order is the expected outcome under the conditions they believe to exist? Each of these will be examined in turn.

The General Orientation of Baran and Sweezy

Paul Sweezy notes, in a preface to *Monopoly Capital* (in the second printing of a Greek translation), that he and Paul Baran "take the labor theory of value for granted and go on from there."[50] Since this position was not explicitly pointed out previously, there had been substantial misunderstanding on this point, though it is not obvious the labor theory of value is relevant to the type of analysis Baran and Sweezy use. Sweezy suggests that a better beginning to the book would have been to present "an exposition of the theory of value as it is presented in Volume 1 of *Capital*" and modify Marx's work by showing how "values as determined by socially necessary labor time . . . are transformed into prices of production, as Marx recognized in Volume 3; and . . . values (or prices of production) are transformed into monopoly prices in the monopoly stage of capitalism . . ."[51]

The central theme contained in *Monopoly Capital* which is used to organize the discussion of the economic and social order is "the generation and absorption of the surplus under conditions of monopoly capitalism."[52] Two points of clarification are necessary here to understand what Baran and Sweezy are saying to determine whether or not it makes sense.

First, the term "monopoly" is not used in the strict neo-Classical sense of being "a single seller of a commodity for which there are no substitutes." The term is intended to include the situation in which a few sellers dominate the markets for products which are generally considered to be substitutes for one another. In conventional economics the term in oligopoly.[53]

To describe the economic structure of the U.S. as one characterized by monopoly capital—accepting the Baran and Sweezy definition—is not an outrageous claim. What they say on this point is not inconsistent with the work of many others and deserves to be quoted at length:

> We must recognize that competition, which was the predominant form of market relations in nineteenth-century Britain, has ceased to occupy that position, not only in Britain but everywhere else in the capitalist world. Today the typical economic unit in the capitalist world is not the small firm producing a negligible fraction of a homogenous output for an anonymous market but a large-scale enterprise producing a significant share of the output of an industry, or even several industries, and able to control its prices, the volume of its production, and the types and amounts of its investments. The typical economic unit, in other words, has the attributes which were once thought to be possessed only by monopolists.[54]

The Characteristics of Monopoly Capitalism

Large scale business enterprise, monopoly capital, is thought by Baran and Sweezy to be at the center of the economic system in terms of influence because of corporate size, wealth, and power. Moreover, this position held by corporations, in their view, is one which is becoming increasingly prevalent. They note some of the key features of the contemporary corporation which make up monopoly capital:

> (1) Control rests in the hands of management, that is to say, the board of directors plus the chief executive officers. . . .
> (2) Management is a self-perpetuating group. . . . Each generation of managers recruits its own successors and trains, grooms, and promotes them according to its own standards and values. . . .
> (3) Each corporation aims at and normally achieves financial independence through the internal generation of funds which remain at the disposal of management. . . .[55]

It is important to point out that these features are included in a chapter entitled "The Giant Corporation." Another implicit feature, presumably, is that the corporation is large-scale in terms of assets, sales, and the number of people it employs.

In short, then, the corporations which make up the system of monopoly capitalism are "huge, management-controlled, [and] financially independent."[56] In addition, "great wealth, or family connections, or large personal or family stockholdings" are "tickets of admission to the inside,"[57] as C. Wright Mills observed earlier.[58] The corporation is part of "an ordered system which selects and rewards according to well-understood criteria."[59] What exists is a system comprised of corporations which are devoid of soul; institutions in the quest of accumulation, granted immortality under law, and given the rights of individuals under court interpretations of the Fourteenth Amendment to the Constitution of the U.S., and united in common goals and interests. The modern corporation, then, is described as the center of an entire *system*—monopoly capitalism.

It is pointed out, however, that this system is unplanned as an entity—a situation very different from that within the corporation where "relations are direct, hierarchical, bureaucratic."[60] Yet while there is no planning for the system as a whole there is an emphasis on maintaining general stability as an aftermath to the huge social trauma of the 1930s. It is a state responsibility not only to keep the whole economic system going but to attempt to strengthen and regularize its operations. The state under monopoly capitalism is rather "the tail that wags the dog," an engine of growth, or, to use Baran and Sweezy terminology, an aid in the maintenance of economic surplus, both in keeping production costs down (through various means, including underwriting the advance of technology) and in keeping production up. The authors present this theory:

> If we provisionally equate aggregate profits with society's economic surplus, we can formulate as a law of monopoly capitalism that the surplus tends to rise both absolutely and relatively as the system develops.[61]

Baran and Sweezy point out that their law of rising surplus is in direct contradiction with Marx's law of a tendency toward a falling rate of profit. They argue that the basis of this contradiction is that the structure of the economy in 20th-century America is quite different from that in 19th-century England. Their analysis, in addition, suggests that a situation of a rising surplus is not necessarily one which can go on indefinitely.

This position on profits does not agree, however, with that advanced by some other Marxian economists and the reason for this seems fairly clear.

> The theory of the reversal of the tendency towards declining profits after the first world war into an apparent tendency to increasing profit has been developed at length by the American Marxist economist Joseph Gillman. And the same author has also highlighted the tremendous increase in sales costs since the appearance of monopoly capitalism, although he draws from it quite another conclusion than Sweezy and Baran (for Gillman, in brief, unproductive expenses such as sales effort at home and

abroad are indispensable for the realization of surplus value, are to be deducted from surplus value to determine "net profit" and thereby, the decline of the rate of net profit continues to be valid).[62]

The Concept of the Economic Surplus

The Baran and Sweezy definition of "economic surplus" needs to be spelled out. For this one must refer to an earlier work of Paul Baran, since the definition in *Monopoly Capital* is quite brief and, unfortunately, is not used consistently, which has been the source of a great deal of controversy. The definition suggested early on in the book is "the difference between what a society produces and the costs of producing it."[63]

Baran's *The Political Economy of Growth* attempts to lay down the concept of economic surplus, a task which he admits is "somewhat tricky," but is defended on the grounds that "it would certainly seem desirable to break with [the] time-honored tradition [in] academic economics of sacrificing the relevance of subject matter to the elegance of analytical method; it is better to deal imperfectly with what is important than to attain virtuoso skill in the treatment of what does not matter."[64] Baran deals with anticipated criticism by ending the chapter with the statement that the "tools" he devises are primitive.

Baran invents "three variants of the concept of economic surplus." First, there is *actual* economic surplus which is defined as "the difference between society's *actual* current output and its *actual* current consumption." He adds, "It is thus identical with current saving or accumulation . . . ."[65] Further, he takes this to be a smaller share of total output than what Marx termed "surplus value" which, Baran recalls, "consists of the entire difference between aggregate net output and the real income of labor."[66] He takes the actual economic surplus to be only that part of surplus value which is being accumulated and does not include "the consumption of the capitalist class, the government's spending on administration, military establishment, and the like."[67] It would seem that this variant is the most important one of the concept of economic surplus in terms of understanding *Monopoly Capital.*

The second variant of economic surplus is *potential* economic surplus which, briefly, is "the difference between the output that *could* be produced in a given natural and technological environment with the help of employable productive resources, and what might be regarded as essential consumption."[68] Baran goes into great detail on this variant and develops subcategories. It is not essential to pursue it here. This variant relates more to what the surplus could be under a smoothly running capitalist system.[69]

The third variant of economic surplus developed in Baran's *The Political Economy of Growth* is *planned* economic surplus. This would be of interest, aside from intellectual curiosity, to those in a society where national and other levels of economic planning were consciously undertaken. Baran defines it as "the difference between society's 'optimum' output attainable in a historically given natural and technological environment under conditions of planned 'optimal' utilization of all available productive resources, and some chosen 'optimal' volume of consumption." Baran notes that the meaning of 'optimum' should be considered to be different from that in conventional economics. He says:

> The meaning and contents of the "optimum" involved are essentially different from those attached to this notion in bourgeois economics. They do not reflect a configuration of production and consumption determined by profit considerations of individual firms, by the income distribution, tastes, and social pressures of a capitalist order; they represent a considered judgment of a socialist community guided by reason and science. Thus as far as resource utilization is concerned, it implies a far-reaching rationalization of society's productive apparatus (liquidation of inefficient units of production, maximal economies of scale, etc.), elimination of redundant product differentiation, abolition of unproductive labor (as previously defined), a scientific policy of conservation of human and natural resources, and the like.[70]

Baran and Sweezy use only the first variant of economic surplus in *Monopoly Capital* which is understandable since this book is a work in political economics which attempts to provide a framework for analyzing the society as it is. In their words:

> The economic surplus, in the briefest possible definition, is the difference between what a society produces and the costs of producing it. The size of the surplus is an index of productivity and wealth, of how much freedom a society has to accomplish whatever goals it may set for itself. The composition of the surplus shows how it uses that freedom: how much it invests in expanding its productive capacity, how much it consumes in various forms, how much it wastes and in what ways. . . .[71]

This use of the concept, obviously, is different from the notion of surplus value as created by Marx (which is the sum of profits, interest, rent, and other less easily identifiable items) because, Baran and Sweezy argue, under monopoly capitalism the matter is more complex than in Marx's day. "The surplus assumes many forms and disguises." Their purpose, they say, is to move beyond Marx's notion of economic surplus and shift the theoretical position to identify the more important existing forms of the economic surplus in present day society.[72]

Joseph D. Phillips compiled a statistical appendix entitled "Estimating the Economic Surplus" for inclusion in *Monopoly Capital*.[73] In this appendix, it is estimated that the economic surplus rose from 46.9 percent of GNP in 1929 to 56.1 percent in 1963 (declining during the early years of the Great Depression and rising sharply during WW II). The portion ordinarily identified with surplus value (profits, interest, and rent) declined greatly during the same period as a percentage of GNP and as a percentage of the total economic surplus. This suggests, Baran and Sweezy say, that "not only the forces determining the total amount of the surplus need to be analyzed but also those governing its differentiation and the varying rates of growth of the components."[74]

A look at the statistical appendix helps to establish a clearer grasp of what is meant by the concept. An attempt is made to break out those parts of GNP which compose the economic surplus. The major components presented by Phillips are (1) property income (income of unincorporated enterprises, excessive depreciation charges, and rent, interest, and other property income), (2) waste in the business process (much of advertising, market research, public relations, etc.), (3) "surplus absorption by government" or all government expenditures, and (4) "penetration of the productive process by the sales effort" (e.g., "the expenses of changing models of automobiles and other durable consumer goods when no fundamental change in quality of usefulness is involved. . . .").[75]

The appendix is introduced with a series of caveats—the base data are flawed (their main source is the U.S. Department of Commerce national income accounts); data are not available or are more difficult to arrange to fit the concept of the economic surplus; value judgments are involved in deciding what is surplus and what is not (what is productive labor and what is not). Though crude, the data presented show that surplus as a percent of GNP has been steadily on the rise since 1929 beginning with 46.9 percent in 1929 and increasing to 56.1 percent in 1963. The war years, 1944, 1945, and into 1946, stand apart from the rate of increase in that surplus as a percent of GNP was very high in those years (71.6 percent in 1944).[76] But what is proved? It is shown that economic activity in the areas of finance, insurance, real estate, advertising, changes in style, "waste" of various kinds, government, and so on are increasing as a percent of GNP, and profit is holding its own (profit data is presented but not thoroughly analyzed by Baran, Sweezy, and Phillips). In retrospect, this omission is not surprising. In part, they are calling attention to what others have since noticed more pointedly—the industrial mix in the U.S. has been changing over time and there has been an increasing percentage of employment in the services and other nonindustrial areas. In addition, a substantial expansion in government as a share of GNP has been a notable feature in this century.

The economic order is seen as one which is dominated by a huge business organization under which the difference between what a society produces and the costs of that production tend to become greater over time. There is a tendency for the surplus to rise. The consequence is, then, an inherent tendency toward depression and stagnation as the channels for surplus absorption become glutted.

A paraphrase of Baran and Sweezy's position on the relationship between the rise of huge corporations and chronic depressions is worth quoting at length:

> The giant corporations charged higher prices and received larger profits than their predecessors. The monopoly power associated with these firms enabled their owners to capture an increasing *share* of corporate income at the expense of workers. As the corporate sector became increasingly dominated by these giants, it increased the tendency for the income of capitalists to grow more rapidly than the wages of workers. This worsening distribution of income created an increasing imbalance between investment expenditures and consumption expenditures. In the short run, owners had a profit incentive to increase investment and thereby enlarge the capital stock. The larger capital stock produced more consumption goods, but the demand for consumption goods did not grow commensurately because wages did not grow as fast as profits. Goods piled up as oligopolistic practices made prices sticky in a downward direction, and this surplus of goods, in turn, reduced investment expenditures. Thus, deficient aggregate demand, which led to depression and stagnation became a natural state of affairs in an economy dominated by monopoly capital.[77]

The theoretical position of Baran and Sweezy is that the economic system of the U.S. is one which is rational at the microeconomic level from the perspective of those who own the means of production, but as a whole it is irrational. It is a system which requires government intervention on a huge scale to keep it functioning and this intervention, they argue, is in spheres which do not threaten or actually enhance the position of those who are owners of capital. Militarism and imperialism are used to protect capital and at the same time provide expenditures necessary to keep the surplus rising. The dynamics are such that an attempt is made to "contain, compress, and eventually destroy the rival socialist system."[78]

Aside from being a system which produces international conflict, domestic irrationality, and manipulation of the population of the society, another main offset to the surplus is the "sales effort" (on advertising, the variance of products' appearance and packaging, model changes, planned obsolescence, credit schemes, and so on).

Baran and Sweezy see a *tendency* toward stagnation under capitalism, the irrational use of resources, and the manipulation of the people of the world. They argue that these tendencies produce opposition and that the drama of our time is world revolution. It is here that *Monopoly Capital* moves from an analysis of the domestic situation to a commentary on global conflicts and their subtitle of *An Essay on the American Economic and Social Order* becomes clearly appropriate. A quotation from the last page of the book gives an intriguing example of the conclusion to which their model is taken:

> As the world revolution spreads and as the socialist countries show by their example that it is possible to use man's mastery over the forces of nature to build a rational society satisfying the human needs of human beings, more and more Americans are bound to question the necessity of what they now take for granted. And once that happens on a mass scale, the most powerful supports of the present irrational system will crumble and the problem of creating anew will impose itself as a sheer necessity. This will not happen in five years or ten, perhaps not in the present century: few great historical dramas run their course in so short a time. But perhaps even fewer, once they are fairly started, change their nature or reverse their direction until all their potentialities have been revealed. The drama of our time is the world revolution; it can never come to an end until it has encompassed the whole world.[79]

A Critique of Monopoly Capital

Now criticism from a variety of circles must be acknowledged. Raymond Lubitz takes *Monopoly Capital* apart both conceptually and methodologically. Lubitz sees the book as a major intellectual force but concludes that if a solid Marxian analysis of the contemporary American economy is possible, it is not this book. Among his most serious charges are that the concept of the surplus is used in different ways at different times and the meaning of it is never clearly defined. Lubitz observes that the term *surplus* is useful if one wants to argue that exploitation is a feature of the system and that it is not obvious that those who get the surplus have a clear-cut right to it. Thus, he argues, it would not be enough to point to the empirical fact of an unequal distribution of income and wealth.[80]

Lubitz sees the work of Baran and Sweezy as a kind of Keynesian/ Marxian meld which stresses the supposed inherent stagnation of the economy. This view was argued in Keynesian terms in the 1930s (by Alvin Hansen and others) and therefore needs no Marxian component to make this point. So, he charges Baran and Sweezy with being unoriginal. But the more serious criticism is that the income and product sides of the national income accounts are mixed together. Since national income is equal, by definition, to national product, one could measure surplus using either. But what Phillips does is add property *income* (including aggregate profits) to various *expenditures* such as those by government, and that undertaken in various forms of "waste" in an attempt to estimate the surplus. Lubitz has serious doubts about this approach though he notes possible defenses with which Baran and Sweezy might counter his argument.[81]

Lubitz has agreement on the issue that some of the wrong things have been added up to arrive at economic surplus. Ernest Mandel says

> one should subtract, not add, depreciation allowances from gross receipts in order to establish corporate "surplus." And this calculation strongly reduces Phillips' statistical demonstration of the "tendency of the surplus to rise."[82]

Mandel, like most critics, is skeptical of the loose way in which Baran and Sweezy use the term Baran invented to analyze the economic system and suggests that they are using the concept much as it is used by anthropologists and students of primitive societies in a most rudimentary way: "that part of social production which exceeds the immediate consumption needs of society."[83]

Ron Stanfield also observes this fundamental error in *Monopoly Capital* where property incomes and "nonessential output" are *added*. "The confusion and intermingling of the two sides of the national accounts is traceable to their desire to have the surplus represent two different magnitudes, unearned incomes and nonessential output."[84]

In sum, then, it would seem that the estimate of surplus in *Monopoly Capital* should be taken with a grain of salt in that it is a quite confused construct.

Lubitz believes that Baran and Sweezy's concept of the surplus is not legitimate but notes that they argue that the "surplus has a 'strong and systematic tendency' to rise." This idea implies that labor's share of total income is declining, but Baran and Sweezy do not prove that this has been the case. Lubitz argues that the reverse has been true, that "profits do not claim the lion's share of productivity's increase; in fact its share is falling." Yet, in a footnote Lubitz notes that "the structure of property income has changed, corporate profits rising, and other forms of property income falling, as proportions of total property income." The corporate profits share of national income has been shown to be greater than levels in the 19th century but constant since 1929. Lubitz ends up concluding that Baran and Sweezy are engaged in "an old vulgar-Marxist game" to "prove tendencies" that are not observable using selected periods of economic history. At best, he argues, the book puts the Keynesian stagnation thesis in Marxian terminology substituting "surplus" for "saving" but fails in making the case that corporations accumulate more than they can spend in alternative ways.[85]

Various commentaries on *Monopoly Capital* which were written for a symposium were published in the journal *Science and Society* not long after the publication of the book. Here the argument that Baran and Sweezy were reviving the stagnation thesis introduced by Alvin Hansen in the 1930s can be seen once again. But beyond this opinion, it is also argued that the model in *Monopoly Capital* does not adequately analyze some phenomena. An important example is that of innovations which, Sharpe argues, can be seen as much a part of capitalism as stagnation. In addition, government is an important institution that is considered by Baran and Sweezy to be somewhat exogenous to their model. Also, Sharpe argues, to see capitalism as inherently prone to stagnation is to ignore periods of prosperity. But Sharpe ends up proclaiming that

> economists will recognize *Monopoly Capital* as a landmark in the development of the stagnation thesis by two of the most distinguished economic critics of our time and will expect a book of this stature to occupy an important place in the history of political economy.[86]

A second member of the symposium notes that there are problems with the use of "monopoly capitalism" which, he claims, probably has its origins in Lenin's *Imperialism*. Although this term may be a catchy one for polemical purposes, it is too general for precise usage in scientific analysis. And Baran and Sweezy themselves do not define monopoly capital more than to say that it is a system consisting of giant corporations.[87]

> It seems very unrealistic to apply a generalized pricing theory to a market structure which . . . is far from being a monopolistic

organism and defies generalization. It is not accident that, as Baran and Sweezy complain, there is very little literature about a monopolistic price *system* while there is a vast amount about the pricing of individual commodities and industries.[88]

Again, criticism of the concept of the economic surplus is to be found. The charge is that this is a very ambiguous formulation which obfuscates the issues more than it clarifies them.

> . . . there is no clarity as to what "economic surplus" actually is; no clarity as to which expenditures the authors believe *should* be financed out of surplus in existing capitalist society or in a society of the future and which expenditures actually *are* so financed; no clarity about what the authors mean by suggesting that expenditures for certain socially unjustifiable purposes, such as excessive advertising, waste in distribution and the military establishment are being financed—as the table in the Appendix also indicates for contemporary American society— out of surplus regardless of whether and how that surplus is being produced; no clarity as to whether surplus would actually have remained unabsorbed if these socially unjustifiable expenditures had not been made; no clarity as to what the repeated statement that "surplus that is not absorbed is also surplus that is not produced" is intended to mean.[89]

The criticisms of Baran and Sweezy's *Monopoly Capital* are formidable and might lead the reader to conclude that the book therefore merits little attention. This would be an error since it would be to ignore the more constructive dialogue which the book sparked and the useful ideas it contains.

David Horowitz is critical of the Baran and Sweezy model for many of the usual reasons: "the failure to articulate the surplus concept more completely [and] to break it down into its constituent components . . ." Another criticism, common to Marxian opinion on the book, is its failure "to make explicit a class analysis directly linked to the process of accumulation."[90] Horowitz points out that the authors were aware of the shallowness of a part of their argument and in fact have covered turf omitted in *Monopoly Capital* elsewhere.[91]

> Despite all criticisms of the model, however, as a model it still represents a theoretical breakthrough of major significance, worthy of the most serious attention of those concerned to understanding contemporary capitalism. The concept of the economic surplus, quite apart from the important and independent thesis advanced by the authors of its tendency to rise in monopoly capitalism, will be certain, as a result of this book, to gain recognition as an indispensable tool of social analysis. In the concept of the economic surplus, as the authors so brilliantly demonstrate, one can see the shape of the integrated so-

cialeconomic system, its dynamics and development . . . . The concept of the surplus allows one to make direct use of the Keynesian income analysis, the Marxian class analysis, and to see (without shifting frameworks) how the forces thus analyzed directly affect and are affected by the *utilization* of social resources determining the whole sociocultural environment.[92]

Elsewhere Horowitz says that Baran and Sweezy did open up possibilities for confusion in not being consistent in their use of the concept of the surplus and for treating it at times as roughly equal to aggregate profits, thereby abandoning the more refined and specific versions of the surplus as developed by Baran in *The Political Economy of Growth,* and using the concept mostly in its "Veblenesque" form (that is, concentrating on waste as a key irrationality of the system which was observed by Thorstein Veblen). Although Horowitz believes this to be a mistake, he also thinks that it was not a fundamental error "since it can be easily overcome by a suitable redefinition of the surplus and an abandonment of the attempt to get all of its features into a linear relationship with one another in a manner of Marx's use of the labor theory of value."[93]

Horowitz goes further and argues that *Monopoly Capital* provides the analytical framework to take an integrated look at the system, from waste in the allocation of resources to the problem of inadequate effective demand. And in so doing its framework—apparently the focus on the generation and absorption of surplus—is close enough to that of the orthodox economists—Keynesians in particular—to be able to distinguish the *real* differences between contemporary socialist analysis and bourgeois theory. In this way Marxists are prevented "from hiding behind the ritualistic invocation of their own orthodox terms and theorems as an excuse for not facing up to the real problems involved in developing a viable socialist theory." And at the same time, it becomes more difficult "for opponents to evade the challenge of the Marxian critique." Thus, Horowitz makes his case for a neo-Marxist theory along the lines conceived of by Baran and Sweezy.[94]

Actually, Baran and Sweezy do not specifically acknowledge the Keynesian influence attributed to them by Horowitz and others though they do compare in one place in the book (pp. 143–144) a part of the stagnation problem of contemporary capitalism to that labeled insufficient "effective demand" by Keynes in *The General Theory.* Rather, the authors of *Monopoly Capital* are very clear on their debt to the work of Michal Kalecki who they recognize (as does Joan Robinson) as having independently discovered the theoretical orientation contained in Keynes' great work. Kalecki, say Baran and

Sweezy, went beyond Keynes by "reintegrating micro and macro theories" and included centralization and concentration in industry in his analysis.[95]

Horowitz seems quite correct in his view that Veblen provided some important ideas for Baran and Sweezy. They cite Veblen a number of times and go so far as to see him as "the first economist to recognize and analyze many aspects of monopoly capitalism . . . ."[96]

Ernest Mandel sees *Monopoly Capital* as

> . . . an interesting and important book. It represents an attempt to explain the contemporary functioning of the capitalist system in the United States, with the Marxist tools of analysis. But it resolutely breaks with the stereotype repetition of the Hilferding-Lenin analysis which is, after all, more than half a century old, and tries to apply the tools in an independent way, to the reality of today.[97]

What is more, according to Mandel, Baran and Sweezy try to be holistic and relate the economic dynamics to the society and to key social problems such as racism, urban decay, mental illness, militarism, and imperialism. Even with these strengths a main difficulty is "the discussion of the problem of 'surplus' absorption and the political perspectives which the authors have drawn from their economic analysis."[98]

Mandel poses the Baran and Sweezy thesis in this way:

> At a certain stage of capital concentration there occurs a decisive change in the way the market operates. Under monopoly capitalism, the dominant corporations are so strong that they can practically suppress price competition and price cutting. But technological innovation continues at the same time, and the dominant corporations continue to respond to strong incentives for cutting production costs. Therefore, there comes into being a widening gap between production costs and selling prices, as a result of which the rate of profit tends to increase sharply. Or, to put it in the author's words: the economic surplus tends to grow constantly.[99]

The problem is that, as Mandel interprets the Baran and Sweezy view, the surplus must be disposed of in some way, outlets for surplus absorption are limited, and consumption by capitalists themselves is nowhere near the amount of surplus appropriated (and dividends as a percentage of corporate profits have, Baran and Sweezy say, been declining). Productive investment is made on the basis of the expectation of profit and with an already deficient aggregate demand (or surplus absorption) problem the result would be an even greater situation of excess capacity. If this is a prolonged state of affairs then new outlets for the surplus must be found. The three main ones pinpointed by Baran and Sweezy are the sales effort, an expansion of government in general as a proportion of total income and product, and growth in military outlays. Along with these comes the increasing irrationality of the system with "more and more people . . . busy producing more and more goods which are either useless or wasteful or outright harmful." And this activity requires that more people and resources be put into convincing members of the society that useless, wasteful, or harmful commodities should be purchased. The implications of this include more aggression abroad which in part serves to defend the investments and interests of large corporations. This tendency could lead to conflict on a world scale and nuclear disaster.[100]

It is possible that Mandel likes this aspect of Baran and Sweezy's argument because he "arrived in the beginning of the sixties at a series of conclusions part of which are similar to those which Sweezy and Baran draw . . . ."[101] But there are some ways in which Mandel's conceptual framwork differs. Mandel

> . . . stressed the appearance of two average rates of profit in the economy of monopoly capitalism: the average rate of *surplus profit* enjoyed by the monopolist corporations; the lower average rate with which the rest of the capitalist entrepreneurs had to be content. [He] drew the conclusion that administered prices and high surplus profit had cut loose the corporations from control by investment banks and made them financially autonomous, their main problem becoming one of disposal of surplus capital. [He] indicated that the main uses for this surplus capital were (1) investment in sales effort and service industries (which have the great advantage of enjoying a lower organic composition of capital), (2) increase in military expenditures and (3) foreign investments. Excess capacity and surplus capital without outlets seemed for [him] as for Sweezy and Baran the main contradictory features of monopoly capitalism.[102]

Mandel also says that it appears that the loose way in which Baran and Sweezy use the idea of the economic surplus results in their mixing together what he calls surplus capital *and* surplus product. To demonstrate that "the 'surplus' (and the rate of profit) has been constantly increasing since 1929" would require first that the two aspects of surplus be disentangled. Mandel argues that this point is not merely terminological but is important for analytical reasons, to get to the root of what he believes to be the main contradictions of capitalism.[103]

It is argued that

[i]n a market economy "surplus product" can be disposed of only through exchange; it assumes the physical form of commodities for which there are no customers. "Surplus capital," on the contrary, is potential purchasing power which, for the moment, finds nothing to buy. . . .

The real problem is a double one: to invest excess capital in such a way as not to further reduce the market for the existing monopolies which operate at less than their full capacity because of insufficient markets; to assure a constant level of capacity utilization for the existing industries, although the laws of motion of capital tend to depress this level of capacity.[104]

Mandel's analysis is that the problem of surplus capital has been dealt with by the growth of the military, service industries, and capital export. The second problem, surplus product, has been handled by the expansion of credit and a persistent inflation. Since the responses to the existence of the two surpluses are different ones they must be separated to avoid "the basic weakness of the Sweezy-Baran analysis."[105]

Still another problem that Mandel sees is the apparent assumption in Baran and Sweezy's book that monopoly capital is a rather monolithic entity which has control of both technological innovation and the avoidance, almost totally, of price competition. Both assumptions seem unwarranted if one takes the world market to be the sphere of involvement by American corporations. Indeed even the expansion of foreign firms into the U.S. in terms of the location of ownership of actual plant and equipment has occurred. Thus, a threat to the full use of productive capacity does exist and unemployment remains a vexing problem in spite of the various ways in which the surplus has been absorbed.[106]

. . . a *temporary* solution of the overproduction problem has been possible only through the erection of a colossal debt structure and of constant inflation. Eventually, this would tend to disorganize any capitalist economy—but it could take a very long time to do so—provided the U.S.A were insulated from the outside world.

But, of course, it is nothing of the kind. Inflation inside the U.S.A.—as a necessary prop against recurrent grave crises of overproduction—has worldwide consequences of which the international capitalist class and its economists are very well aware. The contradiction between the dollar as an instrument for antirecession policies on the U.S. market and the dollar as a means of payment of the world market, is rapidly reaching an explosion point. And the grave international monetary crisis which is in the making will have its consequences on the U.S. economy too.[107]

Mandel comes to conclude, then, that the stability of the economic system in the U.S. is being undermined in a fashion which monopoly capital is somewhat powerless to alter. Baran and Sweezy, on the other hand, see the main challenge to the system as that from the Third World to which some of the problems of capitalism, in their view, have been exported. Mandel sees the main contradiction being a domestic one rooted in the capitalist mode of production and the split between labor and capital.[108]

What all of this disagreement leads to is a heated discussion among Marxian theorists. One anomaly is the general attraction to, and a revulsion for, the integration of Keynesian features into the model. Taking the discussion to the macroeconomic level that this analysis requires relegates the very real condition of the work force to a secondary analysis that cannot be touched adequately using aggregative economics. Baran and Sweezy hoped to maintain a focus on the workers' plight by calling "surplus" the difference between necessary consumption and aggregate income but emerged pierced by serious methodological thorns. The problem has not been resolved and micro- and macroeconomics have not been effectively brought together. Perhaps they cannot be in a single model.

Still another problem that the work of Baran and Sweezy implicitly poses is the rather lethargic or even counterrevolutionary role often played by workers in the U.S. They do not make this claim but see the main strata for change being outside the rank and file of the domestic working class. The major opposition to capitalism becomes world socialist hegemony. This alleged lethargy of the U.S. working class is obviously depressing or thought to be wrong by others who are adherents to the thought of Marx, and the response has been rejoinders and even defensive attacks by the more dogmatic. On reflection, it seems difficult to provide a model which does everything for everyone, (indeed, this is not the function of a model) which intelligently depicts the macroeconomic situation while at the same time discusses exploitation and the response of workers. It would seem that Baran and Sweezy and their reviewers in the general zeal to be totally holistic came to expect too much. *Monopoly Capital* provides a model that works in the abstract but fails when it becomes specific. It is unusual to go so far as to offer a statistical appendix assigning quantitative estimates to a concept such as the surplus. Even Keynes was not so bold in presenting his general theory, and his failure to do so was not based in an absence of confidence in his stance.

Mandel, upon rethinking his position on the idea of the economic surplus, ended up deepening both his appreciation and also his criticism of *Monopoly Capital* and argues in favor of a more classical Marxian perspective emphasizing the labor theory of value to avoid mixing up levels of analysis. What Baran and Sweezy attempt to do is to combine (more implicitly than explicitly) a Marxian theory of value with a "Keynesian" theory of aggregate demand and, in Mandel's view, muddy the waters in the process.

> The main difficulty of *Monopoly Capital* . . . is the authors' failure to deal with the exploitation of labor by capital and their consequent omission of the capitalists' *need* to increase relative surplus value . . . By leaving out of their analysis of monopoly capital the continuous struggle of the capitalist class to maintain and increase the rate of exploitation of the working class, Baran and Sweezy put their whole economic concept of the present functioning of the capitalist system outside the realm of contending social forces, i.e., outside the realm of the class struggle. It is not surprising, therefore, that they end up denying any validity to the anticapitalist potential of the American working class. . . .[109]

Thus, Mandel (through a comparison of his various writings reveals that he is not fully consistent on this point) and the authors of *Monopoly Capital* come to have quite different views on the appropriate conceptual framework to use in analyzing contemporary capitalism. Mandel seems to hold an affinity for *both* the level of analysis that concentrates on the aggregates of surplus capital and surplus product and that concentrates on the more classical notion of surplus value. The latter takes the discussion away from circulation in the economy as a whole and toward the relationship between workers and capitalists. Perhaps this is not a contradiction. It is likely that both levels of analysis are useful, but to combine the two is to become involved in a maze of confusion such as that which runs through both *Monopoly Capital* and responses to it. Indeed, James F. Becker took Baran and Sweezy and Mandel to be saying essentially the same thing. Becker, in fact, raised the same objection to Mandel's analysis in *Marxist Economic Theory* that Mandel posed in his "The Labor Theory of Value and 'Monopoly Capitalism' " about *Monopoly Capital*. Becker concludes this about "monopoly theory" (which he attributes to Baran and Sweezy, Mandel, Joan Robinson, and Harry Magdoff):

> The theory of monopoly by itself cannot provide an adequate portrait of class structure and interrelations within the structure of social labor. Instead it directs our attention to the corporations and to their organization, to the mere agencies of control. For all of the insight provided by individual theorists, the monopoly theory does not tell us with whom we can and must work to bring the class struggle to a successful culmination.[110]

Becker argues that "the theories of monopoly, of competition, and employment—at least in their orthodox versions—can only be ancillaries to the Marxian political economy." This position is taken because, as a socialist, Becker has his sights on the longer view and wishes not to get involved in the short-run ups and downs of capitalism. And he believes that in moving to an analysis of aggregates the "monopoly theorists" have relegated the labor theory of value to a minimal and subsidiary role with the result being the comparative neglect of class analysis and the corresponding absence of a program for change.[111]

It may be that it is not the fault of a "wrong theory" so much as a political void aside from the established Democratic and Republican parties. The focus on exploitation does not seem, to many, to be the most convincing thesis on which to hinge one's argument; and as a matter of fact Becker is mistaken if he thinks that Mandel, for one, does not have at least a primitive theory of change which speculates on the response of workers in general to their material conditions. Let us turn briefly to a discussion of Mandel's view of the internal contradictions in present-day American capitalism.

One View of Change Sparked by Continuing Crisis

Mandel expresses the view that there are powerful forces which could lead to the decline of U.S. workers' support for capitalism since their allegiance, in his view, seems founded on a regularly increased standard of living.

> If one assumes that the dual forces of automation and inflation will introduce growing instability into the American economy, there is at least a reasonable assumption that this instability will eventually undermine the stability of the union bureaucracy and the relative quiescence of the workers. Active opposition to monopoly capitalism which is today largely confined to the Negro movement, the antiwar protest of the student youth, and relative militancy of certain lower-paid wage and salary earners, could readily blossom again into a powerful and unbeatable alliance around the industrial working class.[112]

It is clear that Mandel believes that the promise of a revolutionary overthrow of capitalism would be founded on the fundamental and prolonged instability of the economy and the inability of the state to contain the crisis. In fact, in a later article—which itself sparked a great deal of dialogue on the left—Mandel pointed to six specific forces, six historic contradictions, "which are now destroying the social equilibrium of the capitalist society and bourgeois order of the United States." [113]

First is the decline of unskilled labor and the social roots of black radicalization. The third industrial revolution—automation—has transformed American industry. This created unemployment during the 1950s with productivity rising more quickly than output. This unemployment, therefore, was of a structural nature. In ten years, unskilled labor was reduced radically, an event, according to Mandel, perhaps more revolutionary than any in all of capitalist history. The hardest hit by this in the U.S., of course, are black people. [114] This impact, together with the colonial revolution and emergence of independent states in Black Africa, as well as the war in Vietnam, led to a black revolt. When employment among black youth is at levels at least equivalent to that of the total population during the Great Depression, it is no wonder that unrest exists. This unrest is felt throughout the society and particularly in the inadequate schools. [115]

Second, social roots underlie the student revolt in America. The third industrial revolution has resulted in great upheavals whereby human labor has been expulsed from traditional industry and transferred to other social and economic activity. In Mandel's words,

> . . . [I]n the framework of the third industrial revolution, manual labour is expelled from production while intellectual labour is reintroduced into the productive process on a gigantic scale. It thereby becomes to an ever-increasing degree alienated labour—standardized, mechanized, and subjected to rigid rules and regimentation, in exactly the same way that manual labour was in the first and second industrial revolutions. This fact is very closely linked with one of the most spectacular recent developments in American society: the massive student revolt, or, more correctly, the growing radicalization of students. . . . We are confronted with a colossal transformation which upsets traditional relations between social groups, expelling human labour radically from certain fields of activity, but reintroducing it on a larger scale and at a higher level of qualification and skill in other fields. [116]

Twenty years ago "students were in general either future capitalists, self-employed or agents of capitalism . . . today this pattern is radically changed." With more than 8,000,000 college students (in 1973) it is probable there are not the traditional places for them upon graduation.

> Thus a great number of present-day students are not future capitalists at all, but future salary-earners, in teaching, public administration and at various technical levels in industry and the economy. Their status will be nearer that of the industrial worker than that of management. [117]

Both in Europe and in America there is the same "intense consciousness of alienation among students." The material position is far better among students in America than in Europe.

> Nevertheless, the consciousness of alienation resulting from the capitalist form of the university, from the bourgeois structure and function of higher education and the authoritarian administration of it, has become more and more widespread. It is a symptomatic reflection of the changed social position of the students today in society.[118]

Thus, the potential understanding of social alienation is more likely to push students into becoming anticapitalists than perhaps at any time in American history. A socialist consciousness is prevalent in radical student circles in America, then, just as it is in Europe.

The third force that Mandel points to is that automation has changed the hierarchical structure of the factory. Those in the lower-echelon of management deal with the organization of production while the real bosses discuss "future plans: plans for replacing the existing machinery, plans for financing that replacement, new fields and locations for investment, and so on." The result has been a new process of amalgamation whereby there has been a move toward bringing together previously unrelated companies. A financial empire, worldwide in impact, has come about. Tremendous *power* wielded from above can be invoked. This power, when implemented, creates a contradiction in that the managers of plants, who are comparatively highly educated, are coming to view this power as arbitrary and contrary to the interests of people. Thus, the hierarchical and authoritarian structure, needed by those who hold the power, goes against the local managements' need for cooperation.[119]

A fourth force is that real wages have been eroded by inflation. With the increased rate of growth and declining structural unemployment associated with the economic policies of the Kennedy and Johnson years, there was also an increased rate of inflation. This change is attributed to the growth of the military establishment and the growing private indebtedness of the American society. The result has been the reversal of a trend that existed for 35 years; in 1966 real income among workers began declining. This reversal largely accounts for the dissatisfaction shown for the American Establishment and the support for George Wallace in the 1968 presidential election. Mandel expected this contradiction to be further exacerbated under Nixon's economic policies based on the view that the dollar should be protected at all costs.[120]

A fifth contradiction is one similar to that pointed out by Galbraith in *The Affluent Society* a number of years ago—"public squalor" beside "private affluence." The result of this neglect of the public sector is fiscally troubled and decaying cities, and even financially pinched governments outside of central cities. At the same time the number of public employees continues to grow. The result is that

> [p]ublic employees, who in the past were outside the trade-union movement and indeed any form of organized social activity, are today becoming radicalized at least at the union level. They are organizing, they are agitating, and they are demanding incomes at least similar to those which they could get in private industry. . . .[121]

Further, this radicalization is reinforced by the movement of university students into public administration after graduation. Many of the most radical go into the public sector because they have rejected the other alternatives.[122]

The last contradiction that Mandel discusses is the impact of foreign competition and the assault this impact could have on the real wages of U.S. workers. Essentially, he sees the U.S. losing its "productive monopoly" in the world market. The U.S. export of technology has resulted in European and Japanese productivity approaching that of the U.S. With lower real wages elsewhere than in the U.S., economic consequences will result; U.S. workers' wages are subject to further attack. Further, Mandel argues that since it is the level of wages which brings support for the system, the basis of that support is losing ground.[123]

All of the forces, argues Mandel, lead him to believe that instability is the future of American society. This instability will push a part of the population to seek change.

Monopoly Capitalism, Instability, and the Strata for Change

Mandel is quite specific on the issue of change.

> As long as socialism or revolution are only ideals preached by militants because of their own convictions and consciousness, their social impact is inevitably limited. But when the ideas of revolutionary socialism are able to unite faith, confidence, and consciousness with the immediate material interest of a social class in revolt—the working class—then their potential becomes literally explosive. In that sense, the political radicalization of the working class, and therewith socialism, will become a practical proposition in the United States within the next 10 or 15 years, under the combined impact of all these forces which have been examined here. After the black workers, the young workers, the students, the technicians and the public employees, the mass

of American workers will put the struggle for socialism on the immediate historical agenda in the United States. The road to revolution will then be open.[124]

To Mandel's scenario for change it is easy to retort, "perhaps," especially with respect to his timetable for change. He obviously sees things quite differently from Baran and Sweezy and other American Marxian scholars who show more of a skepticism about the view that a main threat to capitalist hegemony will come from a revolutionary population in the U.S. Yet perhaps it would be more accurate to say that others have been much more reserved about predicting anything at all. In fairness to the Baran and Sweezy trust in the longer view and an increasing socialist solidarity on a world scale, it must be remembered that the genesis of *Monopoly Capital,* really, was the 1950s. In such a bland and depressing era it should come as no surprise that the simple Marxist faith in the industrial proletariat or any other potentially revolutionary strata would be left out of any believable analysis that was in touch with the pulse of the whole nation. In a sense this comparative absence of speculation about the role of U.S. workers with respect to social change is a strength of *Monopoly Capital.* A Marxian analysis that worked in the abstract was presented that became a central part of a literature to be noticed by those uninitiated to radical thought. Many people in the U.S. came to be aware, albeit too slowly and often because of the threat of their own military conscription, of their country's ghoulish involvement in the affairs of other nations. The first wave of response to the shattering myth of the American Dream was that of a profound alienation. But the sense of being exploited in the classical Marxian sense was generally absent and was an issue only to those active in sectarian leftist groups.

Thus, perhaps it is best left to a Belgian Marxian economist, rather than to Baran and Sweezy or other American writers, to offer a commentary on a plausible response to economic conditions by the working people—which is most of us—in the United States. In honesty it must be admitted that most people here, Marxians and others, do not really know where America is going. The country seems often to be a huge amalgam which resists deciphering. The old order appears to be breaking down, but a new sense of direction to which many can relate simply does not exist. Indeed, the flirtation with a revolutionary practice which occurred sometimes in the late 1960s seems in the early 1970s to have been undertaken only randomly. For many, the approach is to do nothing, which may be more attractive than to become politically involved where it seems futile or unwise (which, unfortunately, can often only be determined in retrospect).

The Marxian views presented in this chapter show a remarkable disenchantment with American society. Yet, it is likely that the problems in the political economy and society will not disappear because they are founded on a structure containing generic contradictions. Various methods have been used by the state to contain these contradictions but these methods themselves have become a part of the problem. The answer to these contradictions is socialism.

It is apparent that others have noticed the existence of the centralization and concentration of capital but have not reached the conclusions shared by a number of Marxian social scientists. John Kenneth Galbraith is a prominent economist who is well known for his work in this vein. It will be useful to discuss his view of the structure of the economy at this point to provide a comparative view.

John Kenneth Galbraith and the U.S. Corporate Nexus

Galbraith's *The New Industrial State* appeared shortly after the publication of Baran and Sweezy's *Monopoly Capital* and garnered a great deal of attention. It is an important book on the American corporation more for the reason that it caught on than for a penetrating analysis of the place of the corporation in American society. At its core, it is an ideological tract containing contradictions and is generally supportive of the system. It appeals to those within the corporate nexus to be responsive to the public interest in collaboration with the "educated." Like *Monopoly Capital,* but more so, this particular work is a *partial* analysis looking not at all major components of the system as a whole but only at huge business enterprises. In fact, Galbraith penned a book which supersedes *The New Industrial State,* in which he presents an elaboration of the central ideas about the corporation, a discussion of the "market sector," and changes that *should* be undertaken by government to produce a more harmonious economic system.[125] To the last of these we return in the next chapter.

Here, it is important to grasp the view of Galbraith since he may be capitalism's "next Keynes." What he suggests for government policy flows from his view of what is, which is seriously flawed and utopian.

In *The New Industrial State* (which hereafter will be abbreviated as *NIS* where convenient), in fact, Galbraith compares his approach with that of Keynes. The latter wrote his great work using A. C. Pigou's writings "as a point of departure for disagreement" because "it was the most distinguished exposition of the point of view."[126] Galbraith similarly used the works of Robert Dorfman and Paul Samuelson.[127]

Although Galbraith sees concentration in industry as very evident, he does not see it as threatening for world conflict and domestic economic, social, and political crisis, as do Baran and Sweezy. In fact, he sees a new locus of power emerging, that of "organized intelligence" or the "technostructure" which he defines as being "all who participate in group decision-making or the organization which they form."[128] In addition, he argues that the university is as important to the industrial system as the financier was earlier in the century. He sees capital becoming less powerful.

Rather than world revolution, Galbraith thinks that a convergence of economic systems is occurring, particularly the United States and the Soviet Union. He apparently believes that today's problems, such as poverty, alienation, racial strife, and imperialistic goals in foreign lands (to the extent that he even perceives their existence), are slowly fading away as a powerful group in addition to the technostructure, "the educational and scientific estate," (to use his terms) exercise their new found power.[129]

Galbraith does not see opposition to the dominance of large industry coming from government.

> Only the innocent reformer and the obtuse conservative imagine the state to be an instrument of change apart from the interests of those who comprise it . . . . [T]he line between the industrial system and the state becomes increasingly artificial and indistinct. The technostructure of the large corporation tends to become an extension of those parts of the Federal bureaucracy—notably the armed services, NASA, AEC and other agencies concerned with technological development—on which it most depends. It identifies itself with the purposes of the agency and adopts these to its needs.[130]

Galbraith leaves it to the "college and university community . . . [to] retain paramount authority for the research it undertakes. The needs of the industrial system must always be secondary to the cultivation of general understanding and perception."[131]

Like Baran and Sweezy, Galbraith does not believe in the notion of "consumer sovereignty" which suggests that "all power lies with the consumer" and that there is a "unidirectional flow of instruction from consumer to market to producer."[132] Galbraith refers to this notion, one which he believes to be widespread among economists, as "the Accepted Sequence." He sums it up this way:

> It follows that the accepted sequence is no longer a description of the reality and is becoming less so. Instead the producing firm reaches forward to control its markets and on beyond to manage the market behavior and shape the social attitudes of those, ostensibly, that it serves. For this we also need a name and it may appropriately be called The Revised Sequence.[133]

Galbraith's description of the nature of the industrial system is at first seductive, particularly Chapter 7, which describes the corporation:

> Nothing so characterized the industrial system as the scale of the modern corporate enterprise. In 1962 the five largest industrial corporations in the United States, with combined assets in excess of $36 billion, possessed over 12 percent of all assets used in manufacturing. The fifty largest corporations had over a third of all manufacturing assets. The 500 largest had well over two-thirds. Corporations with assets in excess of $10,000,000, some 2,000 in all, accounted for about 80 percent of all the resources used in manufacturing in the United States. In the mid nineteen-fifties, 28 corporations provided approximately 10 percent of all employment in manufacturing, mining, and retail and wholesale trade.[134]

In terms of sales, it is stated that "The five hundred largest corporations produce close to half of all the goods and services that are available annually in the United States."[135]

What is depicted by the book is a shallow view—a bit of description and some new terminology but little analysis and no core theoretical framework which is clearly stated. Perhaps this is why the book made such a hit. It appears to be profound because it is generally well written and clever and avoids strong criticism of the existing institutions and especially avoids predicting a new social order through a revolutionary segment of the population. In place of prediction, in fact, stands hope.

The New Industrial State is a book about the institutional makeup of the U.S. economy which is controversial only in that it strikes out without the use of neo-Classical economics, reveals a justifiable skepticism about orthodox economics, and focuses not so much on markets but rather on corporations as a force in the economy as a whole. Oligopoly is put in the forefront of the discussion, but what is emphasized is that the productive system is efficient and capable of producing goods of such a great number that it is necessary to create and manipulate demand for them. In a country where the dominant ideology dictates that planning is evil, planning is embraced, at the corporate level particularly, but also in the regulation of demand, as a rational tool. Galbraith offers two main theoretical positions beyond description (where, characteristically and unfortunately, the source of information is rarely presented). One is his theory of motivation for those who work in the new industrial state and the other is his theory of checks on the power of the industrial machinery. They seem at times to be contradictory positions.

The theory of motivation contained in the book is presented primarily in Chapters 12 and 13. In Chapter 12 Galbraith begins with the assumption that power has passed from "capital . . . , in recent times, to the composite of knowledge and skills which comprises the technostructure."[136] The motivation of the technostructure has also gone beyond that of a purely pecuniary nature or compulsion—which he associates with land-based cultures—and has become based on identification with the corporation which requires adaptation.

> A decent respect for reality requires that we recognize that men [sic] serve organizations in response to a complex system of motivations. The mixture will be different in different cases. In the entrepreneurial corporation, in which those in charge have a primary concern for income, pecuniary motivation may be strong throughout the enterprise. In the mature corporation, identification and adaptation may be much more important and this is especially probable if it has strong scientific and technical orientation. And in the mature corporation the motivation will be very different for different levels or kinds of participants.[137]

In Chapter 13 identification is defined as "the voluntary exchange of one's goals for the preferable ones of organization." Adaptation is taken to mean "the association with organization in the hope of influencing its goals to accord more closely with one's own." But Galbraith adds that these motivating factors are obscured because at top management levels there are handsome pecuniary rewards.[138] Corporate executives are seen as organization-minded people working harmoniously together for the good of both the corporation and themselves. In the next chapter, 14, after the invention of "the principle of consistency," executives are depicted as working for the shared goals of society. Conflict is not a part of Galbraith's thinking in this instance. One gets the impression that the new industrial state is inherently quite harmonious. Indeed, in this chapter Galbraith asserts that the place of the technostructure has been strengthened *because* the corporation has a social purpose which is the result of its members' adaptation.

In fairness, it must be said that Galbraith implies that he is thinking of the social purpose as *perceived* by members of the technostructure. For example he notes that the corporation which is engaged in the manufacture of

> a better trigger for a nuclear warhead, attracts the loyalty of its members because their organization is seen to be serving importantly the cause of freedom. It is felt no doubt that human beings, whose elimination these weapons promise, have an inherent tendency to abuse freedom. . . . Much of what is believed to be socially important is, in fact, the adaptation of social attitudes to the goal system of the technostructure. What counts here is what is believed. These social goals, though in fact derived from the

goals of the technostructure, are believed to have original social purpose. Accordingly, members of the corporation in general, and of the technostructure in particular, are able to identify themselves with the corporation on the assumption that it is serving social goals when, in fact, it is serving their own.[139]

Galbraith tends to obscure his position in this chapter and seems hesitant to be controversial. Thus, he *hints* that a greater and greater output of commodities over time may not be at all consistent with the social purpose, such as in this sentence: "What is called a high standard of living consists, in considerable measure, in arrangements for avoiding muscular energy, increasing sensual pleasure and for enhancing caloric intake above any conceivable nutritional requirement. Nontheless, the belief that increased production is a worthy social goal is very nearly absolute."[140] To question this, it is implied, is to be a voice unheard. At the same time "[s]ociety also has goals, stemming from the needs which are unassociated with its major productive mechanism, and which it imposes on the mature corporation. . . . The mature corporation imposes social attitudes as it also responds to social attitudes."[141]

Galbraith reveals his awareness of ideology in economic thought, except for his own. One place he writes "economics, as it is conventionally taught, is in part a system of belief designed less to reveal truth than to reassure its communicants about established social arrangements. . . . Modern economic belief can be understood only as the servant, in substantial measure, of the society which nurtures it."[142] This serves as a foreword to his view of the conventional wisdom as applied to price theory. Quoting Robert Dorfman and Paul Samuelson—who present oligopoly as a very bad form of industrial structure in terms of efficiency, prices, and output—Galbraith observes that this microeconomic observation cannot be reconciled with what is known about macroeconomic performance.

> To the person who insists on asking how this contradiction is resolved, the answer is that it is not. The theory of price-making under oligopoly leads to conclusions that cannot be reconciled with the results on which the theorists themselves agree.[143]

Galbraith argues that the contradiction exists because orthodox price theory does not view prices "in the full context of industrial planning and in full service to the goals of the technostructure."[144] The nature of the system is that prices are controlled and output is planned due to modern technology and a need for the minimization of losses to assure the survival of the corporation and the activities of the technostructure. The main constraints are, in Galbraith's view, that prices must be low enough to attract an adequate number of buyers to expand sales; and at the same time, prices must be high enough to finance growth and keep the stockholders happy. This set of goals, then, "explains" why the performance of a concentrated economy has been "satisfactory." The economy and society are perceived as being under the benevolent wing of the technostructure which seeks corporate survival and the fulfillment of its own goals. These are a meld of corporate goals personified by the technostructure and the goals of society. "It follows that the antitrust laws, in seeking to preserve the market, are an anachronism in the larger world of industrial planning."[145] Therefore, it should be no surprise that these laws continue to exist without being zealously enforced. They are not in tune with economic and social reality.

An important part of the system that Galbraith describes is a network of producers who are oligopolists in the regulation of aggregate demand in the style associated with the Keynesian "Revolution." But this turns out to be planning of a malevolent nature:

> If a large public sector of the economy, supported by personal and corporate income taxation, is the fulcrum for the regulation of demand, plainly military expenditures are the pivot on which the fulcrum rests. Additionally they provide underwriting for advanced technology and, therewith, security for the planning of the industrial system in areas that would otherwise be excluded by cost and risk.[146]

Furthermore, the *NIS* takes the position that economists, such as Samuelson, who believe that Keynesian policy could as easily be of a social welfare as of a military nature have too simplistic a view. First, the public sector needs to be large if it is to effectively regulate demand "and the resources released or absorbed are large enough to count. Military expenditures are what now make the public sector large. Without them, the federal government would be rather less than half its present size. It is most unlikely that this would exercise the requisite leverage on the private economy."[147] Galbraith sees as inadequate the total expenditures that could be undertaken for the underwriting of technology and other expenditures to plan the industrial system along with expenditures on schools, welfare, and the public works. Thus, although Galbraith is not necessarily an adherent of this policy, the new industrial state is one which uses military expenditures as part of its program for the creation of demand for commodities.[148] The new industrial state contains the military-industrial complex.

As far as social class is concerned, Galbraith suggests that new class lines are being drawn between the educated and the uneducated in place of the lines formerly imposed between the owners of capital and the working class. Education is part of the new industrial state, and those rejected by the economic system who are relegated to unemployment are those who do not, by and large, have the necessary skills and credentials. Thus, in addition to unemployment, a shortage of labor exists in some areas. Those who do not have the skills and who migrate in search of employment

> contribute heavily to welfare and unemployment rolls in the communities to which they have moved. The nature of the opprobrium to which they are subject is indicated by the appellations that are applied to them—they are hillbillies, Okies or jungle-bunnies. It is not that they are poorer but that they are culturally inferior. It is such groups, not the working proletariat, that now react in resentment and violence to their subordination.[149]

So those who are unemployed are termed a "resistant core" who are the

> counterpart of . . . a growing number of vacancies for highly qualified workers and a strong bargaining position for those who are employed. This leads to the final source of instability in the industrial system and to yet a further resort to the state.[150]

The instability to which Galbraith refers is that of the wage-price spiral which results from the ability of oligopolistic corporations to pass on wage increases in prices; this has become "an organic feature of the industrial system." The only answer to this spiral (one which Galbraith has reiterated time and time again) is wage and price controls and planning and regulation in the public sector as is the rule in the private sector.[151]

The new industrial state is also characterized by the declining importance of unions. Identification is part of the motivational structure for the technostructure, and loyalty to the organization exists at other levels as well which is adverse to unionism. To underscore his point, Galbraith talks about the numbers of blue-collar workers as compared to white-collar workers ("the category most characteristic of the technostructure"). It is observed that the former decreased dramatically between 1947 and 1965 (by four million) while the latter increased by 9.6 million. In 1965 there were eight million fewer blue-collar than white-collar workers—36.7 million as compared to 44.5 million (included in white-collar occupations are professional, managerial, office, and sales workers).[152]

Galbraith argues that even if white-collar workers are not part of the technostructure, they identify with it and cites a 1957 survey in which three-fourths of such workers saw themselves "as being more closely associated with management than with production workers."[153] This position makes white-collar workers less subject to organization in unions. Still another part of the move away from unionization, it is argued, is the result of power being passed to the technostructure and a corresponding lessening of conflicts of interest between employers and employees.[154]

> In fact the industrial system has not largely encompassed the labor movement. It has dissolved some of its most important functions; it has greatly narrowed its area of action; and it has bent its residual operations very largely to its own needs. Since World War II, the acceptance of the union by the industrial firm and the emergence thereafter of an era of comparatively peaceful industrial relations have been hailed as the final triumph of trade unionism. On closer examination it is seen to reveal many of the features of Jonah's triumph over the whale.[155]

But while "the trade unions retreat, more or less permanently, into the shadows, a rapidly growing body of educators and research scientists emerges."[156] This group stands in relation to the industrial system as did banking in earlier times since Galbraith's view is that for "the mature corporation the decisive factor of production . . . is the supply of qualified talent."[157] Thus, another part of the new industrial state is a huge complex of educational institutions. The members of this complex are "the educational and scientific estate" who, at least potentially, have a great deal of power since they are important to the new industrial state as "the productive agent."[158]

Galbraith *describes* what he calls the new industrial state as a nexus which is far different from the mythical market system in conventional economic thought. He argues not only that a substantial amount of planning exists but that it is necessary for a vibrant economy and society. If the public sector were to follow the lead provided by the private sector in planning, the shortage of adequate transportation and housing could be corrected.[159] What is more the new industrial state has far transcended the Marxian critique of capitalism:

> This too is the result of the intricate web of change which we are here unraveling. The revolution, as delineated by Marx, assumed the progressive immiserization of the working class. Instead of the expected impoverishment there has been increasing affluence. Marxists no longer deny this or convincingly suggest that worker well-being is illusory or transitory. The revolution was to be catalyzed by the capitalist crisis—the apocalyptic depression which would bring an already attenuated structure down in ruins. But the industrial system has, as an integral requirement, an arrangement for regulating aggregate demand which, while permitting it to plan, gives promise of preventing or mitigating

depression. So the danger of an apocalyptic crisis seems more remote. The trade union, militantly expressing the power of the worker, was to be the cutting edge of the revolution. But the industrial system mellows and even absorbs the union. Most important, perhaps, of all, the revolution has occurred in some countries. And there the lineaments of industrialization—planning, large producing organizations, the resulting discipline, the measures of success by economic growth—no longer seem as different as they did in the fears and hopes of a half century ago. Everything on which the revolution seemed to depend, and even the revolution itself, has disintegrated.[160]

These are many of the elements of Galbraith's description. And he is very explicit that his purpose is to provide "the materials for consideration of where [the economic system] has arrived" rather than to predict its future or to advocate change.[161]

It should be evident that Galbraith is not talking about the impact of concentration in industry as used in conventional industrial organization where the focus is the size of the firm in relation to its share of the market in a particular industry. Rather he is talking about a nexus of institutions including the largest corporations which make up what he later (in *Economics and the Public Purpose,* discussed in the next chapter) calls the planning system. The industrial system has, in this view, reached out and grasped the beliefs which enhance its goals and validate the planning which insures its success. This association necessitates a close link with the entire educational system to provide skilled people to do the work. But at the same time a sort of "counterforce" exists in the educational and scientific estate which fosters skepticism and comprehension as well as political pluralism. The educational and scientific estate is powerful because the new industrial state is dependent upon it for manpower.[162] Galbraith is not obscure on this point but reiterates it several times, even saying that one must be cautious about generalizations and predictions but that

> . . . it is safe to say that the future of what is called modern society depends on how willingly and effectively the intellectual community in general, and the educational and scientific estate in particular, assume responsibilities for political action and leadership.[163]

Galbraith also notes that it is not at all certain that this elite will take the lead since "any new political force . . . lacks self-confidence."[164] Of this elite, economists are probably least suited to make pronouncements about social life, he argues, since their perspective is obscured by a narrow view which leads to them being "in the main, the natural allies of the industrial system."[165]

For those who are skeptical of this seeming denouncement of Galbraith's own professional colleagues, an addendum is added to the book on method and the nature of the argument. In particular, it is pointed out how Galbraith's economics differs from conventional economics where it is claimed, among other things, there are few ideas in economics that cannot be got across in plain English as opposed to obscure jargon or quantitative presentations. It is in this addendum that he reveals his preference for handling a big topic more generally and abstractly than to work on a smaller topic more specifically and rigorously (which he sees economists as equating with quantitative expositions). In short, Galbraith is skeptical of economics in its usual form.

Galbraith is a convergence theorist. When comparing the U.S. and the U.S.S.R., he argues that "convergence between the two ostensibly different industrial systems occurs at all fundamental points."[166] It is possible that what Galbraith is observing is the convergence of two systems that are equally undesirable. Yet some observers of world economic systems would argue, as did Nikola Uzunov in a critique of an earlier draft of this work, that the evidence is really not yet available, and we must simply watch the unfolding of events if the objective is to construct a holistic view that lacks prejudice.[167]

Toward the end of the book, Galbraith argues that the "danger to liberty lies in the subordination of belief to the needs of the industrial system." He adds,

> [i]f we continue to believe that the goals of the industrial system—the expansion of output, the companion increase in consumption, technological advance, the public images that sustain it—are coordinate with life, then all of our lives will be in the services of these goals. What is consistent with these ends we shall have or be allowed; all else will be off limits. Our wants will be managed in accordance with the needs of the industrial system; the policies of the state will be subject to similar influence; education will be adapted to industrial need; the disciplines required by the industrial system will be the conventional morality of the community. All other goals will be made to seem precious, unimportant, or antisocial. We will be bound to the ends of the industrial system. The state will add its moral, and perhaps some of its legal, power to their enforcement. What will eventuate, on the whole, will be the benign servitude of the household retainer who is taught to love her mistress and see her interests as her own, and not the compelled servitude of the field hand. But it will not be freedom.[168]

On the other hand, if the industrial system becomes a decreasing part of life there is less reason for alarm. The totality of existence would be more the experience of human beings and even intellectual activity would be more for its own sake than the service it can render to the industrial system. The fetish for commodities would be overcome, and the more aesthetic dimensions of being would flourish. Galbraith concludes this book, then, with the hope that as the industrial system transforms itself, it will also bring into existence the community—the educational and scientific estates, and presumably, at least, parts of the technostructure—that "will reject its [the industrial system's] monopoly of social purpose."[169]

Gaps in the Marxian and Galbraithian Views

The New Industrial State, for whatever reasons, captured a much larger audience than *Monopoly Capital.* Yet this work of Galbraith's cannot be seen as a formidable leap forward in critical social science or as containing the elements of a paradigm that offers a great challenge to the conventional wisdom. The book by Baran and Sweezy in contrast, despite its flaws, is an important part of the literature in critical political economics. Perhaps Galbraith's main contribution is to have argued that the underlying assumptions of the conventional microeconomics are seriously unrealistic. Yet the *NIS* is an essentially vague book and rather inconclusively, and even at times ambivalently, borders on prettifying the world of big business, with the ancillary institutions of an influential educational nexus and a somewhat heavy-handed state which is but an arm of the private sector. The state, in the Galbraithian view, has an applied Keynesian past which was (and is) militaristic the result of which is the state creation of a whole arms industry which is privately owned.

The New Industrial State was written as a complementary volume to Galbraith's *The Affluent Society.* In the latter, thought about private affluence and public deprivation led Galbraith to think about "another and larger world" which "was a world of great corporations in which people increasingly served the convenience of these organizations which were meant to serve *them.*"[170] But Galbraith wavers in this view throughout his long discussion of the structure of American industry.

The main point of agreement in both *The New Industrial State* and *Monopoly Capital* is that the 500 or so largest corporations are the main economic force in the United States. But when the meaning of this observation is spelled out in these alternative analyses very different conclusions are reached.

Galbraith has evolved beyond his views in *American Capitalism* where he argued "The support of countervailing power has become in the last two decades perhaps the major peacetime function of the federal government."[171] And Galbraith no longer views underemployment as a mainly frictional phenomenon as he did in that earlier work.[172] In the *NIS* there is an unemployed and underemployed lumpen proletariat. Curiously, there is, at the same time, a seemingly ill-founded optimism in the "scientific and educational estate" which has close ties with the corporate "technostructure" to act as the stratum for change. In *Monopoly Capital* no powerful *domestic* stratum for progressive change is to be found. But Baran and Sweezy would likely suggest the stratum which Galbraith sees nearly last. Indeed, the experience of the latter two in academia undoubtedly strongly reinforces their view that the "scientific and educational estate" is simply part of the state system which symbiotically works closely with monopoly capital to maintain an inequitable and pernicious status quo (while containing contradictions, like the rest of the system).

Galbraith avoided some of the difficulties encountered by Baran and Sweezy by never attempting to become more theoretically concrete or quantitatively rigorous in his exposition of empirical data. Perhaps the Baran and Sweezy view would not have been as seriously flawed if they had remained at a level of abstraction typical of Galbraith's discussion.

If Baran and Sweezy—as other Marxian critics have charged—can be said to pay inadequate attention to workers in U.S. society, Galbraith can be said to nearly ignore them. But a similarity arises in that each views his own sphere of identification as the strata for change. For Baran and Sweezy, it is the international socialist Movement, and for Galbraith, it is the educational and scientific estate.

There are missing pieces in both books. Both are flawed theoretically and methodologically and cannot be said to grasp the whole. Although to be holistic is a difficult task, other Marxian works and Galbraith's *Economics and the Public Purpose* go significantly beyond analyses discussed in this chapter. However, there is a definite continuity between the literature touched on here and that to be examined in the remainder of this book. Chapter 5 discusses some additional contemporary economic thought in which concentrated and centralized capital is put in the broader context of the economy and society with special emphasis on the state apparatus.

NOTES

1 Karl Marx, Capital, vol. 1, translated by Ernest Untermann, p. 836, the Kerr edition, 1912.

2 James O'Connor pointed out everything in this paragraph and coined the slogan in personal correspondence, dated February 10, 1975.

A specific example of a disconcerting variety of state capitalism—organized by The Federation of Rocky Mountain States, Inc.—is discussed in the next chapter in addition to the theory of the dynamics behind the possible emergence of a national social-industrial complex. Also see Appendix B.

3 On the latter point, see John Maynard Keynes, The General Theory of Employment, Interest and Money (London: Macmillan, 1936), pp. 213 and 214.

4 Stephen Hymer, "Robinson Crusoe and the Secret of Primitive Accumulation," Monthly Review, vol. 23, no. 4 (September 1971), pp. 11–36. James O'Connor notes that this article contains the implicit point (which Hymer made explicit to O'Connor in a conversation) "that the whole bourgeois passion for a science of economizing is useful only when one class is using and exploiting the labor power of another class." The original Robinson Crusoe was written by Daniel Defoe in the early 18th century.

5 See, for example, Robert Heilbroner, ed., "Classical Argument for Free Trade," in The Economic Problem (Englewood Cliffs, N.J.: Prentice-Hall, 1970), pp. 564–566.

6 Karl Marx, Capital, vol. 1, part 8.

7 Hymer, "Robinson Crusoe," pp. 11–12. One criticism of Hymer's article is that the story of Robinson Crusoe exists within the context of precapitalism while Hymer discusses the social relationships as if the context is capitalism (e.g., Friday is a slave rather than a wage earner). Nonetheless, it is useful to use the logic Hymer creates seeing it all symbolically.

8 Ibid., p. 25.

9 Ibid., p. 29.

10 This much-discussed figure in schools of management wrote Principles of Scientific Management (New York: Harper & Row, 1947).

11 Hymer, "Robinson Crusoe," p. 31.

12 Ibid., pp. 13–14 and the whole article.

13 Ibid., p. 35.

14 Ibid., p. 36.

15 "International Telephone and Telegraph Corporation: a Case Study of a Conglomerate," San Jose State University Center for Economics Education, 1972. For a lively popularized discussion see Anthony Sampson, The Sovereign State of ITT (Greenwich, Conn.: Fawcett Publications, 1973).

16 "The Economic Crisis in Historical Perspective," Monthly Review, vol. 26, no. 10 (March 1975), p. 1.

17 *Important in this regard is Douglas F. Dowd,* The Twisted Dream: Capitalist Development in the United States Since 1776 *(Cambridge, Mass.: Winthrop Publishers, 1974). Also see a review of Dowd's book by James O'Connor, "The Twisted Dream,"* Monthly Review, *vol. 26, no. 10 (March 1975), pp. 1–54. A modern classic is William Appleman Williams,* The Contours of American History *(New York: New Viewpoints, 1973), first published in 1961.*

18 Frederic M. Scherer, Industrial Market Structure and Economic Performance *(Chicago: Rand McNally & Co., 1970), p. 41.*

19 *Ibid.*

20 *Ibid., p. 42. The Berle and Means study is* The Modern Corporation and Private Property *(New York: Macmillan, 1932).*

21 "Probing the Structure of the American Economy," *Congressional Record (March 4, 1975), p. S3007. Read into the record by Senator Lee Metcalf of Montana.*

22 *Douglas Dowd,* The Twisted Dream, *p. 70. Dowd gathered this information from John M. Blair,* Economic Concentration: Structure, Behavior and Public Policy *(New York: Harcourt Brace Jovanovich, 1972); Federal Trade Commission,* Economic Report on Corporate Mergers *(Washington, D.C.: U.S. Government Printing Office, 1969); Samuel Richardson Reid,* Mergers, Managers and the Economy *(New York: McGraw-Hill, 1968); Robert T. Averitt,* The Dual Economy *(New York: W. W. Norton, 1968); and from* Fortune, *May 1971, May 1972, and May and June 1973.*

23 *Ibid.*

24 *U.S. Bureau of the Census,* Statistical Abstract of the United States: 1974 *(Washington, D.C.: U.S. Government Printing Office), p. 486.*

25 *Dowd,* The Twisted Dream, *p. 70.*

26 *Ibid.*

27 *Ibid.*

28 *U.S. Bureau of the Census,* 1974 Statistical Abstract, *p. 476.*

29 *Scherer,* Industrial Market Structure, *p. 43.*

30 *Ibid., p. 44.*

31 *U.S. Bureau of the Census,* 1974 Statistical Abstract, *p. 487.*

32 *Ibid., p. 491.*

33 *In addition to works already cited, one could consult the voluminous documents produced by the U.S. Senate Subcommittee on Antitrust and Monopoly of the Committee on the Judiciary, e.g.,* The Conglomerate Merger Problem, *Part 8 of hearings on economic concentration held in November of 1969 and in January and February in 1970 (Washington, D.C.: U.S. Government Printing Office, 1970). Also, there are a couple of decent books based on the work of this subcommittee. There is Richard J. Barber,* The American Corporation: Its Power, Its Money, Its Politics *(New York: E.P. Dutton, 1970). Barber served as counsel for the subcommittee. Also see Morton Mintz and Jerry S. Cohen,* America, Inc. *(New York: Dial, 1971). Cohen also served as counsel on the Senate Antitrust Subcommittee. Another important source is*

Joe Bain's Industrial Organization *(New York: Wiley & Sons, 1959) and for a less thorough but compact and concise treatment using a framework similar to Bain and Scherer see Richard Caves,* American Industry: Structure, Conduct, Performance *(Englewood Cliffs, N.J.: Prentice-Hall, 1972). One of the best sources of information currently is Senator Lee Metcalf. A letter to his office can result in receiving several important documents. One that is informative on the issue of secrecy surrounding disclosure of ownership is the Subcommittee on Reports, Accounting and Management (chaired by Metcalf) of the Committee on Government Operations, U.S. Senate,* Corporate Ownership and Control *(Washington, D.C.: U.S. Government Printing Office, 1975).*

34 Scherer, Industrial Market Structure, p. 59.

35 S. Menshikov, Millionaires and Managers *(Moscow: Progress Publishers, 1969), Chapter 1.*

36 Ferdinand Lundberg, The Rich and the Super-Rich *(New York: Bantom Books, 1968), p. 934.*

37 James C. Knowles, "The Rockefeller Financial Group," ed. Ralph L. Andreano, Superconcentration/Supercorporation *(Andover, Mass.: Warner Modular Publications, 1973), pp. 343–1 to 17. A document which is useful on the ownership question is one prepared by the Subcommittees on Intergovernmental Relations, and Budgeting, Management, and Expenditures of the Committee on Government Operations, U.S. Senate,* Disclosure of Corporate Ownership *(Washington, D.C.: U.S. Government Printing Office, 1974), as well as previously cited Senate Subcommittee material.*

38 Ibid., pp. 343–17.

39 Ibid.

40 James O'Connor, The Corporations and the State *(New York: Harper & Row, 1974), footnote, pp. 59–60. O'Connor criticizes a series of articles by Fitch and Oppenheimer in which they present a theory of finance capital. The critique is a companion one of Baran and Sweezy's Monopoly Capital. O'Connor has added the emphasis. My view is that O'Connor's interpretation is correct; but Baran and Sweezy left themselves somewhat open to misunderstanding. Some of the quotes from* Monopoly Capital *later in this chapter demonstrate what I mean.*

41 Quoted in Paul Sweezy, Modern Capitalism and Other Essays *(New York: Monthly Review Press, 1972), p. 36.*

42 Ibid., pp. 36–37.

43 "The Merger Movement: A Study in Power," Monthly Review, *vol. 21, no. 2 (June, 1969), pp. 19 and 3.*

44 Robert L. Heilbroner, "A Marxist America," New York Review of Books, *vol. 6 (May 26, 1966), p. 22.*

45 Ibid., p. 22.

46 James O'Connor, "Monopoly Capital," New Left Review, *no. 40 (November–December, 1966), pp. 38–39.*

47 Ibid., pp. 39–42.

48 Ibid., p. 42.

49 Paul Baran and Paul Sweezy, Monopoly Capital: An Essay on the American Economic and Social Order (New York: Monthly Review Press, 1966), p. 8.

50 Paul Sweezy, "Monopoly Capital and the Theory of Value," Monthly Review, vol. 25, no. 8 (January 1974), p. 32. This article was reprinted in this journal to clear up misunderstanding of Baran and Sweezy's position on the labor theory of value. One of the most detailed critiques of Monopoly Capital with respect to the labor theory of value is Ernest Mandel, "The Labor Theory of Value and 'Monopoly Capitalism'," International Socialist Review, vol. 28, no. 4 (July–August 1967), pp. 29–42. More on this follows.

51 Ibid. The latter subject, Sweezy points out, was not mentioned extensively by Marx "for the obvious reason that all of Capital was written well before the onset of the monopoly capitalist period."

52 Baran and Sweezy, Monopoly Capitol, p. 8.

53 Ibid., footnote on p. 6. Interestingly, Paul Sweezy authored a now classic article entitled "Demand Under Conditions of Oligopoly," The Journal of Political Economy, vol. 68 (August 1939), pp. 568–573. Sweezy and two English economists—R. L. Hall and C. J. Hitch in "Price Theory and Business Behavior," Oxford Economic Papers, no. 2 (May, 1939), pp. 21–45—independently presented the theory of the kinky demand curve. For more on this see George Stigler and Kenneth E. Boulding, A.E.A. Readings in Price Theory, vol. 6, (Chicago: Richard D. Irwin, 1952), particularly pages 404–414. The theory is that oligopolists will expect their rivals to match price reductions but will hesitate to follow price increases, which causes prices rarely to be reduced and a tendency toward an upward creep even in relatively stable times. Sweezy now uses the term "monopoly capital" to categorize the part of the structure of industry he originally called oligopoly. But monopoly capital also includes pure monopoly which Scherer (Industrial Market Structure, p. 59) thinks generates about 6 or 7 percent of gross national product.

54 Baran and Sweezy, Monopoly Capital, p.6.

55 Ibid., pp. 15–16.

56 Ibid., p. 20.

57 Ibid., pp. 16 and 17.

58 C. Wright Mills, The Power Elite (New York: Oxford University Press, 1956). p. 116.

59 Baran and Sweezy, Monopoly Capital, p. 42.

60 Ibid., p. 53.

61 Ibid., p. 72.

62 Ernest Mandel, "Surplus Capital and Realization of Surplus Value," International Socialist Review, vol. 28. no. 1 (January–February 1967), p. 58. The work by Joseph Gillman to which Mandel refers is The Falling Rate of Profit: Marx's Law and its Significance to Twentieth Century Capitalism (London: D. Dobson, 1957).

63 Baran and Sweezy, Monopoly Capital, p. 9.

64 Paul Baran, The Political Economy of Growth, (New York: Monthly Review Press, 1957), p. 22.

65 Ibid., p. 22.

66 Ibid., footnote.

67 Ibid.

68 Ibid., p. 23.

69 Ibid., pp. 23–41. The only published study I know of which attempts to systematically quantify the surplus uses this variant for reasons that seem mysterious or at least not obvious. Ron Stanfield in The Economic Surplus and Neo-Marxism (Lexington, Mass.: Lexington Books, 1973) even ends up concluding that "the surplus as herein defined and estimated corroborates this thesis [that the surplus rises over time] in both its absolute and relative dimensions. However, little should be made of this since the thesis itself is uninteresting under the definition of the surplus herein employed. Baran and Sweezy in the context of this hypothesis are obviously emphasizing the distributive shares as between earned and unearned income aspect of the surplus. Here, of course, the surplus is not viewed in this context. Viewed in the context of the difference between potential output and essential output, the rising surplus merely implies that technological change is increasing potential output faster than essential consumption is increasing." (p. 87).

70 Baran, The Political Economy of Growth, Monthly Review Press, pp. 41–42.

71 Baran and Sweezy, Monopoly Capital, pp. 9–10.

72 Ibid., p. 10. This is, of course, highly controversial. One criticism is that it does not deal with labor exploitation.

73 Ibid., pp. 369–391.

74 Ibid., p. 11.

75 Ibid., pp. 369–384.

76 Ibid., whole appendix and p. 289 for specific statistics.

77 Robert Keller, "Monopoly Capital and the Great Depression: Testing Baran and Sweezy's Hypothesis," The Review of Radical Political Economics, vol. 7, no. 4 (Winter 1975), p. 65.

78 Baran and Sweezy, Monopoly Capital, p. 191.

79 Ibid., p. 367.

80 Raymond Lubitz, "Monopoly Capitalism and Neo-Marxism," The Public Interest, no. 21 (Fall 1970), p. 167.

81 Ibid., p. 168.

82 Mandel, "The Labor Theory of Value and 'Monopoly Capitalism'," p. 30.

83 Ibid., p. 29.

84 Ron Stanfield, The Economic Surplus and Marxism, p. 86.

85 Lubitz, "Monopoly Capitalism and Neo-Marxism." Entire article. James O'Connor says "Baran and Sweezy implicitly argue that much surplus is embodied in consumer goods (e.g., the trim on a car). Thus constant or rising surplus does not prove what Lubitz claims it does."

86 Myron E. Sharpe, "Marxism and Monopoly Capital: a Symposium," Science and Society, vol. 30, no. 4 (Fall 1966), pp. 461–470. Other members of the symposium were Maurice Dobb, Joseph M. Gillman, Theodor Prager, and Otto Nathan.

87 Otto Nathan, "Marxism and Monopoly Capital," p. 487.

88 Ibid., p. 493.

89 Ibid., p. 492.

90 David Horowitz, "Analyzing the Surplus," Monthly Review, vol. 18, no. 8 (January 1967), p. 58.

91 Ibid., pp. 58–59. Joseph D. Phillips (in a telephone conversation on October 3, 1974) offered the opinion that Sweezy's The Theory of Capitalist Development (New York: Monthly Review Press, 1942) and Paul Baran's The Political Economy of Growth were both better works—conceptually and methodologically—than Monopoly Capital. Unfortunately, neither of these is as relevant to the current situation as Monopoly Capital, though they are relevant.

92 Horowitz, "Analyzing the Surplus," p. 59.

93 David Horowitz, "The Case for a Neo-Marxist Theory," International Socialist Review, vol. 28, no. 4 (July–August 1967), pp. 27–28.

94 Ibid., p. 28.

95 Baran and Sweezy, Monopoly Capital, p. 56. Here Josef Steindl is mentioned in the same vein with Baran and Sweezy saying that "anyone familiar with the work of Kalecki and Steindl will readily recognize that the authors . . . owe a great deal to them." (p. 56). The works of Kalecki they cite are Essays in the Theory of Economic Fluctuations, published in 1939; Studies in Economic Dynamics, published in 1943; and Theory of Economic Dynamics, (New York: Monthly Review Press, 1968). The latter work was completed in 1952, and is a revised and combined edition of the previous two. The Josef Steindl book is Maturity and Stagnation in American Capitalism, (New York: Monthly Review Press, 1974), first published in 1952.

96 Baran and Sweezy, p. 132.

97 Ernest Mandel, "Surplus Capital and Realization of Surplus Value," p. 56.

98 Ibid., pp. 56–57.

99 Ibid., p. 57.

100 Ibid., pp. 57–58.

101 Ibid., p. 58. The earlier work to which Mandel refers is Marxist Economic Theory (New York: Monthly Review Press, 1970), vol. 2, Chapter 14. This was first published in French in 1962.

102 Mandel, "Surplus Capital and Realization of Surplus Value," International Socialist Review, pp. 58–59.

103 Ibid., p. 59.

104 Ibid., pp. 59–60.

105 *Ibid.*, p. 60.

106 *Ibid.*

107 *Ibid.*, p. 61.

108 *Ibid.*, and Monopoly Capital, *especially the last chapter.*

109 Ernest Mandel, "The Labor Theory of Value and 'Monopoly Capitalism'," p. 33.

110 James F. Becker, "On the Monopoly Theory of Monopoly Capitalism," Science and Society, *vol. 35, no. 4 (Winter 1971), p. 437.*

111 *Ibid.*, p. 438.

112 Mandel, "Surplus Capital and Realization of Surplus Value," p. 61.

113 Ernest Mandel, "Where Is America Going?" New Left Review, *no. 54 (March–April, 1969), pp. 3–15. A revised version is in Maurice Zeitlin, ed.,* American Society Inc. *(Chicago: Markham Publishing Co., 1970), pp. 508–524. I will make reference to the latter in the following. The quotation is on page 508.*

114 *Al Szymanski argues that Spanish-speaking people are now at the bottom of U.S. society and that blacks have made gains since the 1960s. For more on this topic, see Szymanski's "Trends in Economic Discrimination Against Blacks in the U.S. Working Class,"* The Review of Radical Political Economics, *vol. 7, no. 3 (Fall 1975). A seeming flaw in his analysis is that Szymanski discusses employment trends quite comprehensively but leaves out an analysis of unemployment by race.*

115 *Ibid.*, pp. 508–510.

116 *Ibid.*, pp. 510–511.

117 *Ibid.*, p. 511. My personal experience working in "management" roles in three major American corporations strongly affirms this view. The higher education data are dated and come from the U.S. Bureau of the Census, *1974 Statistical Abstract, p. 133.*

118 *Ibid.*, pp. 511–512.

119 *Ibid.*, pp. 512–514.

120 *Ibid.*, pp. 514–516.

121 *Ibid.*, pp. 516–519. Others might see this as more traditional trade unionism rather than radicalism.

122 *Ibid.*

123 *Ibid.*, pp. 519–524.

124 *Ibid.*, pp. 523–524.

125 John Kenneth Galbraith, Economics and the Public Purpose *(Boston: Houghton-Mifflin, 1973).*

126 J.M. Keynes, The General Theory of Employment, Interest, and Money *(London: Macmillan, 1936).*

127 John Kenneth Galbraith, The New Industrial State *(Boston: Houghton-Mifflin, 1967), p. x. For sympathetic reviews of this and other works of*

Galbraith see Myron E. Sharpe, John Kenneth Galbraith and the Lower Economics, 2nd ed. (White Plains, N.Y.: International Arts and Sciences Press, 1974).

128 Ibid., p. 71.

129 His more recent views on these issues seem no different. A presentation of some of these views appears in the next chapter.

130 Galbraith, The New Industrial State, p. 379.

131 Ibid., p. 372.

132 Ibid., p. 211.

133 Ibid., p. 212.

134 Ibid., pp. 74–75.

135 Ibid., p. 2. Unfortunately, in a manner characteristic of some authoritative voices, Galbraith doesn't bother to note his sources of information on this score. It should be taken, therefore, very lightly.

136 Ibid., p. 140.

137 Ibid., p. 134.

138 Ibid., pp. 157–158.

139 Ibid., pp. 162, 163.

140 Ibid., p. 164.

141 Ibid., pp. 164–165.

142 Ibid., p. 167.

143 Ibid., p. 183. Some would think that an examination of antitrust legislation and practice as conducted by the Antitrust Division of the U.S. Department of Justice as well as the various regulatory agencies would be appropriate in a work which examines centralized and concentrated capital. My view is simple and needs little elaboration. Antitrust activity, to the extent that it occurs at all, serves the legitimization function of the state giving the illusion that the people are protected from big capital. In short, antitrust bodies serve capitalist ideology. This theme is covered extensively in Chapter 5.

144 Galbraith, The New Industrial State.

145 Ibid.

146 Ibid., p. 229.

147 Ibid., pp. 230–231.

148 Ibid., p. 232.

149 Ibid., p. 245. The assertion that there is a growing number of vacancies in some fields is, of course, controversial and was perhaps more correct in the 1960s than at this writing.

150 Ibid., p. 246.

151 Ibid., Chapter 21.

152 Ibid., p. 267.

153 *Ibid., p. 269.*

154 *Ibid., p. 247.*

155 *Ibid., p. 281.*

156 *Ibid., p. 282.*

157 *Ibid., p. 281.*

158 *Ibid., p. 283.*

159 *Ibid., Chapter 31.*

160 *Ibid., p. 290.*

161 *Ibid., p. 324.*

162 *Ibid., Chapter 33.*

163 *Ibid., p. 381.*

164 *Ibid., p. 382.*

165 *Ibid., p. 384.*

166 *Ibid., p. 391.*

167 *The work of Jan Tinbergen, a Dutch economist, is useful when thinking about convergence theory. See, for example, his "Do Communist and Free Economies Show a Converging Pattern?" in* Soviet Studies 12, no. 4 *(April 1961). Another work on this is Jagdish N. Bhagwati, ed.,* Economics and World Order: From The 1970's to the 1990's *(New York: Macmillan, 1972).*

168 *Galbraith,* The New Industrial State, *pp. 398–399.*

169 *Ibid., p. 399,*

170 *Ibid., p. vii.*

171 John Kenneth Galbraith, American Capitalism: The Concept of Countervailing Power *(Boston: Houghton-Mifflin, 1952), p. 143.*

172 *Ibid., p. 204.*

5

A CRITIQUE OF JAMES O'CONNOR AND J. K. GALBRAITH ON THE DUAL ECONOMY, THE STATE, AND ECONOMIC INSTABILITY

The work of Marxian economist James O'Connor and the work of John Kenneth Galbraith provide an especially good opportunity for a comparative analysis of theories. Both are concerned with many of the same phenomena but differ dramatically in their perspectives. Pointing to the differences and similarities helps to crystalize the issues. This chapter gleans the most persuasive theory of the state possible and develops the discussion of the structural realities of the political economy.

The *first* task is a discussion of the state in general terms to reveal more clearly what the state and theories of the state are. The *second* task is to undertake an analysis of some of the work of James O'Connor on theories of the state and the political economy as a whole. A *third* part of this chapter is a critique of Galbraith's *Economics and the Public Purpose*. Related tasks and a contrast of the Marxian and Galbraithian perspectives emerge in the process. In combination with the preceding chapter a comparatively holistic view of the structure of the whole political economy is sketched. This chapter is a crucial link to the final synthesis in Chapter 6 and an obvious complement to the discussion of centralized and concentrated capital.

The State in Society

Ralph Miliband argues that Western social scientists have had a "theory of the state," but it is a theoretical stance which *"takes as resolved* some of the largest questions which have traditionally been asked about the state, and takes unnecessary, indeed almost precludes any special concern with its nature and role in Western-type societies."[1] Miliband is speaking of political science and political sociology, but it could be argued that his view fits conventional economics as well although it does not apply to anthropology or to Marxian political economics (which appears to take account of anthropological phenomena more than conventional economics).[2]

Miliband is really speaking to the "pluralist" position in his criticism which states that

> everybody, directly or through organized groups, has some power and nobody has or can have too much of it. In these societies, citizens enjoy universal suffrage, free and regular elections, representative institutions, effective citizen rights, including the right of free speech, association and opposition; and both individuals and groups take ample advantage of these rights, under the protection of the law, an independent judiciary and a free political culture.[3]

The result, in the pluralist view, is that "all the active and legitimate groups in the population can make themselves heard at some crucial stage in the process of decision."[4]

The pluralist view—though it may not be taken seriously in recent times—seems naive if the perspective of Marxian political economy has any validity at all. The pluralist view also appears to deny some anthropological evidence about societies historically and cross-culturally. In particular, the pluralist perspective disregards some very formidable perceptions on the nature of the state and industry in capitalist society. This relationship is one which brings together dominant economic organizations, particularly monopoly capital, which have been quite successful in capturing a large share of the state. The latter serves, in the view of more than one contemporary theorist, the functions of accumulation and legitimization (fundamentally, the appropriation of surplus value for dominant social groups while keeping social order of a kind).

But the development of a theory of the state is a complex task. This is true, possibly, because, as Miliband argues,

> "the state" is not a thing . . . it does not, as such, exist. What "the state" stands for is a number of particular institutions which, together, constitute its reality, and which interact as parts of what may be called the state system.[5]

Miliband argues that to equate the government with the state breeds confusion about the nature and incidence of state power and that it is not unusual for this confusion to exist since it is most often the government which operates on behalf of the state[6] (and, as will be repeated later, the *budget* of government can, in fact, be seen as the bare bones of the state). In addition, there are a number of institutions—"the government, the administration, the military and the police, the judicial branch, subcentral government and parliamentary assemblies—which make up 'the state' and whose interrelationship shapes the form of the state system." "State power" exists in these institutions which is "wielded in its different manifestations by the people who occupy the leading positions." Such people are "presidents, prime ministers and their ministerial colleagues; high civil servants and other state administrators; top military men; judges of the higher courts;" and so on (including "the political and administrative leaders of subcentral units of the state").

> It may well be found that the relationship is very close indeed and the holders of state power are, for many different reasons, the agents of private economic power—that those who wield that power are also, therefore, and without unduly stretching the meaning of words, an authentic "ruling class".[7]

In much the same vein Robert McC. Adams says that the state is a notion that centers on the political order.

> For all the acrimonious debate about the essential features of state societies, they may reasonably be defined as hierarchically organized on political and territorial lines rather than on kinship or other ascriptive groups and relationships.[8]

Further, and in more detail, Lawrence Krader argues that the state has the role of "directing the life of the people under it by centralized social power in the hands of a few." In addition the state, according to Krader, is found only in certain societies, and can be viewed apart from government and is also distinct from society. Nonetheless, "It is the central and highest political authority for regulation of the society" within territorial limits. "The state is embedded in a type of society which is stratified by wealth, prestige, and power, and is divided thereby into classes." What is more, Melinowski, according to Krader, held

> . . . in the state, monopoly of coercive power and the delimita-
> tion of territory are connected. This interconnection is an inte-
> gral part of the state, being in and of its nature. Or it may be
> understood historically, as a sequence of events, whereby power
> was asserted in a geographically unified and defined society.
> When a central authority establishes a monopoly of coercive
> force in a society, the limits of extension of that force, which may
> have been vague until then, at this point become precisely
> determined. Those over whom the force or threat of force is
> exercised must accept the state or reject it. There is no middle
> ground.[9]

Thus, it can be said that the state system transcends government per se but is closely related to it. Other institutions such as even the most prestigious private universities are in a sense part of the state. So are many corporations which work under contract to government. In the final analysis just what the state is must be left in an unsatisfactorily vague and abstract place. Yet a concept that cannot be precisely defined can emerge more clearly as it is used in discussing aspects of it.

A key distinction between the views on the state which follow are that O'Connor as a Marxian writer is a conflict theorist who sees the state as a body of institutions and associations which serves dual and contradictory functions. One main function is that of assisting the owners of the means of production in their task of profit seeking. Galbraith's work, on the other hand, is to economics much like R. A. Dahl's perspective is to political science. Curiously, however, Galbraith shows that he is aware that the state has been captured to no small extent by the upper socioeconomic strata. Yet he remains an adherent to the view that the state might serve the purposes of redistribution.

James O'Connor on Economic Dualism, A Theory of the State and the Social-Industrial Complex

The perspective of James O'Connor offers promising directions in the development of a conceptual framework to understand the over-whelming influence of monopoly capitalism and its alliance with the state. Essentially, what is put forth in his recent writings is a theory of the state which should cause those who claim that there is no current satisfactory theory of the state to pause and ponder. The shortcoming in the vacuum of state theory has been approached in some detail in *The Fiscal Crisis of the State* and, to a lesser extent, in a collection of essays entitled *The Corporations and the State*. In addition, O'Connor—as noted earlier—was involved in the creation of a journal, *Kapitalistate,* which (as the title implies) takes as its focus the relationship between contemporary capitalism and the state.[10] Daniel Bell calls *The Fiscal Crisis of the State* "the most ambitious effort to develop a 'sociology of fiscal politics'" and correctly perceives O'Connor's work as being related to the now-classic (but ignored when it was first published in 1925) essay by Rudolf Goldscheid entitled "A Sociological Approach to Problems of Public Finance."[11]

The Fiscal Crisis of the State is not particularly easy reading and it at times is uneven and repetitious though perhaps unavoidably so. The author has attempted to work out a holistic view in the Marxian tradition. The conceptual framework and the analysis (supported by data that is useful to reinforce the general line of reasoning but do not prove it) provide the reader with a challenging view of the political economy as a whole. The book expands upon and works in the Marxian framework and should be seen as a contribution to the development of theory upon which others can build, both conceptually and empirically.

In FCS it is argued that advanced capitalism has tendencies towards crisis (economic, social, and political). Reflections are offered on the societal (particularly governmental) directions that are likely to be pursued to deal with that crisis.

The relationship between the private and state sectors of the economy are discussed in a fashion much different than that typical of Keynesian economics, where government is viewed as a stabilizing force in an economy while leaving major economic decisions to the private sector. In general, O'Connor's perspective sees the economic system as being plagued by fundamental structural contradictions which are manifested in economic, political, and social crises. The main contradiction in the structure of the economy is that the process of production is a social process and the benefits from production are acquired disproportionately by those who own the means of production privately.

Importantly, O'Connor's work is inspired, at least in part, by the perspective of "fiscal sociology," particularly the previously mentioned work of Goldscheid.[12] Goldscheid says, for example, that "the budget is the skeleton of the state stripped of all misleading ideologies." O'Connor does a good job of providing a theoretical framework which attempts to reveal the nature of the "skeleton," the state, and the corresponding class society.

O'Connor notes that a theoretical perspective on the nature of the governmental budget is necessary to understand what he sees as a fiscal crisis (or the tendency for governmental expenditures to "outrace" revenues) "and a method for discovering the meaning for the political economy and society as a whole."[13] This perspective is necessary because, in his view, the U.S. is encountering general instability, including unemployment and inflation, which cannot be corrected by traditional monetary and fiscal policy. Inequality, poverty, racism, sexism, imperialism and war, continued urban ills and "other crises . . . seem a permanent part of daily life." O'Connor adds, "No one is exempt from the fiscal crisis and the underlying social crises which it aggravates."[14]

These main questions arise in *FCS*: (1) Why does the crisis exist? (2) What means are likely to be used by the state in an effort to resolve the crisis? (3) What are the longer run solutions? O'Connor introduces his analysis with a discussion of "traditional economics" and a somewhat thin discussion of his view that it is "theoretically bankrupt." He critiques, for example, the work by Keynesian Evsey Domar who "theorized that government expenditures can be dealt with (1) by assuming that they are exogenous, or determined by forces outside the economic system; (2) by merging them with consumption expenditures; or (3) by assuming them away altogether."[15] He argues that this is unacceptable and says:

> As government expenditures come to constitute a larger and larger share of total spending in advanced capitalist countries, economic theorists who ignore the impact of the state budget do so at their own (and capitalism's) peril. . . . Their premise is that the government budget should and can be increased or lowered to compensate for reduced or increased private spending. Many orthodox economists believe that the volume of federal spending (if not its composition) is determined by and inversely related to the volume of private spending.
>
> As will be seen in the course of this study, the orthodox approach is at best simplistic . . . [16]

Assumptions and Theses in O'Connor's Analysis

To provide an alternative approach to traditional theory, O'Connor begins with the premise that the state in capitalist society must try to fulfill two basic functions, *accumulation* and *legitimization*. In other words, the state must attempt to maintain economic growth (which is related to low unemployment and price stability) while promoting the perception that "the system" is equitable. But this relationship is an awkward one. These goals, O'Connor argues, are contradictory, and, therefore, the state must attempt to justify what it is really doing (e.g., mainly servicing the interests of private property, particularly "monopoly capital") "by calling its policies something that they are not, or it must try to conceal them (e.g., by making them into administrative, not political, issues)."[17]

A second premise is that Marxist economic categories are indispensable to understanding the fiscal crisis. O'Connor explains those categories that are found useful to organize the discussion. Some main categories are *social capital* which is composed of *social investment* and *social consumption;* and *social expenses.*[18] Scholars of Marx's work would observe that O'Connor is not orthodox in his use of categories or methods used by Marx. Rather O'Connor adheres to the Marxian conceptual framework in a loose and general fashion.

O'Connor defines social capital as "expenditures required for profitable private accumulation; it is indirectly productive (in Marxist terms, social capital indirectly expands surplus value)."[19] Of the two subcategories,

> *social investment* consists of projects and services that increase the productivity of a given amount of labor power and, other factors being equal, increase the rate of profit. A good example is state-financed industrial-development parks. *Social consumption* consists of projects and services that lower the reproduction costs of labor and, other factors being equal, increase the rate of profit. An example of this is social insurance.[20]

The second category, *social expenses,* "consists of projects and services which are required to maintain social harmony—to fulfill the state's 'legitimization' function. They are not even indirectly productive." Further, "The best example is the welfare system which is designed chiefly to keep social peace among unemployed workers."[21]

It is then explained that "Because of the dual and contradictory character of the capitalist state, nearly every state agency is involved in the accumulation and legitimization functions, and nearly every state expenditure has this twofold character."[22] This being the case, it is no simple task to untangle the budget of the various levels of the state to spell out the extent to which the state is involved in accumulation and the extent to which it is involved in legitimization.

FCS contains two main theses.

> The first basic thesis presented . . . is that the growth of the state sector and the state spending is functioning increasingly as the basis for the growth of the monopoly sector and total production. Conversely, it is argued that the growth of state spending and state programs is the result of the growth of the monopoly industries. In other words, the growth of the state is both a cause and effect of the expansion of monopoly capital.
>
> More specifically, the socialization of the costs of social investment and social consumption capital increases over time and increasingly is needed for profitable accumulation by monopoly capital. The general reason is that the increase in the social character of production (specialization, division of labor, interdependency, the growth of new social forms of capital such as education, etc.) either prohibits or renders unprofitable the private accumulation of constant and variable capital. The growth of the monopoly sector is irrational in the sense that it is accompanied by unemployment, poverty, economic stagnation, and so on. To insure mass loyalty and maintain its legitimacy, the state must meet various demands of those who suffer the "costs" of economic growth.[23]

This approach is then compared with other perspectives and O'Connor notes that his "view contrasts sharply with modern conservative thought, which asserts that the state sector grows at the expense of private industry." He argues that "the growth of the state sector is indispensable to the expansion of private industry, particularly monopoly industries." He also notes that this thesis contrasts with contemporary liberal thought which, he says, holds "that the expansion of monopoly industries inhibits the growth of the state sector."

On the contrary, it is argued, the growth of monopoly capital coincides with the need for expanding social expenses. "In sum, the greater the growth of social capital, the greater the growth of the monopoly sector, the greater the state's expenditures on social expenses of production." [24]

The second thesis of this book is that "the accumulation of social capital and social expenses is a contradictory process which creates tendencies toward economic, social and political crises."[25]

It is argued that this is so because a "structural gap" has been created by capital costs being socialized more and more *while the "social surplus" is appropriated privately.* "The result is a tendency for state expenditures to increase more rapidly than the means of financing them."[26]

Secondly, it is argued that "the fiscal crisis is exacerbated by the private appropriation of state power for particularistic ends. A host of 'special interests'—corporations, industries, regional and other business interests—make claims on the budget for various kinds of social investment."[27]

In sum, the introduction to *The Fiscal Crisis of the State,* particularly the part entitled "Summation of the Theory of the Fiscal Crisis," is packed with ideas and lays down the directions that are pursued in the remainder of the work.

The Structure of the American Economy

The first chapter of the book, "An Anatomy of American State Capitalism," develops the first thesis presented in the introduction to the work. Here it is argued that economic activity in the U.S. is maintained by two broad groups of organizations: industries organized by private capital and industries organized by the state. Those organized by private capital are characterized as being members of two main types: those that are competitive and those that are monopolistic (in the usual sense the terms are used in political economics). Further, about a third of the work force is estimated to be employed by the competitive sector, the same for the monopoly sector and, as noted earlier, a third is thought to be employed by the state and "industries under contract with the state."[28] These estimates are not documented by O'Connor and must therefore be considered as plausible, but imprecise. O'Connor emphasizes that these sectors are interrelated and collectively form the major structural foundation of the political economy of American society. This society is termed a welfare-warfare economy; a contemporary economic system where the state maintains a peculiar variety of stabilization. The state serves capital by directly and indirectly contributing to the drive to accumulate the riches of the system primarily for the benefit of the owners of the means of production. Private profit is necessary for any production at all to be undertaken. Further, it is theorized that the monopoly sector industries are the engine of economic growth and capital accumulation which requires advancement in science and technology. It is argued that the sector has aided the growth of the monopoly sector and effect of this growth has been to require the growth of the state sector. More and more social capital is required by the nature of the complex monopoly sector which needs skilled administrative and technical workers, increasing amounts of infrastructure, etc. With increased interdependence in production, greater state expenditures are required for social consumption (such as social insurance of various kinds) as well. At the same time, markets do not grow as fast as productive capacity. Part of the problem stems from the low-wage competitive sector whose demand (because of lack of wherewithal) does not rise as fast as that in the higher wage monopoly sector.

Historically, it is argued in the tradition of Marxian imperialism theory, the answer to inadequate demand has been to seek overseas investment and trade (given the internal contradictions of the domestic economy). The involvement of U.S. industry abroad (controlling many world markets) has required a worldwide military establishment, foreign aid and loans, etc. O'Connor argues that the expansion of the surplus population (those who have grave difficulty finding any employment) and surplus productive capacity are part of the same process that occurs to promote the expansion of monopoly capitalism. The growth of the welfare state occurs under the same forces that create the warfare state. O'Connor summarizes his observations on expanding warfare and welfare expenditures in this way:

> The present situation thus is attributable to growing unemployment and poverty and the further development of the welfare state, on the one hand, and growing surplus productive capacity, the drive to expand, protect, and control foreign markets, and the growth of the warfare state, on the other. But whatever the specific conjuncture of forces at any time and in any society, the underlying dynamic of the expansion of welfare and warfare expenses is the process of capital accumulation in monopoly industries. [29]

Capital Accumulation as a Contradictory Process

O'Connor's argument, then, is that capital accumulation is a contradictory process which creates the conditions for an expanded state budget and a dependent population. The automobile industry, for example, is composed of primarily four business corporations in the U.S. and employs thousands of workers directly and millions more indirectly. If auto sales drop dramatically, jobs are lost by workers almost immediately so that auto manufacturers will decrease their variable costs and thus avoid the uneconomic prospect of having revenues less than total costs. The auto industry cannot survive, and would not, unless it makes a profit; the industry (to say the same thing in more Marxian terms) must appropriate the workers' surplus value, or the industry must part ways with the worker if the former relationship cannot be maintained. The state is the workers' primary refuge. It provides unemployment compensation and, if the downturn is prolonged, welfare payments. In the expansionary (and other) phase(s) of the business cycle, the state provided social capital such as education and training, research and development that aided in the development of technology (which resulted in cost savings for industry), and even, recollections of the immediate post-World War II period have it, direct gifts (or for, what is the same thing, a song) of plant and equipment. Further, the industry's product has use value because social capital (infrastructure) was created in the form of a vast network of roads and highways (while neglected in the area of alternative forms of transportation such as railroads). The state also played a part in maintaining corporate profits by direct and indirect purchases of the industry's product. During the economic downturn, the state must, to preserve its assumed legitimacy (and to alleviate genuine human distress), engage in expenditures on social expenses such as welfare. On the one hand, concentration in industry was assisted and not contained; on the other hand, a large number of workers, who are, on the whole, relatively well paid during the best of times, devote their energies to and for the accumulation of four business corporations. The contradiction, as a microcosm of the resultant stabilization problem, is that state expenditures tend to be greater, historically, than state revenues. In the last 100 years of capitalism the state and large corporations have become much more prominant in the everyday activities of everyone. More societal interdependence exists. The population has relocated geographically to create urban society; monopoly capitalism and the state form the main institutional system in which the majority of working people conduct their everyday affairs. This long paragraph raises but a few issues which surround and are part of the process of capital accumulation and which come to mind as a result of O'Connor's description of the structure of the economic system of the U.S. in this second half of the 20th century.

O'Connor's description of "American State Capitalism" seems generally plausible as a very broad overview which is supported by references to some specific examples (such as the entry of large-scale capital into agriculture, an industry pointed to by economists in introductory textbooks, traditionally, as one where the model of perfect competition is comparatively valid). In particular, O'Connor's discussion of the way in which the growth of monopoly capital seems to affect other parts of the structure of the economy is very important. Concurrent with the growth of monopoly capital and its expansion into agriculture, construction, and the services has been declining opportunities for competitive capital. In short, O'Connor's argument is that there is "overcrowding in the competitive sector of the economy." What is more, the competitive sector has resisted union organization at the same time it has provided an outlet for those who would otherwise be "proletarianized." The difficult position of competitive capitalism within the midst of monopoly capitalism requires small businessmen and farmers, as well as workers in these industries, to depend increasingly on the state—"indirectly in the form of fair-trade laws and similar protective legislation, directly in the form of loan guarantees, farm subsidies, and similar programs."[30] Outlays by the state in these areas, he points out, are forms of social expense.

The general argument is that a kind of dual economy exists. The monopoly capital segment is one in which many of the costs of industry are incurred by the state—profits are accumulated privately, costs are "socialized." In this monopoly sector wages tend to be quite high since labor costs can be effectively passed on to consumers. The competitive sector of the economy, on the other hand, tends to be less stable. The competitive sector absorbs, to some extent, the "surplus population" (which is equated with technological unemployment at one point)[31] and appears to be to O'Connor what the secondary labor market represents to dual labor market theorists. In brief, the primary labor market is taken to consist of people who work under favorable and stable conditions, with good pay and strong attachment to their jobs. Those in the secondary labor market are not well paid, their jobs are not secure, and their attachment to their employment is low.[32] This conceptualization of a dual economy is presented as an "ideal type" in O'Connor's work where the "monopoly, competitive, and state sectors are, at the abstract level, characterized by different modes of surplus value production, appropriation, and realization.[33] The different modes can be looked at in the following fashion:

> The competitive sector is mainly based on absolute surplus value production. It can increase profits only by paying low wages, maintaining poor working conditions, keeping hours of work long, etc. This sector has relatively less capacity for productivity upgrading; new firms enter easily, and workers are weakly organized. Productivity gains are passed to the whole economy through the price mechanism and easy entry tends to limit any firm's ability to expand the scale of production. This sector has historically demanded of the state that it adjudicate and expand markets, restrict imports, fix prices, provide social investments like highways, severely discipline labor, and expand foreign trade.[34]

Surplus value in the monopoly sector "tends to be created relatively, although speed-ups and the like are not unknown." Monopoly is materially creative in the sense that it is related to "rapid productivity increases" as applied science is integrated into the production process. With "large amounts of fixed capital, and a 'deal' concluded between dominant capital and bureaucratic trade union . . . produc-

tivity increases in higher wages as well as higher profits [are pre-
served which are] intended to insure capital's control over the
production process."[35] This political relationship, further, is necessary for the concentrated sector of the economy to be what it is.

The Bay Area collective points to the shortcomings of this conceptualization—the monopoly and competitive sectors—in the following
way:

> O'Connor creates multidimensional ideal types based on dif-
> ferences in capital and technology. These are useful, but seem to
> oversimplify the sectoral complexities of the organization of
> production. It is not clear, for example, if his monopoly/competi-
> tive distinction applies to broad economic sectors, particular
> industries, firms, or even jobs. Some industries, for example,
> have both monopolistic and small producers. Some firms employ
> both highly skilled, well-organized workers and unskilled, some-
> times poorly organized workers. O'Connor does not deal ade-
> quately with these questions, and fails to analytically differen-
> tiate between sectoral concepts based on production and circula-
> tion relations. Further, the political determinants of sectoral
> differentiation are not developed. Some labor segmentation
> theorists, for example, have argued that, contrary to O'Connor,
> the proliferation and hierarchical arrangement of job categories
> derives not from technical or capital-related needs, but from a
> *political* strategy to deliberately divide workers. While these
> alternative explanations need not be exclusive, they certainly
> suggest the need for further analysis.[36]

The collective cites Robert Averitt's *The Dual Economy: Dynamics of
American Industry Structure* as well as the "work of Barry Bluestone,
David Gordon, Rick Edwards, Herb Gintis and others on labor market
segmentation" as providing findings which would have sharpened
O'Connor's sectoral analysis had he incorporated them.[37]

O'Connor is very aware of the shortcomings of his conceptualization of industrial structure in *FCS*. He sees a flaw in his discussion
where he defined the competitive sector as being made up of
industries since, he argues, it is actually made up of firms. He cites the
example of the printing industry where there are some large, but
competitive sectors, firms that buy from and sell to monopoly sector
firms and therefore have stable orders, and a relatively stable demand
for workers who are comparatively well paid. He argues that there
are also a lot of small firms in the printing industry that are
characterized by unstable employment conditions and low wages
because they engage, primarily, in transactions with other small
firms. There is a need to specify the sectors more carefully and to
perhaps incorporate the work of dual labor market theorists as well

as the conceptual framework used in John Kenneth Galbraith's *Economics and the Public Purpose* (which is critiqued later in this chapter). With a more refined conceptual framework one could then attempt to verify that the monopoly and competitive sectors do, in fact, exist and the characteristics that distinguish each could be identified. Some characteristics that O'Connor proposes are wage rates and employment stability.[38]

To summarize briefly, the structure of the American economy is seen as interdependent with supporting interaction among the three sectors. Monopoly capital and the state work together to socialize the costs of production and maintain high wages for many of the monopoly sector workers as profits and wages are pegged to the levels possible under monopoly capital's ability to set prices. Those not engaged in the monopoly capital or state sectors of the economy are involved in the competitive sector where there is less security and stability and where wages are lower. In addition, there is a surplus population which is unemployed and underemployed and which generates a need for state outlays in the form of social expenses. Monopoly capitalism, then, as a system generates an increasing amount of expenditures for both social capital and social expenses while the enormous profits of monopoly capital are acquired privately.

Although the structure of the economy is symbiotic, it hardly produces social harmony. To demonstrate O'Connor's analysis on this point, there must first be an elaboration on his conceptualization of the state.

In terms of the production of surplus, which was looked at above in the competitive and monopoly sectors, the state is different in that it does not directly engage in this process "but instead appropriates it to maintain and enhance the conditions necessary for capital accumulation" while maintaining legitimacy which "means in practice that it must provide some broad social benefits."[39] Further, the state sector is an expanding sector but productivity expands less than in the private sector.

> The state sector expands because state agencies and contractors must supply social capital to the monopoly sector and because monopoly sector growth in turn requires that the state devote even more funds to social expenses. Costs of expanding state agencies and programs increase rapidly for two reasons: First, productivity increases are relatively small, and thus a rising portion of the total productive forces must flow into the state sector to maintain a constant level of state services per unit of

growing outputs. Second, wages are relatively high and increase
relatively rapidly. Wages are high because many, if not most,
state services . . . require a skilled and experienced labor force.
And wages increase rapidly because state sector rates tend to be
tied to monopoly sector productivity.[40]

In addition, "Monopoly sector money wages are pegged to productivity and cost of living. This fact has important consequences for
wages, costs, and production in state industries. There is a general
tendency for state sector wages to be driven up to the level prevailing
in the monopoly sector." This point is given substance by the
examples of "workers employed by state contractors . . . and state
agencies" who "receive union pay scales" and who are members of
state and local employee associations that are effective bargaining
agents, as well as the influence felt by increasing unionization among
workers in the state sector and the fact that wages "are determined
politically (rather than by the necessity of surplus value production,
as in the private sector), thus placing a floor on average pay scales, a
floor absent in the competitive sector."[41] The association of wages in
the state industries sector with monopoly sector productivity is, then,
one factor which results in an expanding state budget.

O'Connor argues that if one were seeking to do empirical work on
his formulation of the relationship of the state to private capital "the
main thing to prove statistically . . . is to show how the growth of
social capital creates the demand for the expansion of social expenses."[42] For example, one could ask, does government-sponsored
research and development produce technological unemployment
over time in some industries which results in the expansion of
unemployment compensation, welfare, and other government expenditures to alleviate problems encountered by the (new increment
to the) surplus population? O'Connor believes that the gross statistics
indicate this is true, and he cites the particular example of education
expenditures growing along with welfare.[43] A possible rejoinder is
that the simultaneous growth of various state expenditures does not
in and of itself prove much. More accurately, it is not totally
convincing to argue that both education and welfare expenditures
grew as part of the process where the growth of social capital
generates the conditions for the growth of social expenses. The causal
link is not obvious, at least in this instance. As in Baran and Sweezy's
Monopoly Capital, the conceptual framework of FCS seems more
powerful in the abstract.

Chapter 2 of *FCS*, entitled "Dimensions of the Crisis" provides an
elaboration on the theme that monopoly capitalism is at the root of

economic, social, and political crisis. It is argued that the simultaneous growth of the monopoly sector and the state sector produces serious problems for the political economy as a whole.

There are a number of contradictions (a theme characteristic of Marxian thought) implicit in American capitalism. Again, production is a social process, but the means of production are privately owned; under monopoly capitalism capital costs and social expenses are, in the long run, more and more socialized while profits are accumulated privately. "In the medium run, state sector wage costs become increasingly inflated because wage increases tend to outrace productivity increases." A larger number of people have become dependent on the state as the increasing interdependency of the society as a whole results in a growing "proletarianization." People having nothing but their labor and no other social institutions but the state to turn to in time of an economic downturn.[44]

Further, post-World War II economic growth, O'Connor argues, "has required continuing inflation and a continuing fiscal crisis (or 'inflation' of the state budget)."[45] O'Connor's reasoning is best left in his own words on this point:

> [T]he stability of U.S. capitalist society has depended upon three factors: Economic expansion overseas and worldwide economic hegemony; the maintenance of harmonious production relations in the monopoly sector; and the socialization of monopoly sector production costs and expenses, together with the private appropriation of profits and the absence of the socialization of wage payments. All of these conditions are closely related, and each has proven to be inflationary.[46]

Moderate inflation has not been opposed so long as many people found it acceptable as their real income did not decline. "In sum, until recently, the political balance favored moderate inflation—even though people on fixed incomes, many state employees and state clients, many small businessmen, and others were victimized by inflation."[47]

But as all things tend to pass, so does moderate inflation. Today inflation is a concern—to the point that wage and price controls were undertaken by the Nixon administration in the early 1970s and are seen to be a "permanent" necessity by some economists.[48]

> Today, inflation and fiscal crisis are anathemas to monopoly capital and the state. Reducing inflation and ameliorating the fiscal crisis have become the basic conditions of stability. Monopoly capital and the state must face up to a critical dilemma. On the one hand, monopoly industries must grant increases in money wages to avoid a rupture in relation with labor, even

though unit labor costs and prices continuously rise. On the other, domestic inflation worsens the fiscal crisis and tends to reduce foreign demand for U.S. products, cutting into exports and worsening the balance of trade. In addition, inflation pushed up the interest rate, which in turn, tends to choke off credit-financed spending on housing and consumer durable goods—two mainstays of the private economy. In brief, if monopoly capital keeps prices firm, rising costs cut into profit margins; if it increases prices, falling demand reduces sales and profits . . .[49]

O'Connor points out that, from a theoretical point of view, there are three ways for the state to keep costs down, address the problem of inflation, and deal with the fiscal crisis:

The first is to deflate the economy as a whole by engineering a managed recession. The second is to introduce and enforce wage and price controls. And the third is to cooperate with monopoly capital to increase productivity in the private and state sectors (in order to lower costs and relieve the fiscal crisis within the state sector). Each of these measures has been used to a greater or lesser extent in nearly all of the advanced capitalist countries.[50]

The "only practical long-run option available to the state is to encourage productivity in the monopoly sector (to retain costs and prices and increase production and profits) and in the state sector (to ameliorate the fiscal crisis)."[51] Wage-price controls and managed recession are considered to be highly problematic.

So it is possible, O'Connor argues, that a social-industrial complex[52] may be emerging to deal with the tendencies of contemporary capitalism. For this emergence to happen, it is argued, some political changes would have to occur. First, the ties between monopoly capital and the state will have to become even closer. Second, the influence of competitive capital (which O'Connor assumes to exist), "particularly its influence and power in local and state government and in Congress," would need to be weakened. Third, stronger bonds between monopoly capital and organized labor would be necessary.[53]

Still another set of factors that O'Connor points to appears in an article published more recently than FCS. It is here that a correction exists in what O'Connor termed an "idealist error" (his term, in personal correspondence) which limited the analysis to the factors above.[54]

In this, O'Connor gives more weight to the conditions that emerged during 1965–70 with respect to struggles undertaken by blacks and others who were members of the surplus population which put pressure on welfare (social expenses) spending. The general argument is that what was behind federal expenditures on health, education, and welfare growing from 21.7 percent of the federal budget in 1960 to 25.1 percent in 1965 and then to 32.5 percent in 1972 was the political impact of the surplus population on the state. Essentially O'Connor is arguing that the result of this struggle was the relative income share of the surplus population increasing somewhat with respect to the rest of the working class including organized labor. The implications of this were declining discipline among those in the lowest socioeconomic strata with respect to jobs (many in the competitive sector which also characterizes the industrial setting of the secondary labor market) and a resulting push for even greater centralization and concentration of capital in, for example, agriculture and construction. To paraphrase O'Connor's analysis, antipoverty and related programs tended to push up wages in this particular labor market which had an effect on prices and had some impact of the attractiveness of domestic products and services as compared to those from abroad. This phenomenon in turn exacerbated the fiscal crisis and resulted in a corresponding assault on the antipoverty budget and programs by the Nixon Administration in the first part of the 1970s.[55]

The rectification included a policy of "benign neglect" toward the lowest income strata of society and greater attention to the condition of organized labor and capital. This existed in the setting of antipoverty programs never being intended to eliminate poverty but rather to serve the function, as Piven and Cloward argue, to politically cool out the lowest rung of the socioeconomic strata.[56]

TABLE 3   TRENDS IN MILITARY AND SOCIAL EXPENDITURES

Year	Local, State, and Federal Expenditures as a Percentage of U.S. GNP	Military Expenditures as a Percentage of Local, State, and Federal Expenditures	The Ratio of Federal Social Expenditures to Military Expenditures
1973	37.8	18.5	1.45
1972	37.2	20.8	1.33
1971	35.1	23.7	1.16
1970	34.1	26.7	.96
1969	33.1	28.9	.83
1968	32.8	30.9	.80
1967	32.5	29.8	.78
1965	30.1	26.8	.80
1960	30.0	34.0	.59

*Federal social expenditures are defined as all subsidies to wages (health care, housing, welfare of all kinds, and basic education) and subsidies to capital in the form of interest payments, highways, higher education, manpower training and development of technology, including the space program. Military expenditures include veterans' payments and other military expenditures contained in appropriations of other branches of the government than the Department of Defense.

Source: *The Statistical Abstract for the U.S.*, 1973. Compiled by Al Szymanski, "Review Essay: The Fiscal Crisis of the State and the Unstable Economy," *The Insurgent Sociologist," vol. 4, no. 4 (Summer 1974), p. 82.*

The result of this struggle around the federal budget by different parts of the population, of different parts of labor and capital, has been an intensification of demands on the state and increasing problems of stabilization in the trade-off between unemployment and inflation. The outcome has been the development of more contradictions and a heightened economic, social, and political crisis which is perhaps more in its middle or beginning phase than toward its resolution. This crisis, O'Connor argues, has moved various groups to press for their demands more dramatically. If monopoly capital's domestic policy and budget are the victors in all of this, the frightening prospect of the introduction of American fascism in a less "friendly" fashion might be experienced.[57]

One reviewer questions the view that the state will continue to expand in "peacetime." It is argued that this appeared to be possible before 1968 when a "liberal coalition was emerging around the legacy of the Kennedy family which saw in some form of 'social-industrial complex' a way out of these contradictions."[58] A closer look, however, appears to document O'Connor's case. Table 3 presents data which leads another reviewer to state, "In the years after 1968 Nixon, in spite of his rhetoric, [had] been implementing the program (although not without a lot of foot dragging) of the social-industrial complex."[59] In the table it is seen that in 1960 local, state, and federal expenditures were 30 percent of GNP. By 1973 the Figure was 37.8 percent of GNP. In 1960 military expenditures were 34 percent of local, state, and federal expenditures. The figure was 18.5 percent by 1973. The ratio of federal social expenditures to military expenditures was .59 in 1960 while it was 1.45 in 1973.

Still another look at the expansion of the "public" sector points to these observations: total government purchases of goods and services were 10.8 percent in 1929 as compared to 20.6 percent in 1969. In 1929 state and local government purchases of goods and services were 9.1 percent of GNP and federal expenditures were 1.7 percent of GNP compared with 10.1 percent in the former case and 10.5 percent in the latter in 1969. Further, in 1940 the government share (federal, state, and local) of the total labor force was 8.9 percent as compared with 19.2 percent in 1969.[60] Although these figures do not capture a view that encompasses all of the state, they indicate that government is obviously much more involved in the contemporary economy than it was in earlier years. Whether this constitutes evidence which suggests that there has been the emergence of a social-industrial complex is a matter of interpretation. However, what seems inescapable is that the state is an important component of contemporary society and is something which must be reckoned with by social scientists. It is possible that both the *FCS* and its few reviewers have underestimated the organizational ability of capital and the state and their proximity to each other.

This view emerges from the awareness of an expanded state budget in comparison with all economic activity as well as the observation that increasing expenditures took place in spheres of activity unrelated to the military-industrial complex. Another factor that is instrumental in the formation of the view here that the social-industrial complex is already underway in a profound fashion stems from an awareness of one regional experiment involving state and corporate collaboration. The most striking example—and an admittedly unique one—is that of the Federation of Rocky Mountain States, Inc. which is discussed in some detail in the Appendix B. The Federation is a non-profit corporation which has brought together some 275 corporations and banks and several state governments to undertake a variety of activities using substantial amounts of federal funds. This one example suggests that the notion of monopoly capital should not be applied only in a national context. Firms that are unknown nationally may work quite compatibly with the largest corporations and the state for mutual (privately appropriated) benefit in geographic regions at the subnational level. The Federation of Rocky Mountain States could be seen as a kind of prototype for a national formalized state capitalism or for other regional attempts at the closer integration of capital and the state. Although a sketch of the Federation itself as an example of an emerging state capitalism is left to the Appendix, it is worthwhile to discuss on a theoretical level what a social-industrial complex implies for the society. In other words, it is important to ask: so what if the contradictions of capitalism result in a tighter relationship between the state and capital?

The Conflict Between Accumulation and Sociopolitical Legitimacy with the Social-Industrial Complex[61]

One might suggest that industry seeks to use a portion of the state (in the instance of the Federation funding and services from the federal and state governments as well as direct participation in policy formulation and implementation by its representatives) in an attempt to expand its markets, integrate its influence over the regional labor market, and be in tune with the available resources in the areas of land, energy, minerals, and forests. In addition, the Federation provides information and influence in the area of transportation which provides means (which generate private profit) by which to relate to actual and potential markets. What is more, a sophisticated communications system is in operation and is being further developed to coordinate the economic activity of private industry and information dissemination between private industry and the state, as well as augmenting communication within various parts of the state itself. All of this, it will be argued, is done at the relative expense of the people of the society (the noncapitalists) as a whole, and especially that of the lower socioeconomic strata, in that the social capital is provided by the state which was acquired by the state's appropriation of surplus value.

The contradiction that emerges is that the process of production is social, whereas accumulation is private. It can be pointed out that it is entirely possible that the social-industrial complex involves the redistribution from labor as a whole to the owners of capital through the institution of the state. The state, in addition, serves, on the one hand, to appropriate surplus, and, on the other hand, to actively participate in the use of that appropriated surplus to create social capital which can help to increase the appropriation by capital of relative surplus value as costs are reduced. This, as in the example of the Federation, decidedly appears to be a case of "socialism" for the membership of the Federation and "free enterprise" for the people who live in the Rocky Mountain states and more particularly the work force of the nation and even some parts of capital.

It might be argued that the people of the region stand to benefit from an improved job market and increased productivity in the state sector, and therefore a better return from expenditures by the state. If O'Connor's conceptual framework is accurate, however, the expanding social capital should at the same time generate expanding social expenses. One can only speculate, on the correlation, but the following line of reasoning suggests itself. In the first instance, to the extent that the operations of the social-industrial complex are funded at the federal level, there is a transfer from the entire taxed population to the region under question. More specifically, the transfer is primarily to private capital. It would seem that the distribution of income in the area and the nation may be affected as business profits are increased by the activities of the SIC. That is, successful efforts to expand markets will increase the income and wealth of the owners of the means of production more than anyone else. And, as is known, the upper socioeconomic strata are not taxed progressively.[62] The issue then is that the social-industrial complex benefits those who acquire profit while the activities are funded by everyone who pays taxes.

Another aspect is that the integration of capital and the state may enhance the productivity of the former and thereby, for a given amount of product, require relatively fewer workers. Workers, if they are lucky, are displaced to the secondary labor market or; if they are not so fortunate, they become unemployed. The latter instance requires social expenses and claims on the budget of the state. In the former instance workers enter a lower income bracket and the state appropriates less from them.

It would seem that the line of reasoning above applies to the national macroeconomic level more than to the regional level. What might occur at the regional level is a better employment picture for workers but, as the fallacy of composition suggests, what occurs in part of the system does not necessarily add up to a harmonious whole. As O'Connor points out (in personal correspondence in January 1975) the introduction of the social-industrial complex in the Rocky Mountain region directly implies the expansion of the surplus population in other parts of the system, such as the Midwest and East, which are not, at this writing, engaging in such activity. Here seem to be the seeds of a theory of the *spatial manifestations* of the general argument in *The Fiscal Crisis of the State* which would merit a long exposition which can only be mentioned here.[63]

Although they are not the specific focus here, some rather sobering political implications also emerge. Like corporations generally, be they profit or nonprofit, the Federation of Rocky Mountain States, Inc. is accountable to itself and its membership (not even the possible safeguard of stockholders' ire exists in this instance) and the possible rebuke by grantors (which are mainly part of the federal bureaucracy). The elected political officials are actively involved in a body which is beyond electoral politics and which works directly with representatives from private industry in the task of accumulation at the relative expense of the people. The operations of the Federation, in short, are not so much politically accountable as they are administrative (and to some extent entrepreneurial), and although state governments may come and go, the regional administrative organization of the Federation of Rocky Mountain States remains. Voters appear to be choosing the integration of capital and the state no matter whom they actually vote for, so long as state government participation in the Federation exists.

But the maintenance of sociopolitical legitimacy is not assured given the rather blatant nature of this instance of social-industrial complex, and that issue is a crucial one which is at the root of the actual course of events that will emerge in the Rocky Mountain states or anywhere that the social-industrial complex exists. On the probability of the maintenance of sociopolitical legitimacy one can only speculate since to give this matter the attention it deserves would require extensive detailed analysis of the possible conflicts that are likely to develop based on the socioeconomic composition of the area. O'Connor poses a question worth pondering which outlines some of the issues: "Will industry in [the] Rockies hire the Chicano surplus population in Denver [for example], or what?" Perhaps the issue of legitimacy will not be a huge barrier to the further implementation of the complex inasmuch as the development of the region may be of a capital intensive nature without the corresponding expansion of the surplus population in the Rocky Mountain states (although the expansion of the surplus population is implied elsewhere). The sort of reaction that is probable is especially under question because of the region's comparatively smaller incidence of organized labor. Perhaps an awareness of the state capitalist nature of this particular example of the social-industrial complex, however, would be precisely one factor that would generate an intensified need for labor to organize more thoroughly and quickly.

These arguments strongly suggest that there is every reason to be highly skeptical of this sort of regional organization. It is the brainchild of state capitalism and provides zeal only for corporate liberals. To bring regional industry directly into the process of regional "planning" is like inviting national industry into the process of *direct* participation in national decision-making. While there are many documented instances of the latter it is doubtful that most people would view the federal government as legitimate if this were to obtain. There seems no more reason for this arrangement to exist at the regional level except that the opportunities for mystification seem to manifest themselves more dramatically. Yet a high corporate post seems to make a person powerful in the affairs of society. A national social-industrial complex might be the path of "development" for the U.S. political economy unless opposition emerges to the current existence of state capitalism and additional plans for a more formalized planned capitalism. There are those who are pushing for the creation of a planning body within the executive branch of the federal government. Such a body would usher in a new era in American capitalism and would be equivalent to what O'Connor calls the social-industrial complex at the national level. Although a democratic socialism would be far more appealing than the national socialism implied by the social-industrial complex, it is not at all clear that the social basis exists which would create that democratic socialism. But it seems certain that the usual political mechanisms—such as periodic national elections—are irrelevant to the creation of democratic socialism and are supportive of the creation of an American style national socialism.

This argument should not be taken to mean that a more pronounced American style of national socialism is inevitable. Indeed, an awareness of the possibility could alter that scenario. O'Connor himself has voiced the opinion that fascism in the U.S. is not likely and that the world learned much from the experience of the 1930s and 1940s. Pessimists, however, are quick to point out that the U.S. government was nothing short of fascist in the war against Indochina and that much of the U.S. population was like the "good Germans" during Hitler's reign of terror. One writer holds the opinion, though, that really progressive change *could* be undertaken to transform institutions through existing Constitutional law. Peter Bachrach argues that a central problem in the U.S. is that the "political" is usually viewed narrowly and as being applicable only to official governmental decision-making. Bachrach points out, for example, that although giant corporations are not formally part of the U.S. government, they are similar to the latter in that "they both authoritatively allocate values for the society." General Motors, for example, should be seen as a portion of the political sector in which democratic norms apply. Even though GM is a private firm, it performs a public function. Thus, it is subject to the limitations of the Constitution. The Supreme Court, Bachrach argues, has expanded the notion of "state action" which has resulted in constitutionalizing some "private governments." If corporations were to be considered political institutions, which they are in fact, they would be within the confines of the Constitution and democratic principles.[64]

O'Connor's View of Possible Directions for the U.S. Political Economy

O'Connor's theoretical framework argued that the development of the SIC in a portion of the system may well exacerbate the fiscal crisis of the state so far as the system as a whole is concerned. What may occur, to the extent that the SIC exists in but part of the national political economy, is an interregional redistribution of income with the redistribution from labor to capital being the most striking possibility. No doubt some income redistribution among workers could also occur interregionally. If the social-industrial complex were to be developed nationally, the prospects, so far as economic stabilization is concerned, might be somewhat different. In the last chapter of *The Fiscal Crisis of the State* is a description of the dimensions of a possible social-industrial complex.

> The fiscal crisis of the capitalist state is the inevitable consequence of the structural gap between state expenditures and

revenues. It is our contention that the only lasting solution to the crisis is socialism. However, the state might be able to ameliorate the fiscal crisis by accelerating the growth of the social-industrial complex. Politically, the complex consists of the slowly evolving alliance between sections of monopoly capital and the surplus population, together with low-paid monopoly sector labor. Economically, the complex consists of the transformation of social expenses into social capital by mounting socioeconomic programs both to provide new subsidized investment opportunities for monopoly capital and to ameliorate the material impoverishment of the surplus population. Sociologically, the complex consists of the creation of a new stratum of indirectly productive workers—the small army of technologists, administrators, paraprofessionals, factory and office workers, and others who plan, implement, and control the new programs in education, health, housing science, and other spheres penetrated by social-industrial capital.[65]

This last chapter of *FCS* spots some of the issues surrounding the possible development of a national social-industrial complex that might prohibit or generate it beyond an experimental basis and the meaning that such a complex would have economically, socially, and politically. The full development of such a complex is not viewed as inevitable; but were it to occur, it would require "enormous changes throughout American society, particularly in the contours of the political-economic system."[66]

Further, the meaning of the SIC in terms of economic stability on the macroeconomic level would be, in O'Connor's view, as follows:

The hoped-for long-term effect of the more rapid development of the social-industrial complex is an increase in productivity throughout the economy. Such growth might help alleviate the fiscal crisis because each dollar of government expenditure might be more "efficient" in the sense of adding to the economy's long run productive capacity, thus expanding total income and the tax base and easing the burden of financing the budget. In other words, the fundamental purpose of the complex is to gear the state sector more closely to the monopoly sector—the dynamic sector in terms of growth of production.[67]

O'Connor thinks that the vast changes that would foster the development of the SIC are at least partially underway. In view of the preceding discussion, this might be considered an understatement.

First, monopoly capital, including branches of the military-industrial complex itself, must attempt to solve the fiscal crisis and the problem of inflation, on the one hand, and the problem of insurgency and radical movements among the surplus population on the other.

Second, and related to the first point, movements among the poor, minority groups, women, youth, and other sections of the population are demanding basic changes that will alter the distribution of income and economic opportunities in their favor. Third, Europe and Japan not only are on their feet economically but also in many fields are outcompeting the United States, and increasingly are interested more in world markets (including markets in the socialist countries than in expanding American "protection" against possible "aggression" from the socialist world. In the United States as well, more and more capital is being internationalized, or invested in international corporations which trade and invest with anyone for a profit—including the socialist countries in eastern Europe and the USSR. And a general sense that the American empire has become intolerably expensive in both lives and money is reflected in the growth of neoisolationist sentiment. The state bureaucracy itself signals its willingness to replace some military-complex activity with social-industrial investments and programs. In fact, this combination of factors blocked additional funds for the SST and almost scuttled the Lockheed loan.

Government and business are attempting on a broad front to enlist "allies" in the struggle with those opposed to the social-industrial complex. Urban coalitions that work with black militants have been established. Students and youth are promised that America can reform itself and offered new careers and economic opportunities that will "serve the people." And the regional economic and political infrastructures that are being set up will, it is hoped, take root and provide the framework for the accumulation of social-industrial capital. Other practical and ideological steps include dozens of experimental programs and investments in education, health, transportation, pollution control, and other fields.[68]

These factors (which are themselves subject to a detailed discussion that will not be undertaken here) are not at all monolithic though they are formidable. In opposition to the SIC, or at least not in favor of it, stand competitive sector capital, organized labor, and the military-industrial complex (MIC). These groups stand in opposition, it is argued, because they have little to gain from the closer integration of capital and the state. The competitive sector is labor intensive and will not benefit much from more education expenditures, research and development, and so on. Further, the competitive sector rejects welfare and social programs for ideological reasons and because the owners of competitive enterprises do not wish to pay for them. Organized labor, O'Connor argues, would be opposed to the SIC they would be taxed to finance it, and the bulk of newly created jobs would go to those in the surplus population. In addition, the position of organized labor would be weakened vis-à-vis the rest of the work force if the SIC were to work. As far as the military-industrial complex is concerned, why should those who run the institutions in this complex care if the SIC were to be developed? One reason is that perhaps great changes in current arrangements would have to be experienced. It seems likely that the MIC would be on the side of maintaining the status quo.[69]

The preceding sketch is only a partial one of the ideas contained in *The Fiscal Crisis of the State* on the social industrial complex, which is seen as the more plausible way to abate the fiscal crisis if the economy continues to deteriorate and if both managed recession and wage-price controls prove to be unsatisfactory or unacceptable. It is no revelation to note that the development of a social-industrial complex would not be at all politically neutral and would not lead to the conclusion that it would put an end to discussions of various normative stances. The SIC would represent a more formalized version of monopoly state capitalism which would be quite consistent with a hierarchically ordered society even though the fiscal crises might be contained for a time. The SIC might be simply a more sophisticated form of "friendly fascism."[70] It would be one that would require a particular variety of political "success." Further,

> the social-industrial complex and the move toward decentralization embrace contradictory and potentially explosive goals. If the social crisis that underlies the fiscal crisis is not exacerbated by the emergence of a strong left-wing revolutionary movement (or a right-wing, fascistic movement), a fully developed social-industrial complex is a possibility. But if American politics takes a sharp leftward or rightward turn, it is clear that the social, economic, and political meaning of the complex will be drastically altered.[71]

The last two paragraphs of *The Fiscal Crisis of the State* offer a resounding conclusion to the argument of the book as a whole and are taken here for purposes of transition to a counter thesis on the meaning of the dual economy and the developments which exist in the state, as well as some of the implications for American society.

> In the final analysis, whether a social-industrial complex really gets off the ground, whether divisions between state and private workers grow or narrow, and whether state worker organizations can forge an alliance with organized labor and state dependents, radicals, and revolutionaries will not be able to exploit present opportunities, much less those that might appear in the future, in the absence of a mass socialist movement that cuts across all division within the working class. If monopoly capital's ideological and political hegemony is not effectively challenged, if a unified movement is not organized around opposition to monopoly capital's budgetary priorities, the fiscal crisis will continue to divide all those groups and strata that today fight in dismal

isolation for a greater share of the budget or for a smaller share of the tax burden. Put another way, in the absence of a political movement that transcends particular interests, divisions between monopoly sector workers, state workers, and the surplus population could very well deepen.

Finally, in the absence of a socialist perspective that puts forth alternatives to every facet of capitalist society and that can help people comprehend every issue from the class nature of budgetary control to the nature of tax exploitation to the process by which the uses of technology and science are decided, unionists, organizers, and activists will continue to function in a relative theoretical vacuum. Precisely because we live at a time when all strata of the working class relate to each other more and more politically (and at a time when ultimate contradiction is the use of political or social means to achieve individual ends), what is needed is a socialist perspective that seeks to redefine needs in collective terms. The fact is that even if the working class socialized the entire share of income going to profits, the fiscal crisis would reappear in a new form—unless both social investment and social consumption and individual consumption and individual modes of life are redefined. Stokely Carmichael's saying, "Individualism is a luxury that we can no longer afford," is becoming true in a political as well as economic sense. In the absence of this kind of general historical consciousness, it will not be possible for organizers and activists to come to grips with even direct and immediate budgetary issues, not to speak of questions of authority, bureaucracy, social control, racism, and sexism—or, finally, the question of what will be the new material basis for social existence itself.[72]

The "Practical Politics" of Theoretical Stances

Since there is clearly not an organized socialist movement in the United States which comes anywhere near the political strength of the majority parties, since the emergence of the social-industrial complex should be viewed as being in its infancy, and since even the more critical interpretations of the dynamics of contemporary capitalism, such as O'Connor's, are not widely known and are, in fact, sometimes consciously suppressed,[73] it seems useful at this point to note that there is a more widely received interpretation of the contemporary political economy which is similar in some ways to O'Connor's *FCS* but which might appeal to the more established parts of American society for economic and social change. It is Harvard Professor, former Ambassador, past president of the American Economic Association, and sometime adviser to Presidents, John Kenneth Galbraith's *Economics and the Public Purpose*. A contrast of

The Fiscal Crisis of the State and the Galbraith work seems useful at this point to clarify the issues more fully. It will become even more clear that the Marxian work and the archetype represented by Galbraith's writings differ in important ways that must be understood in order to grasp the meaning of the contemporary situation in the United States and in much of the capitalist world. As a matter of fact, it can be said that Galbraith and the Marxian writers have observed some of the same structural phenomena similarly during this decade and the last but have reached quite different conclusions about what the meaning of these structural features is.

Galbraith's Economics and the Public Purpose

Galbraith's important work, *The New Industrial State*, which was published shortly after Baran and Sweezy's *Monopoly Capital,* offered a quite different interpretation of some similar phenomena (primarily the place of giant industry in American society). The same could be said of *Economics and the Public Purpose* in comparison with O'Connor's *FCS*. Both Marxian analyses appeared in print before the respective Galbraith works but each was, in comparison with the attention given to Galbraith by the media, nearly ignored.[74] Whether or not *The Fiscal Crisis of the State* will receive even the attention given to *Monopoly Capital* remains to be seen, though an impressionistic judgment is that *FCS* has attracted a great deal of attention among those who are attracted to radical and Marxian political economics, as well as others.

The discussion that follows uses an important review of *Economics and the Public Purpose* by Paul Sweezy as well as a discussion of the book offered by Robert Heilbroner.[75] In this latest book, Galbraith expands upon his idea that there is a "new industrial state," which contains the "technostructure" and the "scientific and intellectual estates" (discussed in some detail in the preceding chapter) as transmitters of consciousness by which the economic system, with the help of others, would be "reformed." Galbraith moves quite far beyond these earlier concepts and appears to be attempting to firmly establish his own brand, or tradition, of economic thought. He is obviously critical of neo-classical economics and in fact says, "It will be guessed that the neo-classical system is not a description of reality. And this the ensuing pages will affirm."[76] But he is no adherent to Marxian views either as he clearly demonstrates in an early chapter:

> One consequence of the rejection of the neo-classical model is a renewed interest in Marx. The Marxian system was once the

great alternative to classical economic thought. Numerous of its tenets are in striking contrast with the more implausible assumptions of the neo-classical model. It accords a major role to the large enterprise. . . .

This reaction is not one . . . in which I concur. . . . This is to substitute one insufficient view of economic society for another. Honesty and perhaps also courage are associated with acceptance of what exists.[77]

Like O'Connor, Galbraith sees the existence of two significant segments of the structure of the economy of the U.S.—large industry, particularly the 1,000 largest corporations, and the market system (or competitive enterprises). However, Galbraith regards the largest corporations as constituting a "planning system." It is made up of a thousand or so huge corporations which put out 75 percent or more of industry's production.[78] Also like O'Connor, Galbraith sees the largest corporations—the oligopolistic and monopolistic sector—as the dominant force in the economy as a whole.

Galbraith lays down his view of the private sector in this way:

The planning system seeks to exercise control over its economic environment, and . . . it succeeds. The market system manifests the same desire, is much more visible in its effort and is much less successful. The one system dominates its environment; the other remains generally subordinate to it.[79]

He discusses the market system where it is argued that many services are "the domain of the small firm and thus of the market system."[80] Also, "as services resist organization, so also do the arts."[81] As to the future of the arts in the market system, it is concluded, "they will continue to be a major stronghold of the individual and the small firm."[82] Further, the relationship between the two parts of the privately owned sector is seen as one where "there is . . . exploitation as between parts of the economy. . . ." where, like many Marxian writers, the view is that the existence of competitive capital is seen as not being contrary to the interests of centralized and concentrated capital. In addition, Galbraith's view is that there is an unequal development of the parts.[83] In sum, however, a clear depiction of what the market system really is, is not fully developed. The reader is left, presumably, to deduce what the market system is taken to be by comparing it with the description of the planning system.

This deduction, however, will not be all that easy since the discussion is conducted at a high level of abstraction which is more a rejoinder to neo-classical theory than a solid and plausible description of contemporary economic reality. It appears that Galbraith has not moved beyond *The New Industrial State* in this book as far as his conception of the place of large corporations in American society is concerned. Rather, he has joined this previously constructed view with a more broad and improved outlook that includes a discussion of large corporations and their relationship with government and with competitive enterprise. In essence then, Galbraith is a kind of dual economy theorist, as are O'Connor and others. But Galbraith leaves the reader without a clear and believable theory of the state and offers no succinct criticism of what is wrong with a symbiotic relationship between the different public and private sectors even though an impressive list of contemporary economic problems is compiled including irrationality; the maldistribution of income; maldistribution of power between economic sectors, particularly between "the planning system" and the "market system"; various inequities (such as the most pleasant jobs also paying the most); superfluous production rather than in the areas of greatest need; ecological concerns as they are related to the modern economy; inflation; shortages of some commodities; and so on. Following this list is the observation that it may be possible for the economic system to perfect itself through reforms, since, as is pointed out in the preface to the book, Galbraith is "a reformer and not a revolutionist."[84] One cannot help but feel, after a comparison of the thought of O'Connor and Galbraith particularly, that this latter fact may get in the way of his analysis of society since to lack faith in the capacity to reform the system, by Galbraith's criteria, might result in losing hope itself. Sweezy suggests that this normative stance may in fact underlie Galbraith's theory of the technostructure and its relationship to the planning system.[85]

Heilbroner points out that Galbraith, as a writer within the tradition of political economy, has had the unifying theme of power running through his works.[86] Heilbroner argues that in comparison with *American Capitalism* and *The Affluent Society,*

> *The New Industrial State* (1967) pressed this conception of power further. The themes of massive economic strength, already stressed in *American Capitalism,* and of the manipulation of the private sector, which figured large in *The Affluent Society,* were combined to portray capitalism as a system in which the organizing principle was that of planning, disguised by rhetoric and ideology to appear as "competition." The planning was organized by and for its vast corporate entities—the central repositories of power within the system—and carried out by the operations of the "technostructure," a word that emphasized the

bureaucratic, rather than entrepreneurial, attribute of corporate management.

Galbraith's latest book, *Economics and the Public Purpose*, does not significantly alter this conception of capitalism as a system of disguised private planning.[87]

The feature that sets this book off from other Galbraith writings in Heilbroner's view "is not the diagnosis of, but the suggested response to power. The core of the book, in short, is a bold program designed to cope with the power structure of capitalism."

But to have a program, one must have a realistic appraisal of the situation. Although Galbraith does know that a few hundred corporations turn out a huge percentage of the dollar value of product and services[88] and that a market sector exists along side, he offers no satisfactory theory of the state or even the structure of the economy. A criticism that follows is that Galbraith's economic dualism is one where ideal types that are polar extremes are created, which can also be said of O'Connor's conceptualization. But it seems that the labels chosen by Galbraith are less descriptive of the private economy than is plausible in comparison to O'Connor's choice of words (though whether this matters is open to discussion). Further, as Sweezy argues,

> the picture of a more or less homogeneous "market system" confronting a handful of giant corporations is fanciful in the extreme. Not that the small, exploited, and self-exploiting enterprise doesn't exist in such areas of the economy as agriculture, retail trade, and services; it does exist and it is victimized by the system, just as Galbraith says. But there are also plenty of winners who are by no stretch of the imagination in Galbraith's planning system. To name only a few of the more important categories is to reveal how extensive and significant the phenomenon is: small and medium-sized corporations in manufacturing and trade, locally based construction firms (nearly the whole construction industry), large farmers and ranchers, real estate owners and operators, owners of radio and TV stations, local bankers, professionals (especially doctors and lawyers).[89]

Of course, much of this observation applies to FCS as well.

To the extent that it exists at all, Galbraith's theory of the state is not nearly as useful as his critique of the theory arising out of neo-classical and Keynesian economics. Indeed, given his predilection for reform, Galbraith suggests a variety of ways the state can be used to stabilize the economic system, whereas, curiously, in other places, he recognizes that the state has been captured, in part, by the upper socioeconomic stratum. For example, he argues that the "tax system has . . . come to reflect, increasingly, the preferences of the planning system—and notably the preferences of the higher-salaries members of the technostructure."[90] In addition, Galbraith argues that "any particular intervention by the state is against the public interest. And one must expect that the planning system will at least partly capture any regulatory body for its own purposes. Many have noted that regulatory agencies tend to become the instruments, even the puppets, of the industries they are supposed to regulate. This we see to be normal." The remedy, Galbraith says, is for the state to be broken free from "the power of the planning system."[91] Galbraith sees the "planning sector" as getting what it wants from the state but views the state as not "the executive committee of the bourgeoisie, but it is more nearly the executive committee of the technostructure."[92] In either case, obviously, a problem exists if a transformation from monopoly state capitalism to socialism is the goal (and it is toward this professed goal that Galbraith sketches a program).[93] Galbraith's answer to this difficult problem is that "if there is to be any change for emancipation of the state, there must be a political grouping that accepts the public cognizance and is expressly committed to the public purpose."[94] Galbraith makes the following observations about the strength of the private sector in public affairs:

> In the neo-classical system, as in the popular myth, the voter instructs the legislator and the legislator relays the instruction to the public bureaucracy. The capitalist sought to alter this arrangement, not without success, by winning control of the legislator. The planning system also has a substantial measure of control over the legislature through its management of belief. But it has a much more forthright and direct control of legislators by way of the public bureaucracy.[95]

Galbraith also discusses the ways in which the congressional seniority and committee structure serve to make Congress responsive more to private interests than the public interest and argues that "there should be a presumption not in favor of reelection but against it."[96] It is also argued that the Congress should not be considered part of the public bureaucracy but rather should be motivated "to be responsive to public concerns." If it were, Galbraith says, even a weak President would be moved to pursue the public interest. With this said, he offers a sketch of the areas of public action that are believed to be possible and necessary.[97]

While ideas about the good society and desirable structural reforms may be interesting to ponder one cannot help but notice that Galbraith essentially dances around the specific political mechanisms which would move the U.S. economy and society from where it is to where he suggests that it should be. In fairness, it should be added that this criticism also applies to revolutionary socialists. His view of the state is much more thin and less penetrating than that developed by O'Connor. It may not, in fact, be unreasonable to see his view as somewhat schizophrenic in that he recognizes the enormous power of "the planning system" in both the public and private sectors but then appears to have some faith in traditional political methods to seek change.

A major break from past writings is Galbraith's use of the term "socialism" to describe the sort of changes he would like to see occur. He advocates, for example, the nationalization of selected industrial sectors, although it is not clear precisely which sectors they would be. Of socialism Galbraith says

> This is the new socialism which searches not for the positions of power in the economy but for the positions of weakness. And again we remark that most reliable of tendencies—and the best of tests of the validity of social diagnosis—which is that circumstance is forcing the pace. In all the developed countries governments have been forced to concern themselves extensively with housing, health, and transportation. Everywhere they are already, in large measure socialized. This is true in the United States as elsewhere.[98]

As A. Dale Tussing points out (in personal communication) this is called "dust bin socialism" in England and as O'Connor notes, the *costs* are socialized but the profits are not which is part of the basis for the fiscal crisis of the state.

Galbraith concludes his discussion of socialism in this way:

> For unduly weak industries and unduly strong ones—as a remedy for an area of gross underdevelopment and as a control on gross overdevelopment—the word socialism is one we can no longer suppress. The socialism already exists. Performance as well as candor would be served by admitting to the fact as well as to the need. And in doing so we would be showing that the planning system cannot always make disreputable that of which it disapproves.[99]

This is perhaps the weakest argument in the whole of *Economics and the Public Purpose.* How does a nation have socialism while maintaining capitalism? O'Connor's perspective on big business and the state seems much more to the point when he says that a fundamental feature of capitalism in the U.S. is the joint venture between monopoly capital and the state seeking to accumulate while maintaining the legitimacy of the system. If this is socialism, it is a curious brand of "socialism" for the relatively rich and powerful with "free enterprise" being maintained for everyone else to encounter as a popular myth. It must be concluded that Galbraith seems to step forward advocating a more refined state capitalism. His criticisms of the system seem to run nowhere as deep as that of O'Connor or Baran and Sweezy. Galbraith tends to see the technostructure, not the owners of capital, as those who have power. As Sweezy puts it

> [w]hy call this a utopia rather than what Galbraith doubtless believes it to be, i.e., a hard-headed, realistic, and realizable program of social reform? The reason quite simply is that his conception of the power structure is light years away from the reality of monopoly capitalist society.[100]

Sweezy proves to be a harsh and persuasive critic of the "model" which Galbraith substitutes for "the neo-classical picture of a consumer-dominated and producer-powerless self-adjusting market system which fails to perform satisfactorily only when deluded intellectuals and ignorant politicians meddle with it."[101] One criticism of the Galbraith conception of the dual economy is that the "planning system" does not "do any planning together, and [does] not constitute a system in the usual sense of a collection of entities strongly interrelated among themselves and more weakly related to their environment."[102] Sweezy sees this as an ideological conceptualization in that it points to perpetrating the myth that not the capitalists but rather a large group of specialists, the technostructure, are in control of corporations. Galbraith sees the technostructure as only representative of itself with its power derived largely from "its ability to hoodwink or brainwash most other people into believing that its purposes are identical with the public purpose." The Galbraithian solution to this problem would be to educate people and "break the society's thralldom to the technostructure."[103]

Both Heilbroner and Sweezy point out that Galbraith avoids a discussion of the class interests which are embodied in the contemporary institutions and therefore perpetrates the illusion that a responsive Congress and an informed public will guide the political economy toward a rather nondisruptive better day. Heilbroner says this:

> What lacks in this generalized discussion is an analysis of the underlying purpose for which the technostructure exerts its organizing capabilities under capitalism. *In particular, what lacks is a description of the general class interests that are served by the operation of the technostructure in a capitalist society.*[104]

Heilbroner notes that the notion of class interests and class structure is not an uncontroversial one. But if it has no validity, "how does it happen that so many of the prevailing beliefs and operative institutions in capitalist society are compatible with, or supportive of, the claims of massed property?"[105] Heilbroner's criticism of the Galbraith theory of the technostructure is that

> [c]apitalism as a system cannot be adequately explained—much less reformed—as long as it is viewed as nothing more than a structure of interlocked bureaucracies that display the self-preservative and self-aggrandizing drives of any such structure. Capitalism must be seen as a social system permeated from top to bottom with a belief in the divine rights of property, and therefore as a system whose operation systematically produces and reproduces rewards and privileges for those whose place in society is linked with property.[106]

Sweezy's argument is that "the capitalists dominate the giant corporations of today as completely as they did the smaller enterprises of a hundred years ago."[107] What is suggested, in agreement with Heilbroner, is the need for class analysis. When this analysis is undertaken

> things look rather different. The higher reaches of the government bureaucracies (including the judiciary) are overwhelmingly staffed by members of the dominant economic class and/or people dependent on them and the political party organizations are controlled at every level by the vested interests which stand to gain most from the protection and favors which the local, state, and federal governments are in a position to hand out. These are facts which have been confirmed by innumerable empirical studies of cities, towns, an political institutions, though it is true that not all of the authors of these studies draw the logical conclusion that government in the United States is owned lock, stock, and barrel by exactly the same interests that own most of the country's wealth and control its economic life. These interests, taken together, constitute a ruling class in the fullest sense of the term, the richest and most powerful class in the history of the world.[108] . . .

> The implications of this for Galbraith's strategy of reform are of course devastating. If the enemy is a rootless, upstart technostructure which maintains itself in power mainly by selling a phony ideological bill of goods, then it makes sense to rely on an ideological counterattack followed by an effort to win the Democratic party over to Galbraith's new brand of populism. But if the enemy is in fact an enormously powerful bourgeoisie with two centuries of experience in ruling behind it and absolutely no scruples about using every available means to achieve its ends, then a rather different strategy seems called for.
> Above all, one had better look around for possible allies who could enter upon a struggle to unseat the class now in power with a reasonable prospect of success. And I challenge Galbraith, or

anyone else, to say where such allies might conceivably be found except in the working class, if we use the term in a broad sense to include the great majority of those who must work for a living regardless of the color of their collars. Workers have potential power not because they are in the majority—when the chips are down no ruling class cares for the arithmetic of minorities and majorities—but because they are indispensable to the process of production and hence to the very life of society. [109]

In sum, Galbraith's interpretation seems much less convincing, much more round-about, unsystematic and ideological, and, as Sweezy argues, utopian than O'Connor's. The work of the latter offers a much more specific focus on the structure of the economy, its relationship with the state, and the state itself than does the work of Galbraith in this latest book. O'Connor lays out a theoretical framework that could be helpful, particularly with more conceptual and empirical work, to understand economic reality, [110] and possibly what should and could or is likely to be done about it, how that might occur, and who the principle actors would be.

Toward a Synthesis and Critique of Marxian and Galbraithian Perspectives on the Dual Economy, the State, and Economic Instability in the United States

Both Galbraith and O'Connor present perspectives which are useful in moving toward a rather formidable conceptual framework useful for the understanding of the contemporary political economy of the U.S. The perspective developed by O'Connor is much more convincing than Galbraith's. Although neither author uses the term "dual economy," it seems useful and accurate to see them both as encompassing theories of economic dualism in their analysis. Further, the conceptual scheme of each could be enriched by incorporating more specifically the work of other theorists of economic dualism. If, for example, the work of dual labor market theorists and the notion that there is a dual welfare system [111] were added to the idea that there are distinct sectors of the private portion of the economy, it would seem that powerful advances in theories about the functioning of the political economy might occur. Work toward the development of a conceptual framework might go far toward explaining the complex generic economy-wide forces at work in advanced capitalism and specifically the causes of the vexing problems of unemployment, subemployment, and inflation as well as many other difficulties which are economic and beyond.

Galbraith offers a more thorough critique of neo-classical economics in his work, but he is less successful in putting a new conceptual framework in its place than is O'Connor. The former is aware of a "dual economy," but he may well underestimate the extent to which the concentrated sector is rooted in what Marxian writers would call the ruling class and the extent to which the ruling class has control over, and is very much part of, the state. O'Connor, on the other hand, has put his efforts into creating a new theory of the state using Marxian categories (in a loose way), and enticingly argues that the state seeks to fulfill the functions of accumulation and legitimization but does so with accompanying economic, social, and political instability.

Galbraith's discussion of the contemporary situation is seriously flawed. More accurately it is ideological and supportive of capitalist hegemony. Yet, his view of the dual economy is useful, and his critique of neo-classical economics is persuasive. On balance, the most penetrating analysis of the present situation does not emerge from *Economics and the Public Purpose*. Galbraith, for example, sees depressions as a phenomenon passed when other spheres of observation detect remarkable economic insecurity. There are specific job markets where depressionlike levels of unemployment do seem to exist[112] while there is substantial subemployment in much of the society. Real wages have fallen in recent years, and there appears to be a general perception that the economy has been deteriorating, in a sense beyond but including that reflected in statistical accounts.[113] As A. Dale Tussing put it (at a teach-in on the economy at Syracuse University in February 1975), "if depressions are a 'thing of the past,' so is full employment. We do not get below 5 percent any more. And unemployment figures are increasingly misleading." David Mermelstein (in a surely controversial statement) goes even further when he argues that "there can be no mistake about it: we are in the early stages of a world crisis of historic dimensions. All we know for sure is that hard times loom ahead for the vast majority of the American people."[114] Chapters 2 and 3, which looked at the surface manifestations of the economy, concur in the general perception that the 1970s are ushering in the emergence of prolonged economic problems but also the birth of new possibilities. At the same time, it seems reasonable to suggest that wisdom is on the side of predicting nothing at all.

Interestingly, Galbraith pointed to five areas of weakness in the economy in an interpretation, which first appeared in 1954, of the collapse of the stock market in 1929 and the depression of the 1930s. He argued that there was a "bad distribution of income," a "bad corporate structure," a "bad banking structure," a "dubious state of the foreign balance," and a "poor state of economic intelligence." In short, he thought that the economy was fundamentally unsound. He notes that changes in these areas occurred after the Great Depression but, humble enough to avoid viewing himself as a prophet, he offers no judgment on the likely future stability of the economic system.[115] In this interpretation it is also pointed out that government responses to economic problems were undertaken initially that made things worse. It is no great insight to suggest that the areas Galbraith pinpointed in this work are all areas to ponder in the mid-1970s.

What useful ideas do the recent works of O'Connor and Galbraith offer to explain contemporary problems of economic stability? There are many. Some important elements can be seen by pointing to some main areas of dissonance and agreement that exist between O'Connor's analysis and Galbraith's.

Both see the contemporary economy as troubled, and both present their interpretations for the reasons for these troubles. Galbraith offers a general blueprint of a new relationship between the economy and the rest of society as well as an updated version of what the key features of the economic machinery are. He argues for reform that would be on the side of the "public purpose." But it is at this point that a sharp division arises in the perceptions of the two men. Galbraith tends to use the terms "public" and "private" as fact rather than as conceptions. He believes that less conflict between these two (fictions, one can argue) might be created with education and some tinkering here and there with key institutions, particularly in the relationship between industry and the body politic. O'Connor, on the other hand, suggests that the "public" sector is most often really a disguised portion of private interests—especially capital. The state acts on behalf of groups that are economically and politically powerful, which are rationally exercising their considerable power to maintain and further their economic self-interest. Capitalist society is seen as inherently hierarchical, and production is created by workers but organized by owners who receive a disproportionate share of the resulting income. The owners of capital have struggled for economic profit and have been remarkably successful. They have organized people to make the pie and have devised means by which to enforce and legitimize the distribution of disproportionate pieces of it. O'Connor's two poles are capital and the people, whereas Galbraith's are the private and public interest. The latter polarity, although meaning something in a very abstract way, clouds the issues. To distinguish between those who live by the sale of their labor and those who live by the purchase of labor seems more useful, even if what this distinction really means in all the various aspects of personal and social life is unsatisfactorily vague. But O'Connor's conceptual framework and general argument help clear up the ambiguity.

Galbraith, on the whole, argues that some sort of "social democracy" along the lines of, perhaps, Great Britain would change U.S. society for the better. He suggests that the nationalization of some industrial giants would be a good thing. He suggests that no new political mechanism need be created to achieve this change. He is not talking about the necessity for equality; rather he is seeking to suggest ways in which opportunity could be equalized more satisfactorily. O'Connor, on the other hand, thinks that the only longer run solution to the economic, social, and political crises of the society is the creation of a socialist society which, in his terms, means the abolition completely, or nearly so, of the private ownership of the means of production which results in the existence of two main social classes. As in Marxian thought generally, the population as a whole is seen as being divided into the main categories of owners and nonowners of the means of production. There are monopoly, competitive, and state sector workers, but they are workers all. There are members of the surplus population who are dependent on the state. The latter situation creates social expenses, whereas the relationship of owners and their agents to the state results in a push for state expenditures for the purposes of social capital that expands or maintains privately accumulated profits. Private ownership of the means of production is seen as particularly problematic when a few hundred corporations control the bulk of it. In somewhat elementary Keynesian terms, this structural situation results in leakages from the circular flow at a different pace than injections. With dramatic concentration in industry, the result can be a deteriorating economy, particularly in terms of opportunities for employment, while administered prices even increase as an attempt to maintain profit margins occurs. The state then deals in contradictory ways to deal with inflation and unemployment if traditional fiscal and monetary policies are undertaken. Wage-price controls are one additional unsatisfactory option. Another "alternative" is a managed recession to reduce prices, but this alternative also increases unemployment and arouses a portion of the population. The tighter integration of capital and the state (the emergence of the social-industrial complex) remains as yet another option. It is the strengthening of the social-industrial complex that Galbraith unwittingly advocates rather than socialism in the sense that word is commonly used. Galbraith wants to mold the purposes of the "planning system" more toward the social good. But his list of the areas of necessary public action which, in his view, would follow "the public cognizance and emancipation of the state" would actually redirect the U.S. toward an American-style national socialism.[116] It is instructive to look at Galbraith's program and follow each requirement with counter observations in an attempt to clarify the Galbraithian position and note the ways in which it departs from socialism as that term is used by O'Connor and other Marxian writers. Galbraith presents a seven part program for reform.

His first suggested line of public action would be

> . . . measures to equalize power within the economic system. No remedy is possible that does not enhance the power of the market system or reduce the power of the planning system or both. Equalization of performance and equalization of income both require equalization of power.

Here the argument is not against private ownership of the means of production but is in favor of regenerating the neo-Classical stance of the supposed inherent benefits of laissez faire in a competitive environment which, it may be recalled, requires easy entry into the exit from an industry, good information, a large number of buyers and sellers so that no one or few are powerful enough to regulate prices and the quantity of the available commodity, etc. These requirements are out of tune with the general tendencies in the structure of industry that have occurred in this century as monopoly capital has become stronger and stronger. Antitrust laws have not abated the tendency toward the concentration in economic power. The burden of proof is, it must be insisted, on s/he who would seriously suggest that private ownership of the means of production is consistent with and generates continued competitive capitalism.

Galbraith's second requirement would be

> . . . measures directly to equalize competence within the economic system. Of particular concern here are functions—provision of housing, surface transportation, health services, artistic and cultural services—which do not lend themselves to organization by the planning system and which are not rendered competently by the market system. This defines a major area of social action—or socialism.

At first it must be pointed out that all of these areas are included as issues to be dealt with in the example of state capitalism, the Federation of Rocky Mountain States, sketched in the Appendix. In addition the social-industrial complex theoretically would center on all of the areas Galbraith notes. Engaging in these activities is the business, which is handsomely profitable, of the social-industrial complex. State capitalism should not be confused with socialism.

The third set of proposals in *Economics and the Public Purpose* are

> . . . measures directly to enhance the equality of return as between the market and the planning systems and within the planning system to offset and hopefully to overcome the inherent tendency to inequality.

As the discussion on the dual economy suggested earlier, it would go against the nature of monopoly capital and competitive capital to have their profits equalized. The monopoly sector is more capital intensive and experiences greater rates of increase in productivity. Monopoly capital is a formidable phenomenon which cannot be easily intimidated and which will oppose threats to its position in society and in the world. There are many examples of the lengths to which monopoly capital will go to retain its dominant and highly profitable position, including the participation in the overthrow of elected governments, such as in Chile.

The fourth set of policy suggestions pushes for

> . . . measures to align the purposes of the planning system, as these affect the environment, with those of the public. This includes the regulation or prohibition of such effects of production and consumption—pollution of air and water, damage to landscape—which serve the purposes of the planning system but are in conflict with the purposes of the public.

One might simply observe that industry seeks to maintain its profits, which requires keeping costs down and sales up. To the extent that pollution and other ecological concerns are likely to be tackled by policy, it would usually have to be backed up with a portion of the state budget, either to pay for the necessary changes directly or to enforce the changes upon industry. The removal of the institution of capitalism would remove the main barrier (the quest for private profit) to becoming absolutely serious about rationally planning the use of the earth's scarce physical environment—its land, its petroleum, ores, and minerals, its timber, its water, its air, and even its atmospheric ozone layer. Finally, as A. Dale Tussing points out (in personal communication): There are two main options available for protection of the ecology while capitalism exists. The first is to pay firms not to pollute in the form of tax credits, etc. The second is to tax them for polluting, using effluent fees, etc. The fact that in the U.S. the first option is usually chosen shows who is in charge and how.

Galbraith's fifth requirements to achieve his plan of reform are ". . . measures to control public expenditures to ensure that these serve public purposes as distinct from those of the planning system."

Although it is hard to argue with the sentiment expressed in this stance of advocacy, there is more than enough evidence already in, of which O'Connor's argument is but one example, that this is not the experience under capitalism, and it is difficult to imagine how it could become so. The idea that the state serves the functions of accumulation and legitimization through expenditures for social capital and social expenses provides a set of assumptions that are in touch with reality. That they are suggests that to expect Galbraith's fifth proposal for reform is to construct unrealistic expectations as long as powerful corporations and individuals retain their position in society. The other requirements Galbraith suggests do not resolve this objection.

The sixth requirement is

> . . . measures to eliminate the systemically deflationary and inflationary tendencies of the planning system. These must not, as in the past, be a source of added power for the planning system. They must not discriminate against the market system. And they must be consistent with greater equality in income distribution as between the two systems.

As the Marxian perspectives suggest, monopoly capital exists, is powerful, and would be, to put it mildly, reluctant to share its power and to behave in a way consistent with Galbraith's conception of the public good. Curiously, Galbraith's view is in agreement with O'Connor's that the "planning system" (monopoly capital) generates economic instability (and O'Connor's book is basically a treatise on why that is believed to be so). Galbraith recognizes that centralized and concentrated capital has a magnitude of social influence (by such measures as the percentage of the labor force it employs, the value of its product and services in comparison to GNP, etc.) which is huge, but he believes this influence can be abated by measures of reform. Grounds for skepticism seem well founded.

The seventh and last requirement that Galbraith suggests is a necessary part of public action to complete his program of reform would be ". . . measures to ensure the interindustry coordination of which the planning system is incapable."

Galbraith seems to be suggesting that the planning system is not really a planning system at all if it cannot (practically or legally) plan as an interindustry body but only plans on a corporate basis.

Galbraith would call a slightly revised and more integrated version of the contemporary economic system in the U.S. "socialism." It is with this allegation that Marxian and radical political economists could not agree even if the reform that is suggested were possible.

Galbraith, in short, is actually advocating a more eqalitarian version of what O'Connor calls the social-industrial complex. The seven point program above can be seen as an ideological defense of a more refined and formalized state capitalism. Rather than supporting such a plan, there are grounds for putting the social-industrial complex to much more scrutiny where it already exists (such as in the case of the Federation of Rocky Mountain States).

The contradiction in Galbraith's argument is that he recognizes the power of centralized and concentrated capital, and he is aware that this power extends to the state. Yet the state is called upon to undermine, to some extent, the power of centralized and concentrated capital. At the same time, Galbraith has company in drafting a blueprint for a planned capitalism, and it is likely that he will have even more company to the extent that the problems of the U.S. economic system are not resolved.[117] Thus, a tentative view is that a planned capitalism is a more plausible scenario to expect than revolutionary change. However, it is unlikely that all of Galbraith's suggestions would be acceptable to those who would ultimately decide specifically what policies would be included in a program to save capitalism. As in the case of Keynes, it is likely that a part of the program suggested by Galbraith and the other advocates of a planned capitalism would be accepted while sweeping the redistributive aspects under the rug. A plausible scenario is the assertion of a program for a planning of profit taking while submitting the bulk of the population to continued insecurity and hierarchical institutions.

Unfortunately, *The Fiscal Crisis of the State* does not suggest the way toward a democratic socialism even though the last chapter of the book is an articulate analysis of the interclass and intraclass struggle that is taking place. Although O'Connor concludes that the only lasting solution to the problem of contemporary economic instability is in the implementation of socialism, he does not really explain, first, how this might be done, second, what this socialism would contain as its main characteristics, and third, how more authoritarianism and even totalitarianism could be avoided in these very explosive times. If a pessimistic but not fatalistic question may be posed, is it possible that there will not be enough opposition to the social-industrial complex and that it will come to dominate this geographic region of the earth and its sphere of hegemony for a long time to come? As Alan Wolfe put it, a

> . . . task of a Marxist theory of the state is to explain why the contradiction between the legitimating function of the state and its accumulating function has not exploded. Why is it that a system which so palpably benefits a few has not been thoroughly routed by the forces of the many?[118]

Galbraith's work suggests ways in which state capitalism might be made to function better and more equitably without the creation of new political mechanisms. He may suggest them because, in part, what he wants to happen seems much more modest and, unfortunately, within reach than O'Connor's objectives. Perhaps a part of Galbraith's scheme is occurring in any case, however gradually. Much as Keynes' great classic in economic thought provided rationalizations for government to move in directions in which it was tending anyway, Galbraith's book may provide rationalizations for the further development of the social-industrial complex, for the state to become much more closely knit with industry while using rhetoric claiming that this integration of the state and capital is in the public interest.

This contrast of the views of O'Connor and Galbraith leaves us with an uncomfortable dilemma. One might agree with the main elements of O'Connor's argument, but it does not answer some important questions. Although much of Galbraith's discussion is enlightening and offers a useful comparison to O'Connor's paradigm, it is fundamentally incomplete in its presentation of what contemporary capitalism is all about and where his recommendations for "reform" would lead U.S. society. Yet it is more likely to be heard if only because of the rationalizations it contains for those who would be directly involved in the further implementation of state capitalism.[119]

No apology is put forth for having no answers to this dilemma. As Alan Wolfe put it "the task is a project, in Sartre's sense of the term, work for a generation of scholars. If that generation ever gets to work, it will have James O'Connor to thank for pointing out the directions."[120] But it must be added that the work of scholars is hardly enough unless their message is very clear. On this much there is not reason for pessimism. Much is being done and much more probably will be done.[121] Even if it is the unwanted stepchild of economic thought in this country, the Marxian perspective has made a noticeable impact on those who have taken the time to familiarize themselves with it. But the impact this perspective can make on the people and the society as a whole is yet to be seen. It is the people who will put the theory to the test, who will make the future for good or ill.

NOTES

1 *Ralph Miliband,* The State in Capitalist Society *(New York: Basic Books, 1969), p. 2.*

2 *For example, as in Frederick Engels,* The Origin of the Family, Private Property, and the State, *which first appeared in 1884 and drew upon, among other things, Marx's critical notes on the work of the American anthropologist Lewis H. Morgan.*

3 *Miliband, The State in Capitalist Society, p. 2.*

4 *R. A. Dahl, A Preface to Democratic Theory (Chicago: University of Chicago Press, 1956), pp. 137–138. The adjective "legitimate" is problematic to say the least.*

The nature of power is, of course, the subject of a vast literature in the social sciences. The Marxian perspective is, obviously, very much at odds with the pluralist world view. A few examples of articulate rejoinders to the pluralist position are C. Wright Mills, The Power Elite (New York: Oxford University Press, 1956); various essays in G. William Domhoff and Hoyt B. Ballard, ed., C. Wright Mills and the Power Elite (Boston: Beacon Press, 1968); Domhoff, Who Rules America? (Englewood Cliffs, N. J.: Prentice-Hall, 1967), a book which in the making, story has it, began as an attempt to demonstrate there is no ruling class and ended with the author, a psychologist, believing there in fact is a governing class—"a social upper class which owns a disproportionate amount of a country's wealth, receives a disproportionate amount of a country's yearly income, and contributes a disproportionate number of its members to the controlling institutions and key decision-making groups of the country." (p. 5). One could also see other work by Domhoff and, especially, G. William Domhoff, ed., "New Directions in Power Structure Research," a special issue of The Insurgent Sociologist, vol. 5, no. 3 (Spring 1975). Two other good works are Todd Gitlin, "Local Pluralism as Theory and Ideology," Studies on the Left, vol. 5, no. 3 (1965), pp. 21–45; and Ralph L. Andreano, ed., Superconcentration/Supercorporation: a Collage of Opinion on the Concentration of Economic Power (Andover, Mass: Warner Modular Publications, 1973), particularly the article by James C. Knowles, "The Rockefeller Financial Group," pp. M343-1 through M343-59.

These rejoinders, although most of them are not specifically Marxian, collectively show that the pluralist view is not without major flaws, if not downright incorrect. Or, as E. E. Schattschneider put it in The Semisovereign People (New York: Holt, Rinehart & Winston, 1960), "The flaw in the pluralist heaven is that the heavenly chorus sings with a strong upper-class accent. Probably about 90 percent of the people cannot get into the pressure system." (p. 35).

The notion that the upper socioeconomic strata provides most of those who populate the key decision-making roles appears again in this chapter, mainly as an underlying assumption for which there is a substantial amount of evidence.

5 *Miliband, The State in Capitalist Society, p. 49.*

6 *Ibid.*

7 *Ibid., pp. 540–555.*

8 *Robert McC. Adams, The Evolution of Urban Society (Chicago: Aldine, 1966), p. 14.*

9 *Lawrence Krader, Formation of the State (Englewood Cliffs, N.J.: Prentice-Hall, 1968), pp. viii, 27, and 28. Krader synthesizes and critiques the work of twenty-five writers on the theory of the state (including Morgan and Engels) whose works appeared in the 18th, 19th, and 20th centuries.*

10 *James O'Connor, The Fiscal Crisis of the State (New York: St. Martin's Press, 1973), hereinafter FCS; The Corporations and the State: Essays in the*

Theory of Capitalism and Imperialism *(New York: Harper & Row, 1974). The first issue of* Kapitalistate, *which is an international journal with a "working papers" format, was published in 1973.*

11 Daniel Bell, "The Public Household—on 'Fiscal Sociology' and the Liberal Society," The Public Interest no. 37 (Fall 1974), pp. 30 (footnote) and 37. The Goldscheid essay is in Richard A. Musgrave and Alan T. Peacock, eds., Classics in the Theory of Public Finance(New York: St. Martin's Press, 1967), pp. 202-213.

12 Rudolf Goldscheid, "A Sociological Approach to Problems of Public Finance."

13 O'Connor, FCS, p. 3.

14 Ibid.

15 Ibid., p. 5.

16 Ibid.,

17 O'Connor, FCS, p. 6. O'Connor, as Nikola Uzunov points out, could have been more explicit on what the legitimization function of the state has to do with the distribution of income. My view is that redistribution mainly occurs among workers while capital remains relatively untouched. But there is no solid data, of which I am aware, to support this theoretical position. Two studies which analyze the struggle over who gets what with respect to capital and labor are Howard Sherman, "Inflation, Unemployment, and Monopoly Capital," and Raford Boddy and James Crotty, "Wage-Push and Working Class Power: a Reply to Howard Sherman," both in Monthly Review, vol. 27, no. 10 (March 1976).

18 Ibid., pp. 6-7.

19 Ibid., p. 7.

20 Ibid.

21 Ibid. This, of course, is a superficial view. There will be more on this in the following.

22 Ibid.

23 Ibid., pp. 7-8.

24 Ibid., pp. 8-9.

25 Ibid., p. 9.

26 Ibid. Once more "surplus" emerges as an imprecise term. Here it seems close to surplus value.

27 Ibid.

28 A very good abbreviated account of this description of the magnitude of the state, measured by the number of workers involved, is included in an essay, also entitled "The Fiscal Crisis of the State," which is chapter six of The Corporations and the State, op. cit. The following appears in that work: "In addition to the 11 million workers employed directly by the state, there are countless wage and salary earners—perhaps as many as 25 to 30 million—who are employed by private capital dependent in whole or in part on state contracts and facilities. Workers in such industries as military and

space, branches of capital goods, construction, transportation, and others, are indirectly employed by state capital. Further, tens of thousands of doctors, welfare workers, and other self-employed and privately employed professionals and technicians who use facilities provided by the state are also dependent in whole or in part on the state budget. Finally, tens of millions of men and women are dependent on the budget as clients and recipients of state services; these include nearly all students at all levels of education, welfare recipients, and users of public health, hospital, recreational, and other facilities.

There is no way to measure the total number of people who are related to each other through the state budget, and who are dependent on the budget for their material well-being; everyone is in part dependent on the state, and for millions of poor people, particularly minority people, this dependence runs very deep. Perhaps one-quarter to one-third of the labor force is wholly dependent on the state for basic necessities. And, historically, more and more people have looked to the state for that which they cannot provide themselves."(p. 106)

Still another short version of the general argument of FCS appears in Kapitalistate no. 1 (1/73), pp. 79–83.

29 O'Connor, FCS, p. 29.

30 Ibid., pp. 29–30.

31 Ibid., p. 25. O'Connor is as muddy as Marx on the concept of the surplus population but perhaps unavoidably so. The more compulsive reader would probably like a glossary of terms and precise definitions of all concepts introduced. Sadly or not most books are not written in that manner and definitions usually emerge in the context in which they are used conveying the authors' intended meaning only approximately. O'Connor and Marx are no exception to this general rule, especially with respect to the surplus population.

32 A good introduction to dual labor market theory is provided by David M. Gordon, Theories of Poverty and Underemployment (Lexington, Mass.: D. C. Heath, 1972), especially Chapter 4. In practice, obviously, the categories of primary and secondary labor markets break down like any "ideal types." And it is not certain that the so-called "primary labor market" is the dominant form of employment in the U.S. But the ideal types are used here with O'Connor's full awareness that they are limited.

33 San Francisco Bay Area Kapitalistate Group, "The Fiscal Crisis of the State: a Review," Kapitalistate, no. 3 (Spring 1975), p. 150.

34 From an earlier version of the review noted in the preceding footnote.

35 "The Fiscal Crisis of the State: A Review," p. 151.

36 Ibid., p. 156.

37 Ibid., footnote, p. 157. Robert Averitt's The Dual Economy: Dynamics of American Industry Structure (New York: W. W. Norton and Co., 1968) provides an important contribution to microeconomics. It presents the concepts of "center firms," "periphery firms," and "key industries." Labor markets are also discussed in the context of this conceptualization of the structure of industry. Further, two chapters offer an interpretation of government, its relationship to the private sector and to labor markets.

Published in 1968, this book, the author says, "might be called a micro-economic supplement to the 'new economics' of macro policy." Averitt thought that the beginnings of a new economic era was appearing which was characterized by perpetual full employment. He observed the existence of giant corporations as not being inconsistent with economic stability so long as rational government policy was undertaken. Although there is much of worth in this book insofar as developments in microeconomic theory are concerned, the author appears to have projected economic stability for the system as a whole into the future mistakenly. One might argue that Averitt's theory of the dual economy is useful while not accepting his thesis that the dual economy exists without serious stabilization problems. The argument developed in the rest of this chapter will elaborate on this idea.

38 O'Connor's self-criticism and ideas about developing theoretical clarity come from personal correspondence during October, 1973.

39 Bay Area Work Group, "FCS: A Review," p. 3.

40 FCS, p. 30. Charles Ardolini and Jeffrey Hohenstein, in "Measuring Productivity in the Federal Government," Monthly Labor Review, vol. 97, no. 11 (November, 1974), estimate that, of those organizational units in the agencies sampled (which included more than half of the federal civilian work force), there was a productivity increase in the federal government of 1.6% annually from fiscal year 1967 through fiscal year 1973. This study was undertaken at the behest of the Joint Economic Committee which resulted in the formation of a joint interagency team (from the Office of Management and Budget, the General Accounting Office, and the Civil Service Commission) to do the job. "In the Federal sample, over 850 output indicators have been aggregated by the Bureau of Labor Statistics." "The nature of the indicators varied substantially. They included such diverse items as trademarks disposed, tank repairs, weather observations, square feet of buildings cleaned, electrical power generated, and deportable aliens located." (p. 15).

William Eisenberg, in "Measuring the Productivity of Nonfinancial Corporations," Monthly Labor Review, vol. 97, no. 11 (November, 1974) argues that "Productivity in nonfinancial corporations increased at a 3.1 percent annual rate during the past 25 years, reflecting a 4.4 percent annual increase in output and a 1.3 percent increase in man-hours." (p. 21).

41 O'Connor, FCS, pp. 30–31.

42 Personal correspondence with O'Connor during October, 1973.

43 Ibid. The issues raised in this paragraph are complex and could benefit by both more conceptual work augmented by putting the theory to the test with empirical data. To do this would be a huge task which will not be undertaken here.

44 O'Connor, FCS, p. 40.

45 Ibid., p. 46.

46 Ibid.

47 Ibid., p. 47.

48 For example, Robert Lekachman in "The Inevitability of Controls," Challenge, vol. 17, no. 5 (November/December 1974), pp. 6–8.

49 O'Connor, FCS, p. 47.

50 *Ibid., pp. 47–48. An epistomological observation, which stems from a conversation with Steven Porter, a colleague at the Educational Policy Research Center at Syracuse, on The Fiscal Crisis of the State, is that these policy alternatives to deal with the fiscal crisis exist in relation to time in different ways. Thus the deflation of the economy or the use of wage-price controls may well exist at the same time the state is engaging in more and more activities with and for capital. Although categorical differences in kind exist here, I do not see problems as far as the internal consistency of the argument is concerned.*

51 O'Connor, FCS, p. 51.

52 *O'Connor uses the terms social-industrial complex and state capitalism interchangeably but sees, I think, the former to be a more advanced version of the latter. Further, the term is not completely descriptive of what O'Connor means. His focus is the integration of the state and capital. If one were to try to think of the elements the complex would include from a broad sociological perspective, it would be called perhaps an industrial-communications-police-university-military-welfare, etc. complex. This type becomes very long, incomplete, and awkward.*

53 O'Connor, FCS, pp. 55–57.

54 James O'Connor, "Nixon's Other Watergate: The Federal Budget for Fiscal 1974," Working Papers on the Kapitalistate no. 2 (February 1973), pp. 5–12.

55 Ibid.

56 Frances Fox Piven and Richard A. Cloward, Regulating the Poor: The Functions of Public Welfare (New York: Random House, 1971).

57 O'Connor, "Nixon's Other Watergate."

58 Alan Wolfe, "What Makes the System Perdure?" The Nation, vol. 218, no. 11 (March 16, 1974), p. 345.

59 Al Szymanski, "Review Essay: The Fiscal Crisis of the State and the Unstable Economy," The Insurgent Sociologist, vol. 4, no. 4 (Summer, 1974), p. 82.

60 Richard C. Edwards, Michael Reich, and Thomas E. Weisskopf, eds., "The Expansion of the Public Sector in the United States," The Capitalist System, (Englewood Cliffs, N.J.: Prentice-Hall, 1972), pp. 199–201.

61 *Social-industrial complex will be abbreviated as SIC where convenient in the following.*

62 Joseph Pechman and Benjamin Okner, Who Bears the Tax Burden? (Washington, D.C.: Brookings Institute, 1974).

63 *Many of the issues in this section, when contrasted with the discussion of the SIC in FCS, as they are drawn out later will lead to the conclusion that the Federation of Rocky Mountain States is a case of heavy flirtation with many aspects that would make up a social-industrial complex but it should not be taken to be a full blown SIC. For the SIC to function in the way O'Connor suggests, it must be undertaken on a national level to avoid interregional contradictions. The section of FCS entitled "Suburban Exploitation of the City" particularly, as well as the rest of Chapter 5 (pp. 124–149)*

provides an enticing line of reasoning which could be developed to deal with interregional contradictions and conflicts.

64 Peter Bachrach, The Theory of Democratic Elitism: a Critique *(Boston: Little, Brown, 1967), pp. 102–103.*

65 O'Connor, FCS, p. 221.

66 *Ibid.,* p. 223.

67 *Ibid.,* p. 221.

68 *Ibid.,* pp. 223–224.

69 *Ibid.,* pp. 221–223.

70 See, for example, Bertram M. Gross, "Friendly Fascism: a Model for America," Social Policy, vol. 1, no. 4 (November/December 1970), pp. 44–52. Here Gross sketches the elements of an American style "techno-urban fascism" which has as its theme much more than the managed economy. It extends to management of the whole of society. "Under techno-urban fascism, certain elements previously regarded as inescapable earmarks of fascism would no longer be essential. Pluralistic in nature, techno-urban fascism would need no charismatic dictator, no one-party rule, no mass fascist party, no glorification of the state, no dissolution of legislatures, no discontinuation of elections, no distrust of reason. It would probably be a cancerous growth within and around the White House, the Pentagon, and the broader political establishment." (p. 46) It would be a warfare-welfare-industrial-communications-police complex. Gross tries to scare us in this article and succeeds. But he also tries to avoid incapacitating fear since that "would lead to inaction, spreading the intangible terror that would be the secret weapon of creeping fascism." (p. 52) What he encourages, rather, is dialogue on neofascist tendencies in the U.S. Here I am reminded of Pogo's remark that "we have found the enemy and [s/he] is us."

71 O'Connor, FCS, p. 228.

72 *Ibid.,* pp. 255–256.

73 I suppose every college and university faculty member is at least aware of this if it is not general knowledge. The late C. Wright Mills was never promoted beyond the academic rank of Associate Professor in spite of the best credentials and publishing record and when it was suggested that he be offered a professorship at Stanford University, where Paul Baran taught but not without problems from the administration and others, the Chairman of the Sociology Department said: "But Mills is not a sociologist, he is a Marxist." (This story, and an account of Baran's absence of acceptance in academia, may be found in Paul Sweezy and Leo Huberman, ed., Paul A. Baran: a Collective Portrait, [New York: Monthly Review Press, 1965], esp. p. 53.) A more current account of the problems encountered by radical economists who seek and try to keep academic jobs is that of Lawrence S. Lifshultz, "Could Karl Marx Teach Economics in America?" Ramparts, Vol. 12, no. 9 (April 1974), pp. 27–30 and 52–59. This article is primarily about the job discrimination that radical economists have experienced at a few prestigious Eastern Ivy League universities, particularly Harvard. At some of these schools, it has become chic to invite at times a well-known Marxian scholar, of which there are few in this country, to give a lecture or speech, or

perhaps even a course. Lifshultz notes that the chairman of the Yale Economics Department invited Paul Sweezy to give a graduate seminar in Marxian economics in early 1971. "Sweezy declined the offer and in a letter to Peck stated that he believed there was a larger issue involved. He pointed out that current difficulties could be solved, if the practice of university departments consistently dropping younger qualified Marxists from their staffs was changed."

" 'Every generation of graduate students includes a by-no-means insignificant number of Marxists,' Sweezy wrote to Peck. 'But with very few exceptions they are dropped before acquiring tenure. And the exceptions find it prudent to keep their ideology separate from their teaching and research . . .' " (p. 53).

74 At least twenty-six reviews of Economics and the Public Purpose appeared in the first year after publication of the book, many in the liberal popular press and a few in scholarly journals. In contrast, at this writing only a handful of reviews of O'Connor's The Fiscal Crisis of the State have appeared though it has been cited in Douglas Dowd, The Twisted Dream (Cambridge, Mass.: Winthrop Publishers, 1974) and Daniel Bell, "The Public Household." In addition to reviews by the San Francisco Kapitalistate Collective, Al Szymanski, and Alan Wolfe, there is David Gold, "James O'Connor's The Fiscal Crisis of the State: An Overview," ed., David Mermelstein, The Economic Crisis Reader (New York: Vintage Books, 1975), pp. 123–132.

75 Paul M. Sweezy, "Galbraith's Utopia," The New York Review of Books, vol. 20, no. 18 (November 15, 1973), pp. 3–6; Robert L. Heilbroner, "Galbraith's Progress," Dissent, vol. 21, no. 1 (Winter 1974), pp. 105–108.

76 John Kenneth Galbraith, Economics and the Public Purpose (Boston: Houghton-Mifflin, 1973), p. 26.

77 Ibid., pp. 27–28. It is difficult to avoid comment here on Galbraith's immodesty particularly since he admits to having not seen aspects of economic and social reality previously (see the Foreword, especially, p. X) in his earlier books.

78 Sweezy, "Galbraith's Utopia" p. 3.

79 Galbraith, Economics and the Public Purpose, p. 50.

80 Ibid., p. 55.

81 Ibid., p. 61.

82 Ibid., p. 69.

83 Ibid., p. 66.

84 Ibid., p. xiii.

85 Sweezy, "Galbraith's Utopia," N.Y. Review of Books, p. 3.

86 Robert L. Heilbroner, "Galbraith's Progress," p. 105.

87 Ibid., p. 106.

88 As noted above, Sweezy thinks that the largest 1,000 corporations account for about 75 percent of industrial production. Galbraith does not offer a precise percentage which is not at all uncommon in the literature on

centralized and concentrated capital. It is here that more empirical work would be informative.

89 Sweezy, "Galbraith's Utopia," p. 3.

90 Galbraith, Economics and the Public Purpose, p. 304.

91 Ibid., p. 218.

92 Ibid., p. 172.

93 Though as Sweezy argues and with which I concur, what he actually seems to present is a curious, if unintended, apologetic for monopoly capitalism. This idea will be developed later.

94 Galbraith, Economics and the Public Purpose, p. 243.

95 Ibid., p. 247.

96 Ibid., p. 249.

97 See ibid., pp. 250–251 for his menu of change.

98 Ibid., pp. 279–280.

99 Ibid., p. 285.

100 Sweezy, "Galbraith's Utopia," p. 4.

101 Sweezy, "Galbraith's Utopia," p. 3.

102 Ibid.

103 Ibid., p. 4.

104 Heilbroner, "Galbraith's Progress," p. 107.

105 Ibid.

106 Ibid., pp. 107–108.

107 Sweezy, "Galbraith's Utopia," p. 4.

108 Ibid., p. 5.

109 Ibid., p. 6.

110 Alan Wolfe says that by the test of an intellectual effort enhancing the understanding of society "The Fiscal Crisis of the State will be one of the most important books of the 1970s." (in "What Makes the System Perdure?" p. 344).

111 Some dual labor market theorists were mentioned earlier. The idea that there is a dual welfare system comes from A. Dale Tussing, Poverty in a Dual Economy (New York: St. Martin's Press, 1974).

112 See, for example, Dwayne Ward, "Labor Market Adjustments in Elementary and Secondary Teaching: the Reaction to the 'Teacher Surplus'," Teachers College Record, vol. 77, no. 2 (December 1975).

113 Such as those generated by the U.S. Department of Commerce and others and used, e.g., by the Federal Reserve Bank of New York. In its Monthly Review, it was reported in November 1974 that economic activity had dropped for the third consecutive quarter of the year, in the fashion of postwar recessionary periods, while inflation remained severe—at an annual rate of 15 percent in September—which has not been historically typical

for the U.S. (See "The Business Situation," p. 268). In this same issue Arthur Burns, Chairman of the Board of Governors of the Federal Reserve System, notes that the two largest bank failures in the nation's history occurred in the past year. He argues that economic conditions are "at a reduced, but still very high, level" but shows confidence in bankers and solicits their views after saying this about the structure of American banking: "building upon the existing machinery may not be sufficient, and . . . a substantial reorganization will be required to overcome the problems inherent in the existing structural arrangement." (pp. 263–267).

114 In the preface to David Mermelstein, ed., The Economic Crisis Reader, p. ix. The situation is depicted quite differently, of course, by the media (which is, in general, part of monopoly capital). In 1976 much has been made of so-called recovery from the most severe economic downturn since the Great Depression. Paul Sweezy points out (in a public lecture at California State University, Chico, in March 1976) that to see short run economic "recovery" as a sign that hard times are over would be no more valid currently than during the 1930s. The position here, of course, is that the economic difficulties the U.S. has been encountering are a result of the central contradiction of capitalism (production is social, ownership is private) which led to the structure of monopoly capitalism which, in turn, exacerbates the contradictions of capitalism, which requires more and more state intervention, which further generates centralization and concentration, etc.

115 John Kenneth Galbraith, The Great Crash (Boston: Houghton-Mifflin, 1954), particularly chapter 10.

116 Galbraith, Economics and the Public Purpose, pp. 250–251. The following seven point program appears on the same pages.

117 In addition to those resources already cited, see Arnold R. Weber, "Once More the Talk is of Plans to Plan the Economy," The New York Times, The Week in Review Section (May 25, 1975), p. 2. Weber assesses the situation in this way: "The tattered state of the American economy has stimulated renewed debate over the role of Government planning in a democratic society. Advocates promise relief from the gyrations that have plagued the economy in the past. Opponents condemn planning as a threat to freedom and efficiency." The issues are much deeper than this.

118 Wolfe, "What Makes the System Perdure?" p. 346.

119 A possible irony is that Galbraith himself may be very much a part of O'Connor's legitimating function! It is important to note that so much fits into O'Connor's general theory including even the social function that reformist "critics" of the contemporary political economy serve. In a classic discussion of aborted views of what socialism is about there are these famous lines: "By Socialists, in 1847, were understood, on the one hand, the adherents of the various Utopian systems: Owenites in England, Fourierists in France, both of them already reduced to the position of mere sects, and gradually dying out; on the other hand, the most multifarious social quacks, who by all manners of tinkering, professed to redress, without any danger to capital and profit, all sorts of social grievances, in both cases men outside the working class movement, and looking rather to the 'educated' classes for support." [emphasis added]. Upon re-reading these lines in Frederick Engels'

preface to Marx and Engels famous The Communist Manifesto *(first published in 1848, with this preface added in 1888), I immediately thought of Galbraith's theory of the technostructure and his appeal to the "scientific and educational estates" as key agents of "change." O'Connor's response (in personal correspondence in January of 1975) to reading the first line of this footnote about Galbraith's position is one with which I strongly concur: "there is no agency of change [in Galbraith's scheme], since he has no theory of people and activity."*

120 Wolfe, "What Makes the System Perdure?"

121 See, for example, Dimitrios I. Roussopoulos, The Political Economy of the State *(Montreal: Black Rose Books, 1973). In this work there are many articles which use Marxian theory to provide a conceptual framework to do empirical work on the situation in Canada. Literature that we have not mentioned is surveyed here. Of particular interest is an article by Rick Deaton, "The Fiscal Crisis of the State in Canada," in which the author offers this acknowledgment (footnote 1, p. 55): "Classic works are James O'Connor, 'The Fiscal Crisis of the State,'* Socialist Revolution *parts I and II, January–February, 1970 and April–May, 1970 and Margaret and John Rowntree,* On Revolution in the Metropolis, *unpublished, 1970. The author is deeply indebted to both Prof. O'Connor and the Rowntrees. It is interesting to note that working independently, all these parties by using the same methodology, have arrived at nearly identical conclusions."*

Still another important work which contains an extensive and useful bibliography is "Some Recent Developments in the Marxist Theory of the State," compiled by the San Francisco Kapitalistate Group which was presented at the Union for Radical Economics "Theory of the State" session at the Allied Social Sciences Association convention in San Francisco, December 30, 1974. This appeared as David A. Gold, Clarence Y.H. Lo, and Erik Olin Wright, "Recent Developments in Marxist Theories of the Capitalist State," Monthly Review, *vol. 27, nos. 5 and 6 (October and November 1975). As one who attended the presentation and discussion of this paper, I can only say that this was a very helpful and informative gathering surrounding this extremely important area of inquiry. The quality of discussion that ensued suggests that important developments in the theory of the state are in process and should be anticipated. As the Galbraithian planning perspective gains hold, so will rejoinders from critical political economics.*

6

SUMMARY, SYNTHESIS, AND SEARCH FOR A GENERAL THEORY IN CRITICAL POLITICAL ECONOMICS

A general theory in what has been called critical political economics can be formulated. Such a task can be only a presentation of highlights since to be totally comprehensive would result in an even more voluminous discussion. This chapter, then, is but a sketch of where an inquiry into Keynesian, Galbraithian, Marxian, and radical thought with respect to economic instability, the centralization and concentration of capital, and the state has taken us. What results are some key elements of a grounded theory in political economics which is founded upon a comparative analysis[1] of the four main varieties of thought critiqued as well as the more eclectic work that defies being easily categorized within these main paradigms. The theoretical position presented here is founded in the various empirical investigations in the preceding chapters as well.

There are, of course, problems involved in posing a general theory of the U.S. political economy and calling it critical political economics. No one would call one's own theory apologetic economic, social, or political theory. Yet to suggest a theory which is in essence a synthesis of much of the existing theory and give this synthesis a "new" name is not only terminological. The theoretical position being proposed is at least moderately different in substance from any one existing school of thought in political economics. But the cornerstone of critical political economics is a radical/Marxian meld. On close examination it becomes clear that the synthesis that emerges and the perspective to be proposed in this chapter are an eclectic mix of what are thought to be the more persuasive of the ideas explored in this book.

Three closely related tasks remain to draw a theoretical synthesis together. These segments are what readily come to mind as the more apparent highlights. First, some central aspects relevant to the synthesis and critique of Keynesian, Galbraithian, Marxian, and radical thought which serve as the foundation for critical political economics will be reiterated. A second task is really part of the first but is a more formalized statement of theory in which a plausible account of some key components of the structure of the United States political economy is sketched. A third task is to consider the way in which the political economy theoretically would be expected to perform if it were to be founded upon the structure described.

Toward a Critical Political Economics

All of the ideas in political economics explored in the preceding chapters do not neatly fit into Keynesian, Galbraithian, Marxian, or radical thought. There is a great deal of contemporary literature that is quite eclectic and claims allegiance to no intellectual tradition but draws from—in the minds of the individual authors—whatever works. Indeed, an important variety of thought that overlaps the four main schools discussed is that in theories of economic dualism. Work in economic dualism has been undertaken both by conflict theorists (such as James O'Connor) and economists who perceive the economic order to be essentially harmonious (such as Robert Averitt). Here is seen an eclecticism within a broader framework, with the individual theorists seizing upon powerful ideas even though their general theoretical stance is at odds with others with whom they see areas of shared intellectual worth. But more on this later.

Chapter 1 presented a survey of key literature that should be seen as representative of critical political economics. This survey and the bibliography point to a wealth of literature which provides a critical analysis of the economic system in the United States. It is argued that the central difference between critical political economics and ortho- dox economics is that the latter is deeply involved in policy formula- tion which reinforces, or seeks to reinforce, the economic system of capitalism. The orthodox economists identify themselves with the system seeking ways to make it function more smoothly, often thinking it foolish to take any other stance. An example of one of the more cynical, if clever, comments in this vein was made by Kenneth Boulding at the 1974 annual meeting of the American Economic Association where he said, "Capitalism is a very bad system but socialism is much worse." Boulding noted that he had a lot of good ideas that would serve to reform the system, and it was a pity that they weren't taken more seriously in policy formulation undertaken by the federal government. This position seems typical of those economists apologetic of the system who also hold a naive theory of the state.

It was necessary to focus on archetypes in the preceding discus- sion. Although it is likely that the majority of economists are uncommitted to fierce and rigid ideologies, at least conciously, and primarily do what the established institutions in which they work require of them, in practice economics is the servant of the prevailing economic and social order. Some economists have surfaced as the more zealous spokesmen (and most are men) of the popular para- digm. By and large the popular paradigm is what Samuelson used to call the neo-Classical synthesis in earlier editions of his introductory textbook. This consists of neo-Classical microeconomics and Keynes- ian macroeconomics which is usually not a synthesis at all but rather is the juxtaposition of two different levels of analysis. Samuelson sketched the broad contours of the neo-Classical synthesis in this way:

> [B]y means of appropriately reinforcing monetary and fiscal policies, our mixed-enterprise system can avoid the excesses of boom and slump and can look forward to healthy progressive growth. This fundamental being understood, the paradoxes that robbed the older classical principles dealing with small-scale "microeconomics" of much of their relevance and validity—these paradoxes will now lose their sting. In short, mastery of the modern analysis of income determination genuinely validates the basic classical pricing principles; and the economist is now justified in saying that the broad cleavage between micro- economics and macroeconomics has been closed.[2]

Critical political economics, in contrast, is very skeptical of the U.S. economic system with the practitioners of Marxian economics arguing that the economic system of capitalism is faced with contradictions so fundamental that resolution of them would not leave the system of capitalism intact. Most radical and Marxian economists are, in fact, quite alienated from the established order and find it a painful curiosity typified by conflict and struggle in contrast to the view in economic orthodoxy which either assumes a harmony of interests or that an acceptable harmony of interests can be accomplished through intelligent policy that they are qualified to help construct. Analysis of the political economy with an eye to social class is central to critical political economics and rare in orthodox economics. More correctly, it might be said that orthodox economics contains implicitly, if often unconsciously, policies which benefit capital or at least do not seriously threaten capital.

At first glance critical political economics is a radical/Marxian meld. But Chapter 1 and later analysis present successive stages of materials so that critical political economics comes to include a weighty influence from the more eclectic work of nonradical writers as well as from other branches of social science (especially sociology) and ecology. And it is argued that the economic orthodoxy suffers from faulty assumptions and an absence of a holistic view in comparison. In short, the economic orthodoxy often has as its strength elegance of method but a poverty of significant substance. Critical political economics attempts to view the economy within the whole of society and human existence. Needless to say, it does not totally succeed at this overly ambitious—even embarrassingly grandiose—task. But that is the state of the art in the age of scientism. The context of the view presented is one in which a general skepticism about social science *qua* science is also evident.

A contrast of critical political economics with the archetype represented by the thought of John Kenneth Galbraith is also presented in the preceding discussion. Galbraith's perspective is not a formidable leap forward in persuasive paradigms, but is rather a post-Keynesian apologia for a planned capitalism. The radical/Marxian analyses are seen as much more provocative and scientific than Galbraith's.

Although not enough time has elapsed for an adequate historical perspective, critical political economics is rich with ideas and its identification with the Movement/New Left of the 1960s is its social basis. Its scope is attention to macroeconomic instability, centralization and concentration in industry, theories of the state, inequality, alienation, racism, sexism, irrationality, imperialism, war and alternatives to capitalism. The social bases of the economic orthodoxy are the mainstream of American society and its ruling elite. The social bases of Galbraith's ideas are the liberal wing of the Democratic party and an identification with the intellectual elite.

Chapter 2 develops the theme that the economic orthodoxy is subservient to the established order and criticizes the Keynesian archetype. Although it is a cliché to claim that "Keynesianism is not enough" and that its hegemony is under fire, this obvious point is made in the belief that this stance has not been widely accepted. The view that a theoretical vacuum exists in the economic orthodoxy of Keynesian macroeconomics as compared to the actual system to which it is addressed emerges in this chapter. The argument is that the basis of modern macroeconomics presented by John Maynard Keynes has been lost as this doctrine moved from a short-term set of policy recommendations to applied longer term economic medicine. Worthwhile insights were provided by Keynes. The most significant probably was the argument that Classical economics was faulty in its assumption that the economic system was self-equilibrating. In practice, however, state expenditures to provide the necessary aggregate demand to provide relatively full employment—embodied as a state responsibility in the U.S. by 1946—took a malevolent form with the corresponding growth of the military-industrial complex. Although Keynes' argument that laissez faire was not a sound economic doctrine was well defended by his theoretical discussion and measured economic reality, his thought was to become, in turn, a new orthodoxy. An important omission in Keynes' thought was an analysis of imperfect competition. Such writers as Joan Robinson have argued that Keynesian policy has been a series of expedients to combat economic slumps which avoided the nasty assaults on profits and power wielded by corporations and labor unions (and the former much more than the latter) that would have been necessary to sidestep pressures to inflation as a way of life. Thus, one crisis in economic theory was the inability of theory to explain the level of employment. Even though this crisis itself has not been abated completely, another crisis emerged more recently whereby the content of employment and unemployment is not explained by Keynesianism turned orthodoxy. A segmented society has been promoted by uneven economic development. A policy of growth based on technical progress requiring skilled workers in the concentrated and centralized portion of the economy has existed. Unemployment and underemployment have emerged among the less-educated workers and surplus skilled and educated workers as they have been "thrown out at the bottom." Thus, in addition to an increasing aggregate output, there has been a continuing problem of poverty and inequality. So applied Keynesianism has kept the economy growing over time, but this growth has not assured a place in the work force for everyone. As Joan Robinson puts it, "In short, we have not got a theory of distribution." With this second crisis emerging on top of the unresolved first problem, the legitimacy of applied economics is in question insofar as it does not deal with direct income redistribution and institutionalized power. The questioned hegemony of the economic orthodoxy becomes even more dubious as serious economic problems are not resolved and confusion exists in the policies suggested by the most prestigious economists who fancy themselves to have the ear of the politically powerful.[3]

Chapter 2 points out that still other issues emerge when analyzing Keynesian macroeconomics. A cornerstone of the doctrine is that of economic growth. This idea runs absolutely counter to what is argued by many students of ecology and social scientists influenced by their observations. Although some proponents of the "limits to growth" view have been called members of the lunatic fringe by at least one detractor,[4] at best the argument is unresolved. So it can be said that it is not obvious that economic growth of the U.S. variety can be sustained or should be promoted as a matter of public policy. Nor is it clear that other countries should pursue U.S.-style "development." It is also not obvious that Keynes' notion that the allocation of resources and composition of output is acceptable can be sustained.

Keynes believed his general theory to be quite earthshaking and his perception proved correct. But it cannot be seriously thought that he was proposing *the* general theory or that such an event is possible. The Keynesian paradigm does not contain an adequate theory of the state, and modern Keynesians have not developed such a theory (though a theory of the state is implicit). Moreover, where imperfect competition is brought into the discussion in most textbooks written in the style of the neo-Classical synthesis, the micro- and macroeconomic levels are not brought together demonstrating how one relates to the other. Yet Keynesian doctrine remains the main position contained in the contemporary lower economics. It is in this literature that it becomes very clear that the economic orthodoxy does not seek to stand apart as a neutral science simply explaining events. It would seem that when economics promises so much as a shaper of events, it is due the criticism it has received when the promise cannot be fulfilled. Many economists have not taken kindly to being put in the position of scapegoats for the failures of contemporary economic policies. They have taken defensive postures and made honest and open dialogue less possible. Indeed, radical and Marxian social scientists are not welcome at most American colleges and universities, a fact which is a commentary on the defensive posture of the intellectual orthodoxy.

The main challenge to the economic orthodoxy considered in this work is that in Marxian thought insofar as macroeconomic instability, analyses of the centralization and concentration in industry, and theories of the state are concerned. These areas are the main ones explored here as a limited investigation into critical political economics. It would be very worthwhile to explore the other areas of inquiry in critical political economics as well. A study of alienation as a social phenomenon related to the economic and broader system in particular would be a work supplementary to this one. So would be an insightful and persuasive political sociology in an attempt to determine what form class struggles are likely to take and whether or not democratic socialism is on the historical agenda in the United States.

Chapter 3 draws out some of the more classical antecedents which are a loose foundation for contemporary Marxian analyses. This discussion shows that some areas of similarity exist between Keynesian and Marxian thought, and that each can be called upon to supplement the other. Joan Robinson in particular is an exponent of this view. Many adherents to each school resist the ideas of the other for ideological reasons as well as for fear that to embrace thought from other perspectives might threaten their intellectual identities and their legitimacy among their peers. It would also be a threat to political aims in that for Keynesians to admit the validity of aspects of Marxian thought might be to recognize the transitory nature of the capitalist system. For Marxists to recognize the strength of Keynesian policy would be to acknowledge the depressing prospect of capitalism having much more staying power than they would like to anticipate. Thus, it becomes possible that political hopes are deeply imbedded in much, if not all, of the economic theory that has been criticized even when the attempt has been made to keep the discussion at a scientific level. Perhaps it is because, as Samuel Bowles and Herbert Gintis have claimed, "science has replaced theology in the modern world, and with this change a new basis of social legitimation has come into being."[5]

With the structural transformation of capitalist society, the lines between aspects of the various schools of economic thought have become extremely blurred in some instances. For example, it might be said that Galbraith is to no small extent a Keynesian revisionist who realizes that public intervention into the economy would contain policies directed at the regulation of aggregate demand and business investment but that the state would need to become involved in economic affairs in still more direct ways—such as selective nationalization, public employment, direct income redistribution, and the use of wage-price controls—if economic stability is to obtain and if the realities of centralized and concentrated portions of

American industry are to be dealt with adequately. Galbraith has obviously broken away from traditional microeconomic theory, whereas Keynes was an adherent to the general stance of Alfred Marshall and others in that vein. It may not, in fact, be unreasonable to see Galbraith as a more evolved Keynes who is more attuned to oligopoly as a fact of life. Neither should be seen as socialists, obviously, and both views are quite anti-Marxian to the extent that Marxian ideas are recognized by them at all. Both positions suggest policies which would strengthen economic performance without eliminating the private ownership of the means of production. Both, then, can be seen as advocates and adherents of a state capitalism though Galbraith's version is much more far reaching in its elements and its implications than even contemporary Keynesian thought.

Radical and Marxian economists—in the way in which those terms have been used in the preceding chapters—are much more skeptical of even a highly modified capitalism. The theoretical perspective of radical economists is much more varied than in any of the other categories that have been discussed. But if any generalization is at all accurate, it can be said that radical political economics is characterized by a loose and often unacknowledged Marxism which attempts to integrate noneconomic ideas into its analysis. This radical political economics is thought quite synonymous with that of the Movement or the New Left which is deeply concerned about alienation as well as social injustice in general, both in capitalist countries and in those countries which are experimenting with a variety of socialist models.

There is diversity and disagreement among those who are more explicitly Marxist. A serious difficulty arises out of the fact that they are stuck with analyzing a social order with which they are in opposition at an historic moment when no convincingly solid alternative to it has been yet constructed, though struggles to do so abound and there are a handful of promising models. Signs of the impending breakdown of capitalism are eagerly hoped for and looked for, and a strata in opposition with whom they could form an alliance to move from theory to practice would be a saving grace. But the mass of workers, especially in the United States, have been disappointingly unmoved and are often ignorant of, and resistant to, genuinely socialist aspirations. Thus, the Marxian intellectual is left with an "unhappy consciousness." Those who are lucky enough to have not been ignored or set aside by the intellectual community are left to live in material comfort within a society they intellectually and personally reject.[6] They are socialists in a capitalist world. The strain is difficult to bear, and for many a life of rejection and struggle because of their ideas places restrictions on their productivity (not to mention their longevity). Those Marxists who are able to secure employment seem usually to be more outstanding than is expected of their colleagues who hold more conventional views, and even then they are subject to charges of elitism by the less successful who share their views. The political climate of the U.S. is not at all supportive of work in Marxian social science, and it is well-known that those who hope to secure grants for research keep their more radical perspectives to themselves. Perhaps this is commentary enough on the worth of Marxian thought as well as on the power of the financial, corporate, and state superstructure and the values it supports. Marxian thought is a threat to the established order both in the U.S. and more certainly in the world.

In contemporary Marxian thought there is agreement with Galbraith that centralization and concentration of capital is a stark reality and that it is no longer worthwhile to think in laissez faire terms. At the same time, it is not valid to see competitive enterprise as nonexistent. The evidence and theory support the view that the competitive portion of the political economy serves the interests of the financial and corporate superstructure. But Galbraith should not be credited with much originality in bringing centralized and concentrated capitalism to the forefront of the discussion though credit is due to his having done much to popularize this observation. This view existed among Marxists and others long before Galbraith acknowledged it, and it has simply become greatly reinforced by events since Marx speculated on the idea that "one capitalist kills many," or Lenin wrote, "The enormous growth of industry and the remarkably rapid process of concentration of production in ever-larger enterprises represent one of the most characteristic features of capitalism."[7]

As Chapter 4 depicts, the question of the extent to which capital is centralized and concentrated is a difficult one to answer empirically. There is fairly comprehensive information available on the concentration issue for many specific industrial sectors. It is shown that all manufacturing is highly concentrated by about any measure. A small percentage of manufacturing corporations (393 out of 184,961) held 61.3 percent of manufacturing assets in 1964. In 1970 the largest 200 manufacturing corporations contributed 43 percent of all manufacturing value added. The post-World War II period was one of increasing concentration in manufacturing (if not all industrial sectors) in terms of assets held and value added by the largest manufacturing corporations with respect to all manufacturing. But it must be noted that the merger movement of the 1960s has not been well interpreted at this writing, and it is not an accurate measure of corporate power to speak only of industries. At the same time it must be added that to speak of manufacturing is to focus on one of the more concentrated industrial sectors (with transportation, communications, electric and gas being the most concentrated). Thus, it cannot be concluded that the post-World War II period is a period of increasing concentration for all industries. This phenomenon has not been conclusively proved by anyone, though the hypothesis that concentration has increased is highly plausible. The discussion in Chapter 4 is by necessity very sketchy and the look at industries is much more aggregated than would be ideal since a full discussion is worth at least a large book. When specific parts of manufacturing are broken out, the variance in concentration is much more marked than indicated by the figures cited with some being much more concentrated and others being much less concentrated.

Since information on the centralization and concentration of capital is not comprehensive or conclusive, a reliance must be placed on theoretical and impressionistic studies. Chapter 4 contrasts the contemporary classics—Baran and Sweezy's *Monopoly Capital* and Galbraith's *The New Industrial State*—on the social meaning of big business. Both have their genesis in the same historical period and both focus on corporate power in the economy as a whole. As the discussion in that chapter reveals, neither study is without its problems; but Galbraith's analysis emerges as a tract which suggests that the "educational and scientific estate" could use its countervailing power to keep the largest corporations from running over all of society. Galbraith sees corporate power being exercised by the "technostructure," or those who are actually involved in middle- to high-level corporate positions as technocrats and managers. This view is one in which technical expertise makes decisions. Knowledge is power.

No doubt there is power in knowledge, so Galbraith is plausibly partially correct. But in the *NIS* he goes far enough with this theme that it seems entirely reasonable to suspect that his vision is impeded by an ideology which is at least related to his place in the social structure. Although doomsday books are not popular, it is very difficult to understand how Galbraith arrived at such an optimistic assessment of the power of knowledge against the power of money, property, and position in strategic social institutions. Thus a contrast of the classic work by Baran and Sweezy with Galbraith's discussion of some of the same phenomena presents markedly different interpretations.

Baran and Sweezy see the political economy as one characterized by exploitation, tendencies toward stagnation, imperialism, and irrationality (including "waste") in general. The position of the largest corporations is emphasized to the extent that finance capital stands far in the background in their analysis. Some Marxists have thought the work to be the position of what they have called "Marxist managerialism." That is, Baran and Sweezy are accused of seeing the corporations free from the financial nexus and influence of the very rich. On examination this charge cannot really be sustained, though how some got that impression from *Monopoly Capital* is understandable. Their view of the ruling class is unsatisfactorily vague, perhaps because the ruling class thesis is more an underlying assumption than something which is supported with a rigorous analysis. The definitive work in this area is yet to appear, though there are numerous studies supporting the thesis that power and decision making are concentrated in the hands of those whose positions exist on the foundation of private property accumulated over the generations through the appropriation of surplus value. Other work can serve to supplement that of Baran and Sweezy. The works of S. Menshikov and James C. Knowles are two examples of supplementary studies.

Other criticisms have been leveled by Marxists about the absence of an explicit labor theory of value in *Monopoly Capital*. This assumption is an underlying one which Paul Sweezy clarified long after the book first appeared. Yet, the aggregative approach used by Baran and Sweezy is at a level of abstraction that rather prohibits a discussion of the sociopolitical reaction of workers to the material conditions they experience under the U.S. political economy. More accurately this discussion becomes separate. The book attempts to explain the dynamics of the political economy which is seen as dominated by giant corporations using the state for their ends. Rational at the microeconomic level from the perspective of the owners of the means of production and their higher level agents, the system as a whole is shown as very irrational. Monopoly capital, for example, is viewed as being behind imperialist expansion abroad, pushing the U.S. population into an ideological confrontation with countries trying to create socialism. So while the U.S. population—with notable exceptions that are pointed out—experienced comparative affluence in the post-World War II period and is, therefore, not shouting for change, there emerges from the Baran and Sweezy analysis the idea that this situation is very transitory even though no specific timetable is suggested. It is argued that socialism is the emerging world economic order even if capitalism may last the century or longer.

Galbraith's analysis of the place held in society by the largest 500 corporations is obviously distinctly different from that of Baran and Sweezy. But a point of convergence between the two books is their comparative neglect of both the competitive sector of the economy and the state. More accurately, the analysis of each with respect to these two elements is inadequate. Materials in Chapter 5 attempt to set this inadequacy straight.

A fundamental point of disagreement which seems irresolvable between Keynesian and Galbraithian thought, on the one hand, and radical and Marxian thought, on the other, is the theory of the state which exists among each. For Keynes and Galbraith the state is that body which can be called upon to provide the palliative, though both acknowledge upper socioeconomic stratum influence. How this sector which would create the palliative might receive their rather unequivocal reformist endorsement is a mystery. Both men at times recognize the existence of powerful interests embodied in the state, but they each express a curious confidence that the manipulative powers of the state can be influenced to achieve the social policy objectives they advocate.

In Marxian thought the state is not expected to be a conscious agent of progressive change. But it does fulfill dual and contradictory functions so that it is not surprising that the lower socioeconomic strata and their political allies often seek to use the state to change their material position. In addition, in some Marxian thought the support of the use of the state to stabilize the system is advocated as a strategic tactic.[8] Generally the state is seen as the ancilliary body which manages the common affairs of the upper socioeconomic stratum which lives off the labor of the rest of the population. In Marxian thought social transformation in genuinely socialist directions implies disbanding the capitalist state along with the form of ownership structure whose interests it disproportionately serves. In Marxian thought the state contains formidable contradictions which results in the alleviation and exacerbation of economic, social, and political crises at one and the same time. In James O'Connor's view (the most persuasive theory of the state sketched in this work), the state serves the functions of both accumulation and legitimization which are necessary for capitalist hegemony but which also work in opposite directions fiscally. A third state activity that O'Connor does not draw out is one which can be seen as rather a "trump card." The state can use its police powers when the legitimization function fails. "Stability" results through a ruthless program of the crushing of the opposition to hierarchical society. The most dramatic example of our times, to which a whole generation of children in the U.S. were exposed with daily media accounts, was the struggle for the imposition of capitalist hegemony in Indochina. Another striking example is

	OWNERSHIP	
	Private	Public
CONTROL — Private	Capitalism	Syndicalism
CONTROL — Public	Corporatism	Socialism

Figure 1   Varieties of ownership and control

Source: R. E. Pahl and J. T. Winkler, "The Coming Corporatism," *Challenge*, vol. 18, no. 1 (March–April 1975), p. 31.

former New York State Governor Rockefeller crushing the inmates' rebellion at Attica State Penitentiary in 1971 with state troopers killing prisoners and their prison employee hostages alike. The campaign by various police agencies in the nation against the Black Panthers, in which many armed raids against them resulted in their deaths, imprisonment, or flight to avoid prosecution is still another instance of police state action to supplement an inadequate program of legitimization. Indeed, many Native Americans saw the bicentennial celebration as "200 years of resistance" rather than 200 years about which to be happy.

The economic system in the United States and economic systems in general can be portrayed by a simple chart used by R. E. Pahl and J. T. Winkler, two British sociologists. In Figure 1 are ownership and control possibilities in the public and private sectors of a society. Private ownership and private control constitute the necessary conditions for *capitalism,* a common and popular idea. Public ownership with private control is called *syndicalism.* Public ownership and control are the necessary features of *socialism.* The interesting part of the figure is the introduction of the term *corporatism,* which is characterized by private ownership accompanied by public control. Too often the terms capitalism and socialism are used in too sweeping a fashion—a tendency which exists sometimes in the preceding chapters for the sake of simplicity. It seems useful to use the Pahl/ Winkler categories of economic, political, and social systems. This refinement helps clarify the similarities and differences between social orders.

Pahl's and Winkler's conception of corporatism is very similar, if not synonymous, to Bertram Gross's "friendly fascism" and James O'Connor's social-industrial complex (both discussed in Chapter 5). Corporatism is "fascism with a human face." It is an economic system in which the state directs private enterprise toward order, unity, nationalism, and "success." No longer is the full range of the business cycle tolerated under corporatism with the accompanying risk to profits and the stability on which the status quo's hegemony depends. Prices are stabilized and wages are controlled.[9] Those who deviate from the established order are punished, ignored, imprisoned, or killed (often while evading capture or engaged in self-defense). The ends of society are determined by the state itself which embodies the views of the upper socioeconomic stratum.

In essence, Galbraith's stance is one in which corporatism is embraced—though its implications are not acknowledged or perhaps—though this is hard to believe—even realized. This stance is a Keynesian one come of age, drawn out to its totally logical conclusions after serial short-term policies became structural realities. This is a Keynesianism absent of a critical theory of the state or an analysis of the class nature of capitalist society. Indeed, this is a vulgarized Keynesianism where state intervention has gained popular acceptance, or at least has evaded refusal, because of "practical" necessity.

Corporatism is, of course, not a unique form of modern social organization. It is fast becoming the rule in those countries where private ownership of the means of production remains. It has existed in various forms in various places for much of this century. For example, in Germany during the regime of Adolf Hitler, corporatism existed in a particularly lethal form where the Keynesian notion of "liquidate the rentiers became kill the Jews."[10] Pahl and Winkler say that where contemporary corporatism is implemented

> [w]hat all the major parties have done is to take over the core
> elements of the *economic* strategy which the Italian fascists,

Salazar in Portugal, the Falange in Spain and the Nazis adopted to deal with the interwar crisis. . . . What the parties are putting forward now is an acceptable face of fascism; indeed a masked version of it, because so far the more repugnant *political and social* aspects of the German and Italian regimes are absent or only present in diluted form.[11]

Andrew Shonfield recognized the fact of a transforming and expanding public sector amidst capitalism in the middle 1960s and noted that Germany and the United States stood apart from such countries as Britain, France, Italy, Sweden, and others. In the case of the former "they evince an ostentatious antipathy for the whole process and loudly advocate resistance to it."[12] Galbraith has set out, in his writings, to persuade his audience to favor a more planned approach. Although it is likely that (as in the case of Keynes) Galbraith serves as provider of "scientific" rationalizations to do what the powerful will do for pragmatic reasons of necessity, the distinction between European capitalism (or corporatism—the distinction becomes so muddy in usage) and that in the United States is becoming more and more only nominally different. As Bill Warren puts it,

[F]ormalized medium or long-term economic planning has by now been attempted by all the principal industrialized capitalist countries, including the United States—which with the sweeping wage and price controls introduced by Nixon in late 1971 has belatedly joined the ranks of the other capitalist powers. . . .[13]

In this view the Galbraithian policy recommendations are already powerfully in motion with a far-reaching move beyond Keynesian short-term demand regulation. Planning, however piecemeal, especially in the U.S., is a fact of life. Yet, Warren's analysis

clearly rules out any view of the state as being in some sense more "independent" than before of the capitalist class or its dominant groups. Both the political and the economic motives inducing government to intervene in new ways in the economy were designed directly to preserve the interests (and survival) of the imperialist system in general, and individual capitalist states in particular, against their respective working classes national rivals and the socialist countries. The state possesses no independence, but does exercise a genuine if relative *autonomy,* inherent in its own specific and creative functions, and activity, covering organization, administrative, intellectual, educational and other spheres.[14]

Warren thinks that the evidence shows increasing authoritarianism and a popular distrust of "politics" as well as a collaboration between the state and the powerful corporations. In these circumstances, he argues, social democratic parties have been integrated into this structure so that "even gradualist socialism as a slogan, rules out any possibility of adopting an ambiguous attitude towards such parties." The response should be to

> detach their working-class base from them instead of fostering illusions that they are potential socialist parties. Along side this strategy must go a firm class refusal of any integration whatever into the processes of capitalist planning and management of the economy in general.[15]

Thus capitalist consciousness is the basis of the new corporatist order espoused by Galbraith and many others. Although this scenario was not discussed in the preceding chapters as existing in a mature form, the elements of a social-industrial complex are quite evident and there is, for example, in the Rocky Mountain states, a serious flirtation with this form of state capitalism underway in the U.S. It may be, in fact, not outrageous to believe that a more developed form of this pernicious postcapitalist system is a foregone conclusion—as Bill Warren apparently believes—if state activity continues on its current path.

More on the Structure of the U.S. Political Economy

Figure 2 provides a highly simplified sketch of a few key parts of the U.S. political economy and depicts the general relationships between the parts. The diagram emerges from the materials surveyed in the preceding chapters. Key works which provided analyses leading to this synthesis of the structural components are especially James O'Connor's *The Fiscal Crisis of the State* and Baran and Sweezy's *Monopoly Capital* for a depiction of monopoly capital (Baran and Sweezy) and the relationship between monopoly capital, the competitive sector, the state, and the surplus population (O'Connor). Galbraith's *Economics and the Public Purpose* would label the monopoly sector "the planning system" and the competitive sector "the market system." This depiction of the dual economy is also contained in Robert Averitt's *The Dual Economy* where the firm in the monopoly sector is termed "the center firm" and the firm in the competitive sector is "the periphery firm." The labor force components in Figure 2 come from the dual labor market work of many theorists, which is surveyed in Robert M. Gordon's *Theories of Poverty and Underemployment*. Within the state, the idea of the dual welfare system comes from A. Dale Tussing's *Poverty in a Dual Economy*.[16]

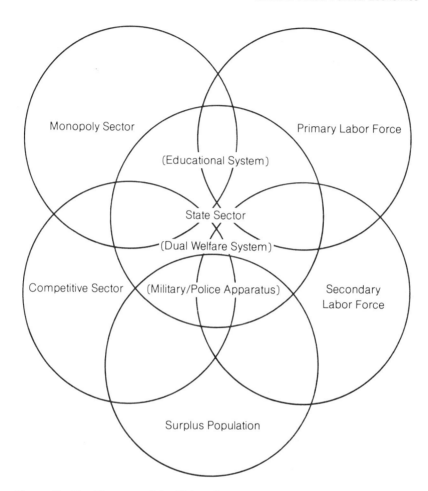

Figure 2 The Structure of the United States Political Economy: Key Components

As Figure 2 depicts, the current structure may be one in which there is a monopolized (centralized and concentrated) sector of the economy (which transcends industries per se) along with a competitive sector. These plus the state create the demand for labor and provide the society's goods and services. Those workers who are employed in the monopolized sector are often part of what dual labor market theorists call the primary labor force (though this term is not flawless). Here employment is comparatively stable and wages are comparatively high, both of which are reflections of this sector's productivity and profitability advantage over the competitive sector. The security existing in this advantageous labor market position has much to do with the monopoly capital sector relationship with the state, which seeks both to provide the basis for accumulation and to legitimize the system as a whole. Force, the threat of force, or simple exclusion are used when parts of the population fail to accept the program.

The competitive sector, on the other hand, overlaps substantially with what dual labor market theorists have called the secondary labor force. Here employment conditions are highly tenuous.[17] Wages and salaries are comparatively low, and job attachment is weak. The competitive sector largely "takes up the slack" when production turns down in the economy as a whole. A classic (if unusual) case is former corporate managers (and others) becoming street vendors during the Great Depression. A more contemporary example would be, perhaps, countercultural artisans selling their wares on a San Francisco streetcorner even though they have teaching credentials. More representative examples are farm workers, car washers, waitresses, etc. Supplementary income or transfer payments are found in the form of food stamps, unemployment insurance (for the very lucky, and only for a few months), and welfare. There is a close identity between those in the competitive sector, the secondary labor force, and the surplus population. Overlap between these three broad structural categories abounds.

The glue that holds all of these sectors—and the political economy as a whole—together is the state sector which provides direct employment under conditions nearly or more favorable as the monopoly sector (in terms of compensation and job security) and welfare of various kinds in addition to expenditures to fulfill the accumulation function. Part of this sector is the entire police/military apparatus which is the state's trump card when the accumulation and legitimization functions prove to be inadequate. Direct attempts at redistribution are thus largely thwarted.

An analysis of the monopoly, competitive, and state sectors with the comparative perspectives of O'Connor and Galbraith has been provided in Chapters 4 and 5. Powerful evidence suggests that these sectors do exist as good, if crude, approximations to social reality. A huge amount of information exists in particular about the centralized and concentrated (monopoly) sector of the economy. This sector, in collaboration with the state and an intertwined financial nexus, appears to dominate all of U.S. society. The competitive sector serves the purposes of monopoly capital and the social class standing behind it, by providing a fluidity in which the displaced can operate and the illusion of freedom can be maintained. For example, the displaced auto worker can dream of starting his or her own business and even conceive of enjoying more freedom than the dull assembly line offers, good wages aside. The long-haired astrologer/attorney who would hardly make a good manager of the affairs of the super-rich in a conventional law firm or bank trust department or even function well in a state agency can seek out a clientele of the like-minded in any countercultural oasis such as in many parts of San Francisco. The consciousness III psychedelic psychiatrist can do his or her free wheeling Jungian/neo-Freudian/Gestalt/primal/bio-energenics/meditation/yoga therapy among the confused and float-ing population in many an urban area and avoid the shirt and tie "profession" or the bureaucratic hospital or clinic. Indeed, the Marxist economist who has grown weary of being fired from colleges and universities can become a freelance (and otherwise under-employed or unemployed) social scientist seeking a book advance, state or foundation funding to do socially relevant and personally fulfilling research, or perhaps (as Paul Sweezy did) start a journal for which an audience exists. It is plausible that competitive sector examples could be found for those of virtually any skills or experi-ence. Indeed, the person who, in capitalist society, finds it more rewarding to relate to plants or animals than people can scrape a living together by being an artichoke or goat farmer on rented or borrowed land. Of course, the dope dealer is probably one of the most commonplace of small entrepreneurs today (and, of course, many are not so small).

Without the competitive sector, it is plausible that the many who are excluded and drift among the surplus population, the secondary labor market, and the competitive sector[18] would be a potential class in revolt. Indeed, it is likely that this group would also include many of those over 65 years of age who were forcibly retired from work they found not only financially but personally fulfilling. If those who are excluded from work in the monopoly or state sectors had no alternatives, it is likely that a more revolutionary population would exist. Thus, the maintenance of competitive enterprise can be seen as quite functional to the continuance of corporate and upper so-cioeconomic stratum hegemony. Those who are not needed or who are so alienated from centralized and concentrated capitalism are not always with absolutely nothing else to do. Coupled with state legitimization policies, starvation becomes comparatively rare, though hardship is common.

The Police/Military Apparatus

Christopher H. Pyle, an attorney and former officer in the U.S. Army Intelligence between 1961 and 1968, made the following observation in testimony before the Senate Subcommittee on Constitutional Rights in 1971.

> Plainly stated, my thesis is that the United States today possesses the intelligence apparatus of a police state. This apparatus is not something of the future; it exists today as a loose coalition of Federal, State, municipal, and military agencies. Together, these law enforcement, counterintelligence, and internal security agencies have developed to the point where authoritarian government is now an operational possibility.
>
> I do not mean to suggest that the emergence of this domestic intelligence community has turned the United States into a police state. On the contrary, I find it somewhat paradoxical that as this apparatus has proliferated, the civil liberties of most Americans have also grown. The reason for this apparent contradiction may be that the men who have developed these agencies are, by and large, decent and well-intentioned men. However, [there] . . . is no guarantee that the apparatus which they have created will not someday come under the control of others for whom the investigatory power is a weapon to be wielded against political and personal foes.
>
> As . . . Justice Brandeis once wrote: "Experience should teach us to be most on our guard to protect liberty when the Government's purposes are beneficient . . . The greatest dangers to liberty lurk in the insidious encroachment by men of zeal, well-meaning, but without understanding."[19]

There have, of course, been objections to the police state apparatus. National data banks, for example, have come under scrutiny due to fears of "men of zeal" having put computer technology to work for purposes of social control. In the process the rights of citizens have been trampled upon.

The agency in the federal government most accused of the misapplication of computer technology is probably the Federal Bureau of Investigation within the Department of Justice. Indeed, FBI Director Clarence M. Kelley is reported to have been aware that the lives of some people are inadvertently ruined or made problematic by easy access to their National Crime Information Center (NCIC) which was begun in 1967, and contained 4.8 million records, and 450,000 criminal history files in 1974 but found the tradeoff between "criminals" captured and ruined lives to favor the former.[20]

> Now . . . NCIC's records are available within minutes to more than 6,000 police agencies . . . its information can be made available to more than 46,000 police, court, and corrections agencies. In five years, NCIC computers will hold 3 million criminal histories and in 10 years the number will swell to 8 million.
>
> Even now, with most systems still in the manual dark ages, credit bureaus and employment agencies have in many instances easily gained access to crime records. Compounding the problem is the fact that arrest records are often disseminated without final

dispositions of the cases. Thus, an arrest can be held against an individual who was found innocent.[21]

In addition to the NCIC there is a nonprofit communications corporation—the National Law Enforcement Teletype System (NLETS)—which is operated by the states.[22] Thus, both federal and state government is actively cooperating to make the police apparatus effective. In the process the accumulation and legitimization functions are supplemented dramatically. Any political force in opposition must realize that given this technology, rebellious parts of the population run the risk of being subdued and apprehended quickly. In essence the nation's police are a domestic military force which numbered 548,000 full-time equivalent officers in 1972, or 28.7 per 10,000 population. Their total expenditures for this same year were almost $7 billion. This amount seems almost trivial in comparison with national military personnel numbering 3.4 million with Department of Defense expenditures of $76.7 billion (also in 1972).[23]

All of the dimensions of the state which reinforce class society can hardly be enumerated here. But two parts of the state where there is support for a segmented society are both the welfare and the educational systems.

The Welfare and Educational Systems

A. Dale Tussing has persuasively outlined the extent to which there is a lower socioeconomic strata welfare system which stands apart from the general welfare system. In the former case usual examples are the various federal, state, and local assistance programs, food stamps, public housing, etc. In the case of the nonpoor there is unemployment insurance, social security, farm subsidies, income tax deductions for homeowners, and so on. Welfare for the poor is at a lower level of support, visible, vulnerable to local politics, restrictive to the lives of the recipients, and does not contain as a feature of the programs incentives for recipients to "succeed" in society. For the nonpoor, the reverse is true.[24] A picture of ideology and class interests coalescing to reinforce capitalist culture and hegemony emerges. But missing from Tussing's analysis is a commentary on the, say, upper income quintile though he says "In reality . . . one does not necessarily come to understand the causes and implications of poverty by studying poor people. In fact, it may even be more fruitful to study the rich. . ."[25]

The educational system is obviously an important and central part of the state. But for whatever reasons, the role of education has proved somewhat elusive and useful to mystify class relations in capitalist society. Education fulfills both O'Connor's accumulation and legitimization functions, occupies much of an otherwise greatly expanded surplus population, and has become a major nexus of human activity—even an industry—in its own right.

In a way, the educational system can be seen as a self-serving industry which but mirrors the hierarchical society it helps to reproduce and of which it is a functional part. The "education ideology" in the United States justifies vast economic inequality (M.D.'s are the foremost example). In the universities—which constitute the apex of the higher learning—their boards of trustees are the equivalent to the corporate board of directors. Indeed, there are many trustees who are also directors. In this regard, it seems unlikely that things have changed at all since Thorstein Veblen, in a highly amusing concluding passage to his book on higher education, struck out against this structure in the early part of the century. Veblen says that it is not likely that the "captain of erudition" can be dispensed with since

> [h]e is too dear to the commercialized popular imagination, and he fits too convincingly into the businessmen's preconceived scheme of things, to permit any such sanguine hope of surcease from skilled malpractice and malversation. All that is here intended to be said is nothing more than the *obiter dictum* that, as seen from the point of view of the higher learning, the academic executive and all his works are anathema, and should be discontinued by the simple expedient of wiping him off the slate; and that the governing board, in so far as it presumes to exercise any other than vacantly perfunctory duties, has the same value and should with advantage be lost in the same shuffle.[26]

Earlier in this paragraph Veblen says that this view has little more than speculative value and that he does not believe the president's office could in fact be abolished along with the governing board. But he obviously enjoyed speculating on the possibility! His sense that it was but speculation is, of course, verified by the continued presence of "captains of erudition."

This should not be taken to imply that it is only at the university level that the capitalist (or corporate) model of hierarchy exists. In fact, this form is the common one of organization in this part of the, primarily, "public" sector. At the elementary and secondary levels, the educational system has not been a noticeable agent of social change. It is likely that it is, in fact, primarily an agent of social control and the maintenance, generally, of the status quo. The ultimate test is how well people fare in their lives, especially what their experience in the educational system has to do with where they end up in the work force.

Of particular concern to educational policy researchers has been the seeming nonresponsiveness of socioeconomic outcomes to compensatory education of various types and the notion that programs addressed to the very disadvantaged (e.g., jobless high school dropouts) have—to the extent that they have been successful—tended to displace others in the secondary labor market to subemployment or unemployment. In other words, work-related compensatory education—not to mention noncompensatory education—may redistribute employment rather than change the situation in the aggregate.[27]

Indeed, the well-known work by Christopher Jencks and associates went so far as to claim that economic success is more related to luck and on-the-job competence than to other factors. "The definition of competence varies from one job to another, but it seems in most cases to depend more on personality than on technical skills."[28] If this phenomenon is true—and to grant this is to gloss over an unresolved controversy—then it is, as Jencks and associates point out, difficult to concoct a set of policy recommendations to equalize competence and even more difficult to think up an equalization of luck strategy. Although this viewpoint has moved some to conclude that it would follow to suggest abandoning efforts to influence socioeconomic outcomes through any educational strategy, it does not appear to have been the key point Jencks, et al. were making. They end up arguing that the redistribution of income would be the most direct method of amelioration. But they also point out that "the selection of a suitable mechanism for equalizing incomes is an interesting but politically irrelevant exercise." Ending on an upbeat note characteristic of writers of books, Jencks and associates express the view that people need to be convinced that the redistribution of income is a legitimate political issue. They need to express that idea through the institution of the federal government, which would need to become responsible not only for the amount of aggregate income but also for its distribution. This expression is likely to occur only if the poor do not believe that their status is just (and presumably also act as if that were the case) and the rich (and especially their children who will themselves, presumably, be the next rich generation) begin to feel guilty about their advantaged place in society.[29]

Although many probably agree with the sentiment expressed by Jencks, et al., it is not at all obvious that the political consciousness of the various parts of the U.S. population will proceed expeditiously in the directions *inequality* poses. In fact, it seems as useful to speculate about the possibility of political action that would create a structure generating equality.

Still another part of the educational system is that beyond compulsory education. Although this topic has been touched on earlier, it has not been put in the framework of economic dualism. Interestingly, dualism seems to exist in this as well as other parts of the political economy discussed earlier. Stanley Moses, for example, has posed the idea that there are a core and periphery in postsecondary education with the core being primarily the conventional activities in colleges and universities (degree-diploma track) and the periphery activities being

> a kaleidoscopic representation of the variety of American society. They include educational activities offered in all places where adults are employed—in agriculture, private business, and industry; the military, and civilian government at all levels; the entire potpourri of programs sponsored by the vast number of private associations; national welfare organizations, professional training societies, and specialized programs for adults carried on in regular educational institutions. They include the new "educational system" of manpower activities carried on by government at all levels, primarily through the subsidization of the Federal Government. They also include programs conducted by the "proprietary" and correspondence schools, and programs of organized instruction through educational television.[30]

But even then, participation in the periphery is positively related to income and formal education.[31] So although the educational periphery stands conceptually apart from the core, it is plausible that it serves essentially the same social functions. Adult learning, to the extent that it is related to the world of work, appears to also be instrumental in the solidification of socioeconomic status though to hypothesize that it serves conflicting and contradictory functions seems more persuasive.

The educational system appears to serve both the accumulation and legitimization functions. It does provide the trained work force necessary for production, and in this way it serves the accumulation function. The educational system also helps to legitimize the system by reinforcing the view that through education vertical mobility is possible. The class nature of society is thereby obscured. Thus one primary purpose the educational system serves is the reproduction of the work force and class society. The supposed promise is that education is widely available to any citizen regardless of class (or barriers can be overcome), and the U.S. is, therefore, not rigid about the class position of its members. Of course, the educational system occupies the time of an otherwise greatly expanded surplus or underemployed population. Those who cannot find a satisfactory place in the work force often become part of the learning force. It is likely that, for example, the huge increase in graduate program enrollments in the U.S. in the post-World War II period is directly related to the discovery by college graduates that a bachelor's degree does not assure a nonalienating or high paying job. Graduate school is an option to one-dimensional state or corporate employment or being relegated to the surplus population or secondary labor market where economic hardship surpasses even alienation. This situation is especially likely to be true of lower socioeconomic status people who do not have the proper "connections" to become part of the corporate or other elite even if they had the credentials on paper.[32]

The main structural features of the American political economy are those of monopoly and competitive enterprises, and the state as well as a financial nexus in terms of those main institutions which turn out the society's products and services make up the monetary superstructure and employ the nation's work force. The private sector is characterized by a structural dualism and there is in relationship to this a dualism in labor markets, the primary and secondary labor markets. In addition, there is a dualism in the state. There is welfare for the affluent and there is still another welfare system for those at the bottom of the socioeconomic hierarchy. Dualism extends to the educational system which also reinforces a segmented society. A large number of people at the lower end of the socioeconomic scale (a derivative fact) can be thought of as members of a surplus population. These main features can be measured in a variety of ways.

Further, the way in which this political economy is structured makes for considerable problems. The income distribution, for example, existing as it does with the top quintile of the socioeconomic stratum receiving a proportionately much larger share than the bottom quintile (45 percent in the former case as compared to about 4 percent in the latter—before taxes and transfers which probably do not alter relative shares—according to U.S. Bureau of the Census data for almost all years since 1921) is not unrelated to problems arising in simple circulation, of preventing the product markets and resource markets from coming together in a fashion so that there is full use of the work force with relatively stable prices. Inequality is built into the structure of the economy and society, and it is likely that basic changes in the structure would be required to remove that inequality.

Contradictions and Conflicts in Economic Performance from the Perspective of Critical Political Economics

It seems very plausible that the economic problems of the U.S. in the 1970s have much to do with the structural dimensions sketched. This idea in turn suggests that the future is not likely to be one of economic, social, and political harmony. Rather, it is likely to be a time of continued conflict between capital and labor with the two struggling to use the state to determine economic, social, and political outcomes and resolve the contradictions of capitalism. It also suggests that the state works primarily on behalf of capital though it serves conflicting and contradictory functions. Some questions are: (1) Can capital maintain its comparative hegemony using the state to socialize costs while privately acquiring profits? (2) Will labor be moved to organize in new ways, taking control of production and perhaps even creating nonhierarchical institutions in the process?

With capital in an unprecedented centralized and concentrated form extending even to the multinational conglomerate variety, it is not at all clear that its legitimacy can be maintained. The rhetoric of "free enterprise" is especially empty in this environment. Yet, the nation's impressive empires are also quite visible as is the class which owns these corporate monoliths. Thus it seems possible that a corresponding vulnerability to the potential power of labor has arisen. This vulnerability is greater to the extent that the system does not function smoothly. The system seems to work less well to the extent that the structure described is maintained. With this structure there seems to exist a tendency for the income share received by the upper socioeconomic stratum to grow more than that of the entire work force with special problems developing in the bottom strata.

However, prolonged and generic inequality seems not enough to spark popular revolt. Rather, economic crisis must be systemwide and engulf the lives or threaten to engulf the lives of much of the laboring population for popular revolt to be likely. With state intervention on both the side of accumulation and legitimization, the extent to which crises extend to the whole of the working class becomes obscured. It would seem that perceptions of threats to well-being are almost as important as actual economic crises themselves, though the two are probably strongly correlated. A serious and endemic contradiction in contemporary America is the division between ownership and labor power. Thus, stabilization problems are something which the state seems somewhat powerless to resolve so long as the contradiction itself cannot be eliminated. At the same time, capitalism cannot be expected to be abandoned without a tremendous amount of opposition in the U.S. It, therefore, seems likely that the forces on the side of building a more formalized social-industrial complex are powerful indeed.

A cautious appraisal seems to be that the best promise for the development of a penetrating critical political economics rests in the work of the few theorists who are constructing a theory of the capitalist state founded upon a meld of reinterpretations of classical

Marxian economics, Marxian studies of recent times, the radical political economics originating in the 1960s, work in theories of economic dualism, along with the best eclectic critical studies in economics, sociology, history, and other social science. At the present time, it is difficult to reach firm impressions about the path ahead; but it seems that a tentative prediction could be that Keynesian policies supplemented by some Galbraithian style recommendations will be embraced by state decision-makers. Critical political economics, in this environment, has the advantage of standing apart from a specific stance of immediately attainable advocacy and is therefore likely to be able to assess the path of society more objectively, if imperfectly. In the course of the maturing of a comparatively holistic theoretical framework in critical political economics, there will undoubtedly be heated discussions as "warring universes of discourse"[33] lock horns. Ideologues of all varieties will be especially vulnerable in this climate of uncertainty. And it is likely that many who seek "power over their own lives [will] get this power only by having power over the lives of others."[34] Thus the future appears to be one in which the contradictions of capitalism will become even more pronounced with the following outlining the issues:

> As a class, the capitalists want a government policy which will reduce working-class needs, wages, and consumption (i.e., increase the rate of exploitation), on the one hand, and increase investment and profits, on the other. But as owners of individual capital units which compete with each other and with foreign and international capital, they all still depend on product innovation, forced obsolescence, and other elements which make up the "sales effort" and which *reduce* the rate of exploitation. This is a supercontradiction, the resolution of which will depend on future political alignments and struggle.[35]

To clarify, the "supercontradiction" of our time is a result of a fundamental change in the economic system of capitalism. In earlier times before the quantitative growth of the state, there was a problem realizing surplus value but no problem producing it by keeping wages low, etc. The current situation is one in which there are fewer problems in realizing surplus value (through the use of Keynesian policies), but there is a problem in producing surplus value. That is, labor is a powerful force to be reckoned with by individual units of capital, and it seems that there is an upsurge of union activity and legitimacy. This supercontradiction has all kinds of international and domestic implications including interregional struggles which are generated by capital in an attempt to produce surplus value. For example, capital in the U.S. moved to the South in recent times in search of cheaper labor. There is also increasing economic activity in the Rocky Mountain region both for cheaper (and unorganized) labor and sources of energy, and anything else to reduce costs.[36]

The existing situation in the U.S. political economy then is one of evident and serious problems with respect to instability that seem to be related to and accelerated by the centralization and concentration of industry. This increased centralization and concentration in turn requires a more dramatic move into the state-aided phase of capitalism with "the state's job under capitalism . . . not to appropriate profits but to socialize losses and see that the system functions smoothly."[37] Thus, it is plausible that

> the present economic crisis and the renewed period of stagnation to which it is the prelude are bound to produce a great leap forward into state capitalism in the United States. This will take the form of extensive salvage operations which in fact are already under way in various sectors of the economy (banking, railroads, etc.). . . . And it may involve more or less serious efforts at national economic planning. But whatever the mix, there can be no mistaking the powerful . . . trend toward ever greater state intervention and participation in the U.S. economy.[38]

To summarize, it is obvious that capitalist society is not capable of functioning smoothly and equitably given the structure which exists. The state serves to promote the subterfuge of ideology which suggests that something akin to stability and equity can be created. Conventional economics is an active participant in the generation of this ideology, which is harmful to the interests of the working class and impairs the creation of a new society. In contrast, the radical and Marxian critiques are persuasive, if underdeveloped. It is time that radical and Marxian thought receive the legitimacy that is their due. But how is this acknowledgement to occur in the midst of a cultural wasteland such as exists in American universities (not to mention American society)? It seems likely that even given its scientific value, a critical political economics founded on a radical/Marxian base will continue to live on, in the short-run, as a minority school of thought in political economics finding its support more in the amalgam which makes up the Movement. Certainly, many establishment social scientists will continue to be "closet radicals" knowing that to emerge will require a political vulnerability that only the more courageous (or, more cynically, foolish) will be able to endure. Indeed, many in academia espousing radical rhetoric are merely a part of an innocuous radical chic who are not engaged in radical practice and who serve the function of legitimizing the universities, of giving the appearance that free thought exists in higher learning. But it is likely that socialist hegemony will grow even without the support of an up-front allegiance from social scientists locked in an ambivalence between theory and practice, between what they hold as their values and what they do in their public lives. It is likely that radical social science will develop and its adherents will come out of the closets only if the social basis of support becomes more obvious and more clear. On this note there seems to be mixed evidence but not reason for total skepticism about an emerging community of identification. This community is not now the ambrosia of those seeking progressive social change, but it does exist in a scattered and underground form throughout the United States and more certainly in the world. So although the structure and performance of the United States political economy stands in support of the domination and control of the population at home and abroad, it also generates the conditions for change. It is likely that the basis of the struggle is already in motion, no matter what any of us want. Critical political economics helps to unravel the material basis of that struggle. What is needed to supplement this critical political economics are more refined analyses which transcend the traditional disciplines in the social sciences. In particular, a critical political sociology is necessary to help chart the path ahead, to see if a critical assessment of society can be transmitted into effective struggle for progressive revolutionary social change.

NOTES

1 *As noted at the outset in the first chapter, this approach is argued for in* Barney G. Glaser and Anselm L. Strauss, The Discovery of Grounded Theory: Strategies for Qualitative Research *(Chicago: Aldine, 1967). It is also the more or less natural form this work took in the process of doing it.*

2 *Paul A. Samuelson,* Economics, *5th ed. (New York: McGraw-Hill, 1961), p. 403. The italics in the original have been dropped.*

3 *Joan Robinson, "The Second Crisis of Economic Theory," ed. Rendigs Fels,* The Second Crisis of Economic Theory *(Morristown, N.J.: General Learning Press, 1972). See Chapter 2 for a more complete discussion.*

4 *Geoffrey Barraclough, "The Great World Crisis I,"* The New York Review of Books, *vol. 21, nos. 21 and 22 (January 23, 1975), p. 25.*

5 *Samuel Bowles and Herbert Gintis, "Class Power and Alienated Labor,"* Monthly Review, *vol. 26, no. 10 (March, 1975), p. 24. James O'Connor points out that an analysis of the specific conditions of the U.S. proletariat would be needed to make sense out of competing economic doctrines. That is, economic thought is a reflection of the concrete material realities of a particular society. For example, Marxian thought is much more accepted in Europe than in the U.S.*

6 In this regard see Jean-Paul Sartre, Between Existentialism and Marxism (New York: Pantheon Books, 1975).

7 V. I. Lenin, Imperialism: The Highest Stage of Capitalism (New York: International Publishers, 1939), p. 16.

8 Victor Perlo, for example, implies this when he says "The attitude of Communists is not to rejoice at the arrival of crises but rather to fight against their harmful consequences for the working class," in The Unstable Economy (New York: International Publishers, 1973), p. 208.

9 R. E. Pahl and J. T. Winkler, "The Coming Corporatism," Challenge, vol. 18, no. 1 (March–April, 1975), pp. 28–35.

10 James O'Connor, from personal correspondence in March, 1975.

11 R. E. Pahl and J. T. Winkler, "The Coming Corporatism," p. 30.

12 Andrew Shonfield, Modern Capitalism: The Changing Balance of Public and Private Power (New York: Oxford University Press, 1965), p. 239.

13 Bill Warren, "Capitalist Planning and the State," New Left Review, no. 72 (March–April, 1972), p. 3. Obviously, the U.S. policy makers have demonstrated more ambivalence on this than other countries attempting to manage capitalism through the public sector inasmuch as wage-price controls were not maintained as a permanent policy. And A. Dale Tussing points out that a big weakness of Nixon's controls was they were not based on planning.

14 Ibid., p. 29.

15 Ibid.

16 See the bibliography for the full citations of these works.

17 As depicted, for example, by Elliot Liebow's Tally's Corner; a Study of Negro Streetcorner Men, (Boston: Little, Brown, 1967).

18 Actually, Figure 2 could be drawn so that the surplus population intersects with the monopoly and state sectors. The way it is presented simply dramatizes the situation. In reality, there are times in history—such as during World War II—when there was a very small surplus population. Currently the depiction of the surplus population as in Figure 2 seems quite accurate. But it should not be taken to suggest that there is no movement between the surplus population and employment in the monopoly and state sectors. The diagram contains both static and dynamic analysis and could benefit from further development.

19 Subcommittee on Constitutional Rights of the Committee on the Judiciary, United States Senate. Federal Data Banks, Computers and the Bill of Rights. Hearings conducted in February and March, 1971 (Washington, D.C.; U.S. Government Printing Office, 1971), pp. 169–170. If anything, Mr. Pyle's testimony should be seen as an understatement. In the mid-1970s the F.B.I. and C.I.A. came under increasing scrutiny, which was widely reported in the press. Voluminous documents emerged from the U.S. Senate Select Committee to Study Governmental Operations With Respect to Intelligence Activities. Film makers, too, looked at the police/military apparatus. One fine example of the latter is State of Siege.

20 Susanna McBee, "Crime Records and Privacy," The Washington Post (March 4, 1974), p. 20.

21 *Ibid.*

22 Susanna McBee, *"Communications Aims of FBI Hit by GAO,"* The Washington Post *(March 5, 1974), p. 2.*

23 U.S. Bureau of the Census, Statistical Abstract of the United States: 1974, *(Washington, D.C.: U.S. Government Printing Office, 1974), pp. 156, 308 and 314.*

24 A. Dale Tussing, Poverty in a Dual Economy, *chapter 4.*

25 *Ibid., p. 1.*

26 Thorstein Veblen, The Higher Learning in America: A Memorandum on the Conduct of Universities by Business Men, *(New York: Sagamore Press, 1957), p. 209. First published in 1918.*

27 These ideas were in the air at the Educational Policy Research Center at Syracuse and stemmed from the work of A. Dale Tussing and others as part of the Education and Work project. The term for the phenomenon pointed to—the redistribution of unemployment—has been called "bumping" by Tussing.

28 Christopher Jencks, et al., Inequality: a Reassessment of the Effect of Family and Schooling in America *(New York: Basic Books, 1972), p. 8.*

29 *Ibid., pp. 263–265.*

30 Stanley Moses, The Learning Force: A More Comprehensive Framework for Educational Policy *(Syracuse: Syracuse University Publications in Continuing Education, 1971).*

31 See Laurence DeWitt, Louis Clark, and Dwayne Ward, A Quantitative Analysis of Adult Part-Time Learners *(Syracuse: Educational Policy Research Center, 1975).*

32 Related ideas are found in Samuel Bowles and Herbert Gintis, Schooling in Capitalist America *(New York: Basic Books, 1976).*

33 A term emerging from Gunter W. Remmling's The Road to Suspicion: A Study of Modern Mentality and the Sociology of Knowledge *(New York: Appleton-Century-Crofts, 1967), chapter 1.*

34 James O'Connor, *"The Twisted Dream,"* Monthly Review, *vol. 26, no. 10 (March, 1975), p. 52.*

35 *Ibid., p. 54.*

36 The theoretical clarification stems from a conversation with James O'Connor on November 17, 1975. For more on the interregional struggle of capital see, e.g., "The Second War Between the States," Business Week *(May 17, 1976).*

37 *"The Economic Crisis in Historical Perspective—Part II,"* Monthly Review, *vol. 26, no. 11 (April, 1975), p. 7.*

38 *Ibid., p. 9.*

APPENDIX A
INTRODUCTION TO
THE KEYNESIAN CROSS

The Keynesian cross is a useful analytic device to use to discuss the basics of Keynesian economics—that school of economic thought the mission of which it is to work for a stabilized "mixed economy" (from the perspective of the Keynesians) or monopoly state capitalism (from the perspective of radical and Marxian economists and social scientists). The foci with respect to economic stability are the employment and price levels—the key problems to which Keynesian economics addresses itself are unemployment and inflation.

It is posited that the 45° line on the diagram can represent aggregate supply, because ultimately what is sold, or supplied, must be equal to what is bought. Expenditures are always equal to income. This equality exists halfway between the 90° from the x axis (income) to the y axis (expenditures). Since expenditures always equal income, equilibrium, as it is called, exists with $Y = E$ at the Y_e level of income and the E_e level of expenditures.

The most important point the diagram attempts to make is that the equilibrium level of income and expenditures does not necessarily occur at full employment. Some other level of expenditures may be consistent with aggregate income large enough to employ the entire work force (in the diagram, Y_f). Expenditures come from four places: consumers; business investment in plant and equipment, inventories, etc.; government; and other countries. Forgetting about foreign trade, we can think of aggregate demand as the total of all domestic expenditures. If income is represented by Y, consumption by C, investment by I, and if government expenditures are represented by G, we can note that $Y = C + I + G$. That is, aggregate income adds up to be what consumers, businesses, and governments spent. No surprise. But this aggregate may have not been enough to generate full employment—as is the case in the diagram.

It is important to note what the aggregate demand function on the diagram implies. It implies that expenditures tend to increase at a slower rate than income—that is, when consumers receive more income they save a portion of it. This savings can be seen as a leakage

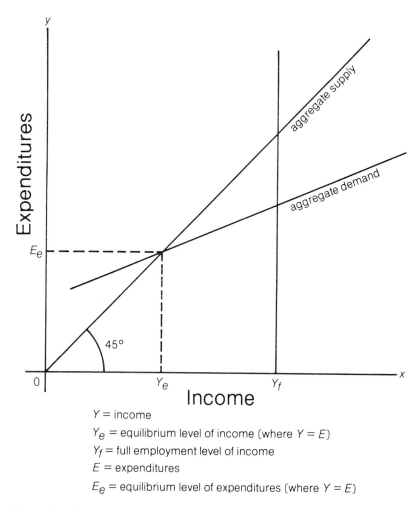

Y = income
Y_e = equilibrium level of income (where $Y = E$)
Y_f = full employment level of income
E = expenditures
E_e = equilibrium level of expenditures (where $Y = E$)

Figure 3   The Keynesian Cross

from the expenditure flow, as are taxes. Injections into the economy occur when the savings are invested and when governments spend and consumers consume. But the only sector of the economy with a lot of flexibility is government. Consumers are faced with a limit so far as their expenditures are concerned—the maximum is somewhere around one's income. Investment occurs only when it is thought that the probability of profits exists. Government spending, on the contrary, can be undertaken at any level policy makers decide. Government can even spend far more than it "has" in tax revenues; it can borrow money or even create it since government has control of the currency printing press and the power to legislate, as well as the formidable power to tax. In short, government has many sources from which to draw to undertake expenditures. If this is done consciously with economic and social objectives in mind (such as low rates of inflation) this is called *fiscal policy*. Fiscal policy can be undertaken to make an impact on such problems as unemployment and inflation. In the diagram it should be apparent that the problem that exists is that the equilibrium level of income and expenditures is not the full employment level of income and expenditures. Fiscal policy, the theory goes, can be used to deal effectively with this problem.

The main point is that fiscal policy can be used to *shift* the entire aggregate demand function. In Keynesian theory the G portion of the C + I + G expenditures could be raised and in the process increase aggregate income and employment. Graphically, the new aggregate demand function might look like this:

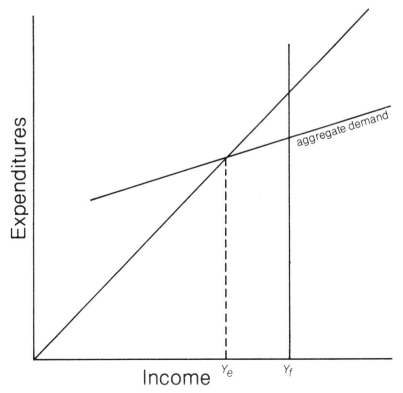

Figure 4

The view constructed above—which is, of course, but a small piece of the whole story—is very important to understand, not because it depicts reality, but because it is the model to which many contemporary policy makers in federal government and economists adhere. More, it is the *paradigm* (which can be defined as a system of thought which attempts to discover reality or aspects of it) which is the most dominant in contemporary macroeconomics. There are many, many grounds on which the simple model of income determination (as depicted by the Keynesian cross) can be called to task. One objection is that policy makers cannot really be as responsive as need be if aggregate demand is to be manipulated as the model suggests it must be to make an impact on the level of employment or prices. Some theory of the state that is plausible is needed aside from a simple mechanical (and technocratic) view as depicted in the model which asserts that government expenditures can simply be determined. Rather, a class analysis is necessary to be in tune with limits that are likely to be applied to Keynesian policies. What is more, it is argued by many that Keynesian policies have become part of the problem in that the state has become a key part of the economy in recent decades in the U. S. and has underwritten the activities of industry so that the centralization and concentration of industry has been intensified.[1] These are but two of many issues. The Keynesian perspective—which without a doubt had captured ideological hegemony in the 1960s among economists—is very much under fire from a variety of circles today. Marxian economics claims it has a paradigm which is more valid. Its adherents argue that it has a plausible theory of the state as well as an understanding of the class nature of U. S. society.[2] It is no overstatement, then to argue that Keynesian theory is useful for a first look at the way government (part of the state) *may* work to make an impact on macroeconomic policy, but it by no means has the final word and its hegemony seems to be on a rapid decline.

NOTES

1 For example, see Joan Robinson, "The Second Crisis of Economic Theory," ed. Rendigs Fels, The Second Crisis of Economic Theory and other selected papers from the American Economic Association Meeting, December 27-29, 1971, (Morristown, N.J.: General Learning Press, 1972). Of utmost importance in this vein is the work of the late Michal Kalecki including "Political Aspects of Full Employment," Political Quarterly, vol. 14 (October–December 1943). A persuasive view, also, is James O'Connor, The Fiscal Crisis of the State (New York: St. Martin's Press, 1973).

2 One very good introductory essay offering alternative interpretations of various Marxian theories of the state is David Gold, Clarence Y. H. Lo, and Erik Wright, "Recent Developments in Marxist Theories of the Capitalist State," Monthly Review, vol. 27, nos. 5 and 6 (October and November 1975).

APPENDIX B

THE FEDERATION OF
ROCKY MOUNTAIN
STATES, INC.:
A Prototype for the Social-
Industrial Complex (SIC)?

The perception that there is an emerging social-industrial complex, based on the conceptual work of Janes O'Connor,[1] is a compelling one. One economist termed the contemporary alliance of industry with the state as a sort of neomercantilism.[2] A careful study of the evolution of capitalism in Europe and elsewhere demonstrated the existence of an economic system far different from the laissez faire model of Adam Smith by the middle 1960s.[3] Even a very casual awareness of the news media between 1968 and the present produces a startling picture of corporate influence on the affairs of government[4] and this relationship moved beyond the blatant during the Nixon years.

What is more, not only capital has sought state assistance. One study group argues, "Historical studies of 19th and 20th century class struggle and political violence have documented that insurgent groups appeared at first to want to smash the state and wound up almost inevitably wanting to use the state.[5] There is at least one dramatic example of a relatively new organization where industry and government work closely together. A sketch of this organization, the Federation of Rocky Mountain States, Inc., suggests that such theorists as Paul Baran and Paul Sweezy in *Monopoly Capital* and James O'Connor in *The Fiscal Crisis of the State* are much more in tune with economic reality than free market advocates such as Milton Friedman or mixed economy enthusiasts such as Paul Samuelson.

The Federation of Rocky Mountain States, Inc. (FRMS), a nonprofit corporation, was begun in the middle 1960s by the governors of Colorado, Idaho, Montana, New Mexico, Utah, and Wyoming (with Arizona as an early member that soon dropped out) at the suggestion of the head of Mountain Bell, a part of American Telephone and

Telegraph.[6] Literature which is available from the Federation unblushingly tells their story.[7]

At first glance, the Federation appears to be a progressive regional organization worried about the exploitation of the area's vast natural resources and is presented in the media as such.[8] There is every reason to be skeptical about this sort of alliance between government and industry. This skepticism is rooted in a rather simple description of the structure and activities of the organization, which appears to be an excellent example of SIC, albeit of a variety more direct and open than most.

By its own account, the Federation "represents a new form of regionalism—a unique combination of governmental officials, educators and business and industry leaders from six states." The Federation has a board of directors composed of 41 members, including 18 officials of the 6 state governments (the governors, 6 state agency directors, 6 state representatives and 2 state senators); 1 official from the federal government (the U.S. Atomic Energy Commission manager of the Idaho office); 4 educators (a university president and 3 college and university deans); and 18 members from the private sector (including 10 corporation presidents and chairmen—from, among others, the communications, power, and transportation industries; 3 bank executives—a president, an executive vice president, and 1 whose position is not indicated; a U.S. Steel Corporation Director of Public Relations from Utah; one law firm attorney; a rancher; a geologist; and a director of an "urban observatory").[9]

"Volunteer vice presidents" are, according to Federation literature, elected from "each state's business membership" (in 1974 they were the president of Mountain Bell, a bank president, the president of a truck line, and the vice president and treasurer of still another corporation). Funds come by appropriations from the six state legislatures and membership dues from business and industry of an equal amount (currently $65,000 annually from each sector), as well as monies from the National Science Foundation, the National Institute of Education, the U.S. Department of Commerce, the Mountain Plains Regional Council, the U.S. Department of Labor, the U.S. Department of Housing and Urban Development, the National Endowment of the Arts, the Four Corners Regional Commission and others. With these funds they engage in the following activities:

> Specific policy and program suggestions are generated by the Federation's councils and their committees . . . Current councils are concerned with market development, telecommunications, natural resources, human resources, transportation, housing, and community development, and the arts and humanities.[10]

The list of private members is included as a later part of this appendix. These members match the basic operating funds provided by the six state legislatures. The list discloses that there are about 275 organizations, including more than 200 corporations, 44 banks, 8 associations, and 1 foundation, from the 6 states affiliated with the Federation. Familiar names such as Exxon, Mountain Bell, Shell Oil, Union Carbide, Western Electric, American Smelting and Refining, FMC Corporation, and the Anaconda Company, to name a few, appear on the list. Further, twelve of the Corporations are listed in more than one state. Mountain Bell is listed in all six states, the Union Pacific Railroad is in five states, Phelps Dodge Corporation and Union Carbide are in four states each and Exxon is listed in three states. Holly Sugar, Ideal Basic Industries, Santa Fe Industries, Colorado Interstate Gas Co., Diamond International, American Smelting and Refining, and Amax Exploration are located in two states each. The list shows that 71 organizations are based in Colorado, 66 in Montana, 47 in New Mexico, 40 in Wyoming, 34 in Utah, and 29 in Idaho.

The operations of the Federation are conducted with the assistance of eight councils of which the Regional Coordinating Council is the most formidable. The members of this council include "each governor's administrative assistant; [the] state planning officer from each state; a private business representative from each state; [and] the chairman of the other Federation councils."[11] The stated functions of the Regional Coordinating Council are to bring together the activities of the other Federation councils, set priorities among the issues entertained, review and provide critiques of all of the policy and program recommendations of the other councils and to consult the board of directors providing "advice and counsel . . . regarding funding levels of various council activities."[12] A specific project underway, at this writing, is "the administration of a $530,000 grant from the National Science Foundation to the Federation to strengthen the councils' efforts to define regional issues, to determine priorities among policy and program recommendations, and to bring new resources to the region."[13]

The Market Development Council, which is composed of businessmen, bankers, ranchers, and state officials and which is, at this writing, chaired by an executive from the Utah Power and Light Company, works to promote "growth in export marketing, industrial development, banking, tourism and agribusiness in the Rocky Mountain area." Efforts in the area of export marketing are reported, by the Federation, to be particularly successful: "more than $70 million in new export activity from the Rocky Mountain states to the Orient was generated by two Federation-sponsored Far East Market Surveys in late 1973 and May 1974. Businessmen traveled to Japan, Taiwan and Korea and spoke daily with Far Eastern firms interested in Rocky Mountain imports, tourism and investments." To promote agribusiness "the Federation co-sponsored a 16-state Western Governors' Conference on Agriculture April 16–19 in Salt Lake City. The purpose of this gathering was to find common ground so that federal farm policies can be influenced."[14]

The Natural Resources Council has as its members the state natural resource director from each state and "representatives of private industry from throughout the region involved in natural resource development." It is involved with matters of land, energy, minerals, and forests. The Transportation Council has as its members "representatives of railroads, truck companies, airlines, transportation associations, state regulatory agencies and state highway officials." It is, at this writing, chaired by the president of a Montana truck line. The stated function of this council is to coordinate "efforts of shippers, carriers, regulatory agencies and state highway officials." The council had a $100,000 grant in 1974 from the U.S. Department of Transportation and the Old West Regional Commission "to examine existing carrier rates and to determine areas where routes need to be developed or expanded."[15] The notion that those being regulated are sometimes in a position to influence regulatory agencies is substantiated by this very graphic example.

There is also the Human Resources Council which has industry representatives, state officials, and educators among its members. Their stated function is "to help the states utilize human resource potential with an emphasis on improving career and job opportunities in the Rocky Mountain region." To do this the Council, in cooperation with the Telecommunications Council is involved in a Satellite Technology Demonstration project, which involves eight states, and a Communications Technology Satellite to develop a regional computerized job bank. The Telecommunications Council, which is made up of "educators," state officials, and representatives of communications companies, and is chaired by the governor of Idaho, also has among its "accomplishments" the formation of "an ad hoc committee to investigate the use of telecommunications by law enforcement agencies in the region," the development of the Rocky Mountain Corporation for Public Broadcasting, and the creation of a funded proposal "to investigate how satellite technology can be used for information collection, storage, retrieval and dissemination." All of this is "To help develop a coordinated telecommunications capability for the Rocky Mountain states that is able to meet present and future needs by staying in the forefront of telecommunications technology and providing states with information and networking capability."[16] A representative of the Federation said that around 80 people are working at the Federation on this project and that their budget is in the neighborhood of four million dollars.[17]

The Housing and Community Development Council is, at this writing, chaired by a bank vice president (from Colorado) and has the state housing administrator from each state and businessmen "involved in housing and community development from each state" as members. This group defines its function as the defining of "regional housing issues and the proposal of policies and programs for the Mountain West."[18]

The Arts and Humanities Council appears to be the least controversial of the lot since it has as its members the directors and chairmen of the state arts commission and has as its stated function "to help the states share cultural resources and to bring major cultural programs to areas that would not otherwise have the opportunity to have them. Emphasis is on providing job opportunities to retain the region's cultural talent." The activities of this council are funded by the National Endowment on the Arts.[19]

Interestingly, the background paper which describes the nature of the Federation, its board of directors, funding, the president and staff, the Regional Coordinating Council and the seven supporting specialized councils dealing with the activities described above ends with this comment:

> All eight Federation councils are designed to work jointly to find solutions to the needs of the Federation member states. Business members, who bring special expertise to regional policy deliberations, recognize the Federation as a way to implement desirable change and generate meaningful communication between the region's public and private sectors.[20]

It may not be surprising to note that the roster of officers lists no women at all, and when asked if there were minority participants in the Federation one representative hesitated and suggested that perhaps there was an Indian or two around somewhere.[21] What is more startling, perhaps, is the total absence of representatives of organized labor among the membership and of any mention of attempts to integrate labor into the Federation. The Federation is overwhelmingly a partnership between capital and the state.[22]

In a Federation pamphlet is found this gem:

> The Federation is a voluntary organization that can only be useful if members actively participate in the council deliberations. The organization has had successes in the past, but with

the recent half million dollar grant from the National Science Foundation, the Federation has an opportunity to realize the decade-old dream of its founders.

The need for this partnership of government, business and education in the Mountain West was best summed up by Robert K. Timothy, president of Mountain Bell and vice-president of the Federation from Colorado: "In my business we are finding anew, almost daily, that problems do not stop at state lines and that good solutions cannot be restricted to a single geographic unit. Our states share the challenge of planning a future consonant with great opportunities and sobering realities. The Federation will help us do that job."[23]

In a section of the previously mentioned pamphlet entitled "A Wide Horizon," the councils and their committees are said to be "the nucleus of the Federation" and that "the Federation is dependent upon active participation of its members, particularly its dues-paying business members" and then concludes that "this difficult concept of multi-state regionalism, itself a bold experiment in cooperation, is one of the Mountain West's best hopes for the challenges of the future."[24] A representative of the Federation himself expressed the same belief when he said that if the Federation could influence the federal government to change the regional boundaries that are established for a variety of programs and if federal regionalism itself were to become more coordinated, "we would be moving towards constructing the best of all possible worlds."[25] It may be no exaggeration to suggest that the founders, members, and participants in the Federation of Rocky Mountain States conceive of it as a sort of prototype for regionalism, and the formalized unification of the state with capital.[26]

FEDERATION OF ROCKY MOUNTAIN STATES, INC.

Officers 1974–1975

Chairman	Governor John D. Vanderhoof, Colorado
Vice Chairman	
Vice Presidents	
Colorado	Robert K. Timothy
Idaho	John M. Dahl
Montana	John S. Rice
New Mexico	T. A. Bonnell
Utah	
Wyoming	Harry T. Thorson

President	Jack M. Campbell, New Mexico
Secretary	George C. Hatch, Utah
Treasurer	Theodore D. Brown, Colorado
Assistant Secretary and Legal Counsel	John Fleming Kelly, Colorado
Staff Executive Vice President	Michael H. Annison
Staff Vice President	Donald W. Galvin
Staff Vice President	William E. Rapp

Board of Directors

Colorado

John D. Vanderhoof
Governor of Colorado

Fred E. Anderson
State Senator

Theodore D. Brown
Executive Vice President
First National Bank of Denver

Robert G. Everett
President
Great Western United
   Corporation

John Fleming Kelly, Attorney
Holland & Hart

Guy T. McBride, Jr.
President
Colorado School of Mines

Dwight E. Neill
Director
Colorado Division of Commerce
   and Development

Robert K. Timothy
President
Mountain Bell

Idaho

Cecil D. Andrus
Governor of Idaho

J. Grant Bickmore
President
Idaho Bank & Trust Company

R. Glenn Bradley
Manager
Idaho Operations Office
U.S. Atomic Energy Commission

Albert Carlsen
Chairman of the Board
Idaho Power Company

John M. Dahl
President
J. R. Simplot Company

Marion Davidson
State Representative

Lloyd D. Howe
Acting Director
Idaho Department of Commerce
   and Development

Montana

Thomas L. Judge
Governor of Montana

Bert E. Arnlund
President
Village Mazda

Byron J. Bennett, Dean
College of Engineering
Montana State University

New Mexico

Bruce King
Governor of New Mexico

Arthur A. Blumenfeld
Director
Albuquerque Urban Observatory

T. A. Bonnell
President
Bank Securities, Inc.

William H. Bertsche
State Senator

Rudyard B. Goode, Dean
School of Business
Administration
University of Montana

John S. Rice
President
Rice Truck Lines

Ronald P. Richards
Director
Department of Intergovernmental
Relations

Jack Daniels
Fidelity National Bank

James H. Koch
State Representative

William Simms
Director
Department of Development

Utah

Calvin L. Rampton
Governor of Utah

David L. Bigler
Director of Public Relations
U. S. Steel Corporation

Mike Dmitrich
State Representative

George C. Hatch
President
Intermountain Network, Inc.

Allan D. Musgrove
President
Sundance Transportation, Inc.

Milton L. Weilenmann
Executive Director
Department of Development
Services

Wyoming

Stanley K. Hathaway
Governor of Wyoming

J. D. "Don" Brunk
Executive Director
Department of Economic Planning
and Development

M. Joseph Burke
Rancher

William H. Curry
Geologist

Harold Hellbaum
State Representative

Edward B. Jakubauskas, Dean
College of Commerce & Industry
University of Wyoming

Harry T. Thorson
President
Toco Corporation

Councils

Regional Coordinating Council

Members Each governor's administrative assistant; state planning officer from each state; a private business representative from each state; the chairman of each of the other Federation councils.

Current chairman: Vincent Horn Jr., assistant to Wyoming Governor Stanley K. Hathaway and state planning coordinator.

Function Coordinates the efforts of all other Federation councils; sets priorities among regional issues; reviews and comments on all policy and program recommendations of the other councils; provides advice and counsel to the board of directors regarding funding levels of various council activities.

Projects Supervises the administration of a $540,000 grant from the National Science Foundation to the Federation to strengthen the council's efforts to define regional issues, to determine priorities among policy and program recommendations, and to bring new resources to the region.

Natural Resources Council

Members State natural resource director from each state, representatives of private industry from throughout the region involved in natural resource development.
   Current chairman: Roy Peck, Wyoming legislator and publisher.

Function Coordinates Federation activity dealing with the orderly development of the Rocky Mountain West's rich natural resources—land, energy, minerals and forests.

Projects In land use planning: disseminating information about national land use planning legislation; calling interstate policy planning workshops; working with Regional Planning Council in drafting and updating land use planning principles from the viewpoint of the Mountain states.
   Developed a series of recommendations approved by Federation state governors which encourage cooperation between the Bureau of Land Management of the U.S. Department of Interior and the state governments.
   In energy: coordinating priorities and energy information within the Rocky Mountain region; collecting, reviewing and disseminating energy studies; drafting proposed energy policies; examining all aspects of energy development in the Rocky Mountain states, with a concern for protecting the environment and the Rocky Mountain way of life.

Market Development Council

Members Businessmen, bankers, ranchers, and state officials.
   Current chairman: Wayne Mulcock, director of area development, Utah Power and Light Company.

Function   Stimulation of quality growth in export marketing, industrial development, banking, tourism, and agribusiness in the Rocky Mountain area.

Projects   In export marketing: more than $70 million in new export activity from the Rocky Mountain states to the Orient was generated by two Federation-sponsored Far East Market Surveys in late 1973 and May 1974. Businessmen traveled to Japan, Taiwan and Korea and spoke daily with Far Eastern firms interested in Rocky Mountain imports, tourism, and investments.

In tourism: cooperative programs are under way by the Federation member-state travel agencies.

In agribusiness: the Federation co-sponsored a sixteen-state Western Governors' Conference on Agriculture in Salt Lake City. The purpose of this gathering was to find common ground so that federal farm policies can be influenced.

Transportation Council

Members   Representatives of railroads, truck companies, airlines, transportation associations, state regulatory agencies, and state highway officials.

Current chairman: John Rice, president, Rice Truck Lines, Great Falls, Montana.

Function   Coordinates efforts of shippers, carriers, regulatory agencies, and state highway officials.

Projects   A council proposal to conduct a motor freight rate study throughout the Federation states, North and South Dakota, and Nebraska, has been funded by the U.S. Department of Transportation and the Old West Regional Commission. $100,000 has been granted to examine existing carrier rates and to determine areas where routes need to be developed or expanded.

Human Resources Council

Members   Educators, business and industry representatives, state officials.

Current chairman: Dr. Dean Talagan, assistant state superintendent, Wyoming Department of Education.

Function   To help the states utilize human resource potential with an emphasis on improving career and job opportunities in the Rocky Mountain region.

Projects   Produced a 25-minute film, "Where Do We Go From Here?", to begin an intensive multi-media campaign urging a career development concept from preschool through adulthood, stressing the various job options available.

In cooperation with the Telecommunications Council, developed the Federation's Satellite Technology Demonstration project, the first of its kind in the world, which will transmit career-planning audio-visual programs from Denver through a communications satellite to fifty-six rural Rocky Mountain schools.

Also in cooperation with the Telecommunications Council, developed a proposal to use the Satellite Technology Demonstration equipment and personnel in connection with the Communications Technology Satellite, to be launched after the conclusion of the STD experiment, for extended programming and the development of a regional computerized job bank.

In addition, hopes to sponsor community education throughout the Rocky Mountain region.

Telecommunications Council

Members   Educators, state officials and representatives of communications companies.

Current chairman: Cecil D. Andrus, governor of Idaho.

Function   To help develop a coordinated telecommunications capability for the Rocky Mountain states that is able to meet present and future needs by staying in the forefront of telecommunications technology and providing states with information and networking capability.

Projects   Developed the Rocky Mountain Corporation for Public Broadcasting and an origination and delay center for airing public broadcasts.

Collaborated with the Human Resources Council in the development of the Federation's Satellite Technology Demonstration, an eight-state project that will beam educational programs from Denver through a communications satellite to remote sites throughout the Mountain West.

Also worked with the Human Resources Council to prepare a proposal that would make use of the expertise developed by the

Satellite Technology Demonstration in connection with the Communications Technology Satellite, to be launched after the conclusion of the STD experiment.

Funds have been granted for a proposal, drafted with Federation assistance, to investigate how satellite technology can be used for information collection, storage, retrieval and dissemination. The University of Denver Graduate School of Librarianship, the University of Kansas Libraries, the Wyoming State Library and the Natrona County (Wyoming) Public Library will participate in an experiment using the new Communications Technology Satellite. One of the technical participants and consultants for the project will be the Federation.

Also helped form an ad hoc committee to investigate the use of telecommunications by law enforcement agencies in the region.

Housing and Community Council

Members   State housing administrator from each state; businessmen involved in housing and community development from each state.

Current chairman: James McKesson, vice president of The First National Bank of Colorado Springs.

Function   To define regional housing issues and propose policies and programs for the Mountain West.

Projects   Newly formed council; now defining common issues and developing a work plan to provide training and technical assistance to states; data collection; generation of additional resources to address multi-state issues.

Arts and Humanities Council

Members   Directors and chairmen of state arts commissions.

Current chairman: David Nelson, executive director of the Montana Arts Council.

Function   To help the states share cultural resources and to bring major cultural programs to areas that would not otherwise have the opportunity to have them. Emphasis is on providing job opportunities to retain the region's cultural talent.

Projects   Works in cooperation with the newly formed Western States Arts Foundation, staffed by persons housed in the Federation's offices. In 1974 will sponsor arts festivals, apprenticeships for young talent, and consulting services to state dance organizations.

The new foundation includes the Federation member-states as well as Arizona, Nevada, Oregon, and Washington.

In 1973, sponsored an eight-state tour of the "Artrain," an art exhibit and museum on rails that stopped for several days in rural communities.

Funding for arts activities is provided by the National Endowment on the Arts.

Private Members

Colorado

Action
Amax Exploration, Inc. (Arizona)
A. P. Green Refractories Co.
Arthur Anderson & Company
Association of Denver Banks Co.
Central Bank & Trust Co.
Climax Molybdenum Co.
Colorado Assn. Commerce & Industry
Colorado Contractors Assn., Inc.
Colorado Interstate Gas Co.
Consolidated Freightways
Conspan of Denver, Inc.
Continental Air Lines
Crissey Fowler Lumber Co.
Curry County Grain & Elevator Co.
Denver & Rio Grande Western Railroad Co.
Eastman Kodak Company
El Pomar Investment Co.
Exxon Company, U.S.A.
Fairchild Industries
Federal Timber Purchasers Assoc.
First National Bank of Colorado Springs
First National Bank of Fort Collins
First National Bank in Grand Junction
First National Bank in Loveland
First National Bank in Trinidad
Frontier Airlines

Garrett Research & Development
Gates Rubber Company
Globe Smelter
Great Western United Corporation
Greeley National Bank
Haskins & Sells
Holland & Hart
Holly Sugar Corporation
Home Light & Power Company
Ideal Basic Industries, Inc.
Illinois-California Express, Inc.
IBM
Johns-Manville Corporation
Kaman Sciences Corporation
Marathon Oil Company
Martin Marietta Corporation
Mountain Bell
Mountain Empire Publishing, Inc.
Mountain States Commerce & Traffic
North Valley State Bank
Peabody Coal Company
Peoples Natural Gas
Phelps Natural Gas
Phelps Dodge Corporation
Public Service Company of Colorado
Ringsby System
Rockmont Envelope Company
Samsonite Corporation
San Isabel Electric Services, Inc.
Santa Fe Industries, Inc.

Science Applications, Inc.
Shell Oil Company
Smith Chemical
Swansea Trading Company
Transportation Technology, Inc.
TRW, Inc.
Union Carbide Corporation

Union Pacific Railroad Co.
Vaughey, Vaughey & Blackburn
Western Colorado Power Co.
Western Electric
Western Gillette, Inc.
Western Nuclear, Inc.
Western Slope Gas Company

Idaho

Albertson's Inc.
America Smelting & Refining
Bank of Idaho
Bunker Hill Company
Diamond International Corp.
Downtowner Motel
First Security Bank of Idaho
FMC Corporation
General Telephone Co. of the
   Northwest
Hecla Mining Company
Idaho Bank & Trust Co.
Idaho First National Bank
Idaho Motor Transport Assn.
Idaho Portland Cement Co.

Idaho Power Company
Intermountain Gas Co.
Inter-Mountain State Bank
Kellwood Company
KTVB, Inc.
Morrison-Knudsen
Mountain Bell
Ore-Ida Foods, Inc.
Pacific Power & Light Co.
Rogers Brothers Company
J. R. Simplot Company
Twin Falls Bank & Trust Co.
Union Pacific Railroad Co.
Valley Bank in Rexburg
Washington Water Power Co.

Montana

Amax Coal Company
American Smelting & Refining Co.
Anaconda Company
Archie Cochrane Motors
Bancorporation of Montana
Builders Transport
Citizens Bank of Montana
Coast Trading Company
Cogswell Agency
Colorado Interstate Gas Co.
Conrad National Bank of Kalispell
Convoy Company
Diamond International Corp.
Dick Irvin, Inc.
Exxon Company U.S.A.
First Metals Bank & Trust Co.
First National Bank & Trust Co.
   Billings
First National Bank & Trust Co.
   Helena
First National Bank in Bozeman

First National Bank in Glendive
First National Bank of Great Falls
First National Bank of Lewistown
Frontier Chevrolet Company
Getter Trucking, Inc.
Glacier Park, Inc.
Grain Terminal Association
Great Falls Gas Company
Great Falls National Bank
Greater Montana Foundation
Hoerner Waldorf Corporation
Holly Sugar Corporation
Ideal Basic Industries, Inc.
Intermountain Land Company
Intermountian Company
H. F. Johnson, Inc.
Kaiser Cement & Gypsum Corp.
Keller Transport, Inc.
Livingston Corporation
Maronick Construction Co.
McLaughlin, Incorporated

Missoula Cartage Co., Inc.
Montana Association of Realtors
Montana Petroleum Assoc.
Montana-Dakota Utilities Co.
Montana Motor Transport Assoc.
Montana Power Company
Montana Railroad Assoc.
Morrison-Maierle, Inc.
Mountain Bell
Northern Tank Line
Northwestern National Bank
Pacific Power & Light Co.
Phelps Dodge Corp.
Phillips Petroleum

Rice Truck Lines
Royal Logging Company
Salt Creek Freightways
Sammons Trucking
Suhr Transport
Union Bank & Trust Co.
Union Pacific Railroad Co.
U.S. Plywood
Valley State Bank
Webb Resources, Inc.
Western Transport Crane &
  Rigging
Yellowstone Truck Div.

New Mexico

Affiliated Supply
Amax Exploration, Inc.
Albuquerque National Bank
American Smelting & Refining
Amrep Corporation
Bank of New Mexico
Bank Securities, Inc.
Citizens Bank
Continental Air Lines, Inc.
Credit Bureau of Albuquerque
Dikewood Corporation
Duke City Lumber Company
Eberline Instrument Corp.
El Paso Electric Company
El Paso Natural Gas Co.
Famariss Oil & Refining Co.
First National Bank in
  Albuquerque
First National Bank in Lea County
First National Bank in Tucumcari
First State Bank at Gallup
First State Bank of Taos
Goodsight, Inc.
Greater Albuquerque Chamber of
  Commerce
Great Lakes Land & Cattle, Inc.
Greer Properties Company
Hood Corp.

Horizon Corp.
Ideal Basic Industries, Inc.
Jemez Mountains Electric
  Cooperative Inc.
Kerr-MeGee Nuclear Corp.
Marathon Oil Company
Molybdenum Corporation of
  America
Mountain Bell
New Mexico Bank & Trust
  Company
New Mexico Cattle Growers
  Association
Phelps Dodge Corporation
Plateau, Inc.
Public Service Company of New
  Mexico
Roswell Chamber of Development
  & Commerce
Roswell State Bank
Sandia Corporation
Santa Fe Industries Inc.
Santa Fe National Bank
Southern Union Gas Company
Southwestern Public Service
  Company
Tequesquite Ranch
Union Carbide Corporation

Utah

Aldirita Logging Co., Inc.
American Smelting & Refining Co.

Arnold Machinery Co., Inc.
Beneficial Management Corp.

California-Pacific Utilities Co.
Denver & Rio Grande Western
   Railroad Co.
Deseret News
ETMF Freight System
Great Salt Lake Minerals &
   Chemicals Corp.
Ideal Basic Industries, Inc.
IML Freight, Inc.
Intermountain Network, Inc.
Kearns-Tribune Corporation
Kennecott Copper Corporation
KUTV, Inc.
Laughlin Investment Co.
E. A. Miller & Sons Packing Co.,
   Inc.
Moon Lake Electric Assn., Inc.

Mountain Bell
Mountain States Resources
   Corporation
Phelps Dodge Corporation
Phillips Petroleum Company
Prudential Federal Savings &
   Loan Assn.
Sierra Lingerie Company
O. C. Tanner Jewelry Company
Terra Tek, Inc.
Texas Gulf
Union Carbide Corporation
Union Pacific Railroad Company
United States Steel Corporation
Utah Citizens Rate Assoc.
Utah-Idaho Sugar Company
Utah Power & Light Company
Walker Bank & Trust Company

Wyoming

Allied Chemical Corporation
Amax Coal Company
American National Bank
American Oil Company
Associated General Contractors of
   Wyoming
Bank of Laramie
Belle Fourche Pipeline Co.
Burlington Northern, Inc.
Carter Oil Company
Cheyenne Light, Fuel & Light Co.
Colorado Interstate Gas Co.
William H. Curry
Exxon Company, U.S.A.
First National Bank, Riverton
First National Bank & Trust
   Company of Wyoming
First National Bank of Casper
First National Bank of Laramie
Holly Sugar Corporation
Husky Oil Company
Jackson State Bank
Kaycee Bentonite Corporation

Kerr-McGee Nuclear Corporation
Marathon Oil Company
Materi Exploration Inc.
Montana-Dakota Utilities
   Company
Mountain Bell
Pacific Power & Light Company
Stockmen's Bank
Toco Corporation
Union Carbide Corporation
Union Pacific Railroad Company
United States Steel Corporation
Updike Brothers, Inc.
U.S. Plywood Corporation
Utah Power & Light Company
Western Standard Corporation
Wyoming Farm Bureau
   Federation
Wyoming Minerals Dept.
Wyoming National Bank of
   Casper
Wyoming Trucking Assoc., Inc.

NOTES

1 James O'Connor, The Fiscal Crisis of the State, (New York: St. Martin's Press, 1973).

2 Martin Primack at San Jose State University.

3 Andrew Shonfield, Modern Capitalism, (New York: Oxford University Press, 1965).

4 As a CBS documentary on Phillips Petroleum demonstrated so graphically in 1973. At the time it appeared, some responded with the query: if one large corporation (CBS) has revealed so much about the ties of another corporation to government and a President, it leads one to wonder if the impact of private capital on the state is far greater than can be imagined on the basis of information which is currently available.

5 San Francisco Bay Area Kapitalistate Collective review of FCS, Working Papers on the Kapitalistate, No. 3 (Spring 1975), p. 157, footnote 6.

6 According to a representative of the Federation as reported in a phone conversation on November 5, 1974.

7 A packet of documents describing the purpose, organizational structure, board of directors, officers, and membership was received from the Federation. Annual reports are also part of the public record and one Ph.D. dissertation ("The Federation of Rocky Mountain States: a Test of Regionalism," by Donald Galvin, the University of Colorado, 1969) was written about the Federation. Galvin compares the Federation with the Tennessee Valley Authority and the New England Council which are both quite different in that the TVA is "public," the New England Council is "private" and the Federation is distinctly "public-private."

8 See, for example, James P. Sterba, "Worry Mounts that Rockies Face Pollution and Crowds," The New York Times (September 26, 1974), pp. 31 and 37. The Federation, according to this article, "devoted a good deal of time during its 10th annual meeting . . . to a stark portrayal of what was under way and what was in store. Using a hypothetical boom town called Resource City, Rocky Mountains, officials of the federation painted a picture of unsightly landscapes, intolerable living conditions, increasing crime and growing mental illness."

9 Federation of Rocky Mountain States, Inc., "Background," mimeo., 1974, p. 1.

10 Ibid., p. 2.

11 Federation of Rocky Mountain States, Inc., "Councils," mimeo., 1974, p. 1.

12 Ibid.

13 Ibid.

14 Ibid., p. 3.

15 Ibid., p. 2.

16 Ibid., p. 6.

17 Phone conversation with a Federation representative, November 5, 1974.

18 FRMS, "Councils," p. 7.

19 *Ibid., p. 8.*

20 FRMS, "Background," p. 5.

21 From a telephone conversation with an FRMS representative, November 5, 1974.

22 It is unlikely that James O'Connor would share my initial surprise on this point. He argues, on page 222 of FCS, that "Organized labor . . . is opposed or indifferent to the more rapid development of the social-industrial complex. Unions in the competitive sector (primarily the construction trades) stand to lose everything and gain nothing. Monopoly sector unionized workers are at best indifferent and at worst opposed to the complex because their taxes will finance social-industrial investments and programs and because unorganized surplus-population workers will receive the bulk of new jobs. Certainly, the 'free' collective bargaining developed since World War II in the monopoly sector will have to be changed substantially (perhaps dismantled entirely) to make the complex work."

When one Federation representative was cautiously asked if some might think it improper for government officials to work so directly with corporate executives and bankers it was answered that "you've simply got to include them." Further, Arizona's exit from the Federation during its early years was attributed to their "reactionary" political stance. The general tone of the Federation representatives was one of enthusiasm for their activities. If any label for their ideology is appropriate it would be that of "corporate liberalism."

23 FRMS publication entitled "Regional Growth in the Rocky Mountain West," p. 14.

24 *Ibid., p. 15.*

25 Telephone conversation with a Federation representative November 6, 1974.

26 It must be emphasized that FRMS represents but the "tip of the iceberg" as far as state capitalism in the Rocky Mountain region is concerned. It is also not the only regional organization in the area. Montana, for example, is also affiliated with the Western Interstate Nuclear Board, the Pacific Northwest River Basin Planning Commission, and the Missouri Policy Office. Montana Governor Thomas L. Judge expressed the view (in a letter to the author dated September 14, 1976) that "the Federation . . . has lost sight of its original purpose" and that a task force "composed of representatives of ten western Governors is reviewing regional organizations including the Federation." Judge said, "[i]t is my hope that the Task Force will serve to cut down the proliferation of regional organizations by consolidation and by elimination of ineffective groups. I am anticipating the creation of an umbrella-type organization to provide an oversight mechanism to insure policies of the various multi-state groups are not contrary to those of the Governors. Some of the features of the Federation, such as private sector participation, are being considered for the new organization."

It was reported in High Country News, the environmental bi-weekly from Lander, Wyoming (December 17, 1976), on p. 12, that "governors of Western states decided . . . to consolidate the functions and the staffs of the Western Interstate Nuclear Board, the Western Governors Conference," and the Western Governors Regional Policy Office. They also decided, "to dissolve the federation of Rocky Mountain States." This decision is consistent with Governor Judge's comments and seems to indicate that the form of social-industrial complex represented by the Federation of Rocky Mountain states is being consolidated and streamlined, though FRMS itself will no longer exist.

State activity in the Rocky Mountain region seems, at this writing, to be occurring at an unprecedented level. For example, the State of Montana is working in collaboration with a myriad of federal agencies (particularly various arms of the U.S. Department of the Interior) in the area of energy related resources, especially coal. It is around the energy issue that the contradictory functions of various parts of the state apparatus seem nearly explosive. For example, the federal government seems on the side of encouraging the strip mining of coal, and in the process enriching those corporations doing the actual extraction and selling of the coal. The State of Montana, on the other hand, seems to be fighting a rather classic conservative battle. More accurately, factions of the Montana population are pushing the state to avoid rapid coal extraction, the disruption of communities, the influx of transient population, and the destruction of the environment. But the outcome remains to be seen. It is possible that Montana could go the way of much of the rest of the nation in terms of the rape of its natural and social environment. This, I think, would be the result of the corporations having their way (endorsed by the federal government rationalizing that the nation needs the coal for, primarily, generating electricity). On the other hand (there is always "the other hand"), it is just possible that the environmentalists, the ranchers, and perhaps even some of those in state government (along with other parts of the population) will become aware enough of corporate activity in time to thwart it. But this force in opposition cannot expect society to stand still and life to enter a period of laissez faire bliss. Rather, those opposed to corporate/state determination of events and realities will have to have a program, a vision of the kind of society they want for themselves, their children, and their friends. I can see no other vision fitting the bill, in the face of contemporary corporate power, than that of democratic socialism. It could be a great irony that those seeking a conservative holding action might well be forced to push for a democratic socialism.

BIBLIOGRAPHY

Adelman, M. A. "The Two Faces of Economic Concentration." *The Public Interest,* no. 21 (Fall 1970).

Andreano, Ralph L., ed. *Superconcentration/Supercorporation: A Collage of Opinion on the Concentration of Economic Power.* Andover, Mass.: Warner Modular Publications, 1973.

Ardolini, Charles, and Hohenstein, Jeffrey. "Measuring Productivity in the Federal Government." *Monthly Labor Review,* vol. 97, no. 11 (November 1974).

Averitt, Robert. *The Dual Economy: Dynamics of American Industry Structure.* New York: W. W. Norton & Co., 1968.

Babson, Steve, and Brigham, Nancy. *Popular Economics: Why Do We Spend So Much Money?* Somerville, Mass.: Popular Economics Press, 1975.

Bachrach, Peter. *The Theory of Democratic Elitism: a Critique.* Boston: Little, Brown & Co., 1967.

Bain, Joe. *Industrial Organization.* New York: John Wiley & Sons, 1959.

Balbus, Isaac. "Ruling Elite Theory vs. Marxist Class Analysis." *Monthly Review,* vol. 23, no. 1 (May 1971).

"Banks: Skating on Thin Ice." *Monthly Review,* vol. 26, no. 9 (February 1975).

Baran, Paul A. *The Longer View: Essays Toward a Critique of Political Economy.* Edited by John O'Neill. New York: Monthly Review Press, 1969.

———. *The Political Economy of Growth.* New York: Monthly Review Press, 1957.

Baran, Paul A., and Sweezy, Paul M. *Monopoly Capital: an Essay on the American Social and Economic Order.* New York: Monthly Review Press, 1966.

Barber, Richard J. *The American Corporation: Its Power, Its Money, Its Politics.* New York: E. P. Dutton & Co., 1970.

Barnet, Richard J. *Roots of War.* Baltimore: Penguin Books, 1972.

Barraclough, Geoffrey, "The Great World Crisis I." *The New York Review of Books,* vol. 21, nos. 21 and 22 (January 23, 1975).

Becker, James F. "On the Monopoly Theory of Monopoly Capitalism." *Science and Society,* vol. 35, no. 4 (Winter 1971).

Bell, Daniel. "The Public Household—on 'Fiscal Sociology' and the Liberal Society." *The Public Interest,* no. 37 (Fall 1974).

Berger, Peter L. and Luckmann, Thomas. *The Social Construction of Reality; a Treatise in the Sociology of Knowledge.* Garden City, N. Y.: Doubleday, 1966.

Berle, Adolf, and Means, Gardiner. *The Modern Corporation and Private Property.* New York: Macmillan, 1932.

Bhagwati, Jagdish N., ed. *Economics and World Order: From the 1970's to the 1990's.* New York: Macmillan, 1972.

Birnbaum, Norman. *The Crisis of Industrial Society.* New York: Oxford University Press, 1969.

Blackburn, Robin, ed. *Ideology in Social Science: Readings in Critical Social Theory.* New York: Random House, 1973.

Blair, John M. *Economic Concentration: Structure, Behavior and Public Policy.* New York: Harcourt Brace Jovanovich, 1972.

Blumenberg, Werner. *Portrait of Marx: an Illustrated Biography.* New York: Herder and Herder, 1972.

Boddy, Raford and Crotty, James. "Wage-Push and Working-Class Power," *Monthly Review,* vol. 27, no. 10 (March 1976).

Bowles, Samuel and Gintis, Herbert. "Class Power and Alienated Labor." *Monthly Review,* vol. 26, no. 10 (March 1975).

——. *Schooling in Capitalist America: Educational Reform and the Contradictions of Economic Life.* New York: Basic Books, 1976.

Braverman, Harry. *Labor and Monopoly Capital: The Degradation of Work in the Twentieth Century.* New York: Monthly Review Press, 1974.

Bronfenbrenner, Martin. "Japan's Galbraithian Economy." *The Public Interest,* no. 21 (Fall 1970).

——. "Radical Economics in America: a 1970 Survey." *Journal of Economic Literature,* vol. 8, no. 3 (September 1970).

——. "Samuelson, Marx, and Their Latest Critics." *Journal of Economic Literature,* vol. 11, no. 1 (March 1973).

——. "A Skeptical View of Radical Economics." *The American Economist,* vol. 17, no. 2 (Fall 1973).

——. "What the Radical Economists are Saying." *Harvard Business Review,* vol. 51, no. 3 (September-October 1973).

Burkhead, Jesse, and Miner, Jerry. *Public Expenditure.* New York and London: Macmillan Press, Ltd., 1971.

Carnoy, Judith, and Weiss, Marc, eds. *A House Divided: Radical Perspectives on Social Problems.* Boston: Little, Brown & Co., 1973.

Caves, Richard. *American Industry: Structure, Conduct, Performance.* Englewood Cliffs, N. J.: Prentice-Hall, 1972.

Clecak, Peter. *Radical Paradoxes: Dilemmas of the American Left: 1945–1970.* New York: Harper & Row, 1973.

Coddington, Alan. "What Did Keynes Really Mean?" *Challenge,* vol. 17, no. 5 (November-December 1974).

Cohen, Hyman R. "Dialectics and Scientific Revolutions." *Science and Society,* vol. 37, no. 3 (Fall 1973.)

Commoner, Barry. *The Closing Circle: Nature, Man and Technology.* New York: Alfred A. Knopf, 1971.

Dahl, Robert A. *A Preface to Democratic Theory.* Chicago: University of Chicago Press, 1956.

Dahrendorf, Ralf. *Class and Class Conflict in Industrial Society.* Stanford, Calif.: Stanford University Press, 1959.

Deutscher, Issac. *Marxism in Our Time.* Edited by Tamara Deutscher. Berkeley: The Ramparts Press, 1971.

De Vroey, Michel. "The Separation of Ownership and Control in Large Corporations." *The Review of Radical Political Economics,* vol. 7, no. 2 (Summer, 1975).

DeWitt, Laurence; Clark, Louis; and Ward, Dwayne. *A Quantitative Analysis of Adult Part-Time Learners.* Syracuse: Educational Policy Research Center, 1975.

Domhoff, G. William. "New Directions in Power Structure Research." *The Insurgent Sociologist,* vol. 5, no. 3 (Spring 1975).

——. *Who Rules America?* Englewood Cliffs, N. J.: Prentice-Hall, 1967.

—— and Ballard, Hoyt B. *C. Wright Mills and the Power Elite.* Boston: Beacon Press, 1968.

Donovan, John C. *The Cold Warriors: A Policy-Making Elite.* Lexington, Mass.: D. C. Heath & Co., 1974.

Douglas, Jack D. "The Rhetoric of Science and the Origins of Statistical Social Thought: the Case of Durkheim's Suicide." In *The Phenomenon of Sociology: A Reader in the Sociology of Sociology,* edited by Edward A. Tiryakian. New York: Appleton-Century-Crofts, 1971.

Dowd, Douglas F. *The Twisted Dream: Capitalist Development in the United States Since 1776.* Cambridge, Mass.: Winthrop Publishers, 1974.

Eckstein, Otto; Heller, Walter W.; Keyserling, Leon; Okun, Arthur M.; Samuelson, Paul A.; Schultze, Charles L.; and Tobin, James with a separate statement by John Kenneth Galbraith and Robert Lekachman. "Toward a Democratic Economic Policy." *Challenge,* vol. 17, no. 4 (September-October 1974).

"The Economic Crisis in Historical Perspective." *Monthly Review,* vol. 26, no. 10 (March 1975).

"The Economic Crisis: Part II." *Monthly Review,* vol. 26, no. 11 (April 1975).

Edwards, Richard C., et al. "A Radical Approach to Economics: Basis for a New Curriculum." *American Economic Review* (May 1970).

——; Reich, Michael; and Weisskopf, Thomas E., eds. *The Capitalist System: a Radical Analysis of American Society.* Englewood Cliffs, N. J.: Prentice-Hall, 1972.

Eisenberg, William M. "Measuring the Productivity of Nonfinancial Corporations." *Monthly Labor Review,* vol. 97, no. 11 (November 1974).

Elliott, John E. and Cownie, John, eds. *Competing Philosophies in American Political Economics.* Pacific Palisades, Ca.: Goodyear Publishing Co., 1975.

Engels, Frederick. *On Capital.* New York: International Publishers, 1937.

——. *The Origin of the Family, Private Property, and the State.* New York: International Publishers, 1942.

Federal Trade Commission. *Economic Report on Corporate Mergers*. Washington, D.C.: U.S. Government Printing Office, 1969.

Fels, Rendigs, ed. *The Second Crisis of Economic Theory and Other Selected Papers from the American Economic Association Meeting, December 27-29, 1971*. Morristown, N.J.: General Learning Press, 1972.

Fischer, George, ed. *The Revival of American Socialism: Selected Papers of the Socialist Scholars Conference*. New York: Oxford University Press, 1971.

Fitch, Robert, and Oppenheimer, Mary. "Who Rules the Corporations?" *Socialist Revolution*, vol. 1, nos. 4, 5, and 6 (July-August, September-October, and November-December, 1970).

Friedman, Milton. *Capitalism and Freedom*. Chicago: The University of Chicago Press, 1962.

Fromm, Eric, ed. *Socialist Humanism*. New York: Doubleday, 1966.

Fusfeld, Daniel R. "The Basic Economics of the Urban and Racial Crisis." *Conference Papers of the Union for Radical Political Economics*. Ann Arbor, Mich.: The Union for Radical Political Economics, 1968.

——. *The Basic Economics of the Urban Racial Crisis*. New York: Holt, Rinehart & Winston, 1973.

——. "Post-Post-Keynes: The Shattered Synthesis." *Annual Readings in Economics '73/'74*. Guilford, Conn.: Dushkin Publishing Group, 1973.

Galbraith, John Kenneth. *The Affluent Society*. Boston: Houghton-Mifflin Publishing Co., 1968.

——. *American Capitalism: The Concept of Countervailing Power*. Boston: Houghton-Mifflin Publishing Co., 1952.

——. *Economics and the Public Purpose*. Boston: Houghton-Mifflin Publishing Co., 1973.

——. *The Great Crash, 1929*. Boston: Houghton-Mifflin Publishing Co., 1954.

——. *The New Industrial State*. Boston: Houghton-Mifflin Publishing Co., 1967.

——. "Solving Unemployment Without Inflation." *Social Policy*, vol. 5, no. 3 (September-October 1974).

Galvin, Donald. "The Federation of Rocky Mountain States: A Test of American Regionalism." Ph.D. dissertation, The University of Colorado, 1969. Ann Arbor: University Microfilms.

Gillman, Joseph. *The Falling Rate of Profit: Marx's Law and its Significance to Twentieth Century Capitalism*. London: D. Dobson, 1957.

Gitlin, Todd. "Local Pluralism as Theory and Ideology." *Studies on the Left*, vol. 5, no. 3 (1965).

Glaser, Barney G., and Strauss, Anselm L. *The Discovery of Grounded Theory: Strategies for Qualitative Research.* Chicago: Aldine Publishing Co., 1967.

Gold, David A.; Lo, Clarence Y. H.; and Wright, Erik Olin. "Recent Developments in Marxist Theories of the Capitalist State." *Monthly Review*, vol. 27, nos. 5 and 6 (October and November 1975).

Goldscheid, Rudolf. "A Sociological Approach to Problems of Public Finance," *Classics in the Theory of Public Finance*, edited by Richard A. Musgrave and Alan T. Peacock. New York: St. Martin's Press, 1967.

Gordon, David M., ed. *Problems in Political Economy: An Urban Perspective.* Lexington, Mass.: D. C. Heath & Co., 1971.

——. "Recession is Capitalism as Usual." *The New York Times Magazine.* (April 27, 1975).

——. *Theories of Poverty and Underemployment: Orthodox, Radical, and Dual Labor Market Perspectives.* Lexington, Mass.: D. C. Heath & Co., 1972.

Gouldner, Alvin W. *The Coming Crisis of Western Sociology.* New York: Basic Books, 1970.

Gray, Lois, and Corwin, R. D. "The Corporate Elite." *Society*, vol. 9, no. 4 (February 1972).

Green, Gil. *The New Radicalism: Anarchist or Marxist.* New York: International Publishers, 1971.

Gross, Bertram M. "Friendly Fascism: a Model for America." *Social Policy*, vol. 1, no. 4 (November-December 1970).

Gurley, John G. "Federal Tax Policy (a Review Article)." *National Tax Journal*, vol. 20, no. 3 (September 1967).

——. "The Future of American Capitalism." *Quarterly Review of Economics and Business*, vol. 12, no. 3 (Autumn 1972).

——. "The State of Political Economics." *American Economic Review*, vol. 61, no. 2 (May 1971).

Habermas, Jurgen. *Legitimation Crisis.* Boston: Beacon Press, 1975.

Hall, R. L. and Hicks, C. J. "Price Theory and Business Behaviour." *Oxford Economic Papers*, no. 2 (May 1939).

Hansen, Alvin H. *A Guide to Keynes.* New York: McGraw-Hill, 1953.

Harrington, Michael. *Toward a Democratic Left.* New York: Macmillan, 1968.

Harrod, R. F. *The Life of John Maynard Keynes.* New York: St. Martin's Press, 1951.

Hayden, Tom. *Trial.* New York: Holt, Rinehart & Winston, 1970.

Heilbroner, Robert L. *Between Capitalism and Socialism: Essays in Political Economics.* New York: Random House, 1970.

———. *The Economic Problem.* Englewood Cliffs, N. J.: Prentice-Hall, 1970.

———. *The Future as History.* New York: Harper & Row, 1959.

———. "Galbraith's Progress." *Dissent,* vol. 21, no. 1 (Winter 1974).

———. *The Great Ascent.* New York: Harper & Row, 1963.

———. *An Inquiry Into the Human Prospect.* New York: W. W. Norton & Co., 1974.

———. *The Limits of American Capitalism.* New York: Harper & Row, 1966.

———. *The Making of Economic Society.* Englewood Cliffs, N. J.: Prentice-Hall, 1962.

———. "A Marxist America." *New York Review of Books,* vol. 6 (May 26, 1966).

———. Second Thoughts on the Human Prospect." *Futures,* vol. 7, no. 1 (February 1975).

———.*The Worldly Philosophers.* New York: Simon & Schuster, 1967.

Heilbroner, Robert L., and Bernstein, Peter L. *A Primer on Government Spending.* New York: Vintage Books, 1963.

Heilbroner, Robert L., and Ford, Arthur, eds. *Economic Relevance: A Second Look.* Pacific Palisades, Calif.: Goodyear Publishing Co., 1976.

Heller, Walter W. *New Dimensions of Political Economy.* New York: W. W. Norton & Co., 1967.

Hession, Charles H. *John Kenneth Galbraith and His Critics.* New York: New American Library, 1972.

HEW Taskforce. *Work in America.* Cambridge, Mass.: MIT Press, 1971.

Horkheimer, Max. *Critical Theory.* New York: Herder and Herder, 1972.

Horowitz, David. "Analyzing the Surplus." *Monthly Review,* vol. 18, no. 8 (January 1967).

———. "The Case for a Neo-Marxist Theory." *International Socialist Review,* vol. 28, no. 4 (July-August 1967).

——, ed. *Marx and Modern Economics.* New York: Monthly Review Press, 1968.

Howard, Dick and Klare, Karl E. *The Unknown Dimension: European Marxism Since Lenin.* New York and London: Basic Books, 1972.

Hunnius, Gerry; Garson, G. David; and Case, John, eds. *Workers' Control: A Reader on Labor and Social Change.* New York: Vintage Books, 1973.

Hunt, E. K. *Property and Prophets: the Evolution of Economic Institutions and Ideologies.* New York: Harper & Row, 1975.

Hunt, E. K., and Schwartz, Jesse G., eds. *A Critique of Economic Theory.* Baltimore: Penguin Books, 1973.

Hunt, E. K., and Sherman, Howard J. *Economics: An Introduction to Traditional and Radical Views.* New York: Harper & Row, 1972.

Hunt, E. K., and Sherman, Howard J. *Economics: An Introduction to Traditional and Radical Views,* 2nd ed. New York: Harper & Row, 1975.

Hymer, Stephen, "The Multinational Corporation and Uneven Development." in *Superconcentration/Supercorporation: A Collage of Opinion on the Concentration of Economic Power,* edited by Ralph L. Andreano. Andover, Mass.: Warner Modular Publications, 1973.

——. "Robinson Crusoe and the Secret of Primitive Accumulation." *Monthly Review,* vol. 23, no. 4 (September 1971).

Initiative Committee for National Economic Planning. "For a National Economic Planning System." *Challenge,* vol. 18, no. 1 (March-April 1975).

International Telephone and Telegraph Corporation: A Case Study of a Conglomerate. San Jose: San Jose State University, Center of Economics Education, 1972. (Mimeographed.)

Jacobs, Paul, and Landau, Saul. *The New Radicals.* New York: Vintage Books, 1966.

Jay, Martin. *The Dialectical Imagination: a History of the Frankfurt School and the Institute of Social Research 1923-1950.* Boston: Little, Brown & Co., 1973.

Jencks, Christopher, et al. *Inequality: A reassessment of the Effect of Family and Schooling in America.* New York: Basic Books, Inc., 1972.

Kalecki, Michal. *Essays in the Theory of Economic Fluctuations.* New York: Farrar and Rinehart, 1939.

——. *The Last Phase in the Transformation of Capitalism.* New York: Monthly Review Press, 1972.

——. "Political Aspects of Full Employment." *Political Quarterly,* vol. 14 (Oct.-Dec. 1943). Reprinted in *Selected Essays on the Dynamics of the Capitalist Economy, 1933-1970.* Cambridge: Cambridge University Press, 1971.

——. *Selected Essays on the Economic Growth of the Socialist and the Mixed Economy.* Cambridge: Cambridge University Press, 1972.

——. *Studies in the Theory of Business Cycles: 1933–1939.* New York: Augustus M. Kelley Publishers, 1969.

——. Theories of Growth in Different Social Systems." *Monthly Review,* vol. 23, no. 5 (October 1971).

——. *Theory of Economic Dynamics: An Essay on Cyclical and Long-Run Changes in Capitalist Economy.* New York: Monthly Review Press, 1968.

Keller, Robert R. "Monopoly Capital and the Great Depression: Testing Baran and Sweezy's Hypothesis." *Review of Radical Political Economics,"* vol. 7, no. 4 (Winter 1975).

Keynes, John Maynard. *Essays in Persuasion.* New York: Harcourt, Brace and Co., 1932.

——. *The General Theory of Employment, Interest and Money.* London: Macmillan, Ltd., 1936.

Klein, Lawrence R. *The Keynesian Revolution.* 2nd ed. New York: Macmillan, 1966.

Knowles, James C. "The Rockefeller Financial Group." *Superconcentration/Supercorporation: A Collage of Opinion on the Concentration of Economic Power,* edited by Ralph L. Andreano. Andover, Mass.: Warner Modular Publications, 1973.

Krader, Lawrence. *Formation of the State.* Englewood Cliffs, N. J.: Prentice-Hall, 1968.

Kuhn, Thomas S. *The Structure of Scientific Revolutions.* Chicago: The University of Chicago Press, 1970.

Lampman, Robert J. *The Snare of Top Wealth-Holders in National Wealth, 1922–1956.* Princeton, N.J.: Princeton University Press, 1962.

Lasch, Christopher. *The Agony of the American Left.* New York: Random House, 1968.

Lekachman, Robert. *Economists at Bay: Why the Experts Will Never Solve Your Problems.* New York: McGraw-Hill, 1976.

——. "The Inevitability of Controls." *Challenge,* vol. 17, no. 5 (November-December 1974).

——, ed. *Keynes' General Theory: Reports of Three Decades.* New York: St. Martin's Press, 1964.

Lenin, V. I. *Imperialism: The Highest Stage of Capitalism.* New York: International Publishers, 1939.

Levison, Andrew. *The Working Class Majority.* New York: Coward, McCann and Geoghegan, 1974.

Lewis, John. *The Life and Teaching of Karl Marx.* New York: International Publishers, 1965.

Liebow, Elliot. *Tally's Corner: a Study of Negro Streetcorner Men.* Boston: Little, Brown and Co., 1967.

Lifschultz, Lawrence F. "Could Karl Marx Teach Economics in America?" *Ramparts,* vol. 12, no. 9 (April 1974).

Lindbeck, Assar. *The Political Economy of the New Left: an Outsider's View.* New York: Harper & Row, 1971.

Lo, Clarence Y. H. "The Conflicting Functions of U.S. Military Spending After World War II," *Working Papers on the Kapitalistate,* no. 3 (1975).

"The Long-run Decline in Corporate Liquidity." *Monthly Review,* vol. 22, no. 4 (September 1970).

Long, Priscilla, ed. *The New Left: a Collection of Essays.* Boston: Porter Sargent Publishers, 1969.

Lubitz, Raymond. "Monopoly Capitalism and Neo-Marxism." *The Public Interest,* no. 21 (Fall 1970).

Lundberg, Ferdinand. *The Rich and the Super-Rich.* New York: Bantam Books, 1968.

McAdams, Robert. *The Evolution of Urban Society: Early Mesopotamia and Prehispanic Mexico.* Chicago: Aldine Publishing Co., 1966.

McLellan, David. *Karl Marx: His Life and Thought.* New York: Harper & Row, 1974.

Magdoff, Harry. *The Age of Imperialism: The Economics of U.S. Foreign Policy.* New York and London: Monthly Review Press, 1969.

Mandel, Ernest. *Decline of the Dollar: a Marxist View of the Monetary Crisis.* New York: Pathfinder Press, 1972.

——. *Europe vs. America? Contradictions of Imperialism.* London: N. L. B., 1970.

——. *The Formation of the Economic Thought of Karl Marx.* New York and London: Monthly Review Press, 1971.

——. *An Introduction to Marxist Economic Theory.* New York: Pathfinder Press, 1970.

——. "The Labor Theory of Value and 'Monopoly Capitalism'." *International Socialist Review,* vol. 28, no. 4 (July-August 1967).

——. *Marxist Economic Theory.* 2 vols. New York: Monthly Review Press, 1970.

——. "Surplus Capital and Realization of Surplus Value." *International Socialist Review* (January-February 1967).

——. "Where is America Going?" *New Left Review*, no. 54 (March-April 1969).

Mannheim, Karl. *Ideology and Utopia: An Introduction to the Sociology of Knowledge.* New York: Harcourt, Brace & World, 1936.

Marcuse, Herbert. *Counter-Revolution and Revolt.* Boston: Beacon Press, 1972.

——. *An Essay on Liberation.* Boston: Beacon Press, 1969.

——. *One-Dimensional Man.* Boston: Beacon Press, 1964.

Marx, Karl. *Capital: A Critical Analysis of Capitalist Production.* Edited by Frederick Engels. Reprint, n.d. 3 vols. Moscow: Foreign Languages Publishing House. First publication 1887.

——. *Contribution to the Critique of Political Economy.* New York: International Publishers, 1970.

Marx, Karl, and Engels, Frederick. *The Collected Writings in the New York Daily Tribune.* Edited and with notes and introduction by A. Thomas Ferguson, Jr. and Stephen J. O'Neil. 4 vols. New York: Precedent Publishing, 1973.

——. *The Communist Manifesto.* New York: International Publishers Co., 1948. First publication 1848.

Mattick, Paul. *Marx & Keynes: The Limits of the Mixed Economy.* Boston: Porter Sargent Publisher, 1969.

Mayer, Martin. *The Bankers.* New York: Weybright and Talley, 1975.

Meadows, Donella; Meadows, Dennis L.; Randers, Jorgen; and Behrens, William W., III. *The Limits to Growth.* New York: Signet, 1972.

Meeropol, Michael. "A Radical Teaching a Straight Principles of Economics Course." *The Review of Radical Political Economics*, vol. 6, no. 4 (Winter 1975).

Melman, Seymour. *American Capitalism in Decline: The Cost of a Permanent War Economy.* New York: Simon & Schuster, 1974.

——. *Pentagon Capitalism: The Political Economy of War.* New York: McGraw-Hill, 1970.

Melville, Keith. *Communes in the Counter Culture: Origins, Theories, Styles of Life.* New York: William Morrow & Co., 1972.

Menshikov, S. *Millionaires and Managers.* Moscow: Progress Publishers, 1969.

"The Merger Movement: A Study in Power." *Monthly Review*, vol. 21, no. 2 (June 1969).

Mermelstein, David, ed. *The Economic Crisis Reader.* New York: Vintage Books, 1975.

——, ed. *Economics: Mainstream Readings and Radical Critiques.* New York: Random House, 1973.

Miliband, Ralph. "Professor Galbraith and American Capitalism." In *The Socialist Register, 1968,* edited by Ralph Miliband and John Saville. New York: Monthly Review Press, 1968.

——. *The State in Capitalist Society.* New York: Basic Books, 1969.

Mills, C. Wright. "Letter to the New Left." In *Power, Politics and People: the Collected Essays of C. Wright Mills.* edited by Irving Louis Horowitz. New York: Oxford University Press, 1963.

——. *The Marxists.* New York: Dell, 1962.

——. *The Power Elite.* New York: Oxford University Press, 1956.

——. *The Sociological Imagination.* New York: Oxford University Press, 1959.

Mintz, Morton, and Cohen, Jerry S. *America, Inc.* New York: Dial, 1971.

"Monopoly and Inflation." *Dollars & Sense,* no. 2 (December 1974).

Moore, Stanley W. *The Critique of Capitalist Democracy: An Introduction to the Theory of the State in Marx, Engels, and Lenin.* New York: Paine-Whitman Publishers, 1957.

——. *Three Tactics: The Background in Marx.* New York: Monthly Review Press, 1963.

Morishimo, Michio. *Marx's Economics: a Dual Theory of Value and Growth.* New York and London: Cambridge University Press, 1973.

Moses, Stanley. *The Learning Force: A More Comprehensive Framework for Educational Policy.* Syracuse: Syracuse University Publications in Continuing Education, 1971.

Myrdal, Gunner. *Critical Essays on Economics.* New York: Pantheon Books, 1973.

Nasser, Alan G. "Where the Highest Standard of Living Went." A review of Ernest Mandel's *Europe vs. America: Contradictions of Imperialism. The Nation,* vol. 218, no. 11 (March 16, 1974).

Nearing, Scott. *The Making of a Radical: A Political Autobiography.* New York: Harper & Row, 1972.

Neihardt, John G. *Black Elk Speaks: Being the Life Story of a Holy Man of the Oglala Sioux.* Lincoln: University of Nebraska Press, 1961.

O'Brien, James. "A History of the New Left, 1960–1968." *Radical America,* (May-June, September-October, and November-December, 1968).

O'Connor, James. *The Corporations and the State: Essays in the Theory of Capitalism and Imperialism.* New York: Harper & Row, 1974.

——. "Financial Capital or Corporate Capital?" *Monthly Review,* vol. 20, no. 7 (December 1968).

——. *The Fiscal Crisis of the State.* New York: St. Martin's Press, 1973.

——. "Monopoly Capital." *New Left Review,* no. 40 (November-December 1966).

——. "Nixon's Other Watergate: The Federal Budget for Fiscal 1974." *Kapitalistate,* no. 2 (1973).

——. *The Origins of Socialism in Cuba.* Ithaca and London: Cornell University Press, 1970.

——. "Summary of the Theory of the Fiscal Crisis." *Working Papers on the Kapitalistate,* no. 1 (1973).

——. "The Twisted Dream." A review of *The Twisted Dream* by Douglas F. Dowd. *Monthly Review,* vol. 26, no. 10 (March 1975).

——. "The University and the Political Economy." *Leviathan,* vol. 1, no. 1 (1969), and *Maxwell Review,* vol. 6, no. 1 (Winter 1970).

——. "Who Rules the Corporations? The Ruling Class." *Socialist Revolution,* vol. 2, no. 1 (January-February 1971).

Offe, Claus. "The Abolition of Market Control and the Problem of Legitimacy." *Working Papers on the Kapitalistate,* no. 1 (1973).

Office of Management and Budget. *The United States Budget in Brief: Fiscal Year 1977.* Washington, D.C.: U.S. Government Printing Office, 1976.

Pahl, R. E., and Winkler, J. T. "The Coming Corporatism." *Challenge,* vol. 18, no. 1 (March-April 1975).

Peabody, Gerald E. "Scientific Paradigms and Economics: an Introduction." *The Review of Radical Political Economics,* vol. 3, no. 2 (July 1971).

Pechman, Joseph and Okner, Benjamin. *Who Bears the Tax Burden?* Washington, D.C.: Brookings Institute, 1974.

Perlo, Victor. *The Unstable Economy: Booms and Recessions in the U. S. Since 1945.* New York: International Publishers, 1973.

Piven, Frances Fox, and Cloward, Richard A. *Regulating the Poor: The Functions of Public Welfare.* New York: Random House, 1971.

Polanyi, Karl. *The Great Transformation: the Political and Economic Origins of Our Time.* Boston: Beacon Press, 1957.

"Probing the Structure of the American Economy." *Congressional Record,* vol. 121, no. 34 (March 4, 1975).

"Prospects for American Radicalism." *New Politics,* vol. 7, no. 2 (Spring 1968).

Reid, Samuel Richardson. *Mergers, Managers, and the Economy.* New York: McGraw-Hill, 1968.

Remmling, Gunter W. *Road to Suspicion: a Study of Modern Mentality and the Sociology of Knowledge.* New York: Appleton-Century-Crofts, 1967.

——, ed. *Towards the Sociology of Knowledge: Origin and Development of a Sociological Thought Style.* New York: Humanities Press, 1973.

"Review of the Month: Keynesian Chickens Come Home to Roost." *Monthly Review,* vol. 25, no. 11 (April 1974).

Review of Radical Political Economics. "Special Issue on Radical Paradigms in Economics," vol. 3, no. 2 (July 1971).

Riddell, Tom. "A Note on Radical Economics and the New Economists." *The Review of Radical Political Economics,* vol. 5, no. 3 (Fall 1973).

Robinson, Joan. *Economics: An Awkward Corner.* New York: Random House, 1967.

——. *An Essay on Marxian Economics.* New York and London: MacMillan Press, Ltd., 1966.

——. "Marx and Keynes." In *Marx and Modern Economics,* edited by David Horowitz. New York: Monthly Review Press, 1968.

——. *Marx, Marshall and Keynes.* Delhi, India: The Delhi School of Economics, University of Delhi, 1955.

——. *On Re-reading Marx.* Cambridge, England: Students' Bookshops, 1953.

Roll, Eric. *A History of Economic Thought.* Englewood Cliffs, N. Y.: Prentice-Hall, 1953.

Ronan, Thomas. "Seven Nobel Laureates Urge Search for Alternative to Capitalism." *The New York Times* (January 26, 1975).

Roosevelt, Frank. "Cambridge Economics as Commodity Fetishism." *The Review of Radical Political Economics,* vol. 7, no. 4 (Winter 1975).

Roszak, Theodore. *The Making of a Counter Culture: Reflections on the Technocratic Society and Its Youthful Opposition.* Garden City, N. Y.: Doubleday, 1969.

Roussopoulos, Dimitrios I., ed. *The Political Economy of the State.* Montreal: Black Rose Books, 1973.

Rubin, Jerry. "Inside the Great Pigasus Plot." *Ramparts,* vol. 18, no. 6 (December 1969).

Rudner, Richard S. *Philosophy of Social Science.* Englewood Cliffs, N. J.: Prentice-Hall, 1966.

Sampson, Anthony. *The Sovereign State of ITT.* New York: Stein and Day, 1973.

Samuelson, Paul A. *Economics.* New York: McGraw-Hill, Tenth Edition, 1976.

San Francisco Kapitalistate Collective. "Review: The Fiscal Crisis of the State." *Working Papers on the Kapitalistate,* no. 3 (Spring 1975).

Sarte, Jean-Paul. *Between Existentialism and Marxism.* New York: Pantheon Books, 1975.

Scaduto, Anthony. *Bob Dylan: An Intimate Biography.* New York: Grosset & Dunlap, 1971.

Schattschneider, E. E. *The Semisovereign People.* New York: Holt, Rinehart & Winston, 1960.

Scherer, Frederic M. *Industrial Market Structure and Economic Performance.* Chicago: Rand McNally & Co., 1970.

Schumacher, E. F. *Small is Beautiful: Economics as if People Mattered.* New York: Harper & Row, 1974.

Schumpeter, Joseph A. *Capitalism, Socialism and Democracy.* New York: Harper & Row, 1950.

——. *History of Economic Analysis.* New York: Oxford University Press, 1954.

Sharpe, Myron E. *John Kenneth Galbraith and the Lower Economics.* 2nd ed. White Plains, N. Y.: International Arts and Sciences Press, 1974.

Sharpe, Myron E.; Dobb, Maurice; Gillman, Joseph M.; Prager, Theodor; and Nathan, Otto, "Marxism and Monopoly Capital: a Symposium." *Science and Society,* vol. 30, no. 4 (Fall 1966).

Sherman, Howard. "Inflation, Unemployment, and Monopoly Capital." *Monthly Review,* vol. 27, no. 10 (March 1976).

——. *Radical Political Economy: Capitalism and Humanism from a Marxist Humanist Perspective.* New York: Basic Books, 1972.

Shonfield, Andrew. *Modern Capitalism: The Changing Balance of Public and Private Power.* New York: Oxford University Press, 1965.

Smith, Adam. *An Inquiry into the Nature and Causes of the Wealth of Nations.* New York: Modern Library, 1937.

Soares, G. A. D. "Marxism as a General Sociological Orientation." *British Journal of Sociology,* vol. 19 (1968).

Stanfield, Ron. *The Economic Surplus and Neo-Marxism.* Lexington: Lexington Books, 1973.

——. "A Revision of the Economic Surplus Concept." *The Review of Radical Political Economics,* vol. 6, no. 3 (Fall 1974).

Stark, Werner. *The Sociology of Knowledge: an Essay in Aid of a Deeper Understanding in the History of Ideas.* London: Routledge & Kegan Paul, 1958.

Steindl, Josef. *Maturity and Stagnation in American Capitalism.* New York: Monthly Review Press, 1974.

Stigler, George J., and Boulding, Kenneth E., eds. *A.E.A. Readings in Price Theory.* Chicago: Richard D. Irwin, 1952.

Stone, Alan. "How Capitalism Rules." *Monthly Review,* vol. 23, no. 1 (May 1971).

Subcommittee on Antitrust and Monopoly of the Committee on the Judiciary, United States Senate, 91st Congress. *The Conglomerate Merger Problem.* Part 8 of the subcommittee hearings on economic concentration. Washington, D.C.: U.S. Government Printing Office, 1970.

Subcommittee on Constitutional Rights of the Committee on the Judiciary, U.S. Senate. *Federal Data Banks, Computers and the Bill of Rights.* Hearing conducted in February and March, 1971. Washington, D.C.: U.S. Government Printing Office, 1971.

Subcommittee on Intergovernmental Relations, and Budgeting, Management, and Expenditures of the Committee on Government Operations, United States Senate, 93rd Congress. *Disclosure of Corporate Ownership.* Washington, D.C.: U.S. Government Printing Office, 1974.

Subcommittee on Reports, Accounting and Management of the Committee on Government Operations, U.S. Senate. *Corporate Ownership and Control.* Washington, D.C.: U.S. Government Printing Office, 1975.

Sweezy, Paul M. "Demand Under Conditions of Oligopoly." *The Journal of Political Economy,* vol. 68 (August 1939).

——. "Galbraith's Utopia." *The New York Review of Books,* vol. 20, no. 18 (November 15, 1973).

——. "John Maynard Keynes." In *Keynes' General Theory: Reports of Three Decades,* edited by Robert Lekachman. New York: St. Martin's Press, 1964.

——. *Modern Capitalism and Other Essays.* New York: Monthly Review Press, 1972.

——. "Monopoly Capital and the Theory of Value." *Monthly Review,* vol. 25, no. 8 (January 1974).

——. "On the Theory of Monopoly Capitalism." *Monthly Review,* vol. 23, no. 11 (April 1972).

——. "The Resurgence of Financial Control: Fact or Fancy?" *Monthly Review,* vol. 23, no. 6 (November 1971).

——. *The Theory of Capitalist Development.* Modern Reader Paperback Edition. New York: Monthly Review Press, 1968.

——. "Toward a Critique of Economics." *Monthly Review,* vol. 21, no. 8 (January 1970).

——. "Toward a Critique of Economics." *The Review of Radical Political Economics,* vol. 2, no. 1 (Spring 1970).

—— and Huberman, Leo, eds. *Paul A. Baran (1910–1964): A Collective Portrait.* New York: Monthly Review Press, 1965.

—— and Magdoff, Harry. *The Dynamics of U.S. Capitalism.* New York and London: Monthly Review Press, 1972.

Szymanski, Al. "The Fiscal Crisis of the State and the Unstable Economy." *The Insurgent Sociologist,* vol. 4, no. 4 (Summer 1974).

——. "Trends in Economic Discrimination Against Blacks in the U.S. Working Class." *The Review of Radical Political Economics,* vol. 7, no. 3 (Fall 1975).

Tanzer, Michael. "Depression Ahead." In *Economics: Mainstream Readings and Radical Critiques,* edited by David Mermelstein. New York: Random House, 1973.

Taylor, F. W. *Principles of Scientific Management.* New York: Harper & Brothers, 1947.

Terkel, Studs. *Hard Times: An Oral History of the Great Depression.* New York: Avon Books, 1970.

——. *Working: People Talk About What They Do All Day and How They Feel About What They Do.* New York: Pantheon Books, 1974.

Tinbergen, Jan. "Do Communist and Free Economies Show a Converging Pattern?" *Soviet Studies,* vol 12, no. 4 (April 1961).

Tiryakian, Edward, ed. *The Phenomenon of Sociology.* New York: Appleton-Century Crofts, 1971.

Tussing, A. Dale. "Education, Foreign Policy and the Popeye Syndrome." *Change,* vol. 3, no. 6 (October 1971).

——. "Emergence of the New Unemployment." *Intellect,* vol. 103, no. 2363 (February 1975).

——. *Poverty in a Dual Economy.* New York: St. Martin's Press, 1975.

"Twenty-Five Eventful Years." *Monthly Review,* vol. 25, no. 13 (June 1974).

Union for Radical Political Economics, The. *The Conference Papers of the Union for Radical Political Economics.* Ann Arbor, Michigan, 1968.

——. *Reading Lists in Radical Political Economics.* 2 vols. Ann Arbor, Michigan, 1971.

——. *Resource Materials in Radical Political Economics.* 2 vols. Ann Arbor, Michigan, 1974.

U.S. Bureau of Census. *Historical Statistics of the United States, Colonial Times to 1957.* Washington, D.C.: U.S. Government Printing Office, 1960.

——. *Statistical Abstract of the United States: 1974,* 95th ed. Washington, D.C.: U.S. Government Printing Office, 1974.

U.S. Department of Commerce. *Historical Statistics of the United States: Colonial Times to 1970.* 2 volumes. Washington, D.C.: U.S. Government Printing Office, 1975.

United States Government Manual 1973/74. Office of the Federal Register National Archives and Records Service General Services Administration. Washington, D.C.: U.S. Government Printing Office, 1973.

Veblen, Thorstein. *The Higher Learning in America: A Memorandum on the Conduct of Universities by Business Men.* New York: Sagamore Press, 1957.

——. *The Theory of the Leisure Class: An Economic Study of Institutions.* New York: Macmillan Co., 1899. 6th Printing. New York: New American Library, 1962.

von Hoffman, Nicholas. "Money on the Brink." A review of Martin Mayer, *The Bankers. The New York Review of Books,* vol. 22, no. 3 (March 6, 1975).

Ward, Benjamin. *What's Wrong With Economics?* New York: Basic Books, 1972.

Ward, Dwayne. "Labor Market Adjustments in Elementary and Secondary Teaching: the Reaction to the 'Teacher Surplus'," *Teachers College Record.* vol. 77, no. 2 (December 1975).

Warren, Bill. "Capitalist Planning and the State." *New Left Review,* no. 72 (March-April, 1972).

Watts, Alan. *In My Own Way: an Autobiography, 1915-1965.* New York: Random House, 1972.

Weather Underground. *Prairie Fire: the Politics of Revolutionary Anti-Imperialism.* San Francisco: Prairie Fire Organizing Committee and Communications Co., 1974.

Weaver, James H. "The Union for Radical Political Economics." *Maxwell Review,* vol. 6, no. 2 (Spring 1970).

Weintraub, Andrew; Schwartz, Eli; and Aronson, J. Richard, eds. *The Economic Growth Controversy.* White Plains, N. Y.: International Arts and Sciences Press, 1973.

Weisskopf, Thomas E. "The Problem of Surplus Absorption in a Capitalist Society." In *The Capitalist System,* edited by Richard C. Edwards, Michael Reich, and Thomas E. Weisskopf. Englewood Cliffs, N. J.: Prentice-Hall, 1972.

Weisskopf, Walter A. *Alienation and Economics.* New York: E. P. Dutton, 1971.

Wellmer, Albrecht. *Critical Theory of Society.* New York: Herder and Herder, 1971.

Williams, William Appleman. *The Contours of American History.* New York: New Viewpoints, 1973.

Wolfe, Alan. "What Makes the System Perdure?" A review of James O'Connor, *The Fiscal Crisis of the State. The Nation,* vol. 218, no. 11 (March 16, 1974).

Wolfe, Robert. "Editorial Statement: Beyond Protest." *Studies on the Left,* vol. 7, no. 1 (January-February 1967).

"Women and the Economy." *The Review of Radical Political Economics,* vol. 8, no. 1 (Spring 1976).

Worland, S. T. "Radical Political Economy as a 'Scientific Revolution'." *Southern Economic Journal,* vol. 39, no. 2 (October 1972).

Zeitlin, Maurice, ed. *American Society, Inc.: Studies of the Social Structure and Political Economy of the United States.* Chicago: Markham Publishing Co., 1970.

Zilg, Gerard Colby. *DuPont: Behind the Nylon Curtain.* Englewood Cliffs, N. J.: Prentice-Hall, 1974.

INDEX